Purpose, Pattern, and Process

Ninth Edition
Revised Printing

Lennis Polnac

Arun John

Austin Community College

Kendall Hunt
publishing company

(continued on page 345)

Contents

Part 2: Pattern 101

6: Description 141

7: Narration 163

Part 4: Additional Readings and Student Writing 263

Preface

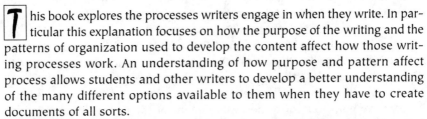

*T*his book explores the processes writers engage in when they write. In particular this explanation focuses on how the purpose of the writing and the patterns of organization used to develop the content affect how those writing processes work. An understanding of how purpose and pattern affect process allows students and other writers to develop a better understanding of the many different options available to them when they have to create documents of all sorts.

As in previous editions of this book, I have based the organization and much of the content on the theories developed by James Kinneavy in his groundbreaking work *A Theory of Discourse*. Kinneavy's theory is especially useful as a way of organizing a composition course. It gives students a comprehensive theoretical framework that allows them to explore a variety of different kinds of writing in a systematic way and to make informed decisions about their own writing.

The "Introduction" defines the basic terminology used in the book. In addition, it shows how the three concepts—purpose, pattern, and process—are interconnected.

Part I, "Purpose" (Chapters 1 through 4), covers four kinds of writing defined by the purposes of the message—expressive, literary, persuasive, and referential. Each chapter presents a further classification by discussing four perspectives of expressive writing, four approaches of literary writing, four appeals of persuasive writing, and four focuses of referential writing. Examples of each type of writing are analyzed for their distinctive characteristics.

Part II, "Pattern" (Chapters 5 through 8), covers the four basic patterns of organization—classification, description, narration, and evaluation. The chapters dealing with classification, description, and narration include a number of variations of the basic patterns. Three kinds of classification (organizing by categories) are included in Chapter 5: formal classification, comparison and contrast, and definition. In addition to physical descriptions (of people, of places, and of things), Chapter 6 includes two other methods of arranging parts within a whole: division and analysis. Finally, Chapter 7 on narration includes three alternative patterns of organization by time order: narration of event, narration of process, and cause and effect. These additional organizational patterns in Chapters 5, 6, and 7 provide writers with a variety of models for imitation and analysis. Furthermore, the four chapters that discuss the patterns of organization (5–8) include examples of writing that combine each purpose with each pattern. The examples of the combinations are analyzed according to the characteristics of the purposes discussed in Chapters 1–4 and the principles of organization presented in Chapters 5–8.

Part III, "Process" (Chapters 9 through 12), covers the process of writing by explaining four necessary activities—getting ideas, creating details, focusing writing, and refining the language. Each chapter provides suggestions for accomplishing those activities.

Part IV, "Additional Readings and Student Writing" (Chapter 13), provides twenty selections that illustrate the principles discussed in the earlier parts of the book. Selections with similar content are grouped together.

I would like to thank the many colleagues and students who, over the years, have contributed to the development of this work. In particular, I would like to thank Anita Howard, with whom I shared an office for many years, for her wise counsel about the ideas I ought to include in the book and for her practical advice about the words I ought to use to communicate those ideas; Tom Cameron and Lyman Grant for their clear, insightful guidance through some perplexing theoretical questions; and Deborah Green, my wife, for her untiring assistance, for her vital encouragement, and, most of all, for her infinite patience during the many revisions.

Lennis Polnac
Austin, Texas

Introduction

Writing is the natural, and no doubt inevitable, consequence of our ability as humans to speak and to use language. With the creation of writing, civilization began to develop more rapidly than it ever had before because people were able to gain access to more information. In fact, in many ways writing made progress possible. Before writing had been developed, information could only be transmitted orally, and the amount of knowledge that could be passed along from one person to another in that way was necessarily restricted by the limitations of human memory. Writing gave human beings a powerful tool. It allowed them to make use of the knowledge accumulated by previous generations as well as to benefit from the wisdom derived from other cultures. At the same time, writing made it possible for people to add to their store of knowledge systematically.

Now, as a result of this process of preserving and passing along information in written form, a vast body of data, which is still continuously expanding, can be found in libraries, museums, archives, and various other repositories of knowledge throughout the world. This enormous reservoir of the collected knowledge and wisdom of the ages, recorded in written form, makes up the fabric of our modern world and enables our various social institutions—business, industry, science, technology, government, education—to function and to progress continually.

The high level of technological development that we enjoy today is the result of the continuing increase in the amount of information available to our society, and at the base of it all is the written word.

Ironically, even though our world in the twenty-first century is more advanced technologically than it has been at any time in history, in some ways we seem to have devalued writing. Letter writing seems to be a lost art in the age of the telephone; time that people may once have devoted to reading is now spent watching movies and TV. Yet in other ways the ability to communicate clearly and effectively in writing continues to be an important, if not an essential, skill in our hi-tech world. As we become more and more dependent on computers, our ability to manipulate written language becomes ever more crucial. In many ways, communicating by e-mail, in chat rooms, and with faxes is making writing more important than it has ever been. As a result, more than ever before, those who read well and write effectively will have a decided competitive advantage in today's society.

In this textbook we will look closely at how writing works by examining the processes that we all go through when we create written communications. Specifically, as the title of the book suggests, we will consider how the **purpose** of any piece of writing and its **pattern** of organization fit into the writing **process** and how an understanding of that process can help us write more effectively.

Any communication, whether it is written or oral, will have a purpose. It would be impossible to conceive of a message that did not have a purpose. Even though we may not always be aware of it, whenever we communicate, a purpose controls practically every aspect of writing: how the message is created, what details are included and excluded, and how those details are organized.

In addition to its purpose, any message we create will have a pattern of organization. When we generate details, we must arrange them in some way. That arrangement will depend on both the purpose of the message and the subject matter being addressed.

Finally, we can think of writing as a process, a series of activities we go through each time we create a message. These activities vary, depending on the personality, work habits, and experience of the writer. In general, however, the process involves selecting a topic, defining a purpose, generating details, and organizing them. An understanding of how this writing process works will enable any writer to have more control over the final product.

PURPOSE

Anytime we speak or write, that communication will have one of four purposes: to express the self, to entertain, to persuade, or to explain. Writing that reveals the self of the writer is **expressive**; writing that entertains is **literary**; writing that attempts to convince an audience is **persuasive**; writing that explains a topic is **referential**.

Each of the following examples illustrates one of these four purposes.

1. I hate cats. They're always in the way. Sometimes I'd like to get rid of every cat in the world. They're such slobs, always lying around. Good for nothings. Cats. You can have 'em.
2. The cat moved stealthily through the shadows, making no sound. It crouched, entirely immobile, its tail twitching rhythmically, watching a bird that cavorted in the grass, oblivious to the impending danger.
3. Cats are adorable, fluffy animals that make wonderful pets. They love to be rubbed and petted, and when you pet them, they make a purring sound to show their affection. Get a cat and you'll never be lonely or unloved again.

4. The cat is a domesticated carnivore that has been a popular pet for centuries. It is a curious, often affectionate animal, but somewhat independent. Although it is often kept to rid a house of mice, it will kill birds, snakes, and lizards as well.

You will notice that each example above, even though it addresses the same general topic, is different in content, organization, and style. The differences occur in part because each example has a different purpose. Example 1 is expressive; 2 is literary; 3 is persuasive; 4 is referential.

These four purposes can be explained in terms of the Communication Triangle (Fig. 1).

All written messages have four elements: a writer, a reader, a topic, and words. Each one of the four purposes emphasizes one of the elements of the Communication Triangle. Expressive writing emphasizes the writer. Literary writing emphasizes the words. Persuasive writing emphasizes the reader. Referential writing emphasizes the topic (the subject matter).

The purpose is like a *filter* through which every word to be included in the written communication must pass. Such elements as humor, imagery, objective words, jargon, emotional language, and slang are included in or excluded from any particular piece of writing depending on what purpose is at work. For example, when writing up the results of an experiment, a scientist would select language that is neutral as opposed to language that is emotionally charged. A writer creating a poem would probably select figurative imagery and avoid technical language. It is the purpose that controls a writer's choices about what kinds of words and devices of language to use in a composition.

DEFINITIONS

Writing that has any one of the four purposes will have distinctive characteristics that will be apparent in particular forms of discourse.

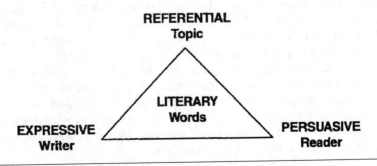

Figure 1 □ The Communication Triangle

Expressive Writing

Writing that has an expressive purpose is the most personal of all writing. It communicates an impression of what the writer is like. Expressive writing is about the writer, and it reveals how the writer looks at the world. Examples of expressive writing are diaries, journals, and personal letters.

Literary Writing

The literary purpose produces writing that is meant to be entertaining, or in some way pleasing to the reader. This kind of writing creates an aesthetic response in the reader because of the way the writer has structured the language. Short stories, novels, plays, poems, and humorous essays are examples of literary writing.

Persuasive Writing

Persuasion is an effort on the part of the writer to change the reader's mind about some issue and in some cases to move the reader to take some action based on a conviction of the rightness of the writer's position. Some examples of persuasive writing are political pamphlets and advertisements.

Referential Writing

Referential writing has as its purpose to explain a topic. That focus on the subject matter creates a need for accuracy and clarity. As a result, writing that has a referential purpose will usually be somewhat more formal than writing that has one of the other purposes. Textbooks, news stories, and business letters are examples of referential writing.

CHARACTERISTICS AND COMBINATIONS

In Chapters 1, 2, 3, and 4 we will examine each of the four purposes in more detail by looking at four major characteristics of each. For each purpose we will discover how writers present the *main idea*, how they provide *substantiation* of the main idea by the elaboration of detail, how they provide *authentication* of those details, and how they make choices about the *language* to be used.

Not every piece of writing fits neatly into these categories. Most writing will have characteristics of more than one purpose. Some persuasive writing may be made up of parts that are purely referential; some literary writing may have some elements that are persuasive. Usually, however, we can identify a **primary** purpose. That is, most of the characteristics of the work will reflect one of the four purposes. If characteristics of another purpose are present, they can be regarded as **secondary**.

The term **argument** is often used when we talk about writing that has either a referential interpretive purpose or a persuasive rational appeal.

Although both forms involve argumentation, the requirements of authentication for each differ drastically. A persuasive claim cannot be proved in the same way that a referential thesis can be. For example, an argument that *too much stress can cause health problems* would be very different from an argument that *we should reduce stress in our lives*. The first, a referential thesis, would demand demonstrable evidence with a high probability of certainty to validate the assertion. Scientifically validated studies would be required. The second, a persuasive claim advocating that the audience take some action, would not require an argument that had a high level of certainty. Whatever the audience would accept in support of the argument would be enough. Although the evidence used to prove the referential thesis might be part of the persuasive argument, it would not be essential to success of that argument. For some audiences, the evidence that stress may cause health problems might not be important enough to convince them to reduce stress in their lives.

It is important to distinguish between referential arguments and persuasive arguments because the kind of information demanded for each is quite different. We lose precision and accuracy in our discussions when we fail to pay attention to those distinctions.

PATTERN

Whenever we create details, we arrange them in some way. Patterns of organization are ways of structuring our experiences and perceptions. They reflect the different ways we think about the world around us. We may classify, describe, narrate, or evaluate. With **classification** we organize by putting things into categories; with **description** we tell what something is like; with **narration** we record events; and with **evaluation** we make value judgements. Which of the four patterns we use in any given piece of writing is affected by the nature of the topic, by the purpose, and by the situational context.

Although generally one dominant pattern will be used to organize the entire work, several different patterns may be, and usually are, present in a single piece of writing. For example, narrations usually have some descriptive elements in them. The categories of a classification system may be developed by description, narration, or further classification. Evaluations necessarily involve the use of another pattern: the subject to be evaluated must be presented to the reader by means of narration, description, or classification.

Each of the following examples illustrates a different pattern.

1. There are many kinds of cats. Most people are familiar with the popular breeds, such as Persians, Himalayans, Siamese, and the American Shorthair (sometimes mistakenly referred to as "alley cats"). These breeds, and other less familiar kinds of cats, can be grouped into three general classes: longhairs, shorthairs, and Rex. The longhairs include the ever popular

Persians and Himalayans. Siamese and the American Shorthair, as well as other less well-known breeds like Burmese, Abyssinian, Russian Blue, and Manx, are included in the shorthair category. Finally, the Rex, a new breed, has hair that is somewhat short but which is also wavy.

2. Our cat has four white feet, but the rest of her fur is solid black. She is a small cat, dainty and retiring, shy around people she doesn't know. She has a small, squeaky voice.

3. The cat crept along the fence staring intently into the vines that grew along the edge of the yard. It could see something that I couldn't. Suddenly it froze, tensing its body and twitching its tail. Then it jumped forward and seemed to have trapped something with its paws. After a moment it began hopping around and slapping the undergrowth with its claws. Finally, it pounced at the bottom of the fence as the elusive prey apparently escaped under the fence.

4. Himalayans make great pets. They are playful and somewhat unpredictable. Their long fur is so soft that it feels like an expensive fur coat. The only drawback to Himalayans is that they leave that wonderfully soft fur on everything they touch.

In each example above, cats are presented in different ways because the writing is organized in a different way. Example 1 is organized by classification; example 2, by description; example 3, by narration; example 4, by evaluation.

The four basic patterns of organization are shown by the diagram below (Fig. 2).

We can think of the patterns of organization as different ways of seeing the subject matter depicted by the writer. Both description and classification represent the subject matter as a static reality, like a snapshot frozen in time. Narration creates a dynamic picture because the details presented change from one event to another. Evaluation is also dynamic because the judgments made are based on assumptions about how the subject being evaluated functions or behaves.

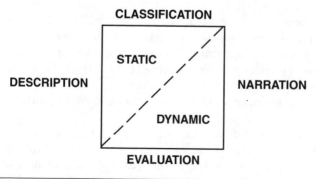

Figure 2 □ Patterns of Organization

DEFINITIONS

In addition to purpose, any piece of writing will also have a pattern, or patterns, of organization. These patterns help make writing understandable and predictable to the reader.

Classification

When we classify, we are organizing the details of our writing into general categories of things. Classification is the arrangement of the details of a subject into classes or kinds. The organizing principle for classification is the **relationship between categories in a system**.

Description

Description is an attempt to make the reader understand how some physical reality or concept is structured. The most obvious use of description is to show physical relationships in space. Space order shows how the different parts of the whole description are related to each other. The organizing principle for descriptions is the **relationship between parts within the whole**.

Narration

Narrations tell a story. All narrations show how events are related in time, so they are arranged in time order. One event follows another, and the resulting sequence of events can be seen as a whole narrative. The organizing principle for narration is the **relationship between events in time**.

Evaluation

When we use evaluation, we make judgments about the subject being evaluated. That is, we say that it is relatively good or bad, or something in between. The organizing principle is the **relationship between values and judgments**.

CHARACTERISTICS AND COMBINATIONS

For each purpose, any pattern of organization or combination of patterns may be used. For example, a paper with a persuasive purpose may achieve that purpose through the use of description, classification, narration, or evaluation. Remember that *all writing will have both purpose and pattern of organization*.

PROCESS

Writing is not always easy. In fact, it usually never is. In his poem "East Coker," T. S. Eliot observes that writing is "a raid on the inarticulate/with shabby equipment always deteriorating. . . ." These images capture some of the inevitable struggle that most writers go through. At times it does seem that writing is almost like a battle between the writer and the language. We must drag each word, kicking and screaming, onto the page and try to make it fit. If the words don't work the way we want them to, we throw them out and find new ones.

When we sit down to write, each of us goes through a process, a certain way of generating ideas, arranging them, and putting them into written form. Although this writing process varies with each individual, some basic elements are always present. The process is recursive. That is, the various parts are repeated again and again so that the whole process moves from one element to another, back and forth. It looks something like the diagram in figure 3.

When we write, we have an idea we want to communicate to our readers, and that idea usually suggests a general purpose (either to express the self, to entertain, to persuade, or to explain a topic). We also define the purpose more specifically by creating a main idea, a specific statement of what the writing is about. (In expressive writing the main idea is a *self-definition*; in literary writing it is a *theme*; in persuasive writing it is a *claim*; and in referential writing it is a *thesis*.) The general purpose and the main idea, then, enable us to generate details that we put into writing. After, or even while, we generate the details, we begin to organize them by using one or a combination of the patterns—classification, description, narration, and evaluation.

This organizing process may make us generate details that we left out when we first began. And this additional organizing and inventing may actually cause us to change our purpose (the main idea or the general purpose or both) and that may in turn cause us to recognize that we need different details that must also be organized and reorganized. So we continually repeat the parts of the process—organizing, generating details, and reorganizing—until we feel that the paper is finished or until we run out of time and have to hand it in. If details are added, they may affect the organization or the purpose. If we move some material from one place to another, we may also change our purpose somewhat.

There are no rules governing this process. The parts of the process may occur in a different order, or there may be more or fewer of them, depending

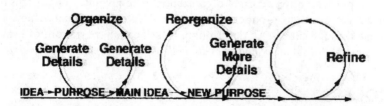

Figure 3 □ The Writing Process

on the experience of the writer and the nature of the writing task. Writing a technical report, for example, would certainly involve a more complicated process than writing an interoffice memo.

The process may occur mostly on paper (or on screen) or almost entirely in the mind, depending on the personality of the writer. That is, some people put down everything they can think of and work through a great many drafts. Others may do most of the editing in their heads before they put a single word on paper. Most of us probably fall somewhere in between these two extremes. Though we alternate between thinking and writing, we will tend to follow all the steps of the process fairly completely.

In general, writers who are more aware of the process will have more control over their writing. As a result, a simple awareness of the steps of the process is a powerful tool.

DEFINITIONS

Even though the nature of the process (or, more accurately, processes) is unique to each individual, there are four discrete kinds of activities that most writers accomplish: getting ideas, generating details, focusing the details, and refining the content. These four activities may occur in any order, or even simultaneously; however, most writers tend to perform each of the four in the order outlined here.

Ideas

The writing process begins with ideas, and even though ideas are all around us, writers sometimes have difficulty coming up with one that is workable or shaping it so that it can be presented in written form.

Details

The details arise from the idea and are controlled by the general purpose and the main idea (specific purpose) of the work. In the initial stages of the process, the writer may generate content sporadically, almost at random, some of which may later be discarded. But it is often necessary to create more content than can actually be used in the final product.

Focus

As more and more content is generated, the work will inevitably begin to have a focus. During that process of focusing, the writer will begin to settle on some patterns of development for the work. Some of those arise naturally from the nature of the topic. At other times, the writer will make conscious decisions to employ a particular method of development.

Refinement

Even though most writers are primarily interested in generating details and in organizing those details in each draft, they usually do some refining all along. For example, even in an initial draft many writers will tend to spell most words correctly, insert punctuation where they think it should go, and make decisions about style. Toward the end of the process, this kind of activity will increase.

CHARACTERISTICS AND COMBINATIONS

Even though the writing process as it has been presented here is dominantly recursive, it also has some linear aspects. That is, the process repeats itself while at the same time moving from beginning to end, from initial draft to final draft. It is helpful to be aware of both aspects.

PART 1

Purpose

Expressive Writing

Literary Writing

Persuasive Writing

Referential Writing

Expressive Writing

*T*he desire to express ourselves with words seems to be an intrinsic part of human nature. Indeed, the urge to communicate who we are as individuals may be basic to the way we think. The noted psychologist Abraham Maslow has suggested that the highest of all human needs is the need for self-actualization, that is, understanding who we really are and acting on that understanding. Expressive writing would seem to be a manifestation of that need for self-actualization and, at least to some degree, a means of achieving it. Expressive writing allows us to engage in a process of self-exploration and self-discovery, to find out who we are and even, perhaps, who we are going to be.

The dominant feature of all expressive writing is that it reveals the writer's identity and individuality. Everything in an expressive work reflects those perceptions and attitudes unique to the person who created it. Each subject addressed is considered, not on its own terms, but rather in terms of how it fits into the writer's personal vision of things. What we see when we read expressive writing is, in essence, a depiction of the mind of the writer, a subjective representation of the world according to the creator of the message.

Examples of self-expression include not only writing by individuals—like diaries, autobiographies, and personal letters—but also documents that are more public and are often collective expressions of a group consciousness, like creeds, declarations, and manifestoes. No matter what forms self-expression may take, however, all of them have certain characteristics in common. In practically any example of expressive writing, we can see these same general features: self-definition, emotional responses, an expression of values, and subjective language.

GENERAL CHARACTERISTICS

❑ A self-definition is formulated or suggested.
❑ Emotional responses are made.
❑ Values are expressed.
❑ Subjective language is used.

SELF-DEFINITION

Defining the *self* is an integral part of the ongoing process of expressing our-selves and trying to understand who we are. A self-definition in expressive writing may include one or more of the dimensions that make up the writer's identity. When any of those facets of the writer's personality are revealed, a self-definition is the result. No matter what the definition is, it reveals how the writer sees the self. We may define ourselves in any number of terms that are most significant to us at the time. For example, statements like

"I am an American,"
"I am an extrovert,"
"I am a woman,"
    and
"I am a rebel"

reflect aspects of a self-definition.

There is no formula for defining the self. Creating a self-definition occurs naturally when we examine our thoughts and feelings. The simple revelation of the writer's thoughts and feelings may suggest a self-definition. Indeed, it would be impossible to record thoughts and feelings without, at least par-tially, defining the self as well. A self-definition is implied by what we choose to say, what thoughts and feelings we choose to reveal. For example, an essay that involves a discussion of "my education" would suggest that the writer thinks of himself or herself as a student. Such a discussion might, in fact, lead to a specific definition of the self, like "I am a student."

How we see ourselves, and define ourselves, is determined in part by past experiences, the culture we live in, the specific circumstance that produces the occasion for self-expression, and the many individual needs, desires, and fears that control our perceptions, attitudes, and beliefs.

In addition to our conception of ourselves at the present moment, we all have some vision of ourselves in the future—what kind of job we want to have, what kind of house we want to live in, what kind of car we want to drive, or what kind of clothes we want to wear. Such projections of ourselves into the future form a part of the idea of who we will be and who we want to be. The process of self-definition and the articulation of a value system may give rise to, and may actually shape, our goals—those things we want to ac-complish either immediately or in the long term. For instance, someone who says, "I am a student," would value things associated with that self-definition. As a result, we wouldn't be at all surprised to hear a "student" say, "I'm go-ing to stay in school until I get a degree," a statement of a goal reflecting the values of a person whose self-definition is "I am a student."

EMOTIONAL RESPONSES

Self-expression reveals the writer's emotions. These emotions are expressed with emotional words as well as exaggerated or imperative language such as exclamations, commands, or sweeping generalizations. Very often the personality of the writer or the situation being written about, or both, provokes an emotional response.

Emotional Language

The writer may reveal emotions directly by using words like *love, hate, hope,* or *fear*—words that express emotions. Through this language, the inner world of the writer is revealed to the reader.

In addition, the writer may use words that have strong connotations. Connotations are the associated, emotional meanings of words. (Denotations are the literal dictionary definitions.) Some words have positive connotations; that is, they create good feelings in most readers. Others, that have negative connotations, create unpleasant feelings in the reader. For instance, the words *thrifty, stingy,* and *economical,* although they have similar meanings, have very different connotations.

Exclamations

An exclamation is a sentence that expresses strong feeling, like "I love this place!" (These sentences are usually followed by an exclamation point.)

Commands

A command is an order or a direction like "Take this away." (Notice that there is an implied *you* at the beginning of the command, so that the sentence means, "You take this away.")

Sweeping Generalizations

Generalizations are statements that include a great many individual cases. A statement like "Everybody likes baseball" is a sweeping generalization because it doesn't allow for any exceptions. Obviously the statement can't be literally true, but in expressive writing such a statement may be an accurate reflection of the feelings of the writer. In addition to *everybody,* words such as *all, everything, everyone, none, no one,* and *nothing* may create sweeping generalizations.

EXPRESSION OF VALUES

The responses we have to events in the world around us shape and are shaped by what we value. Generally speaking, values are those principles, standards, or qualities considered worthwhile or desirable by an individual or a society. We couldn't understand ourselves fully or express the true nature of our identities without understanding the values that influence us. Our values tell us who we are, affect how we see the world around us, and control how we respond to it.

When we say that something is good or bad, or use some synonym for degrees of *goodness* or *badness*, we are revealing values. Superlatives, words that end in *-est*, also indicate that a value judgment is being made, as in the statement, "That's the great*est* book I've ever read." The writer's system of values, either stated explicitly or implied by the judgments made, is present in all expressive writing. Whether those values represent an individual response or the demands of the culture, they are a part of the writer's expression of the self. Values control self-definition.

Attempts at self-definition are invariably connected to a discussion of values and are frequently couched in the terminology of values. The self-defined student who values education highly might say something like "Getting an education is a great opportunity and opens many doors," thus revealing a part of the larger value system.

SUBJECTIVE LANGUAGE

The subjective nature of expressive writing can be seen in the writer's choice of words and phrases. This stylistic feature is part of the revelation of who the writer is.

One of the first things we notice when we read a piece of expressive writing is the first person pronouns (*I, me, my, mine, we, us, our, ours*). The use of these pronouns is consistent with the subjective nature of the self-expression. It would be hard to imagine a piece of expressive writing without these first person pronouns.

Since the self is the dominant element in expressive writing, most of the language used reflects the writer's personality. The writer is expressing his or her identity. The writer's own particular way of using language (called an *idiolect*) controls the selection of words. As a result, expressive writing may have informal features like slang expressions and a conversational style. These characteristics may appear because they are a part of the writer's personality; they honestly express the writer's identity.

Slang and Dialect

Slang expressions are those words and phrases that have special meanings in certain cultures and subcultures. For instance, someone may say that something is *cool*, referring not to its temperature, but to how desirable it is.

Dialect usually refers to regional or social variety in the use of certain forms of language, especially if they deviate from standard usage (although strictly speaking, standard usage is also a dialect). In personal writing, we tend to use language that we are comfortable with, the language we used as children or the language we use in casual conversations with close friends and relatives, even though those forms may not conform to the rules of standard usage.

Conversational Style

A conversational style has a naturalness of tone and ease of expression that helps the writer to communicate emotional reactions. In other words, the conversational style sounds like conversation, as if the writer were speaking aloud spontaneously without thinking too much about such things as word choice, sentence construction, or the particulars of standard usage.

AN EXAMPLE

The following excerpt from John Graves' book entitled *Hard Scrabble* illustrates how the writer's value system and his emotional responses work to create a self-definition. Graves, in creating a definition of himself, also projects goals for the future. In this autobiographical work, Graves gives us a look at his farm in Somervell County, Texas where he has made a transition from urban to rural life. His record of that transition gives us a glimpse of Graves' identity as it has been shaped by the hard scrabble land of central Texas.

The Way

JOHN GRAVES

Nothing else on the place generates quite as much friction with the order of things as goats do, though nearly all the Syndrome's activities generate some. Chickens are proverbially attractive to carnivores, but ours at present, a hen house and yard not having been built, are scrub games, true Darwinian fowl that roost here and there in the barn and get along without even being fed anything except what they can steal by pecking holes in sacks or can glean from larger animals' feed. Sneaking nests in cubbyholes, chasing grasshoppers far out into the pastures, they have managed to raise some chicks and to increase a little every year despite the good red-yolked brown eggs the children find by searching and bring to the house, and the young roosters we take for meat, and an occasional specimen grabbed and eaten by a gray fox that lives up the horse-trap's fenceline. I have intentions of doing battle with this fellow if I ever get the chance, but I rather like him too and somehow never have a gun around when I catch a glimpse of him. For that matter his toll is minimal; the games can fly like quail and even the cockerels I kill for the table have to be shot sportingly in the head from a distance, with a twenty-two. . . . They could probably cope with hawks too, for when buzzards fly over low they give the hollow hawk-warning call and dart for cover. One man I used to know had a gamecock that would fly up in the air to meet and fight a diving hawk, which I daresay the hawk found disconcerting. . . . But sadly hawks are not much of a problem these days, DDT and other sweet agents of profit and progress having decimated their numbers in a brief few years, since in the late fifties I saw the great "hawk storm" on White Bluff. I miss them and am glad to see the few that still show up, nor would I shoot one now if he killed every chicken I have.

Deer love the winter grainfields and graze them hard at times. Here on the creek there aren't yet enough to worry much about, and an occasional loin or haunch of venison is recompense for what damage they do. But at the Soft Scrabble place a few miles south, near big ranches where the current deer explosion is centered, they are already making it nearly impossible to raise certain crops. Though I leased the tract for hunting to friends last winter to hold down depredations a bit, the hunters' light legal take affected them not at all, and at the height of the season a neighbor counted fifty in one bunch amid the ruined oats and vetch I had sowed to make spring hay. . . .

Rabbits have sometimes been rough on the vegetable garden's lettuce and things, but a good tight poultry-wire fence now keeps most of them out, and predators hold their numbers down, so that maybe by not shooting the gray up the fence I am just swapping an occasional fowl for lettuce and cabbage and greens. Coons, barred access to our garbage by dogs at the house, climb over the garden fence at the wild end, and for two or three years made it impossible to harvest any sweet corn—ripping it off the stalks just before it was prime, eating some ears and discarding others scornfully on the ground. I tried lanterns and ticking clocks and cans of urine and other O. F.-recommended techniques but they did no good, and at last I put a sheepdog bitch down there one night, which led to a fine, squalling, barking battle at four in the morning, three grown coons and the bitch and the bitch's son Blue, and me dancing around in my shorts with a flashlight and a club.

But I don't really dislike coons that much—not at all, in fact—and when the big tough boar specimen that did not survive the battle had been buried shallowly amid my ravaged corn (where he would be, like Old Speck the erstwhile goat-killing dog, a fertility in the soil, a dying and reborn god), I found by accident what seems to be a peaceful solution for the problem. As the smell of coonish mortality seeps gently roundabout in that area of the garden, it serves as a reminder to other trespassing coons of their own mortality. Like their human brethren they appear not to care for such reminders and thenceforth stay away, at least till the smell dies out. Nor do you have to resort to further coon-murder to get hold of a corpse to bury; a stretch of morning highway will often yield one or two, freshly slaughtered by last night's passing cars.

(There is perhaps a problem about what to say to acquaintances who may come along and catch you scavenging dead things from the roadside, but an O. F. learns furtive swooping skill in such activity, and a certain amount of shamelessness. He finds it possible to feel not only unashamed but proud of something like a heaped pickup-load of chicken poot. . . .)

> The Way's real Sunday punch at vegetable gardens, though, is delivered by bugs. Squash bugs, stink bugs, cabbage loopers, hornworms, cutworms, army worms, nematodes, grasshoppers, crickets, cucumber beetles of two sorts, aphids of a dozen, leafhoppers, corn earworms, pill bugs, Colorado potato beetles, root maggots, and any number of other such skillful and hungry destroyers . . . All true O.F.s distrust poisons, and hence from year to year we base new hopes on Rodalian "organic" approaches and concoctions—ladybugs and mantids, fireplace ashes, garlic-and-pepper water, companionate plantings, compost and mulch and garbage and manure to firm up the plants' resistance, mineral oil, salt water, beer. . . . Some work surprisingly well at times, and at other times none seem to do much, and impurity invades the O. F. and maybe he guiltily slathers some poison around, but even then of nonresidual sorts, preferably the old botanicals like rotenone and nicotine and sabadilla dust. Or maybe at such times he just lets the bugs take over, or replants enough stuff for them and him both.

This excerpt shows how an expressive purpose reveals the author's value system and how that value system is connected to the author's emotional reactions and a self-definition. Graves reveals a value system based on minimum human impact on nature. Emotional responses like "I rather like him [the fox] too" and the implicit self-definition *I am a nature lover* are closely associated with his value system.

FOUR KINDS OF EXPRESSIVE WRITING

All expressive writing has the general characteristics discussed above, but can be further divided into four groups, each with characteristics different from the others. Each one creates a different perspective on the process of self-expression. They can be called personal, autobiographical, ritual, and interpersonal.

THE PERSONAL PERSPECTIVE

Personal self-expression, which includes diaries and journals, is the least restrictive and perhaps the most characteristically expressive of all the forms of expressive writing. It has four identifying features.

- ❏ Immediate impressions and perceptions are recorded.
- ❏ Matters of importance to the writer are dealt with.
- ❏ The nature of the self is explored.
- ❏ Associations are made and/or episodes are recounted.

Immediate Impressions and Perceptions

Diaries and journals are usually records of the daily experiences of the writer. As a result, they reflect a sense of immediacy more than the other forms of self-expression. The writer records impressions and perceptions of ordinary, everyday things and common events.

Matters of Importance

The writer deals with ideas and beliefs he or she thinks are of the utmost importance. Things that may, upon reflection, seem trivial, nevertheless seem important at the moment they are recorded. If the writer considers something to be important, then it is important. Each individual's value system determines what is important for that person.

Exploration of the Self

In personal writing, the general characteristic of giving a self-definition usually involves an examination of motives and desires, often explained in terms of values. An understanding of the values that underlie motives and goals is an essential part of self-exploration. That kind of understanding can provide important clues for understanding actions, thoughts, and emotional responses.

Associations and Episodes

Because personal writing tends to focus on recent experiences, it follows a pattern of development that reflects the working of the writer's consciousness. Our mental processes usually follow a stream of consciousness—thoughts, impressions, memories, and ideas connected by personal associations. When this process is put down in writing, as it is in a diary or a journal, the result is usually associative. That is, one idea suggests another. Even when a narrative is recorded, it may well be in the form of a disconnected series of episodes.

AN EXAMPLE

From 1660 to 1669 Samuel Pepys kept a secret diary in a shorthand he devised. In his diary he recorded many of the events of his life. Now it is one of the most famous diaries in English literature because of the candor with which it reveals life in seventeenth-century England. The following excerpts give an idea of its content and illustrate the characteristics of personal self-expression.

Diary

SAMUEL PEPYS

July 1, 1660 (Lord's day.)—Infinite business, my heart and head full. Met with Purser Washington, with whom and a lady, a friend of his, I dined at the Bell Tavern in King Street, but the rogue had no more manners than to invite me, and to let me pay my club. This morning come home my fine camlet cloak, with gold buttons, and a silk suit, which cost me much money, and I pray God to make me able to pay for it. In the afternoon to the Abbey, where a good sermon by a stranger, but no Common Prayer yet.

October 13, 1660.—I went to Charing Cross, to see Major-General Harrison hanged, drawn, and quartered; which was done there, he looking as cheerful as any man could do in that condition. He was presently cut down, and his head and heart shown to the people, at which there was great shouts of joy. It is said, that he said that he was sure to come shortly at the right hand of Christ to judge them that now had judged him; and that his wife do expect his coming again. Thus it was my chance to see the King beheaded at White Hall, and to see the first blood shed in revenge for the King at Charing Cross. Setting up shelves in my study.

January 1, 1662.—Waking this morning out of my sleep on a sudden, I did with my elbow hit my wife a great blow over her face and neck, which waked her with pain, at which I was sorry, and to sleep again. . . .

October 2, 1662.—At night, hearing that there was a play at the Cockpit, and my Lord Sandwich, who come to town last night, at it, I do go thither, and by very great fortune did follow four or five gentlemen who were carried to a little private door in a wall, and so crept through a narrow place, and come into one of the boxes next the King's, but so as I could not see the King or Queen, but many of the fine ladies, who yet are not really so handsome generally as I used to take them to be, but that they are finely dressed. Then we saw *The Cardinall*, a tragedy I had never seen before, nor is there any great matter in it. That company that come in with me into the box were all Frenchmen, that could speak no English; but, Lord! what sport they made to ask a pretty lady that they got among them, that understood both French and English, to make her tell them what the actors said.

January 6, 1664 (Twelfth Day.)—This morning I began a practice, which I find, by the ease I do it with, that I shall continue, it saving me money and time; that is, to trimme myself with a razer: which pleases me mightily.

August 7, 1664 (Lord's Day.)—My wife telling me sad stories of the ill, improvident, disquiet, and sluttish manner, that my father and mother and Pall do live in the country, which troubles me mightily, and I must seek to remedy it. . . .

October 16, 1665.—. . . God knows what will become of all the King's matters in a little time, for he runs in debt every day, and nothing to pay them looked after. Thence I walked to the Tower; but, Lord! how empty the streets are and melancholy, so many poor sick people in the streets full of sores; and so many sad stories overheard as I walk, everybody talking of his dead, and that man sick, and so many in this place, and so many in that. And they tell me that, in Westminster, there is never a physician and but one apothecary left, all being dead; but that there are great hopes of a great decrease this week; God send it! . . .

September 2, 1666 (Lord's day.)—Some of our maids sitting up late last night to get things ready against our feast today, Jane called us up about three in the morning, to tell us of a great fire they saw in the city. So I rose and slipped on my night-gown, and went to her window; and through it to be on the backside of Marke-lane at the farthest; but, being unused to such fires as followed, I thought it far enough off; and so went to bed again, and to sleep. About seven rose again to dress myself, and there looked out at the window, and saw the fire not so much as it was, and further off. So to my closet to set things to rights, after yesterday's cleaning. By and by Jane comes and tells me that she hears that above 300 houses have been burned down tonight by the fire we saw, and that it is now burning down all Fish Street, by London Bridge. So I made myself ready presently, and walked to the tower; and there got up upon one of the high places . . . and there I did see the houses at the end of the bridge all on fire, and an infinite great fire on this and the other side the end of the bridge; which, among other people, did trouble me for poor little Michell and Sarah on the bridge. So now with my heart full of trouble, to the lieutenant of the Tower, who tells me that it begun this morning in the King's baker's house in Pudding-lane, and that it hath burned St. Magnus's Church and most part of Fish Street already. . . .

September 5, 1666.—I lay down in the office again upon W. Hewer's quilt, being mighty weary, and sore in my feet with going till I was hardly able to stand. About two in the morning my wife calls me up, and tells me of new cries of fire, it being come to Barking Church, which is the bottom of our land. I up; and finding it so, resolved presently to take her away, and did, and took my gold, which was about £2350, W. Hewer and Jane down to Proundy's boat to Woolwich; but, Lord! what a sad sight it was by moonlight to see the whole city almost on fire, that you might see it plain at Woolwich, as if you were by it. There, when I come, I find the gates shut, but no guard kept at all; which troubled me, because of discourse now begun, that there is plot in it, and that the French had done it. I got the gates open, and to Mr. Shelden's, where I locked up my gold, and charged my wife and W. Hewer never to leave the room without one of them in it, night or day. So back again, by the way seeing my goods well in the lighters at Deptford, and watched well by people. Home, and whereas I expected to have seen our house on fire, it being now about seven o'clock, it was not. But to the fire, and there find greater hopes than I expected; for my confidence of finding our office on fire was such, that I durst not ask anybody how it was with us, till I come and saw it not burned. But going to the fire, I find, by the blowing up of houses, and the great help given by the workmen out of the King's yards, sent up by Sir W. Pen, there is a good stop given to it, as well as at Marke Lane end as ours; it having only burned the dial of Barking Church, and part of the porch, and was there quenched. I up to the top of Barking steeple, and there saw the saddest sight of desolation that I ever saw; everywhere great fires, oil-cellars, and brimstone, and other things burning. I became afeard to stay there long, and therefore down again as fast as I could, the fire being spread as far as I could see it; and to Sir W. Pen's, and there eat a piece of cold meat, having eaten nothing since Sunday, but the remains of Sunday's dinner. . . .

September 17, 1666.—Lay long in bed, talking with pleasure with my poor wife, how she used to make coal fires, and wash my foul clothes with her own hand for me, poor wretch! in our little room at my Lord Sandwich's; for which I ought for ever to love and admire her, and do; and persuade myself she would do the same again, if God should reduce us to it. . . .

May 31, 1669.—. . . And thus ends all that I doubt I shall ever be able to do with my own eyes in the keeping of my Journal, I being not able to do it any longer, having done now so long as to undo my eyes almost every time that I take a pen in my hand; and therefore, resolve, from this time forward, to have it kept by my people in long-hand, and must be contented to set down no more than is fit for them and all the world to know; or, if there be any thing, I must endeavour to keep a margin in my book open, to add, here and there, a note in short-hand with my own hand.

And so I betake myself to that course, which almost as much as to see myself go into my grave: for which, and all the discomforts that will accompany by being blind, the good God prepare me!

You can see in these excerpts that Pepys communicates both the insignificant and the momentous happenings of his daily life. He selects those details that are important to him. Such apparently trivial incidents as beginning the practice of shaving himself (January 6, 1664), accidentally hitting his wife in the head (August 7, 1664), and going to the theater (October 2, 1662) are recorded along with accounts of such historically significant events as a hanging (October 13, 1660), the plague (October 16, 1665) and the great fire of London (September 2, 5, & 17, 1666). But at the particular time they occurred, even those seemingly inconsequential details were important enough to Pepys for him to record them.

Many of those details of daily life reflect values and goals. Some of the passages can be regarded as attempts at self-exploration, self-definition, and a statement of goals for the future. Notice particularly the entry of February 25, 1667 in which he expresses his love and admiration for his wife. Also, in the last entry (May 31, 1669), he reflects on his journal and his failing eyesight.

Throughout the diary, the entries illustrate the associative and episodic structure of personal self-expression. He recounts three separate narratives on July 1, 1660. On October 13, 1660 he comments on the apparently trivial event of setting up shelves in his study after he has recorded a rather unsettling description of the hanging of Major General Harrison.

The Autobiographical Perspective

Autobiographical writing is seen in autobiographies, memoirs, and reminiscences. Such writing results from a consideration of and a reflection on major events in the life of the writer. Although the content is much like personal writing, the events are given more order. The presentation is not as random as it is in journals and diaries. The following specific characteristics are apparent.

- ❑ Experiences from the past are recounted.
- ❑ Significant events in the life of the writer are explored.
- ❑ An effort is made to explain the writer's personality or character.
- ❑ The writer's past actions are rationalized or justified.

Experiences from the Past

The writer of autobiography may look to the distant past as well as to the immediate past. An adult may relate events from childhood. An understanding of the self, as it relates to a person's formative years, provides a basis for explaining recent actions and current values.

Significant Events

In looking back over past events, the writer of autobiography will select those events that are the most significant, those that, for some reason (perhaps because of subsequent events), retain an importance in the writer's memory. These memories may be focused on significant places or important people, for example.

Explanation of the Writer's Personality

The writer of autobiography may make an attempt to explain his or her identity and perhaps tell how that identity developed as a result of significant events. The events and experiences of the past form a pattern that adds up to the present personality.

Rationalization of Actions

Since the gap between the time when the events occur and the time when they are recorded is greater in autobiographical self-expression than it is in personal writing, the goals and values of the writer may have changed. Consequently, there is an effort to make the past actions fit into the present value system. When experiences from the past are recalled, they may be somewhat distorted by time and changed by the process of recording them.

AN EXAMPLE

In the following excerpt from Book I of *Confessions* written by Jean Jacques Rousseau in 1783, we can see how a significant event from Rousseau's childhood is explained and rationalized in light of his values as an adult. Through his recollection of the event, we get a better understanding of Rousseau's personality. The characteristics of autobiographical self-expression are clearly illustrated in the selection.

The End of Childhood

JEAN JACQUES ROUSSEAU

One day I was learning my lesson by myself in the room next to the kitchen. The servant had put Mademoiselle Lambercier's combs in front of the fireplace to dry. When she came back to fetch them, she found one with a whole row of teeth broken. Who was to blame for the damage? No one except myself had entered the room. On being questioned, I denied that I had touched the comb. M. and Mademoiselle Lambercier both began to admonish, to press, and to threaten me; I obstinately persisted in my denial; but the evidence was too strong, and outweighed all my protestations, although it was the first time that I had been found to lie so boldly. The matter was regarded as serious, as in fact it deserved to be. The mischievousness, the falsehood, the obstinacy appeared equally deserving of punishment; but this time it was not by Mademoiselle Lambercier that chastisement was inflicted. My uncle Bernard was written to and he came. My poor cousin was accused of another equally grave offence; we were involved in the same punishment. It was terrible. Had they wished to look for the remedy in the evil itself and to deaden forever my depraved senses, they could not have set to work better, and for a long time my senses left me undisturbed.

They could not draw from me the desired confession. Although I was several times brought up before them and reduced to a pitiable condition, I remained unshaken. I would have endured death, and made up my mind to do so. Force was obliged to yield to the diabolical obstinacy of a child—as they called my firmness. At last I emerged from this cruel trial, utterly broken, but triumphant.

It is now nearly fifty years since this incident took place, and I have no fear of being punished again for the same thing. Well, then, I declare in the sight of heaven that I was innocent of the offence, that I neither broke nor touched the comb, that I never went near the fireplace, and had never even thought of doing so. It would be useless to ask me how the damage was done; I do not know, and I cannot understand; all that I know for certain is, that I had nothing to do with it.

Imagine a child, shy and obedient in ordinary life, but fiery, proud, and unruly in his passions: a child who had always been led by the voice of reason and always treated with gentleness, justice, and consideration, who had not even a notion of injustice, and who for the first time becomes acquainted with so terrible an example of it on the part of the very people whom he most loves and respects! What an upset of ideas! what a disturbance of feelings! what revolution in his heart, in his brain, in the whole of his little intellectual and moral being! Imagine all this, I say, if possible. As for myself, I feel incapable of disentangling and following up the least trace of what then took place within me.

I had not sense enough to feel how much appearances were against me, and to put myself in the place of others. I kept to my own place, and all that I felt was the harshness of a frightful punishment for an offence which I had not committed. The bodily pain, although, severe, I felt but little; all I felt was indignation, rage, despair. My cousin, whose case was almost the same, and who had been punished for an involuntary mistake as if it had been a premeditated act, following my example, flew into a rage, and worked himself up to the same pitch of excitement as myself. Both in the same bed, we embraced each other with convulsive transports: we felt suffocated; and when at length our young hearts, somewhat relieved, were able to vent their wrath, we sat upright in bed and began to shout, times without number, with all our might: Carnifex! carnifex! carnifex!

While I write these words, I feel that my pulse beats faster; those moments will always be present to me though I should live a hundred thousand years. That first feeling of violence and injustice has remained so deeply graven on my soul, that all the ideas connected with it bring back to me my first emotion; and this feeling, which, in its origin, had reference only to myself, has become so strong in itself and so completely detached from all personal interest, that, when I see or hear of any act of injustice— whoever is the victim of it, and wherever it is committed—my heart kindles with rage, as if the effect of it recoiled upon myself. When I read of the cruelties of a ferocious tyrant, the crafty atrocities of a rascally priest, I would gladly set out to plunge a dagger into the heart of such wretches, although I had to die for it a hundred times. I have often put myself in a perspiration, pursuing or stoning a cock, a cow, a dog, or any animal which I saw tormenting another merely because it felt itself the stronger. This impulse may be natural to me, and I believe that it is; but the profound impression left upon me by the first injustice I suffered was too long and too strongly connected with it, not to have greatly strengthened it.

With the above incident the tranquillity of my childish life was over. From that moment I ceased to enjoy a pure happiness, and even at the present day I feel that the recollection of the charms of my childhood ceases there.

In this selection Rousseau looks at an event from his past—an unfair punishment for a misdeed he was wrongly accused of. It is an event that affected him dramatically and changed him significantly, so much so that he says that with that event "the recollection of the charms" of his "childhood" cease. The significance of the event is understood retrospectively.

THE RITUAL PERSPECTIVE

Ritual self-expression includes not only documents that are individual and personal (e.g. wills and prayers), but also writing that is the collective expression of a group (e.g. creeds, declarations, and manifestoes). All self-expression with a ritual perspective has the following characteristics.

- ❏ The self is presented in terms of an agreed upon value system.
- ❏ A repetitive or parallel structure is used.
- ❏ The importance of the document is emphasized.
- ❏ Traditional language and/or traditional forms are used.

An Agreed Upon Value System

The content of ritual self-expression conforms to whatever set of values the writer has adopted. Those values usually tend to reflect a value system agreed upon by a culture or a society.

The following example, "The Apostle's Creed," illustrates such a set of values, values and beliefs found in the doctrine of the Catholic Church. The document, many centuries old, is a collective affirmation of the traditions of the Christian faith.

> I believe in God the Father Almighty, Creator of Heaven and earth; And in Jesus Christ, His only son, our Lord; Who was conceived by the Holy Ghost, born of the Virgin Mary, suffered under Pontius Pilate, was crucified, died, and was buried; He descended into hell; the third day He rose again from the dead; He ascended into Heaven, sitteth at the right hand of God, the Father Almighty; From thence He shall come to judge the living and the dead. I believe in the Holy Ghost, the Holy Catholic Church, the communion of saints, the forgiveness of sins, the resurrection of the body, and Life everlasting.

Repetitive or Parallel Structure

Repetitive or parallel writing structures very often reflect and underscore the group's value system. Repetitive words, phrases, and sentence patterns reveal the ritual nature of the writing and emphasize what the writer considers to be important. Repeated words or phrases focus the reader's attention on key elements of that value system. Notice the repetition of the word "I believe" in the example above.

Importance of the Document

Ritual self-expression is most often solemn. This tone emphasizes the importance of the document to the group and to the culture as a whole. The subject matter of such writings has great significance to the people who preserve the traditions on which the works are based.

Traditional Language and Traditional Forms

Certain words and phrases that have special meanings are used. This traditional language makes us aware that the document itself is important. Works of this kind use language that has appeared over and over in similar documents previously and that reflects the values of the traditions that have produced those works.

AN EXAMPLE

In Franklin's will we can see that the distribution of his estate reveals not only his loyalty to his family and friends but also his feeling of responsibility to certain institutions that exist for the public good.

Wills, even though they tend to be highly formalized, reveal a set of values at the core of a person's belief system. Benjamin Franklin's will gives us an intriguing look at the mind of one of the most original thinkers in Revolutionary America.

The Last Will and Testament of Benjamin Franklin

BENJAMIN FRANKLIN

I, Benjamin Franklin, of Philadelphia, printer, late Minister Plenipotentiary from the United States of America to the Court of France, now President of the State of Pennsylvania, do make and declare my last will and testament as follows:

To my son, William Franklin, late Governor of the Jerseys, I give and devise all the lands I hold or have a right to, in the province of Nova Scotia, to hold to him, his heirs, and assigns forever. I also give to him all my books and papers, which he has in his possession, and all debts standing against him on my account books, willing that no payment for, nor restitution of, the same be required of him, by my executors. The part he acted against me in the late war, which is of public notoriety, will account for my leaving him no more of an estate he endeavoured to deprive me of.

Having since my return from France demolished the three houses in Market Street, between Third and Fourth Streets, fronting my dwelling-house, and erected two new and larger ones on the ground, and having also erected another house on the lot which formerly was the passage to my dwelling, and also a printing-office between my dwelling and the front houses; now I do give and devise my said dwelling-house, wherein I now live, my said three new houses, my printing-office and the lots of ground thereto belonging; also my small lot and house in Sixth Street, which I bought of the widow Henmarsh; also my pasture-ground which I have in Hickory Lane, with the buildings thereon; also my house and lot on the North side of Market Street, now occupied by Mary Jacobs, together with two houses and lots behind the same, and fronting on Pewter-Platter Alley; also my lot of ground in Arch Street, opposite the church-burying ground, with the buildings thereon erected; also all my silver plate, pictures, and household goods, of every kind, now in my said dwelling-place, to my daughter, Sarah Bache, and to her husband, Richard Bache, to hold to them for and during their natural lives, and the life of the longest liver of them, and from and after the decease of the survivor of them, I do give, devise, and bequeath to all children already born, or to be born of my said daughter, and to their heirs and assigns forever, as tenants in common, and not as joint tenants.

And, if any or either of them shall happen to die under age, and without issue, the part and share of him, her, or them, so dying, shall go to and be equally divided among the survivors or survivor of them. But my intention is, that, if any or either of them should happen to die under age, leaving issue, such issue shall inherit the part and share that would have passed to his, her, or their parent, had he, she, or they been living. And, as some of my said devisees may, at the death of the survivor of their father or mother, be of age, and others of them under age, so as that all of them may not be of capacity to make division, I in that case request and authorize the judges of the Supreme Court of Judicature of Pennsylvania for the time being, or any three of them, not personally interested, to appoint by writing, under their hands and seals, three honest, intelligent, impartial men to make the said division, and to assign and allot to each of my devisees their respective share, which division, so made and committed to writing under the hands and seals of the said three men, or any two of them, and confirmed by the said judges, I do hereby declare shall be binding on, and conclusive between the said devisees.

All the lands near the Ohio, and the lots near the centre of Philadelphia, which I lately purchased of the State, I give to my son-in-law, Richard Bache, his heirs and assigns forever; I also give him the bond I have against him, of two thousand and one hundred and seventy-two pounds, five shillings, together with the interest that shall or may accrue thereon, and direct the same to be delivered up to him by my executors, canceled, requesting that, in consideration thereof, he would immediately after my decease manumit and set free his Negro man Bob. I leave to him, also, the money due to me from the State of Virginia for types. I also give to him the bond of William Goddard and his sister, and the counter bond of the late Robert Grace, and the bond and judgment of Francis Childs, if not recovered before my decease, or any other bonds, except the bond due from —— Killian, of Delaware State, which I give to my grandson,

Benjamin Franklin Bache. I also discharge him, my said son-in-law, from all claim and rent of moneys due to me, on book account or otherwise. I also give him all my musical instruments.

The king of France's picture, set with four hundred and eight diamonds, I give to my daughter, Sarah Bache, requesting , however, that she would not form any of those diamonds into ornaments either for herself or daughters, and thereby introduce or countenance the expensive, vain, and useless fashion of wearing jewels in this country; and those immediately connected with the picture may be preserved with the same.

I give and devise to my dear sister, Jane Mecom, a house and lot I have in Unity Street, Boston, nor or late under the care of Mr. Jonathan Williams, to her and to her heirs and assigns for ever. I also give her the yearly sum of fifty pounds sterling, during life, to commence at my death, and to be paid to her annually out of the interests or dividends arising on twelve shares which I have since my arrival at Philadelphia purchased in the Bank of North America, and, at her decease, I give the said twelve shares in the bank to my daughter, Sarah Bache, and her husband, Richard Bache. But it is my express will and desire that, after the payment of the above fifty pounds sterling annually to my said sister, my said daughter be allowed to apply the residue of the interest or dividends on those shares to her sole and separate use, during the life of my said sister, and afterwards the whole of the interest or dividends thereof as her private pocket money. I give the right I have to take up to three thousand acres of land in the State of Georgia, granted to me by the government of that State, to my grandson, William Temple Franklin, his heirs and assigns forever. I also give to my grandson, William Temple Franklin, the bond and judgment I have against him of four thousand pounds sterling, my right to the same to cease upon the day of his marriage; and if he dies unmarried, my will is, that the same be recovered and divided among my other grandchildren, the children of my daughter, Sarah Bache, in such manner and form as I have herein before given to them the other parts of my estate.

The philosophical instruments I have in Philadelphia I give to my ingenious friend, Francis Hopkinson.

To the children, grandchildren, and great-grandchildren of my brother, Samuel Franklin, that may be living at the time of my decease, I give fifty pounds sterling, to be equally divided among them. To the children, grandchildren, and great-grandchildren of my sister, Anne Harris, that may be living at the time of my decease, I give fifty pounds sterling to be equally divided among them. To the children, grandchildren, and great-grandchildren of my brother James Franklin, that may be living at the time of my decease, I give fifty pounds sterling to be equally divided among them. To the children, grandchildren, and great-grandchildren of my sister, Sarah Davenport, that may be living at the time of my decease, I give fifty pounds sterling to be equally divided among them. To the children, grandchildren, and great-grandchildren of my sister, Lydia Scott, that may be living at the time of my decease, I give fifty pounds sterling to be equally divided among them. To the children, grandchildren, and great-grandchildren of my sister, Jane Mecom, that may be living at the time of my decease, I give fifty pounds sterling to be equally divided among them.

I give to my grandson, Benjamin Franklin Bache, all the types and printing materials, which I now have in Philadelphia, with the complete letter foundry, which, in the whole, I suppose to be worth near one thousand pounds; but if he should die under age, then I do order the same to be sold by my executors, the survivors or survivor of them, and the moneys be equally divided among all the rest of my said daughter's children, or their representatives, each one on coming of age to take his or her share, and the children of such of them as may die under age to represent and to take the share and proportion of, the parent so dying, each one to receive his or her part of such share as they come of age.

With regard to my books, those I had in France and those I left in Philadelphia, being now assembled together here, and a catalogue made of them, it is my intention to dispose of them as follows: My "History of the Academy of Sciences," in sixty or seventy volumes quarto, I give to the Philosophical Society of Philadelphia, of which I have the honour to be President. My collection in folio of "Les Arts et les Metiers," I give to the American Philosophical Society, established in New England, of which I am a member. My quarto edition of the same, "Arts et Metiers," I give to the Library Company of Philadelphia. Such and so many of my books as I shall mark on my said catalogue with the name of my grandson, Benjamin Franklin Bache, I do hereby give to him; and such and so many of my books as I shall mark on the said catalogue with the name of my grandson, William Bache, I do hereby give to him; and such as shall be marked with the name of Jonathan Williams, I hereby give to my cousin of that name. The residue and remainder of all my books, manuscripts, and papers, I do give to my grandson, William Temple Franklin. My share in the Library Company of Philadelphia, I give to my grandson, Benjamin Franklin Bache, confiding that he will permit his brothers and sisters to share in the use of it.

I was born in Boston, New England, and owe my first instructions in literature to the free grammar schools established there. I therefore give one hundred pounds sterling to my executors, to be by them, the survivors or survivor of them, paid over to the managers or directors of the free schools in my native town of Boston, to be by them, or by those person or persons, who shall have the superintendance and management of the said schools, put out to interest, and so continued at interest forever, which interest annually shall be laid out in silver medals, and given as honorary rewards annually by the directors of the said free schools belonging to the said town, in such manner as to the discretion of the selectmen of the said town shall seem meet. Out of the salary that may remain due to me as President of the State, I do give the sum of two thousand pounds sterling to my executors, to be by them, the survivors or survivor of them, paid over to such person or persons as the legislature of this State by an act of Assembly shall appoint to receive the same in trust, to be employed for making the river Schuylkill navigable.

And what money of mine shall, at the time of my decease, remain in the hands of my bankers, Messrs. Ferdinand Grand and Son, at Paris, or Messrs. Smith, Wright, and Gray, of London, I will that, after my debts are paid and deducted, with the money legacies of this my will, the same be divided into four equal parts, two of which I give to my dear daughter, Sarah Bache, one to her son Benjamin, and one to my grandson, William Temple Franklin.

During the number of years I was in business as a stationer, printer, and postmaster, a great many small sums became due for books, advertisements, postage of letters, and other matters, which were not collected when, in 1757, I was sent by the Assembly to England as their agent, and by subsequent appointments continued there till 1775, when on my return, I was immediately engaged in the affairs of Congress, and sent to France in 1776, where I remained nine years, not returning till 1785, and the said debts, not being demanded in such a length of time, are become in a manner obsolete, yet are nevertheless justly due. These, as they are stated in my great folio ledger E, I bequeath to the contributors to the Pennsylvania Hospital, hoping that those debtors, and the descendants of such as are deceased, who now, as I find, make some difficulty of satisfying such antiquated demands as just debts, may, however, be induced to pay or give them as charity to that excellent institution. I am sensible that much must inevitably be lost, but I hope something considerable may be recovered. It is possible, too, that some of the parties charged may have existing old, unsettled accounts against me; in which case the managers of the said hospital will allow and deduct the amount, or pay the balance if they find it against me.

My debts and legacies being all satisfied and paid, the rest and residue of all my estate, real and personal, not herein expressly disposed of, I do give and bequeath to my son and daughter, Richard and Sarah Bache.

I request my friends, Henry Hill, Esquire, John Jay, Esquire, Francis Hopkinson, Esquire, and Mr. Edward Duffield, of Benfield, in Philadelphia County, to be the executors of this my last will and testament; and I hereby nominate and appoint them for that purpose.

I would have my body buried with as little expense or ceremony as may be. I revoke all former wills by me made, declaring this only to be my last.

In witness thereof, I have hereunto set my hand and seal, this seventeenth day of July, in the year of our Lord, one thousand seven hundred and eighty-eight.

B. Franklin

Signed, sealed, published, and declared by the above named Benjamin Franklin, for and as his last will and testament, in the presence of us.

Abraham Shoemaker, John Jones, George Moore.

Franklin defines himself in several ways at the beginning of his will, as a printer, as a diplomat, and as a politician. His values are revealed both by his possessions and by the people he leaves them to. The language of the document reflects the traditional wording of wills, a repetitive form indicating how the decedent's estate should be handled. Because it is a legal document, the will is of obvious importance.

THE INTERPERSONAL PERSPECTIVE

Although, at first glance, *interpersonal self-expression* might seem to be a contradiction in terms, it is an appropriate name for personal correspondence and friendly letters because this kind of writing involves a relationship between two people, and while the message is addressed to another person, it is, at the same time, a revelation of the writer's *self*. It is because of the close relationship between the two people involved that such writing tends to be expressive. The writer feels free to open up to the other person. Interpersonal self-expression has the following characteristics.

- ❏ Matters of mutual interest to the writer and reader are addressed.
- ❏ An ongoing relationship is revealed.
- ❏ A level of intimacy is established or maintained between the writer and reader.
- ❏ A personal or social obligation is fulfilled.

Matters of Mutual Interest

The content of interpersonal writing focuses on topics that the writer and reader have in common. A bond between the two is created by shared values or shared experiences. The interpersonal communication itself intensifies the bond by contributing a new set of shared experiences and by reinforcing the values the correspondents have in common.

Ongoing Relationship

Since the communication in friendly letters usually occurs because the two people involved are living apart and perhaps because they have been separated for a period of time, the content of such writing may involve asking and answering questions. There is an implicit assumption that the correspondence will be ongoing and that the questions will probably be answered at sometime in the future. Even if no questions are asked, there is an implicit expectation of a continuing dialogue.

Level of Intimacy

Depending on the relationship between the writer and the reader, a certain level of intimacy is established or maintained. Because of this intimacy, the writer feels comfortable sharing emotional responses with the reader. At times, if the people involved are intimate enough, they share a private language known only to the two of them.

Personal or Social Obligation

Letters between two friends may fulfill a social obligation between them. Expectations are created and fulfilled by the correspondence. Just as a conversation between two people assumes certain rules of etiquette, so does interpersonal correspondence.

AN EXAMPLE

The following personal letter reveals Georgia O'Keeffe's spontaneous emotional feelings and illustrates how interpersonal self-expression involves a sharing of those feelings.

Letter to Anita Pollitzer

GEORGIA O'KEEFFE

[Canyon, Texas, 11 September 1916]

Tonight I walked into the sunset—to mail some letters—the whole sky—and there is so much of it out here—was just blazing—and grey blue clouds were rioting all through the hotness of it—and the ugly little buildings and windmills looked great against it.

But some way or other I didn't seem to like the redness much so after I mailed the letters I walked home—and kept on walking—

The Eastern sky was all grey blue—bunches of clouds—different kinds of clouds—sticking around everywhere and the whole thing—lit up—first in one place—then in another with flashes of lightning—sometimes just sheet lightning—and sometimes sheet lightning with a sharp bright zigzag flashing across it—.

I walked out past the last house—past the last locust tree—and sat on the fence for a long time—looking—just looking at the lightning—you see there was nothing but sky and flat prairie land—land that seems more like the ocean than anything else I know—There was a wonderful moon—

Well I just sat there and had a great time all by myself—Not even many night noises—just the wind—

I wondered what you are doing—

> It is absurd the way I love this country—Then when I came back—it was funny—roads just shoot across blocks anywhere—all the houses looked alike—and I almost got lost—I had to laugh at myself—I couldnt tell which house was home—
>
> I am loving the plains more than ever it seems—and the SKY—Anita you have never seen SKY—it is wonderful—
>
>   Pat.

In this letter, Georgia O'Keeffe is writing about herself. The main idea is a implied self-definition: *I am a lover of the plains.* She uses intimate personal language and she reveals an emotional response of becoming aware of how she is "loving the plains." She reveals an ongoing relationship when she says, "I wondered what you are doing." She assumes that what interests her, her emotional response to the plains and her aesthetic values, will also interest Anita Pollitzer.

COMBINATIONS

The different kinds of self-expression blend together rather easily. In a diary, elements of autobiography may appear. In friendly letters, the writer may communicate the kinds of minor details of life that we see in diaries and journals. "The Way" by John Graves, although primarily autobiographical, exhibits some characteristics of personal self-expression as well.

WRITING STRATEGIES

If your purpose is expressive, all you have to do is write whatever you want to write. Sometimes that's harder to do than you would think. To begin, write down whatever comes into your head. Get words down on paper in whatever order they come to you. You can arrange them later. Think of expressive writing as a sort of laboratory where you can experiment with language. You have the freedom to say whatever you want to say.

As you think about your topic, consider the following questions.

- How do you feel about the topic—what emotions does it arouse?
- How does it affect you?
- How does it make you feel when you think about it?
- What do you want to do when you think about it?
- What events in your life do you associate with your topic?
- Why do you think you feel the way you do?
- How does it relate to your value system?
- How does it affect your goals for the future?

2

Literary Writing

From the myths and songs in primal cultures to modern poetry and fiction, artists have created structures with language that please and delight their audiences. All literary works, no matter how different they may seem, have one thing in common: the writer has deliberately arranged the words so that the effect produced in the reader or audience is one of pleasure.

In this respect, literature is like other art forms. They all please us, or at least have as their purpose to please. One of the outcomes of the aesthetic pleasure that art gives us is this: a work of art will bear repetition. We listen to music we like over and over. We may go back to see again a movie we especially enjoyed. We hang paintings or posters on our walls and look at them, or at least see them, almost everyday. So it is with literary writing. We may reread a poem or a story many times and get just as much pleasure from it each time.

It is the arrangement of words in literary writing that appeals to our aesthetic sensibilities. The literary structures created by the various combinations of words and images please us when we read them. Even if the images themselves may not be appealing, as in the case of horror stories, the structuring of them in a dramatic form may produce enjoyment in many readers.

Literature is most commonly classified by genre: poetry, drama, the short story, and the novel. A major distinction is usually made between poetry and prose. Poetry is traditionally defined as a rhythmical use of language. Everyone is familiar with the rhythms and rhymes of traditional verse, a regular repetition of stresses and sounds. Prose, on the other hand, more closely resembles the patterns of ordinary, everyday speech and is the kind of language used in fiction. In modern literature, however, the distinction between prose and poetry has diminished. Modern poetry relies less on strict metrical rhythms and modern fiction has become increasingly poetic. Some nonfiction may be literary if its purpose is to entertain. Humorous essays are clearly literary.

No matter what form it takes, literary writing has as its purpose to create an aesthetically pleasing effect with language. To produce this effect a literary work will have theme, tension, verisimilitude, and aesthetic language.

GENERAL CHARACTERISTICS

- ❑ Theme and artistic unity are apparent.
- ❑ Tension is created.
- ❑ Verisimilitude is present.
- ❑ Language that creates an aesthetic response is used.

THEME AND ARTISTIC UNITY

In a work called *Poetics*, the Greek philosopher Aristotle said that a literary work must have a beginning, a middle, and an end. Although it may seem to be a statement of the obvious, it nevertheless describes an important feature of literary art. This statement means that a literary work is unified, that the ending of the work comes inevitably out of what has come before. Each part of the work is connected to every other part. The recognition of that interconnectedness of the events is called unity of plot. In addition to plot, time and place have also been traditionally regarded as unities, especially in drama.

In modern literature, we usually recognize other elements that unify a work, such as characterization, style, symbolism, and theme. When we talk about the *theme* of a literary work, we are recognizing the unity of the work that allows us to identify a theme. For instance, a theme commonly developed in Renaissance poetry is that art is timeless and immortal. A theme expresses in a single statement the combined effect that all elements in a literary work produce.

TENSION

The structure of literary writing creates tension. Some elements, such as dramatic action, create tension through conflict. A character in a story may be involved in either physical, social, or psychological conflict. A physical conflict is usually external, with one character pitted against another character or against the forces of nature. A social conflict occurs when a character is at odds with the conventions or mores of society. Psychological conflict is internal, caused by a dilemma in the mind of the character.

Tension is also created when two contrasting elements are juxtaposed, when two things that are different are put side by side. For instance, when two characters who are very different from each other are put into a plot together, they serve to create such a contrast. Even if no overt physical conflict is developed, the difference between the two characters creates tension.

VERISIMILITUDE

The author of a literary work presents events or scenes by using a variety of literary devices that shape the reader's perception of the experiences recorded in the work. Elements such as a setting, dialogue, and characterization are used to create a plot or a scene. These devices allow the reader to identify with the settings and events depicted in the work. A graphic description of the setting, a vivid portrayal of a character, or a conversation between characters will enable the reader to become a part of the imaginative world of the writer.

AESTHETIC LANGUAGE

A literary artist deliberately selects words that have an aesthetic effect on the reader. This is the hallmark of literary writing and is especially apparent in the author's use of imagery, symbolism, connotations, rhythm, and sound patterns.

Imagery

Imagery involves choosing a word or phrase that engages the senses. When we read an image in a work of literature, that image involves us in the work in a way that is different from our objective understanding of the meaning of the word or words used to create the image. Images are of two types: literal and figurative.

Literal Images

As the word implies, these images mean exactly what they say. In literary writing, however, the writer presents them to the reader in an unusual way. They are graphic and vivid and take advantage of the connotations of the words used to create them. Instead of saying, "I saw a beautiful sunset," the literary artist might say something like, "I saw a brilliant orange sunset streaked with clouds of rose and plum." Instead of saying, "I touched a tree," the literary artist might say, "I rubbed the rough bark of the tree, fingering the tiny bits of it that crumbled in my hand and inhaling its pungent aroma." Notice that even though the images are literal, the second wording is more concrete and vivid. The images of the second version in each case engage our senses with more specific detail and take advantage of the connotative meanings of the words.

Figurative Images

Figurative language is a prominent feature of much literary writing, although literary works certainly can be written without using any figures of speech at all. Still, the use of figurative language is one of those features that tells us that we may be looking at a work which is primarily literary. In contrast to literal images, figurative images can be thought of as non-literal images because the impressions they present to the reader are not intended to be realistic. The three most commonly used figurative images (figures of speech) are the simile, the metaphor, and personification.

A simile is a comparison between two different objects or concepts using the word *like* or *as*. Look at the following example:

The clouds look like fluffy balls of cotton.

The comparison is figurative, not literal. Clouds and cotton balls are not in the same class of things, but the comparison seems appropriate because it calls our attention to the similarity in the appearance of the two things and deepens our response by allowing us to associate the image of clouds with the sense of touch, the feel of cotton balls.

The comparison made in the metaphor is more direct, as in the following example:

Look at those fluffy balls of cotton floating in the sky.

The effect of the metaphor is more startling than the effect of the simile, but the comparison is the same.

Personification gives human characteristics to animals, plants, objects, or abstractions, as in the following example:

The clouds are smiling at us.

Clouds don't smile; people do. The comparison is figurative.

Symbolism

A symbol is an object, a person, a place, or an action that stands for something else in addition to its literal meaning in the literary work. In other words, the symbol suggests a meaning beyond itself. There are universal symbols and symbols that are particular to the literary work itself. A universal symbol has the same meaning in a number of different literary works because of some qualities inherent in the symbol itself. For instance, the ocean is often used as a symbol of time or eternity.

In literature almost anything can be a symbol, depending on how it is used in the work. John Keats, in his "Ode on a Grecian Urn," used the image of an urn with figures depicted on it to symbolize the timelessness of art.

Connotative Language

As we saw in Chapter 1, connotations are the associated, emotional meanings of words. (Denotations are the literal dictionary meanings.) Authors of literary works are very sensitive to the connotations of words and deliberately select language that will have an emotional effect on the reader.

Rhythm and Sound Patterns

Literary works, particularly poems, are characterized by the use of sound patterns and rhythms that help create mood and tone. The following excerpt from John Keats' "La Belle Dame sans Merci" illustrates how rhythm and rhyme help create a feeling of sadness and despondency.

> O what can ail thee, knight at arms,
> Alone and palely loitering?
> The sedge has wither'd from the lake,
> And no birds sing.

Although the regular pattern of stressed and unstressed syllables creates an even emotional tone throughout the stanza, the shortened last line makes the mood suddenly somber. Coupled with the words "alone," "palely," and "wither'd," this use of rhythm creates the impression of a plaintive, mournful scene.

The rhyme scheme follows the traditional structure of the ballad stanza, the second and fourth lines rhyming. The repetition of the sound *-ing* focuses our attention on the words "loitering" (suggesting passivity) and "sing" (suggesting activity). The last line, however, tells us that the activity of singing is absent and this reinforces the dominant impression of sadness.

An Example

The following excerpt from John Gardner's novel entitled *October Light* illustrates how the literary narrative creates tension and interest through conflict as well as through imagery, both literal and figurative.

An Interlude

JOHN GARDNER

While his great-aunt Estelle was thinking of Notre Dame, Terence Parks stood in the old man's sitting room-bedroom, turning the French horn around and around, emptying water from the tubing. He was as shy a boy as ever lived, as shy as the girl seated now on the sagging, old fashioned bed with her hands on the flute in her lap. She, Margie Phelps, gazed steadily at the floor, her silver-blonde hair falling straight past her shoulders, soft as flax. Her face was serious, though she was prepared to smile if he should wish her to. She wore a drab green dress that was long and (he could not know) expensive, striped kneesox, and fashionably clunky shoes. As for Terence, he had brown hair that curled below his ears, glasses without which he was utterly helpless, and a small chin. He had, at least in his own opinion, nothing to recommend him, not even a sense of humor. He therefore dressed, always, with the greatest care—dark blue shirts, never with a shirttail hanging out, black trousers, black shoes and belt. He fitted the mouthpiece back into the horn and glanced at Margie. He had had for some time a great, heart-slaughtering crush on her, though he hadn't told her that, or anyone else. In his secret distress, he was like the only Martian in the world. As if she'd known he would do it, Margie looked up for an instant at exactly the moment he glanced at her, and immediately—blushing—both of them looked down.

He set his horn down carefully on the chair and went over to the window at the foot of the bed to look out. A noisy, blustering wind had come up, pushing large clouds across the sky, a silver-toothed wolf pack moving against the moon, quickly consuming it, throwing the hickory tree, the barn and barnyard into darkness. He could hear what sounded like a gate creaking, metal against metal.

"Is it raining yet?" she asked, her voice almost inaudible.

As she came up timidly behind him, Terence moved over a little to give her room at the window.

Her hand on the windowsill was white, almost blue. He could easily reach over and touch it. In the living room behind them—the door was part way open—the grown-ups were laughing and talking, DeWitt Thomas still picking his guitar and singing. You couldn't hear the words. He looked again at her hand, then at the side of her face, then quickly back out at the night.

"Rain scares me," she said. Though her face turned only a little, he could feel her watching him.

The moon reappeared, the black clouds sweeping along like objects in a flood. Terence put his hand on the windowsill near hers, as if accidentally. He listened for the sound of someone coming into the room and realized only now that the door to his left went to the back entryway and, beyond that, the kitchen. He felt panic, thinking they might go out that door unmissed. Something white blew across the yard, moving slowly, like a form in a dream.

"What's that?" she asked, startled, and put her hand on his. Her head came slightly closer and, despite the violence of the storm in his chest, he smelled her hair.

"Fertilizer bag, I think," he said.

"What?" she said.

He said it again, this time loud enough to hear. She did not draw her hand away, though the touch was light, as if at the slightest sign she would quickly remove it. His mind raced almost as fast as his heart, and he pressed closer to the window, pretending to follow the white thing's ghostly flight. Again he smelled her hair, and now her breath—a warm scent of apple.

As for Dr. Phelps' granddaughter Margie, her heart thudded and her brain tingled; she half believed she might faint. Her friend Jennifer at school had told her weeks ago that Terry Parks had a crush on her, and she hadn't doubted it, though it seemed to her a miracle. When he played his French horn in the school orchestra or at the Sage City Symphony, his playing gave her goosebumps, and when they had answering parts in the woodwind quintet, she blushed. Finding him here at the Pages tonight had been a kind of confirmation of the miracle, and when the grown-ups had suggested that the two of them might play duets together, and had sent them here, so that the adults could talk . . .

Now another cloud, larger than those before it, was swallowing the moon. The noise of the wind half frightened, half thrilled her. The barn stood out stark, sharply outlined. The white thing—fertilizer bag, that was right—was snagged in a fence, gray as bone, suddenly inert.

He moved his hand a little, closing it on hers. She drew her breath in sharply. Was someone coming?

"You kids want baked apples?" Virginia Hicks called from the doorway behind them.

They parted hands quickly and whirled around, frightened and confused.

"I'll leave them here on the bedside table," Virginia said, smiling. She seemed to have seen nothing. "You two make beautiful music together," she said, and smiled again, with a wave of her cigarette.

Neither of them spoke, heads spinning, smiling at the floor. Virginia left them.

Something thudded hard against the house, a small limb, perhaps, but no window broke, the walls did not sway, and so they laughed, embarrassed by their momentary fear. As they laughed they walked toward the bedside table where the baked apples stood oozing juice.

"Mmm, baked apples," Margie said softly. She picked up her plate and seated herself primly on the bedside, eyes cast down. Terence came and sat beside her.

"Listen to that wind," he said. The night howled and thudded like an orchestra gone wrong, dissonant and senseless, dangerous, but Margie was happy, for once in her life utterly without fear, except of him. She laid her hand casually on the cover beside her, conscious of the laughter and talk in the next room and also now a sound like arguing, coming from upstairs. She glanced at Terence and smiled. Smiling back, secretive and careful, he put his hand over hers.

Even though this excerpt was taken from a longer work, it has a unity that allows us to think of it as complete. Indeed, within the structure of the novel, it is almost an aside that has little to do with the movement of the plot of the novel as a whole. This beautifully written little scene illustrates all the general characteristics of literary writing outlined above.

Gardner creates verisimilitude through the physical descriptions of the two characters, Terence and Margie, and through the description of the setting. With the characterizations and the creation of a realistic setting the author gives us the feeling that the characters are real and that the events depicted actually happened. We develop some sympathy for Terence and Margie. We willingly involve ourselves as readers in the fiction that the author has created and participate in the events along with the characters. The dialogue also helps us to feel the reality of the scene.

The tension developed in this narrative derives from the characters and the circumstances they find themselves in. Their shyness creates some tension since they are thrown together in a bedroom. Since neither one of them has ever expressed the feelings they have for the other, the internal conflict builds as the plot moves forward. Tension is also increased because the two of them feel isolated: the adults are in the other room and the storm is going on outside.

This episode has artistic unity. Each element—characterization, setting, dialogue, figurative language, and symbolism—moves the plot along towards its inevitable conclusion. Gardner's use of language that evokes an aesthetic response is particularly effective. The description of the clouds as "a silver-toothed wolf pack" is a threatening image that increases the tension of the plot. The symbolism of the storm is effective because it suggests not only turmoil and disorder outside the house, but also reflects the internal conflict, especially in Terence when we are made aware of "the violence of the storm in his chest. . . ."

FOUR KINDS OF LITERARY WRITING

We can divide literary writing into four categories, regardless of the genre. These categories reflect four different approaches to a literary work. These approaches embody the theoretical principles a writer uses to select and organize the content of the work. (Writers may or may not realize that they are using a particular approach.) Some writers consciously adhere to a theory, deliberately following its principles of construction; others simply follow the prevailing literary conventions or imitate what other writers have done without ever consciously adopting a unified, consistent theory. The four approaches to literary writing—expressive, imitative, objective, and pragmatic—address different aspects of the question, "What is literature?"

THE EXPRESSIVE APPROACH

As the name suggests, the expressive approach produces a highly personal kind of literature, similar in some ways to the expressive writing discussed in Chapter 1. The expressive approach became important in England in the nineteenth century when a group of writers that we now call Romantics began to emphasize the importance of recording their emotional responses in the poetry they wrote. The following characteristics are usually found in literature that has been written according to an expressive approach.

- ❏ Personal experiences are recorded.
- ❏ Personal images and/or symbols are used.
- ❏ First person pronouns are used.
- ❏ Emotional reactions are expressed.

Personal Experiences

The writer creates the literary work out of personal experiences. Those events that are most memorable to the writer are transformed into literary language.

Personal Images and/or Symbols

The imagery and/or symbolism found in a literary work using the expressive theory of art are based on the personal experience of the writer. These personal images and symbols have meaning to the writer even though they may be almost incomprehensible to the reader.

First Person Pronouns

Almost invariably, works using the expressive theory are written in the first person. The use of first person pronouns is the natural result of the personal focus of the expressive theory of art.

Emotional Reactions

The words the writer uses express emotional reactions to the experiences recorded. As a result, such writing may seem similar to expressive writing.

AN EXAMPLE

John Keats was one of those nineteenth-century English Romantics who saw poetry as an expression of emotion. The following sonnet records Keats's reactions when, at the age of twenty-one, he read George Chapman's translation of Homer's *Iliad* and *Odyssey*. (Chapman's translation was published between 1598 and 1616.)

On First Looking into Chapman's Homer

JOHN KEATS

Much have I travell'd in the realms of gold,
  And many goodly states and kingdoms seen;
  Round many western islands have I been
Which bards in fealty to Apollo hold.

> Oft of one wide expanse had I been told
>   That deep-browed Homer ruled as his demesne;
>   Yet did I never breathe its pure serene
> Till I heard Chapman speak out loud and bold:
> Then felt I like some watcher of the skies
>   When a new planet swims into his ken;
> Or like stout Cortez when with eagle eyes
>   He stared at the Pacific—and all his men
> Looked at each other with a wild surmise—
>   Silent, upon a peak in Darien.

In this poem, Keats uses a traditional poetic form, the Italian sonnet (rhyme scheme abba,abba,cdc,dcd). Usually a kind of poem associated with themes of romantic love, Keats has transformed this sonnet into an expression of his own love of poetry. Through his use of first person pronouns and in his recounting of his personal experience with literature, we feel the presence of the poet. He expresses his emotional reaction in his use of the word "felt" and in his sense of wonder when he compares himself to a "watcher of the skies" who discovers a "new planet." He also expresses an emotional response when he refers to the "wild surmise" of those who discovered the Pacific Ocean. (Keats mistakenly thought that Cortez discovered the Pacific. It was actually Balboa. Obviously, accuracy is not a necessary characteristic of literary writing.)

THE IMITATIVE APPROACH

The writer using an imitative approach attempts to imitate or mirror reality. A preponderance of the works of modern fiction use the conventions of realism and so reflect the imitative approach. The following characteristics are apparent.

❑   Real life situations are presented.
❑   Realistic language is used.
❑   Realistic, often ordinary, people are depicted.
❑   Realistic settings are described.

Real Life Situations

Situations that have the feel of reality are presented to the reader. The writer attempts to present the events of the plot in a way that seems to be consistent with similar events that take place in everyday life and so creates an impression of reality.

Realistic Language

Characters in a literary work that has an imitative approach will use language that seems appropriate to that character. In other words, the words used fit with the way we might expect the character to speak if we were to really meet him or her. Even though the dialogue in a literary work may not be exactly the way people say things, it does give the reader the *impression* that the characters are real.

Ordinary People

The characters are like those we might expect to meet in real life. The physical descriptions of the characters add to an overall impression of reality. Further, the writer may make the reader aware of the thoughts of the characters.

Realistic Settings

Settings are described in some detail with an eye toward accurately recreating the place where the action occurs. These descriptions reinforce the impression that the characters are like those we would expect to meet in our everyday existence and that the events narrated are probable.

AN EXAMPLE

Frank Norris was an early twentieth-century American writer whose novels were influenced by naturalism, a literary movement that, among other things, emphasized an accurate portrayal of human beings and the environmental forces that shape them. The following excerpt illustrates an attention to an imitative presentation, writing that imitates life.

Spring Plowing

FRANK NORRIS

The plowing, now in full swing, enveloped him in a vague, slow-moving whirl of things. Underneath him was the jarring, jolting, trembling machine; not a clod was turned, not an obstacle encountered, that he did not receive the swift impression of it through all his body; the very friction of the damp soil, sliding incessantly from the shiny surface of the plowshares, seemed to reproduce itself in his finger-tips and along the back of his head. He heard the horse-hoofs by the myriads crushing down easily, deeply, into the loam, the prolonged clinking of trace-chains, the working of the smooth brown flanks in the harness, the clatter of wooden hames, the champing of bits, the click of iron shoes against pebbles, the brittle stubble of the surface ground crackling and snapping as the furrows turned, the sonorous, steady breaths wrenched from the deep, laboring chests, strap-bound, shining with sweat, and all along the line the voices of the men talking to the horses. Everywhere there were visions of glossy brown backs, straining, heaving, swollen with muscle; harness streaked with specks of froth, broad, cup-shaped hoofs, heavy with brown loam, men's faces red with tan, blue overalls spotted with axle-grease; muscled hands, the knuckles whitened in their grip on the reins, and through it all the ammoniacal smell of the horses, the bitter reek of perspiration of beasts and men, the aroma of warm leather, the scent of dead stubble—and stronger and more penetrating than everything else, the heavy, enervating odour of the upturned, living earth.

Norris' description focuses on details that create a vivid impression of the actions associated with plowing a field using a hand plow and horses. Norris engages each of our senses in turn. With the man we feel "the jarring, jolting, trembling machine" and "the friction of the damp soil." We hear the sound of the horse-hoofs "crushing down . . . into the loam . . . the clinking of trace-chains . . . the click of iron shoes," and "the voices of the men." We see the "glossy brown backs" of the horse, "men's faces red with tan," and "knuckles whitened in their grip of the reins. . . ." We smell "the ammoniacal smell of the horses . . . the aroma of warm leather," and the "odour of the upturned, living earth." These images make the scene seem real.

THE OBJECTIVE APPROACH

A writer who is influenced by the objective approach sees literature as existing for its own sake. You may have heard the phrase "Art for Art's Sake" used to characterize this theory. Edgar Allan Poe made reference to it when he spoke of the dignity and nobility of a "poem per se—[a] poem which is a poem and nothing more—[a] poem written solely for the poem's sake." In England during the last part of the nineteenth century, Oscar Wilde reflected the influence of this aesthetic theory in his brilliantly witty dramas. In twentieth-century American poetry a group of poets called the Imagists are a notable example of the influence of this approach. The objective approach has four characteristics.

- ❏ The focus on the experience depicted is sharp and limited.
- ❏ Structural unity is emphasized.
- ❏ The sound and/or appearance of words is emphasized.
- ❏ Exact images are used.

Sharp and Limited Focus

The writer operating from the objective approach tends to focus on limited areas of experience or on a small parts of a setting using sharp, precise images. There is a concentration of focus. Rather than offering complete explanations, the work may suggest or intimate.

Structural Unity

Everything in the work is unified. The writer strives to use words and images that contribute to the overall aesthetic effect of the work. Often the unity is created by the imagery used or by symbolism.

Emphasis on Sound and/or Appearance of Words

The writer pays special attention to each word, not only to its denotative and connotative meanings, but also to its sound and perhaps even its appearance on the page. Rhythms are often used to create a certain mood.

Exact Images

The writer using an objective approach strives for concreteness and exactness. All the images presented support the aesthetic whole.

AN EXAMPLE

Haiku is a traditional Japanese form of poetry having three lines and a set number of syllables—5, 7, 5. Many haiku incorporate references to a season of the year, and all haiku please the reader because they contain evocative imagery. Here are four examples.

Four Haiku

I
Music from a flute
Asks me to stop and listen
To the soft spring rain.

II
Silver clouds touch earth—
My summer-tired feet and eyes
Must know more than dirt.

> **III**
> Rabbit disappears
> Hiding among brittle weeds:
> Small clouds drift away.
>
> **IV**
> A tree stands cold, still,
> Reaches upward for the sky—
> I know only now.

These four haiku illustrate how poetry can create a complex set of meanings through a compressed structure. The connotations of the images produce many connections with other images in each of the poems.

In the first haiku, for instance, the image of music is associated with the flute and also, by implication, with the sound of the rain. The music "asks" the poet to "stop and listen." We become aware of both action (listening) and inaction (stopping). In the same moment of realization we discover that the sound of "the soft spring rain" has an aesthetic quality and that is something to be appreciated as we would enjoy hearing the music "from a flute."

In the second poem "silver clouds" exist in contrast to the heat and the "dirt" of summer. And yet the contrast is overcome because the clouds "touch the earth" forming a kind of bond between clouds and earth. The poet is allowed to transcend the oppressiveness of the summer.

The third haiku presents us first with the image of a rabbit disappearing and "hiding among the brittle weeds." The disappearance of the rabbit is somehow connected to the drifting away of the small clouds. The image of "brittle weeds" reinforces the impression that the situation is transitory, and may suggest the coming of autumn, the season of transition from summer to winter.

In the last haiku the impression of yet a fourth season, winter, is suggested by the word "cold." The tension between earth and sky is emphasized by the image of the tree reaching "upward for the sky." Confronted by the stark reality of the barren tree, the poet is struck by the importance of being aware of the present moment.

THE PRAGMATIC APPROACH

The pragmatic approach (also known as the didactic theory) is generally discounted in modern literature; nonetheless, modern literary criticism recognizes its existence by acknowledging the tendency of literature to focus on theme. Certainly, the theory has been important in the history of literature.

Aesop's fables are a notable example. Allegories, like John Bunyan's *The Pilgrim's Progress*, are frequently didactic. The characteristics of this approach are these.

- ❏ A lesson is taught or a theme is drawn from the experiences reported.
- ❏ The experience presented is related to the theme.
- ❏ A value system is adopted and/or rejected.
- ❏ Harmony is achieved.

A Lesson or Theme

The lesson in a pragmatic literary work may actually be appended to the story or poem in the form of a moral which confirms or rejects social mores. In *Paradise Lost* John Milton says that his purpose in writing the poem is to "justify the ways of God to man." Such a statement reflects the universal scope of the work and reinforces many of the religious tenets of Milton's society.

Relation of Experience to Theme

The theme is often presented by references to moral principles or codes of behavior. If characters are involved, it is through the action of the characters that the writer shapes our attitudes.

A Value System Is Adopted

The lesson or moral of a pragmatic work of literature reflects a referenced value system. Part of the intent of the work is to give support to the values expressed in the work. Satire, making fun of some set of values, is often used to debunk something, frequently some custom or social institution that the writer finds offensive or ridiculous.

Harmony

Harmony means that in the resolution of the narrative, order is restored or maintained. Even though harmony may be disrupted, the ultimate conclusion of works based on a pragmatic theory is a restoration or maintenance of a world consistent with the lesson being taught.

An Example

Written in 1838, the following poem by Henry Wadsworth Longfellow reflects the poetic values of his age. By following a pragmatic approach, he was able to express in his poetry what Americans wanted and yearned for. He delivered moral statements and uplifting sentiments exalting the work ethic and family relationships.

A Psalm of Life: What the Heart of the Young Man Said to the Psalmist

HENRY WADSWORTH LONGFELLOW

Tell me not in mournful numbers,
Life is but an empty dream!—
For the soul is dead that slumbers,
And things are not what they seem.

Life is real ! Life is earnest!
And the grave is not its goal;
Dust thou art, to dust returneth,
Was not spoken of the soul.

Not enjoyment, and not sorrow,
Is our destined end or way;
But to act, that each to-morrow
Finds us farther than to-day.

Art is long, and Time is fleeting,
And our hearts, though stout and brave,
Still, like muffled drums, are beating
Funeral marches to the grave.

In the world's broad field of battle,
In the bivouac of Life,
Be not like, dumb, driven cattle!
Heart within, and God o'er head!

Lives of great men all remind us
We can make our lives sublime,
And, departing, leave behind us
Footprints in the sands of time;

Footprints, that perhaps another,
Sailing o'er life's solemn main,
A forlorn and shipwrecked brother,
Seeing, shall take heart again.

Let us, then, be up and doing,
With a heart for any fate;
Still achieving, still pursuing,
Learn to labor and to wait.

The poem's title makes its didactic purpose evident. Longfellow intends to give the reader some moral lesson. His attention to the reader is evident throughout the poem by his use of first person plural pronouns (*we, us, our*) and the imperative mood (use of commands). Many of the lines in the poem sound like proverbs or bits of advice given to the reader; indeed they sound like the advice a parent might give to a child. In addition, the values expressed in the poem, extolling the work ethic, were values held by many people in American society at the time the poem was written. Those values represent a connection to a widely held cultural myth.

COMBINATIONS

Finding a work of literature that embodies only one of the approaches is rare. For example, even a highly expressive work may reveal a realistic view of the world and draw our attention to concrete images.

WRITING STRATEGIES

If you plan to write a literary piece, there are some things to consider before you begin. Go through your memories, your childhood and adolescence, people you remember. Try to recall an outstanding event and think it through—when it began, what happened, how it ended. Or if you prefer, invent something entirely out of your imagination.

As you think about your literary project, consider these questions.

❑ What is your story about?
❑ What are the major events?
❑ Who are the characters in the story?
❑ What do the characters look like?
❑ What conflict is occurring?
❑ When does the moment of crisis occur?
❑ How is the conflict resolved?
❑ Where does the conflict take place?
❑ What are the physical details of the setting?
❑ Over what period of time does the story take place?

Persuasive Writing

e encounter persuasion every day. It would be difficult to imagine living in the modern world without coming into contact with attempts to persuade us. We see and hear communication intended to affect or to change our opinions everywhere we turn—on billboards by the side of the road, in magazines, in newspapers, and in conversations with friends, acquaintances, or even total strangers. We are exposed to persuasion probably more than to communications that have any of the other purposes. Someone always seems ready to sell us something or impose an opinion on us.

In persuasion, the writer attempts to change the reader's attitudes or beliefs and may even try to move the reader to some action based on that change in beliefs. The basis of that attempt is called an issue and is a reflection of attitudes and opinions. An issue is a point of disagreement, a statement of the opposing points of view, a debatable proposition. An issue usually embodies a matter of public concern, a matter of discussion, debate, or dispute.

Such an issue may be expressed in terms of that disagreement, that is, whether or not some position should be adopted or followed. Issues involve those matters that cannot be resolved by the application of scientific logic. They deal with attitudes and opinions, questions of morality, ethics, and values. Examples of persuasive issues include the following: whether or not abortion ought to be legal, whether or not nuclear reactors ought to be built, what U.S. foreign policy should be. Many questions like these are decided by the government or by other social institutions through a process that involves consideration of the arguments on all sides of the issue.

Persuasion deals with attitudes and opinions, questions that cannot be settled with the same degree of certainty that topics addressed in referential writing can. Nevertheless, many of the issues considered in persuasive writing are extremely important and deserve careful consideration. In fact, persuasion is often the only tool, short of physical force, that we have available to influence and change people's behavior.

In persuasion the argument consists of a claim defending a position on some issue (a debatable proposition). The claim is supported by substantiating details and by appeals to the reader. The argument is authenticated by a warrant (a general belief that the reader will accept) and is presented with language appropriate to the reader, language the reader can relate to.

GENERAL CHARACTERISTICS

❑ A claim is made.
❑ Support for the claim is offered.
❑ A warrant (a general belief) is present.
❑ Reader-oriented language is used.

CLAIM

A claim is an assertion about the rightness of the writer's position on the issue. In effect, a claim (usually stated as a general statement and sometimes called a thesis statement) is what the writer wants the reader to accept. For example, a claim derived from the issue of whether or not nuclear power plants ought to be built would be either that *the building of nuclear power plants ought to be continued* or *the building of nuclear power plants ought to be stopped*. These two assertions represent opposing claims made about the issue.

SUPPORT AND GROUNDS

Direct support is an assertion that is made to convince the audience that the claim is a sound one. For instance, the claim that *the building of nuclear power plants ought to be stopped* could be supported by the assertion that *they are dangerous and represent a threat to the environment and to human beings*. Such assertions provide the reasons that directly support the argument.

In addition, the argument must have *grounds*, the underlying foundation for the argument. Depending on the claim and the kind of argument, the grounds may be such things as experimental data, common knowledge, observations, or statistics.

Other support comes in the form of personal experience, slogans, or other devices that appeal to the audience. These *motivational supports*, in the form of appeals, are discussed later.

WARRANT AND BACKING

Warrants are those beliefs that give authenticity to the support and make it relevant to the claim. A warrant is a general belief or principle that most people take for granted. Warrants are often expressed as cultural or social myths.

A social or cultural myth is a value system accepted by a majority of people in a society or culture. If a particular belief is not accepted in a culture, some arguments cannot be made. For instance, in some cultures, throughout history and even in modern times, an argument to support the claim "women should have an education" could not be made because the warrant "all people are created equal" is not part of the belief system of the culture.

A successful persuasive writer shows an understanding of the myths present in a culture. The advertising industry is very sensitive to these myths and uses them to sell products. Changes in public values are reflected almost immediately in advertising.

Warrants are not self-evident, so they may require additional backing to make them acceptable to the audience. Usually such backing establishes a broader context for the principles expressed by the warrant.

READER-ORIENTED LANGUAGE

The writer of persuasion usually has a specific audience in mind, so he or she uses language appropriate to that reader. By using language that the reader finds familiar, the writer has an easier time getting the reader to agree with the claim, so any kind of language that promotes that end is used. As a result, the writer may use everyday speech, slang, jargon, or Standard Edited American English, if that is what the reader expects and will accept. The language is also appropriate to the situational context, that is, the occasion for the writing. A situational context tells the writer what kind of audience is being addressed and, as a result, it influences the kind of language used.

The writer may also personalize the language by using second person pronouns (*you, your, yours*) or imperative sentences (commands) to draw the reader into the argument and gain identification with the reader. It is important for the writer to know who the reader is.

AN EXAMPLE

The following article by Anna Quindlen illustrates the characteristics of persuasive writing.

Death Penalty's False Promise: An Eye for an Eye

ANNA QUINDLEN

Ted Bundy and I go back a long way, to a time when there was a series of unsolved murders in Washington State known only as the Ted murders. Like a lot of other reporters, I'm something of a crime buff. But the Washington Ted murders—and the ones that followed in Utah, Colorado and finally in Florida, where Ted Bundy was convicted and sentenced to die—fascinated me because I could see myself as one of the victims. I looked at the studio photographs of young women with long hair, pierced ears, easy smiles, and I read the descriptions: polite, friendly, quick to help, eager to please. I thought about being approached by a handsome young man asking for help, and I knew if I had been in the wrong place at the wrong time I would have been a goner.

By the time Ted finished up in Florida, law enforcement authorities suspected he had murdered dozens of young women. He and the death penalty seemed made for each other.

The death penalty and I, on the other hand, seem to have nothing in common. But Ted Bundy had made me think about it all over again, now that the outlines of my 60s liberalism have been filled in with a decade as a reporter covering some of the worst back alleys in New York City and three years a mother who, like most, would lay down her life for her kids.

Simply put, I am opposed to the death penalty. I would tell that to any judge or lawyer undertaking the voir dire of jury candidates in a state in which the death penalty can be imposed. That is why I would be excused from such a jury. In a rational, completely cerebral way, I think the killing of one human being as punishment for the killing of another makes no sense and is inherently immoral.

But whenever my response to an important subject is rational and completely cerebral, I know there is something wrong with it—and so it is here. I have always been governed by my gut, and my gut says I am hypocritical about the death penalty. That is, I do not in theory think that Ted Bundy, or others like him, should be put to death. But if my daughter had been the one clubbed to death as she slept in a Tallahassee sorority house, and if the bite mark left in her buttocks had been one of the prime pieces of evidence against the young man charged with her murder, I would with the greatest pleasure kill him myself.

The State of Florida will not permit the parents of Bundy's victims to do that, and in a way, that is the problem with an emotional response to capital punishment. The only reason for a death penalty is to exact retribution. Is there anyone who really thinks that it is a deterrent, that there are considerable numbers of criminals out there who think twice about committing crimes because of the sentence involved? The ones I have met in the course of my professional duties have either sneered at the justice system, where they can exchange one charge for another with more ease than they could return a shirt to a clothing store, or they have simply believed that it is the other guy who will get caught, get convicted, get the stiffest sentence. Of course, the death penalty would act as a deterrent by eliminating recidivism, but then so would life without parole, albeit at greater taxpayer expense.

I don't believe that deterrence is what most proponents seek from the death penalty anyhow. Our most profound emotional response is to want criminals to suffer as their victims did. When a man is accused of throwing a child from a high-rise terrace, my emotional—some might say hysterical—response is that he should be given an opportunity to see how endless the seconds are from the 31st story to the ground. In a civilized society that will never happen.

And so what many people want from the death penalty, they will never get.

Death is death, you may say, and you would be right. But anyone who has seen someone die suddenly of a heart attack and someone else slip slowly into the clutches of cancer knows that there are gradations of dying.

I watched a television re-enactment one night of an execution by lethal injection. It was well done; it was horrible. The methodical approach, people standing around the gurney waiting, made it more awful. One moment there was a man in a prone position; the next moment that man was gone. On another night I watched a television movie about a little boy named Adam Walsh, who disappeared from a shopping center in Florida. There was a re-enactment of Adam's parents coming to New York, where they appeared on morning talk shows begging for their son's return, and in their hotel room, where they received a call from the police saying that Adam had been found: not all of Adam, actually, just his severed head, discovered in the waters of a Florida canal. There was nothing anyone could do that is bad enough for an adult who took a 6-year-old boy away from his parents, perhaps tortured, then murdered him and cut off his head. Nothing at all. Lethal injection? The electric chair? Bah.

And so I come back to the position that the death penalty is wrong, not only because it consists of stooping to the level of the killers, but also because it is not what it seems. Just before Ted Bundy's most recent execution date was postponed, pending further appeals, the father of his last known victim, a 12-year-old girl, said what almost every father in his situation must feel. "I wish they'd bring him back to Lake City," said Tom Leach of the town where Kimberly Leach had lived and died, "and let us all have at him." But the death penalty does not let us all have at him in the way Mr. Leach seems to mean. What he wants is for something as horrifying as what happened to his child to happen to Ted Bundy. And that is impossible.

In this essay Anna Quindlen defends the claim that we should not practice capital punishment. She states her argument explicitly at the beginning of the last paragraph: "the death penalty is wrong, not only because it consists of stooping to the level of the killers, but also because it is not what it seems." That argument is initially suggested to the reader by the title "Death Penalty's False Promise."

Throughout the work she cleverly supports the claim with examples and her own personal experiences. The warrant that makes her support credible is that our society is civilized and that a civilized society cannot exact the retribution that our emotions tell us that criminals who are convicted of horrible crimes deserve.

FOUR KINDS OF PERSUASIVE WRITING

The success of persuasive writing depends on whether or not the reader accepts the writer's position. As we have seen, the initial support for the claim comes in the form of direct support, an assertion that explains why the writer is making the claim. In addition, to gain that acceptance, the writer of persuasion may use any of four appeals. Each of these four appeals (personal, emotional, rational, and stylistic) focuses on a different aspect of the problem of persuasion.

THE PERSONAL APPEAL

Personal appeal focuses on the credibility of the writer. A positive image of the writer is put forth. If the writer can be presented in a favorable light, then the audience is more likely to accept the argument. The following characteristics can be found in writing using the personal appeal.

❑ The writer's identification with the reader is shown.
❑ The writer is presented as an expert on the issue.
❑ The writer's good intentions are revealed.
❑ The writer's honesty is asserted.

Reader Identification

The persuasive writer using a personal appeal appears to be part of the same group as the reader, using the same language and sharing the same values. The writer may use slang and jargon that the audience would use or accept. If the writer is successful at establishing this identification with the reader, then the task of persuasion is much easier.

Expertness

The writer appears to know what he or she is talking about. If the writer is accepted as an expert, the reader is more likely to believe any statements the writer makes. Three ways of making the writer appear to be an expert are by referring to personal experience, by citing some authority, and by endorsements.

Sometimes writers tell us about *their own experiences* as evidence of their expertise. The writer says "I've been there; I know what it's like."

Other writers introduce themselves as *authorities*. They claim to have studied the issue and areas that relate to it.

In advertising we see products *endorsed* by celebrities who are probably not experts on anything. The fact that they are celebrities, nevertheless, gives credibility to the product they are promoting.

Good Intentions

The writer expresses the intention of helping the reader. In fact, the writer might say "I have your best interests at heart." If the audience believes that the writer is working for them, they are more likely to accept the writer's argument.

Honesty

The writer asserts that he or she is honest and might even say, "I'm being honest with you." That the reader sees the writer as truthful is important to the success of the persuasion. As readers, we aren't likely to accept the arguments of anyone we believe to be dishonest.

An Example

In this speech, delivered in 1775 by Patrick Henry to the Virginia Convention, we can see an extensive use of personal appeal. Henry addresses the issue of whether or not Americans should unite against the British and go to war if necessary. An important part of his strategy to gain support for the Revolution is to present himself as a credible person.

Speech Before the Virginia Convention

Patrick Henry

No man thinks more highly than I do of the patriotism, as well as abilities, of the very worthy gentlemen who have just addressed the house. But different men often see the same subjects in different lights; and, therefore, I hope it will not be thought disrespectful to those gentlemen, if, entertaining as I do opinions of a character very opposite to theirs, I shall speak forth my sentiments freely, and without reserve. This is no time for ceremony. The question before the house is one of awful moment to this country. For my own part, I consider it as nothing less than a question of freedom or slavery. And in proportion to the magnitude of the subject, ought to be the freedom of the debate. It is only in this way that we can hope to arrive at truth, and fulfill the great responsibility which we hold to God and our country. Should I keep back my opinions at such a time, through fear of giving offence, I should consider myself as guilty of treason towards my country, and of an act of disloyalty toward the majesty of Heaven, which I revere above all earthly kings.

Mr. President, it is natural to man to indulge in the illusions of hope. We are apt to shut our eyes against a painful truth and listen to the song of that syren, till she transforms us into beasts. Is this the part of wise men, engaged in a great and arduous struggle for liberty? Are we disposed to be of the number of those, who having eyes, see not, and having ears, hear not, the things which so nearly concern their temporal salvation? For my part, whatever anguish of spirit it may cost, I am willing to know the whole truth; to know the worst, and to provide for it.

I have but one lamp by which my feet are guided; and that is the lamp of experience. I know of no way of judging of the future but by the past. And judging by the past, I wish to know what there has been in the conduct of the British ministry for the last ten years, to justify those hopes which gentlemen have been pleased to solace themselves and the house? Is it that insidious smile with which our petition has been lately received? Trust it not, sir; it will prove a snare to your feet. Suffer not yourselves to be betrayed with a kiss. Ask yourselves how this gracious reception of our petition comports with those warlike preparations which cover our waters and darken our land. Are fleets and armies necessary to a work of love and reconciliation? Have we shown ourselves so unwilling to be reconciled, that force must be called in to win back our love? Let us not deceive ourselves, sir. These are the implements of war and subjugation, the last arguments to which kings resort.

I ask, gentlemen, sir, what means this martial array, if its purpose be not to force us to submission? Can gentlemen assign any other possible motive for it? Has Great Britain any enemy in this quarter of the world, to call for all this accumulation of navies and armies? No, sir, she has none. They are sent over to bind and rivet upon us those chains, which the British ministry have been so long forging. And what have we to oppose to them? Shall we try argument? Sir, we have been trying that for the last ten years. Have we any thing new to offer upon the subject? Nothing. We have held the subject up in every light of which it is capable, but it has been all in vain. Shall we resort to entreaty and humble application? What terms shall we find, which have not been already exhausted? Let us not, I beseech you, sir, deceive ourselves longer. Sir, we have done every thing that could be done, to avert the storm which is now coming on. We have petitioned, we have remonstrated, we have supplicated, we have prostrated ourselves before the throne, and have implored its interposition to arrest the tyrannical hand of the ministry and parliament. Our petitions have been slighted; our supplications have been disregarded; and we have been spurned, with contempt, from the foot of the throne. In vain, after these things, may we indulge the fond hope of peace and reconciliation. There is no longer any room for hope. If we wish to be free, if we mean to preserve inviolate those inestimable privileges for which we have been so long contending, if we mean not basely to abandon the noble struggle in which we have been so long engaged, and which we have pledged ourselves never to abandon, until the glorious object of our contest shall be obtained, we must fight!—I repeat it, sir, we must fight!! An appeal to arms and to the God of Hosts is all that is left us!

They tell us, sir, that we are weak, unable to cope with so formidable an adversary. But when shall we be stronger? Will it be the next week or the next year? Will it be when we are totally disarmed, and when a British guard shall be stationed in every house? Shall we gather strength from irresolution and inaction? Shall we acquire the means of effectual resistance by lying supinely on our backs, and hugging the delusive phantom of hope, until our enemies shall have bound us hand and foot? Sir, we are not weak, if we make proper use of those means which the God of nature hath placed in our power. Three millions of people, armed in the holy cause of liberty, and in such a country as that which we possess, are invincible by any force which our enemy can send against us. Besides, sir, we shall not fight our battles alone. There is a just God who presides over the destinies of nations, and who will raise up friends to fight our battles for us. The battle, sir, is not to the strong alone; it is to the vigilant, the active, the brave. Besides, sir, we have no election. If we were base enough to desire it, it is now too late to retire from the contest. There is no retreat, but in submission and slavery! Our chains are forged. Their clanking may be heard on the plains of Boston! The war is inevitable—and let it come!! I repeat it, sir, let it come!!

It is vain, sir, to extenuate the matter. Gentlemen may cry, peace, peace—but there is no peace. The war is actually begun! The next gale that sweeps from the north will bring to our ears the clash of resounding arms! Our brethren are already in the field! Why stand we here idle? What is it that gentlemen wish? What would they have? Is life so dear, or peace so sweet, as to be purchased at the price of chains and slavery? Forbid it, Almighty God! I know not what course others may take; but as for me, give me liberty or give me death!

Patrick Henry begins this speech by trying to present a positive image of himself. In the first two sentences, he tries to establish a common ground with his opponents by acknowledging their patriotism. Later in the first paragraph, he puts himself in a high moral position by saying that he would think of himself as "guilty of treason" if he did not speak.

In the second paragraph he presents himself as an honest man in search of the truth when he says, "For my part, whatever anguish of spirit it may cost, I am willing to know the whole truth. . . ." He reinforces the impression of honesty by pursuing the truth when, in the third paragraph, he says, "Let us not deceive ourselves. . . ."

Throughout the speech he exhibits an identification with the audience by his continual use of first person plural pronouns *(we, us, our, ourselves).* In that way, he makes *his* statements *their* statements.

He asserts his position as an authority by referring to the "lamp of experience" by which his "feet are guided." His recounting of the past experiences of the colonies reinforces the idea that he knows what he is talking about.

Finally, in the famous concluding sentence, Henry asserts his good intentions and his highly moral position by saying, "I know not what course others may take; but as for me, give me liberty or give me death!"

THE EMOTIONAL APPEAL

The emotional appeal is the most direct of the four appeals of persuasive writing. With it, the writer seeks to arouse the reader's emotions and thereby affect how the reader sees the issue in question. It is a very powerful appeal and so it is sometimes abused by unscrupulous writers. The following characteristics are apparent in persuasive writing with an emotional appeal.

- ❑ The reader's desires, needs, and/or fears are appealed to.
- ❑ The importance of the issue is shown.
- ❑ The benefit to be derived from accepting the writer's position on the issue is shown.
- ❑ The good intentions of the writer are supported.

Appeal to Desires, Needs, and Fears

By using the emotional appeal, the writer presents images that have a strong emotional context, appealing to desires, needs, or fears. For example, we all want to belong to some group and we fear being seen as an outcast. If the writer can make us feel that having a certain belief or owning a particular product will make us *belong*, we may be more likely to accept the argument that goes along with the appeal. Almost any emotion can be manipulated by the clever writer.

Importance of the Issue

The appeal to the emotions of the reader emphasizes the importance of the issue. Because emotions are engaged, the reader *feels* the urgency of the persuasive claim.

Explanation of the Benefits

The benefit to the reader of accepting the writer's position supposedly will be that the reader's fears won't become a reality or the reader's desires will come true. This offering of a benefit helps to reinforce the claim.

Support for Good Intentions

The emotions aroused in the reader may support the good intentions of the writer; that is, they provide evidence that the writer is trying to help. The writer is seen as an instrument for achieving the reader's desires or needs.

AN EXAMPLE

Jonathan Edwards was one of the most famous Puritan ministers in Colonial America. Noted for his effectiveness in the pulpit, he was a master of the use of emotional appeals. The following example is from "Sinners in the Hands of an Angry God," the best-known sermon in American history. It illustrates how a skilled writer and speaker can manipulate the emotions of an audience.

Sinners in the Hands of an Angry God

JONATHAN EDWARDS

Your wickedness makes you as it were heavy as lead, and to tend downwards with great weight and pressure towards hell; and if God should let you go, you would immediately sink and swiftly descend and plunge into the bottomless gulf, and your healthy constitution, and your own care and prudence, and best contrivance, and all your righteousness, would have no more influence to uphold you and keep you out of hell, than a spider's web would have to stop a falling rock. Were it not that so is the sovereign pleasure of God, the earth would not bear you one moment; for you are a burden to it; the creation groans with you; the creature is made the subject to the bondage of your corruption, not willingly; the sun does not willingly shine upon you to give you light to serve sin and Satan; the earth does not willingly yield her increase to satisfy your lusts; nor is it willingly a stage for your wickedness to be acted upon; the air does not willingly serve you for breath to maintain the flame of life in your vitals while you spend your life in the service of God's enemies. God's creatures are good, and were made for men to serve God abused to purposes so directly contrary to their nature and end. And the world would spew you out, were it not for the sovereign hand of Him who hath subjected your heads, full of the dreadful storm and big with thunder; and were it not for the restraining hand of God, it would immediately burst forth upon you. The sovereign pleasure of God, for the present, stays His rough wind; otherwise it would come with fury, and your destruction would come like a whirlwind, and you would be like the chaff of the summer threshing floor.

The wrath of God is like great waters that are dammed for the present; they increase more and more, and rise higher and higher, till an outlet is given; and the longer the stream is stopped, the more rapid and mighty is its course when once it is let loose. It is true that judgment against your evil works has not been executed hitherto; the floods of God's vengeance have been withheld; but your guilt in the meantime is constantly increasing, and you are every day treasuring up more wrath; the waters are continually rising and waxing more and more mighty; and there is nothing but the mere pleasure of God that holds the waters back that are unwilling to be stopped and press hard to go forward. If God should only withdraw His hand from the floodgate, it would immediately fly open, and the fiery floods of the fierceness and wrath of God would rush forth with inconceivable fury and would come upon you with omnipotent power; and if your strength were ten thousand times greater than it is, yea ten thousand times greater than the strength of the stoutest, sturdiest devil in hell, it would be nothing to withstand or endure it.

The bow of God's wrath is bent, and the arrow made ready on the string and justice bends the arrow at your heart and strains the bow, and it is nothing but the mere pleasure of God, and that of an angry God, without any promise or obligation at all, that keeps the arrow one moment from being made drunk with your blood. Thus are all you that never passed under a great change of heart, by the mighty power of the Spirit of God upon your souls; all that were never born again, and made new creatures, and raised from being dead in sin, to a state of new, and before altogether unexperienced light and life, are in the hands of an angry God. However you may have reformed your life in many things, and may have had religious affections, and keep up a form of religion in your families and closets, and in the house of God, it is nothing but His mere pleasure that keeps you from being this moment swallowed up in everlasting destruction. However unconvinced you may now be of the truth of what you hear, by and by you will be fully convinced of it. Those that are gone from being in the like circumstances with you see that it was so with them; for destruction came suddenly upon most of them; when they expected nothing of it and while they were saying, "peace and safety;" now they see that those things that they depended for peace and safety, were nothing but thin air and empty shadows.

The God that holds you over the pit of hell, much as one holds a spider or some loathsome insect over the fire, abhors you and is dreadfully provoked: His wrath towards you burns like fire; He looks upon you as worthy of nothing else but to be cast into the fire; He is of purer eyes than to bear to have you in His sight; you are ten thousand times more abominable in His eyes than the most hateful and venomous serpent is in ours. You have offended Him infinitely more than ever a stubborn rebel did his prince; and yet it is nothing but His hand that holds you from falling into the fire every moment. It is to be ascribed to nothing else, that you did not go to hell the last night; that you were suffered to awake against in this world, after you closed your eyes to sleep. And there is no other reason to be given why you have not dropped into hell, since you have sat here in the house of God, provoking His pure eyes by your sinful wicked manner of attending. His solemn worship. Yea, there is nothing else that is to be given as a reason why you do not this very moment drop down into hell.

O sinner! Consider the fearful danger you are in: it is a great furnace of wrath, a wide and bottomless pit, full of the fire of wrath, that you are held over in the hand of that God, whose wrath is provoked and incensed as much against you, as against many of the damned in hell. You hang by a slender thread, with the flames of divine wrath flashing about it and ready every moment to singe it, and burn it asunder; and you have no interest in any Mediator and nothing to lay hold of to save yourself, nothing to keep off the flames of wrath, nothing of your own, nothing that you ever have done, nothing that you can do to induce God to spare you one moment.

Edwards establishes the importance of the issue—eternal damnation. He tries to convince his audience—those who have "never passed under a great change of heart," those who have never been "born again, and made new creatures"—that they are in "fearful danger." To persuade them of this, Edwards presents a frightening picture of eternal damnation and God's wrath. Such images as God holding the sinner over "the pit of hell . . . as one holds a spider or some loathsome insect over the fire" and the sinner hanging "by a slender thread with flames of divine wrath flashing around it" are calculated to arouse the emotions of fear and disgust. Those emotions may have had a powerful effect on Edwards' audiences, convincing them to examine their lives for evidence that they are one of God's elect.

THE RATIONAL APPEAL

Rational appeal is an attempt to persuade by using language structures that are associated with mental processes we call logical. The following characteristics appear in persuasive writing that uses rational appeal.

- ❏ Assertions are made and the opposing view may be refuted.
- ❏ The expertness of the writer is supported.
- ❏ Common sense is appealed to.
- ❏ Logical structures are used.

Assertions and Refutations

An assertion is a statement supporting the issue. The writer may make a direct assertion like, "My position is correct" or "My proposal will benefit you." Such unsupported assertions have a power of their own. In addition to making assertions, the writer may attack the opposing view and try to refute the arguments of the opposition.

Expertise

The use of logic (or that which appears to be logical) supports the impression that the writer is an expert. Indeed, anyone's expertise depends on having facts and logical proofs at hand. The writer of persuasion may present facts without intending to use them in a logical way. The presentation of facts and statistics may have an effect on the undiscriminating reader, even if the information is not relevant to the issue.

Common Sense

The appeal to common sense is an effort to take advantage of what people may regard as native good judgment, those ideas that emphasize the common feelings of humanity. When people say, "It's just common sense," they mean that their assertions should be obvious to everybody and that anyone who doesn't see the obvious, doesn't have any common sense. Such assertions seem to stand on their own without needing any support.

Logical Structures

Using logical structures involves the application of the principles of deductive and inductive reasoning.

Deductive Reasoning

Deductive reasoning is the kind of logical process that draws particular truths from general truths. The structure of the deductive process can be seen most clearly in the syllogism.

A **syllogism** consists of three statements: a major premise, a minor premise, and a conclusion. If the major and minor premises are true, then the conclusion must be true. It cannot be otherwise. The following illustrates the structure of a syllogism.

> *Major Premise*: All men are foolish.
> *Minor Premise*: Harvey is a man.
> *Conclusion*: Therefore, Harvey is foolish.

An **enthymeme** is an abbreviated syllogism in which one of the premises is omitted. The enthymeme often appears in persuasive writing because the writer may not want the reader to be aware that one of the premises is missing. In addition, the reader may grow impatient with a full blown deductive argument. In the following enthymeme, derived from the syllogism above, the major premise is omitted.

> Harvey is foolish because he is a man.

Slogans, proverbs, aphorisms, and adages represent another abbreviated form of deduction. Such statements seem to ring true when we hear them, but the problem with them is obvious when we pair one with another one that contradicts it.

> Absence makes the heart grow fonder.
> *but*
> Out of sight, out of mind.
>
> You're never too old to learn.
> *but*
> You can't teach an old dog new tricks.

Never put off till tomorrow what you can do today.
> *but*

All things come to those who wait.

Inductive Reasoning

Inductive reasoning moves from particular to general. That is, a general truth (conclusion) is derived from particular instances (**evidence**).

Evidence is a compilation of facts, observations, and data that supports the inductive thesis. Reasoning from evidence is the kind of inductive reasoning we are concerned with in interpretive writing. (This kind of reasoning will be discussed more extensively in Chapter 4.) Although evidence may be presented in practically any form, facts are often given numerical values and used in the form of statistics.

Evidence may be used as a part of an inductive persuasive argument, but a relevant **example**, selected for its appropriateness to the claim, may be more convincing to the reader than a mass of facts and figures. Examples represent an abbreviation of evidence and typically appear in persuasive writing.

Used as a rational appeal, an **analogy** can be quite persuasive, but it can only be pushed to the limits the reader will accept. For instance, we might argue that the principles of law that govern the business world and professions like medicine and law ought to apply to education, that schools ought to be held accountable for negligence and failure to perform. Such an argument is an analogy. Whether or not that argument will be accepted depends, at least in part, on the audience being addressed.

AN EXAMPLE

Susan B. Anthony was a driving force in the movement to get the vote for women in America. The following speech, reportedly her favorite, reflects a commitment not only to the suffrage movement, but also to remedying the economic exploitation of women. In it she makes extensive use of the rational appeal.

Woman Wants Bread, Not the Ballot!

SUSAN B. ANTHONY

Wherever, on the face of the globe or on the page of history, you show me a disfranchised class, I will show you a degraded class of labor. Disfranchisement means inability to make, shape or control one's own circumstances. The disfranchised must always do the work, accept the wages, occupy the position the enfranchised assign to them. The disfranchised are in the position of the pauper. You remember the old adage, "Beggars must not be choosers;" they must take what they can get or nothing! That is exactly the position of women in the world of work today; they can not choose. If they could, do you for a moment believe they would take the subordinate places and the inferior pay? Nor is it a "new thing under the sun" for the disfranchised, the inferior classes weighed down with wrongs, to declare they "do not want to vote." The rank and file are not philosophers, they are not educated to think of themselves, but simply to accept, unquestioned, whatever comes.

Years ago in England when the working men, starving in the mines and factories, gathered in mobs and took bread wherever they could get it, their friends tried to educate them into a knowledge of the causes of their poverty and degradation. At one of these "monster bread meetings," held in Manchester, John Bright said to them, "Workingmen, what you need to bring to you cheap bread and plenty of it, is the franchise;" but those ignorant men shouted back to Mr. Bright, precisely as the women of American do to us today, "It is not the vote we want, it is bread. . . ."

But at length, through the persistent demands of a little handful of reformers, there was introduced into the British Parliament the "household suffrage" bill of 1867. . . . The opposition was championed by Robert Lowe, who presented all the stock objections to the extension of the franchise to "those ignorant, degraded working men," as he called them, that ever were presented in this country against giving the ballot to the negroes, and that are today being urged against the enfranchisement of women. . . . But notwithstanding Mr. Lowe's persistent opposition, the bill became a law; and before the session closed, that same individual moved that Parliament, having enfranchised these men, should now make an appropriation for the establishment and support of schools for the education of them and their sons. Now mark you his reason why! "Unless they are educated," said he, "they will be the means of overturning the throne of England." So long as these poor men in the mines and factories had not the right to vote, the power to make and unmake the laws and lawmakers, to help or hurt the government, no measure ever had been proposed for their benefit although they were ground under the heel of the capitalists to a condition of abject slavery. But the moment this power is placed in their hands, before they have used it even once, this bitterest enemy to their possessing it is the first man to spring to his feet and make this motion for the most beneficent measure possible in their behalf—public schools for the education of themselves and their children. . . .

The great distinctive advantage possessed by the workingmen of this republic is that the son of the humblest citizen, black or white, has equal chances with the son of the richest in the land if he takes advantage of the public schools, the colleges and the many opportunities freely offered. It is this equality of rights which makes our nation a home for the oppressed of all the monarchies of the old world.

And yet, notwithstanding the declaration of our Revolutionary fathers, "all men created equal," "governments derive their just powers from the consent of the governed," "taxation and representation inseparable"—notwithstanding all these grand enunciations, our government was founded upon the blood and bones of half a million human beings, bought and sold as chattels in the market. Nearly all the original thirteen States had property qualifications which disfranchised poor white men as well as women and negroes. . . .

It is said women do not need the ballot for their protection because they are supported by men. Statistics show that there are 3,000,000 women in this nation supporting themselves. In the crowded cities of the East they are compelled to work in shops, stores and factories for the merest pittance. In New York alone, there are over 50,000 of these women receiving less than fifty cents a day. Women wage-earners in different occupations have organized themselves into trades unions, from time to time, and made their strikes to get justice at the hands of their employers just as men have done, but I have yet to learn of a successful strike of any body of women. The best organized one I ever knew was that of the collar laundry women of the city of Troy, N.Y., the great emporium for the manufacture of shirts, collars and cuffs. They formed a trades union of several hundred members and demanded an increase of wages. It was refused. So one May morning in 1867, and for three long months not one returned to the factories. At the end of that time they were literally starved out, and the majority of them were compelled to go back, but not at their old wages, for their employers cut them down to even a lower figure.

In the winter following I met the president of this union, a bright young Irish girl, and asked her, "Do you not think if you had been 500 carpenters or 500 masons, you would have succeeded?" "Certainly," she said, and then she told me of 200 brick layers who had the year before been on strike and gained every point with their employers. "What could have made the difference? Their 200 were but a fraction of that trade, while your 500 absolutely controlled yours." Finally she said, "It was because the editors ridiculed and denounced us." "Did they ridicule and denounce the bricklayers?" "No." "What did they say about you?" "Why, that our wages were good enough now, better than those of any other working women except teachers; and if we weren't satisfied, we had better go and get married. . . . It must have been because our employers bribed the editors. . . ." In the case of the bricklayers, no editor, either Democrat or Republican, would have accepted the proffer of a bribe, because he would have known that if he denounced or ridiculed those men, not only they but all the trades union men of the city at the next election would vote solidly against the nominees advocated by that editor. If those collar laundry women had been voters, they would have held, in that little city of Troy, the "balance of power". . . .

There are many women equally well qualified with men for principals and superintendents of schools, and yet, while three-fourths of the teachers are women, nearly all of them are relegated to subordinate positions of half or at most two-thirds the salaries paid to men. . . . Sex alone settles the question. . . .

And then again you say, "Capital, not the vote, regulates labor." Granted, for the sake of argument, that capital does control the labor of women . . .

but no one with eyes to see and ears to hear, will concede for a moment that capital absolutely dominates the work and wages of the free and en-franchised men of this republic. It is in order to lift the millions of our wage-earning women into a position of as much power over their own labor as men possess that they should be invested with the franchise. This ought to be done not only for the sake of just women, but to the men with whom they compete; for, just so long as there is a degraded class of labor in the mar-ket, it always will be used by the capitalists to checkmate and undermine the superior classes.

Now that as a result of the agitation for equality of chances, and through the invention of machinery, there has come a great revolution in the world of economics, so that wherever a man may go to earn an honest dollar a woman may go also, there is no escape from the conclusion that she must be clothed with equal power to protect herself. That power is the ballot, the symbol of freedom and equality, without which no citizen is sure of keeping even that which he hath, much less of getting that which he hath not.

In this speech Anthony uses rational appeal to support her claim that women's need for the right to vote is a necessary prerequisite for correcting the conditions of working women in America. Throughout the speech she uses examples to support her claim that the right to vote is essential if women are to improve their situation in the workplace.

Her reference to the "household suffrage bill," passed by the British Par-liament in 1867, supports her position by showing how even the opponents of the bill, as a result of its passage, began to support educational reform.

She uses a second example, a failed strike by the collar laundry women of Troy, New York, to show that the right to vote is essential for economic independence.

THE STYLISTIC APPEAL

The stylistic appeal convinces by presenting pleasing images that entice the reader to accept the claim of the persuader. The following characteristics are usually present in a stylistic appeal.

❑ Aesthetically pleasing images and/or symbols are presented.
❑ Concrete, graphic imagery is used.
❑ Startling, unusual images and/or dramatic situations to get the attention of the reader are used.
❑ Images that are consistent with the social or cultural myths are used.

Aesthetically Pleasing Images

Those images that are pleasing tend to make the reader accept the message being presented. Such images are frequently the kinds used in literary writing.

Concrete Imagery

Concrete, graphic imagery is used because it arrests the reader's attention. If the reader is intrigued by and subsequently engaged in the images presented, then the persuasive claim is enhanced.

Startling, Unusual Images, Dramatic Situations

The images designed to get the attention of the reader work because they present ideas that are startling and unusual. Dramatic episodes that have the appearance of literary narratives are also used to get the reader's attention.

Images Consistent with Social or Cultural Myth

Images that are consistent with a current social or cultural myth will be readily accepted by the reader. The reader, more than likely, already has accepted the cultural myth. If the writer can show that his or her position is in line with the accepted myth, the reader will be more willing to accept the argument.

AN EXAMPLE

The following advertisement illustrates the use of stylistic appeal.

Crisscross Cord Shirt

THE TERRITORY AHEAD

If you're shy, this isn't the shirt for you. The fabric—a richly colored, cross-hatched cotton corduroy—is so supremely soft and texturey, it has a tendency to attract unsolicited attention. In fact, when our V.P. of Merchandising wore it on a recent trip, an otherwise well-mannered young woman had to be gently dissuaded from stroking his sleeve long enough for him to board his plan home. Details include a spread collar; button-through patch pockets; handsome, wood-style buttons; and a box pleat in back. Imported in Olive; Barn Red; Amber; Blue-Gray; Plum.

Reg. Sizes: S–XXL. 143004 $59.50
Tall Sizes: MT–XXLT. 143181 $65.50

The descriptive detail "supremely soft and texturey," together with the intriguing narrative about "unsolicited attention," create a compelling stylistic appeal. The description is created to prompt the reader to imagine himself wearing one of the "richly coloured" shirts and having to "gently" discourage the attentions of a "young woman."

COMBINATIONS

Personal appeal and stylistic appeal rarely appear alone. They are most often used in combination with rational and emotional appeals. Some appeals inevitably appear with others. For instance, an example used as a rational appeal may have a strong emotional appeal as well. The use of all four appeals in the same piece of persuasive writing is not at all unusual.

WRITING STRATEGIES

The most important consideration in creating a persuasive argument is to know the audience. Remember that persuasion is the most pragmatic of the kinds of writing. The purpose of persuasion is the practical matter of convincing the reader of the rightness of your position and perhaps moving the reader to act on that conviction. The appropriateness of the appeals you use depends upon your understanding of the nature of the audience. As a result, an important part of the process of writing persuasion is to figure out the values and beliefs of the specific audience you are addressing.

Consider these questions as you begin drafting your persuasive paper.

- ❏ Who is your audience?
- ❏ How can you create interest in your topic?
- ❏ How can you establish your credibility as an authority?
- ❏ What values do your readers have that would predispose them to agree with your position?
- ❏ What issue are you addressing?
- ❏ What is your position on this issue?
- ❏ State your position as a thesis statement.
- ❏ What background will your audience need to understand your argument?
- ❏ What appeals could you use to support your thesis?
- ❏ What reasons support your argument?
- ❏ How would you answer objections to your position?
- ❏ What are the implications of your argument?
- ❏ What emotional appeal best supports your argument?

AN OUTLINE FOR PERSUASION

The persuasive structure reflected in the following outline has been used for thousands of years and is still an effective way to present a persuasive argument.

I. Introduction
   A. Create interest in the topic.
   B. Establish your credibility as an authority.
   C. Establish common ground for both you and the reader.
   D. Show fair-mindedness.
   E. State the claim.

II. Background—give factual information about the topic (may include statistics).

III. Lines of Argument
   A. Present rational and/or emotional appeals.
   B. Present reasons in order of importance.
   C. Show that your position is in the readers' best interest.

IV. Refutation of Any Opposing Arguments
   A. Consider any opposing views.
   B. Note advantages and disadvantages of opposing views.
   C. Refute the opposing positions.

V. Conclusion
   A. Summarize the argument.
   B. Elaborate on the implications of the argument.
   C. Make clear what you want readers to think and do.
   D. Make a final emotional appeal, but don't overdo it.

Referential Writing

Referential writing overwhelms us in modern life. At no time in history has there been such a profusion of documents designed to explain our world. Business, industry, science, academia, government, and the news media all produce massive quantities of information. Libraries devote an enormous amount of space to the storage of reference works, research materials, scholarly journals, government publications, scientific treatises, news reports as well as other kinds of referential writing. When we call ours the *Information Age*, we are referring in large part to this explosion in the production of referential writing.

In all its various forms, the purpose of referential writing is to explain a topic. The explanation will have four features: thesis, evidence, validity, and topic-oriented language.

GENERAL CHARACTERISTICS

❑   A thesis is present.
❑   Evidence consistent with the thesis is offered.
❑   The validity of the evidence is apparent.
❑   Topic-oriented language is used.

THESIS

A thesis is a generalization about the content of the work that tells the reader what the focus of the presentation will be. In other words, the thesis indicates how the topic will be explained. Although a thesis statement may appear anywhere in the work, it is usually included in the introduction where the scope of the discussion is set out. The nature of the thesis depends on the kind of subject matter presented.

The following are examples of referential thesis statements.

❑   A number of European countries have abandoned the use of nuclear reactors as a way to produce electricity.

❏ Dietary changes can improve health for many people.
❏ Many new immigrants to the United States still believe in the "American Dream."

Each of these statements is a generalization indicating the main idea to be addressed in a paper.

A thesis in referential writing differs from a claim in persuasion in that the referential thesis focuses on an examination of the subject matter rather than presenting a defense of one side of an issue. For example, the referential thesis that there is a high correlation between fast driving and accidents is different from the persuasive claim that people ought to slow down when they drive. Even though some of the same information might be included in a paper on each subject, the intent of the two would be different. One would be referential and the other would be persuasive.

EVIDENCE

Evidence included in referential writing will provide support for the thesis. Evidence may take the form of facts, questions, or other details to help explain the topic. The evidence needed in the paper is implicit in the thesis. A paper explaining the changes in the use of nuclear energy in Europe would include evidence giving specific examples of countries in Europe where the change had occurred. A paper about the connection between diet and health might have evidence consisting of empirical studies that show a correlation between the nutrition people had and the state of their health. A paper about immigrants' views of the "American Dream" would probably include reports of interviews with new American immigrants about their attitudes or the results of surveys designed to collect information about those attitudes.

VALIDITY

The evidence presented in referential writing has validity. The validity of that evidence is apparent to the reader, either because the facts themselves are indisputable or because the logic of the presentation is clear. Validity is ensured by an attention to data that can be supported in some way, either by some authority (the credibility of the writer) or by logic.

In most cases we assume that the information included in referential writing is accurate and that if false information is presented, it will be corrected. For instance, when a credible newspaper prints a story, we assume that the report is valid because of our previous dealings with that newspaper. When a scientist publishes research findings, we assume that the information reported is valid because of our knowledge of the nature of scientific investigation. And in both cases we assume that any distorted information or inaccurate data will be quickly corrected or explained.

In addition, if facts presented by the writer correspond to what we already know about the subject, that is, conform to common knowledge, then we have more confidence in the information presented. For example, if the writer refers to historical events that we already have some knowledge of, then the validity of the information will be reinforced.

TOPIC-ORIENTED LANGUAGE

The language used in referential writing will be appropriate to the topic; as a result the topic will control the kind of language used. The information presented will be accurate and concepts will be clearly stated. Third person pronouns are typically used. Conventions of standard usage are followed and unambiguous terms are used.

The degree of formality in referential writing will depend on how the topic is treated. Some kinds of referential writing are more formal than others. Articles in academic journals and scientific studies, for instance, usually demand a fairly formal presentation. News reports, though less formal than scholarly works, are more formal than feature articles, human interest stories, and speculative essays, which may allow some degree of subjectivity and authorial intrusion.

AN EXAMPLE

In the following example, the famed naturalist John Muir offers an explanation of a body of evidence to support his thesis. This example illustrates the general characteristics of referential writing.

Where the Sequoia Grows

JOHN MUIR

It is generally believed that this grand Sequoia was once far more widely distributed over the Sierra; but after long and careful study I have come to the conclusion that it never was, at least since the close of the glacial period, because a diligent search along the margins of the groves, and in the gaps between, fails to reveal a single trace of its previous existence beyond its present bounds. Notwithstanding, I feel confident that if every Sequoia in the range were to die today, numerous monuments of their existence would remain, of so imperishable a nature as to be available for the student more than ten thousand years hence.

In the first place we might notice that no species of coniferous tree in the range keeps its individuals so well together as Sequoia; a mile is perhaps the greatest distance of any straggler from the main body, and all of these stragglers that have come under my observation are young, instead of old monumental trees, relics of a more extended growth.

Again, Sequoia trunks frequently endure for centuries after they fall. I have a specimen block, cut from a fallen trunk, which is hardly distinguishable from specimens cut from living trees, although the old trunk-fragment from which it was derived has lain in the damp forest more than 380 years, probably twice as long. The time measure in the case is simply this: when the ponderous trunk to which the old vestige belonged fell, it sunk itself into the ground, thus making a long, straight ditch, and in the middle of this ditch a Silver Fir is growing that is now four feet in diameter and 380 years old, as determined by cutting it half through and counting the rings, thus demonstrating that the remnant of the trunk that made the ditch has lain on the ground *more* than 380 years. For it is evident that to find the whole time, we must add to the 380 years the time that the vanished portion of the trunk lay in the ditch before being burned out of the way, plus the time that passed before the seed from which the monumental fir sprang fell into the prepared soil and took root. Now, because Sequoia trunks are never wholly consumed in one forest fire, and those fires recur only at considerable intervals, and because Sequoia ditches after being cleared are often left unplanted for centuries, it becomes evident that the trunk remnant in question may probably have lain a thousand years or more. And this instance is by no means a rare one.

But admitting that upon those areas supposed to have been once covered with Sequoia every tree may have fallen, and every trunk may have been burned or buried, leaving not a remnant, many of the ditches made by the fall of the ponderous trunks, and the bowls made by their upturning roots, would remain patent for thousands of years after the last vestige of the trunks that made them had vanished. Much of this ditch-writing would no doubt be quickly effaced by the flood-action of overflowing streams and rain-washing; but no inconsiderable portion would remain enduringly engraved on the ridge-tops beyond such destructive action; for, where all the conditions are favorable, it is almost imperishable. Now these historic ditches and root bowls occur in all the present Sequoia groves and forests, but as far as I have observed, not the faintest vestige of one presents itself outside them.

We therefore conclude that the area covered by Sequoia has not been diminished during the last eight or ten thousand years, and probably not at all in post-glacial times.

In the first paragraph of this essay the author states the thesis—that the Sequoia were never more widely distributed over the Sierras than they are now. In this way the scope of the topic is defined and the kind of evidence needed to prove the thesis is suggested. Throughout the rest of the essay, the author presents evidence relevant to the thesis.

The evidence presented includes personal observations about the current range of the Sequoia groves, the existence of a trunk fragment that had been lying on the ground for over 380 years, and the absence of ditches and root bowls created by fallen trees outside the current range. All the evidence taken together proves the thesis and makes Muir's conclusion highly probable. The evidence is valid because it is logically connected to the thesis. The validity of Muir's factual observations is self-evident. The language used to present the information is formal and objective. There is no subjective bias in the presentation.

FOUR KINDS OF REFERENTIAL WRITING

Referential writing can be divided into four groups—informative, interpretive, exploratory, and reflective—each with a different focus for explaining the topic.

THE INFORMATIVE FOCUS

In referential writing with an informative focus, the writer presents the information, but does not do anything more with that information. The objective of such writing is simply to present the facts to the reader.

Referential writing with an informative focus has four characteristics.

- ❏ The thesis is a summative generalization of the content.
- ❏ Factual language is used.
- ❏ The evidence is comprehensive.
- ❏ Surprise value is maintained.

Summative Generalization

As with all referential thesis statements, an informative thesis will be a generalization. The informative thesis will present the most general information on the topic. For example, the following thesis statement would be the most general statement included in a report about a train wreck: *A train derailed after hitting a truck at a railway crossing in northern Illinois this weekend.* The statement would provide the basis for other evidence that would follow it. More specific evidence would be needed to fill in the details of the accident and provide a full explanation.

An informative thesis would not contain inferences or ask questions about the evidence, but instead would simply be a summation of the details of the written work.

Factuality

A fact is anything that is verifiable or that has real, demonstrable existence. If something is a fact, it can be verified. For instance, the Preface to *Webster's Third New International Dictionary* says that the volume contains 450,000 words. The fact, the number of words in the dictionary, is something that can be verified objectively (by counting them). Most people probably wouldn't actually count the number of words in the dictionary. They would simply accept the word of the publisher. That's how most of us deal with information. As readers, we don't usually set about trying to verify everything we read. If we read something in the newspaper, we probably accept the item as factual (assuming that we believe that the newspaper is a credible source of information and that the paper would print a correction if it had made an error). Our past experiences with publishing tell us which sources are credible and which are not. We are always aware that if a bit of information is a fact, it can be verified.

Attributions (telling where the information comes from) are not necessary if the facts are common knowledge. If the facts being presented are not common knowledge, identifying the source of the information is essential. Research papers exemplify this feature.

In research papers using the MLA style of documentation, complete information on the sources used is given on the last page of the paper under "Works Cited." In the body of the paper the only information that needs to be given is the exact page number from which the information is taken and any other information that is necessary (usually the name of the author) to enable the reader to find the source in the "Works Cited" list.

Comprehensiveness

A work is comprehensive if it contains all the information necessary to inform the reader about the topic. But just how much is enough? This is sometimes a difficult question to answer. Part of the answer depends on the pattern of organization used (see Chapters 5-8). For example, to be comprehensive, a physical description of a person, a place, or an object would need to include enough detail so that a reader would be able to visualize the thing being described. A narrative would need to include all events necessary so that the reader could understand the entire sequence. When writing news stories, journalists make sure that they answer the questions: who? what? when? where? why? and how? The answers to those questions ensure that the basic facts of an event are reported in the story.

Comprehensiveness may also be determined by how the information is to be used. For instance, many dictionaries have far fewer than the 450,000 words contained in *Webster's Third New International Dictionary*, and yet they achieve comprehensiveness because their use is limited to looking up the most commonly used words.

Another consideration that determines whether or not a work is comprehensive is the audience for whom the work is intended. For example, although the *World Book Encyclopedia* contains much less information than the *Encyclopedia Britannica*, it does achieve comprehensiveness because it's aimed at a much younger audience that presumably would find it more difficult to use a work as comprehensive as the *Encyclopedia Britannica*.

Surprise Value

Surprise value is the extent to which reader interest is maintained. Information is *surprising* if the reader has an interest in the facts presented. Those facts are surprising if the reader's response to the information is "I didn't know that." Once the information is known, the surprise value diminishes for that particular reader. But another reader, unfamiliar with the same information, may find it surprising. Informative writing does not bear repetition in the way that literary writing does. We may read a news story again, but only because we want to see the information again, not because we find it aesthetically pleasing.

The arrangement of the facts in a news story usually reflects the emphasis on surprise value. The most important facts, those with the most surprise value, are given first. Less important facts follow and may be skipped over by the reader (or omitted by the editor before the story is printed).

AN EXAMPLE

In this informative excerpt from *Wild Heritage* (1965), Sally Carrighar presents facts about the field of ethology. By explaining what ethologists do, she develops an extended definition of the term *ethology*.

Ethology

SALLY CARRIGHAR

By . . . the 1920's and 1930's, there was a new generation of biologists and many were ready to listen. While some of them have preferred to do their work in laboratories, others have gone out of doors, to make a real science of animal observation. They call themselves, these co-operating indoor and outdoor men, ethologists, and it is largely due to their efforts that we now have a reliable body of knowledge about our animal forebears.

For laymen ethology is probably the most interesting of the biological sciences for the very reason that it concerns animals in their normal activities and therefore, if we wish, we can assess the possible dangers and advantages in our own behavioral roots. Ethology also is interesting methodologically because it combines in new ways very scrupulous field observations with experimentation in laboratories.

The field workers have had some handicaps in winning respect for themselves. For a long time they were considered as little better than amateur animal-watchers—certainly not scientists, since their facts were not gained by experimental procedures: they could not conform to the hard-and-fast rule that a problem set up and solved by one scientist must be tested by other scientists, under identical conditions and reaching identical results. Of course many situations in the lives of animals simply cannot be rehearsed and controlled in this way. The fall flocking of wild free birds can't be, or the homing of animals over long distances, or even details of spontaneous family relationships. Since these never can be reproduced in a laboratory, are they then not worth knowing about?

The ethologists who choose field work have got themselves out of this impasse by greatly refining the techniques of observing. At the start of a project all the animals to be studied are live-trapped, marked individually, and released. Motion pictures, often in color, provide permanent records of their subsequent activities. Recording of the animals' voices by electrical sound equipment is considered essential, and the most meticulous notes are kept of all that occurs. With this material other biologists, far from the scene, later can verify the reports. Moreover, two field observers often go out together, checking each other's observations right there in the field.

Ethology, the word, is derived from the Greek *ethos*, meaning the characteristic traits or features which distinguish a group—any particular group of people or, in biology, a group of animals such as a species. Ethologists have the intention, as William H. Thorpe explains, of studying "the whole sequence of acts which constitute an animal's behavior." In abridged dictionaries ethology is sometimes defined simply as "the objective study of animal behavior," and ethologists do emphasize their wish to eliminate myths.

Perhaps the most original aspect of ethology is the way that field observation is combined with experimentation in laboratories. Although the flocking of birds cannot be studied indoors, many other significant actions of animals that are seen only infrequently in the field, or seen only as hints, may be followed up later with indoor tests. Likewise investigations made first in laboratories can be checked by observations of animals ranging free in their normal environments.

Suppose that a field man, watching marked individuals, notes that an infant animal, *a*, is nursed by a female, *B*, known not to be its mother. Later he sees other instances of such maternal generosity. Is this willingness on the female's part a case of inherited behavior, or has it been picked up as one of the social customs of the species; that is, is it *learned*? Does it mean that all the adult females of this species feel some responsibility for the young, and if so, is such a tendency innate, or could behavior like that be acquired?

Elephant mothers are among those which give milk to offspring not their own. A group of elephants cannot very well be confined in a laboratory; but if the field worker is concerned with a species of smaller animals, he can bring newborn young into captivity, raise them and mate them there, and then note the behavior of the new mothers. Since they never have seen other females nursing young, their actions will be innate, inherited. And if it does turn out that one of these females will nurse any young that come to her, it will further have to be determined whether she recognizes her own. That question too can be answered in the laboratory; it is an easy problem for an experimental psychologist. By such techniques it has been found, for example, that in the species of small brown bats called *Myotis myotis* the mothers do know their own young and likewise will nurse any hungry infant regardless of blood relationship. This

> maternal behavior could have been observed in a colony of animals kept for generations indoors, but since the habitat there is artificial, the only way to know whether the behavior is normal to the species was to observe it first in animals living free in their natural world. Only by such a combination of laboratory and field work can instincts and acquired characteristics be distinguished. The value of knowledge like that is so great that the wonder is why such cooperation had not developed much earlier.

This work presents the reader with facts about the field of ethology, addressing both the derivation of the word itself and the processes used by ethologists in their study of animal behavior. The comprehensiveness of the topic is controlled by the limitations of her definitions. She develops the work by using examples of the work done by ethologists. These examples help give the work its validity. Her use of a specialized vocabulary also contributes to the validity of the work as well as to the objectivity of its tone.

THE INTERPRETIVE FOCUS

Referential writing with an interpretive focus is an attempt to explain the meaning of the evidence presented. The writer, through the use of logic, attempts to prove the validity of the interpretation. Scholarly works in all the academic disciplines usually have an interpretive focus. Biologists explain the laws governing life on Earth; literary critics interpret novels and poems; psychologists analyze the functioning of the human mind; physicists explore the forces controlling matter and energy. No matter where we look in the academic world, scholars and scientists are trying to offer logical explanations of the various subjects studied in their disciplines.

Four characteristics define referential writing with an interpretive focus.

- ❏ The thesis is an inference about the meaning of the evidence.
- ❏ Proof is provided by the evidence.
- ❏ Objective language is used.
- ❏ Evidence is presented deductively and/or inductively.

Inference

The thesis is an inference that explains in general terms what the evidence means. For example, the thesis statement "Some industries are causing water pollution by discharging toxic chemicals" is an inference that would explain the meaning of evidence gathered through a scientific analysis of any affected bodies of water.

Proof

The evidence presented in interpretive writing provides the proof supporting the inference that is implicit in the thesis. All the evidence included is necessary so that the reader can understand the legitimacy of the thesis. For example, to prove that a particular industry was causing water pollution, a researcher would have to present evidence that toxic chemicals produced by the industry were present in the water in large amounts. The evidence would probably contain data derived from an analysis of the water in question.

Objectivity

The presentation of evidence in interpretive writing is objective. The writer uses denotative language. Language that is biased and slanted is excluded. Conventions of standard usage are followed and unambiguous terms are used.

Any specialized terms must be defined accurately because the definition of a term may affect the validity of the proof. In many academic disciplines certain words have very special meanings that are different from common definitions.

Deductive and Inductive Reasoning

Deductive and inductive reasoning are methods for logical reasoning. They have been discussed to some degree already in Chapter 3, but in this chapter we look at these concepts as they are used in proving the validity of interpretations.

Deductive Reasoning

Deductive reasoning is a purely logical process moving from the general to the specific. The syllogism reflects this aspect of deductive reasoning. Deduction draws particular truths from some general truth. The conclusion is implicit in the premises. The kind of syllogism examined in Chapter 3 is called a **categorical syllogism** because it sets up a category and shows that some individual case does or does not fit into the category.

Another kind of syllogism is called the **hypothetical syllogism**. This kind of syllogism sets up a hypothesis, an *if-then* statement. The logic of the syllogism is such that if part of the *if-then* statement is true, then the conclusion must follow. The following example from Charles Darwin's *Origin of Species* illustrates how both categorical and hypothetical syllogisms may appear in a deductive interpretation of a natural phenomenon.

> How will the struggle for existence . . . act in regard to variation?
> Can the principle of selection, which we have seen is so potent in
> the hands of man, apply in nature? I think we shall see that it can
> act most effectually. Let it be borne in mind in what an endless

number of strange peculiarities our domestic productions, and, in a lesser degree, those under nature, vary; and how strong the hereditary tendency is. Under domestication, it may be truly said that the whole organization becomes in some degree plastic. Let it be borne in mind how infinitely complex and close-fitting are the mutual relations of all organic beings to each other and to their physical conditions of life. Can it, then be thought improbable, seeing that variations useful to man have undoubtedly occurred, that other variations useful in some way to each being in the great and complex battle of life, should sometimes occur in the course of thousands of generations? If such do occur, can we doubt (remembering that many more individuals are born than can possibly survive) that individuals having any advantage, however slight, over others, would have the best chance of surviving and of procreating their kind? On the other hand, we may feel sure that any variation in the least degree injurious would be rigidly destroyed. This preservation of favorable variations and the rejection of injurious variations, I call Natural Selection. Variations neither useful nor injurious would not be affected by natural selection, and would be left a fluctuating element. . . .

In written prose the deductive argument may be more complex than a single syllogism. The essence of the deductive reasoning in Darwin's passage about natural selection can be seen in the following statements:

❏ Offspring vary endlessly.
❏ Beings have a close-fitting relationship to their environment.
❏ Variations useful to man occur.
❏ Variations useful to each being occur in nature.
❏ More individuals are born than can survive.
❏ Individuals with an advantage have the best chances of surviving and procreating.
❏ Individuals with variations that would be injurious would be destroyed.
❏ Favorable variations are preserved.
❏ Injurious variations are rejected.

A number of these assertions can be converted to syllogisms.

Hypothetical Syllogism

❏ *Major Premise:* If many variations are produced, then some will be useful.
❏ *Minor Premise:* Many variations are produced.
❏ *Conclusion:* Some are useful.

Categorical Syllogism

❑ *Major Premise:* Those individuals with any advantage have a better chance of surviving.
❑ *Minor Premise:* Individuals with favorable variations have an advantage.
❑ *Conclusion:* Individuals with favorable variations have a better chance of surviving.

Categorical Syllogism

❑ *Major Premise:* Variations passed to offspring are preserved.
❑ *Minor Premise:* Favorable variations are passed to offspring.
❑ *Conclusion:* Favorable variations are preserved.

Inductive Reasoning

Inductive reasoning moves from the specific to the general. It involves making inferences (generalizations) based on observations (specific statements). A general truth becomes known through particular, empirical observations.

The conclusions in inductive reasoning are not as certain as the conclusions arrived at by deductive reasoning. Inductive conclusions are at best highly probable. The advantage of induction is that it is self-correcting; that is, new evidence or additional evidence may alter the conclusions drawn previously.

Analogy is a simple form of induction, but its application is fairly limited. The two things being compared in an analogy have to be very similar for the inference to be valid. For example, if I bought a new pair of jeans, I could reason by analogy that since the new jeans were similar in style, price, and material to an old pair I had, then the new pair should wear about as well as the old ones did. (Analogy as a pattern of organization is also discussed in Chapters 3 & 5.)

The **inductive generalization** is more widely applicable than analogy. A valid inference can be made if observed events are in agreement. For instance, a field biologist might make observations about the conditions necessary for a particular species of animal to live in a given location. If the presence of certain conditions (say a limited temperature range) coincided with the presence of the animal, and the absence of those conditions coincided with the absence of the animal, then the biologist might logically conclude that the condition (temperature range) determined whether the animals would live in the habitat. Furthermore, the biologist would probably record the observations as statistics, i.e. numbers of animals, temperatures, and other variables that might affect the study.

For an inference to be valid, it must be generalizable. For instance, it would be a mistake to say that because some women between the ages of 25 and 30 leave their jobs to have children, all women between the ages of 25 and 30 will leave their jobs to have children. Such a generalization would not be very dependable.

The following example from Charles Darwin's *The Descent of Man* illustrates how interpretations are made by using an inductive reasoning process.

> Most of the more complex emotions are common to the higher animals and ourselves. Every one has seen how jealous a dog is of his master's affection, if lavished on any other creature; and I have observed the same fact with monkeys. This shows that animals not only love, but have desire to be loved. Animals manifestly feel emulation. They love approbation or praise; and a dog carrying a basket of his master exhibits in a high degree self-complacency or pride. There can, I think, be no doubt that a dog feels shame, as distinct from fear, and something very like modesty when begging too often for food. . . . Several observers have stated that monkeys certainly dislike being laughed at; and they sometimes invent imaginary offenses.

Reduced to the bare essentials of the evidence presented, Darwin's **inductive reasoning** would look something like this:

- ❑ Animals love and desire to be loved.
- ❑ Dogs show jealousy.
- ❑ Monkeys show jealousy.
- ❑ Animals feel emulation and pride.
- ❑ A dog carrying a basket shows self-complacency.
- ❑ Animals feel shame and modesty.
- ❑ Dogs show modesty when begging too often for food.
- ❑ Monkeys dislike being laughed at.
- ❑ *Conclusion:* Most of the more complex emotions are common to higher animals and ourselves.

The **hypothetico-deductive** method is an inductive technique that involves setting up a hypothesis to explain certain facts gathered by observation and then deducing new conclusions from the hypothesis and testing those conclusions by experiment. Newton's theory of gravitation is an example of the use of this method. It is the basic method of research used in the advanced sciences.

Statistics are often used as evidence to prove a thesis in writing that has an interpretive focus. Using statistical methods allows us to collect, organize, and interpret numerical information in a meaningful way. If, for instance, we were studying the problem of solid waste disposal, we might report the increase in the amount of waste disposed of in our society by converting the numbers to percentage increases per year, or to increases per person. Such a use of statistics would make the information more meaningful.

Statistics is usually divided into two classes: descriptive statistics and inferential statistics. Descriptive statistics refers to methods used to describe and summarize numerical information that has been collected. Writers often use tables, charts, and graphs to depict the summarized data. Inferential statistics (also known as inductive statistics and sampling statistics) refers to methods that allow us to make inferences about a larger group from the data collected on a smaller group. Opinion polls and experimental research studies make use of the techniques of inferential statistics.

When you use statistics to support interpretations, you should make sure that you have not misused statistical information. Errors of inference in the use of statistics are not always apparent because of the mathematical language used to present the information. Remember Disraeli's comment, "There are three kinds of lies: lies, damned lies, and statistics." However, you should also remember that when misuse of statistics occurs, the problem is neither with the statistics nor with statistical methods, but with their careless use.

The following excerpt from Charles Darwin's *Origin of Species* illustrates how a scientific interpretation made from a body of evidence uses the hypothetico-deductive method. Note that Darwin sets up an experiment and uses statistics to support the inductive generalization that there is a great interdependence among animals and plants in nature.

I am tempted to give one more instance showing how plants and animals, remote in the scale of nature, are bound together by a web of complex relations. I shall hereafter have occasion to show that the exotic Lobelia filgens is never visited in my garden by insects, and consequently, from its peculiar structure, never sets a seed. Nearly all our orchidaceous plants absolutely require the visits of insects to remove their pollen-masses and thus to fertilize them. I find from experiments that humble-bees are almost indispensable to the fertilization of the heartsease (*Viola tricolor*), for other bees do not visit this flower. I have also found that the visits of bees are necessary for the fertilization of some kinds of clover; for instance, 20 heads of Dutch clover (*Trifolium repens*) yielded 2290 seeds, but 20 other heads protected from bees produced not one. Again, 100 heads of red clover (*T. pratense*) produced 2700 seeds, but the same number of protected heads produced not a single seed. Humble-bees alone visit red clover, as other bees cannot reach the nectar. It has been suggested that moths may fertilize the clovers; but I doubt whether they could do so in the case of the red clover, from their weight not being sufficient to depress the wind-petals. Hence we may infer as highly probable that, if the whole genus of humble-bees became extinct or very rare in England, the heartsease and red clover would become very rare, or wholly disappear. The number of humble-bees in any district depends in a great measure on the number of field-mice, which destroy their combs and nests; and Col. Newman, who has long attended to the habits of humble-bees, believes that "more than two-thirds of them are thus destroyed all over England." Now the number of mice is largely dependent as everyone knows, on the number of cats; and Col. Newman says, "Near villages and small towns I have found the nests of humble-bees more numerous than elsewhere, which I attribute to the number of cats that destroy the mice." Hence it is quite credible that the presence of a feline animal in large numbers in a district might determine, through the intervention first of mice and then of bees, the frequency of certain flowers in that district!

AN EXAMPLE

In this 1981 essay Ellen Goodman explains the historical changes that have occurred in the relationship between school and work in American society and discusses how that change has affected our attitudes about young people.

The Long Transition to Adulthood

ELLEN GOODMAN

"When I was a child, I spake as a child, I understood as a child, I thought as a child: but when I became a man, I put away childish things." (I Corinthians 13:11)

What about the years in between childhood and adulthood? How do we speak then? How do we think? How do we become men and women?

For most of history there was no in-between, no adolescence as we know it. There was no such lengthy period of semi-autonomy, economic "useless-ness," when the only occupation of a son or daughter was learning.

In the eighteenth century, Americans weren't legally adults until they turned twenty-one, but they did important work on farms by seven or eight. When they were physically grown, at only thirteen or sixteen, they had virtually the same jobs as any other adult.

In those days, education was irregular at best, but each child had his or her own vocational guidance teacher: the family. So the transition to adulthood was handled—though not always easily or without tension—through a long ap-prenticeship, on the farm or in a craft, by people who could point out a direct social path to adulthood.

It was industrialization that changed all that. In the nineteenth century, mills and factories replaced farms, and cities replaced the countryside. Children didn't automatically follow their parents' occupations and so family relations be-came less important for job training than something called school.

In that century, the need for child labor on farms diminished and the hor-rors of industrial child labor became widespread. So we passed laws against child labor and in favor of mandatory education. Decade by decade we have raised both ages.

School has replaced work not just out of our benevolence. There are also deep economic reasons. In 1933, at the height of the Depression, the National Child Labor Committee put it as baldly as this: "It is now generally accepted that the exploitation of children, indefensible on humanitarian grounds, has become a genuine economic menace. Children should be in school and adults should have whatever worthwhile jobs there are."

School became the place of reading and writing and certification. It provided the necessary paper for employment. School not only kept young people out of the marketplace but promised "better" jobs if they stayed and studied.

The result of all this is clear: Today, school is what young people do for a living.

In 1870, less than 5 percent of the high school age group were in high school. In 1976, 86.1 percent of those fourteen to seventeen were in school. In 1977, nearly one-third of the eighteen to twenty-one-year-olds were in college.

There has been a 129 percent increase in college enrollment in this country since 1960. In many places today, community colleges are entered as routinely as high schools.

While a high school diploma or a college degree no longer guarantees a job, there are more and more jobs you can't even apply for without them. So the payoff is less certain, but the pressure is even greater to go to school longer and longer, to extend the state of semi-autonomy further and further.

The irony is that society worries more when the young try to grasp at adult "privileges" than when they remain in the passive fraternity-house state of mind. We worry about teenage drinking and driving and pregnancy—all perhaps misguided attempts at "grown-up behavior." Yet we offer few alternatives, few meaningful opportunities for adulthood training. We have virtually allowed sex, drinking and driving to become rites of passage.

School just isn't enough. It demands only one skill, tests only one kind of performance. From a pre-med dorm to an Animal House, it is a youth ghetto where adults are only authority figures, where students don't get the chance to test their own identities, their own authority, their own responsibility to others.

Without enough alternatives, we have left schools the job of producing adults. But schools are where the young are kept, not where they grow up.

Adolescence isn't a training ground for adulthood now. It is a holding pattern for aging youth.

1981

Goodman's analysis of the change in American society is an interpretation of the role of school in America today. She proves the thesis that adolescence is not a training ground for adulthood anymore. She offers evidence based on the historical change from apprenticeship to schools as a way of training youth. Her use of statistics and the common knowledge most readers have of the operation of schools gives her work validity. The focus on topic-oriented language makes the tone objective.

THE EXPLORATORY FOCUS

Writing that has an exploratory focus is speculative. The writer engaging in exploration may go beyond the standard interpretations.

Four characteristics are found in exploratory writing.

❏ The thesis is presented as a question or questions.
❏ Alternative explanations are offered.
❏ Tentative solutions are suggested.
❏ Informal style is used.

Questions

Exploratory writing emphasizes discovery. This emphasis is reflected in the process of asking questions about the subject matter being considered. The problems presented cannot be explained by available theories. This kind of thinking is the first step in scientific investigation. Notice how the following statements of an exploratory thesis suggest a range of possible answers.

❏ What can human beings do to allow a polluted environment to regenerate itself?
❏ What can increase students' success in school?

Alternative Explanations

Alternative explanations are offered. Exploratory writing allows the writer to put forth possible explanations that may seem unusual or startling. An unusual alternative explanation or several possible explanations of the topic provide the evidence to support the exploratory thesis.

Tentative Solutions

Although solutions are suggested and conclusions are drawn, they are tentative. That is, they are subject to change. It is this tentativeness that gives the speculation in exploratory writing its validity.

Informal Style

Exploratory writing is more subjective than other forms of referential writing. This subjectivity is reflected in the language used. First person pronouns sometimes appear and the style is probably more informal than most interpretive writing.

Tentative language is used. Words like *it seems* and *perhaps* indicate that the writer is offering explanations that are based on speculation rather than incontrovertible logic.

An Example

The following article from *The Smithsonian* magazine illustrates the range of questions that can be addressed in referential writing with an exploratory focus.

Daydream

JOHN P. WILEY

A dark forest used to stand silent just inside the National Museum of Natural History, a growth of hemlocks four to five feet in diameter. Through the trees you could see a river, a wooded island on the right, and acres of wild rice to the left. No bridges crossed the river. It was the spot where Rock Creek empties into the Potomac River in Washington, and you were seeing it as the Indians saw it before the Europeans arrived. Malls and memorials stand now where once the wild rice grew; a sea wall keeps the river in its place.

When I walk the seawall, I try to see the river as it was. I do the same on Chesapeake Bay or along the Hudson River, remembering accounts of the extraordinarily abundant fish and wildlife found by the early explorers. And I wonder how well they might recover if we went away for a few centuries. Would hemlocks grow again in what is now a boathouse parking lot at Rock Creek?

My only empirical data comes from a 5-by-20-foot bank alongside my driveway. A rock garden planted with lilies and irises when I moved in six years ago, I abandoned it in the press of other business. Today, thanks to the wind and the birds, it is crowded with oaks, maples, dogwoods and a yellow poplar already 15 feet high. A living wall. All I had to do was stand back out of the way.

To find out what would happen on a larger scale, one could consult the literature on plant succession, study abandoned highways, visit ruins in Mexico, travel to lost cities in Asia. Or one could make evacuating the entire Earth the premise for a science-fiction story, and let the special-effects people fill in the details when the story is snapped up for a major motion picture. New York City 10,000 years after the last human left would be a new challenge for the model makers.

The scenario goes something like this: the time comes when, despite our best efforts, the only way left to save Earth is to leave it. Everybody. For a long time. So many species have been lost, so many ecosystems impoverished, that the whole biological life-support system is close to collapse. The natural waste-removal systems, the recyclers, the air filters and water holder are being overwhelmed.

In this fantasy future, field biologists are the new elite. They are paid more than Congressmen, although less than basketball players. Biologists have been multiplying as fast as species have been disappearing. In 1980 one expert had told Congress that there were only 1,500 people in the world competent to identify tropical organisms; when brown leafhoppers destroyed several billion dollars worth of rice in Southeast Asia in the late 1970s, only a dozen people in the world could distinguish with certainty the 20,000 species that make up the insect group.

Now, some decades later, armies of biologists carry on with a wartime intensity, desperate to learn more about how the natural systems work before they disappear. The need to know not only what should be saved first on Earth, but what should be added to the recycling systems on the space colonies and asteroid mines overhead which, like some of the most carefully assembled home aquariums, do not quite work. By now humans live as far away as the moons of Jupiter, but all the secrets of life remain on Earth.

At some point it becomes clear that the race is being lost. True, human numbers are dropping. Heavy industry has moved into space. But so much tropical forest has already been cut, so many watersheds destroyed, so much topsoil washed away that the biological decline has unstoppable momentum. It is too late for management, no matter how wise.

Thus a decision once made by bands and tribes, to pack up and move, is now made by the population of the planet. The actual mechanics are a little fuzzy in my fantasy, except that more and more people would move into space.

With a little suspension of disbelief one can see the story unfold. Grass appears in the boathouse parking lot. A small section of the seawall collapses and, with no one around to fix it, the river moves in like a silent bulldozer. The noblest experiment of all has begun.

Now the story moves in fast-forward, time-lapse photography; we watch nature reclaim itself through the eyes of appropriate creatures. Early on we see city streets through the eyes of a rat; we follow the feral dogs and cats that roam the suburbs along with the racoons and skunks. A century later a coyote hunts in the streets of Manhattan; five centuries after that a panther uses the pinnacle of a rubble pile to search for prey. A pigeon's eye view of a city changes to a falcon's.

Humans will not be able to leave the planet completely alone, of course, any more than an editor can pass on a manuscript without making a mark. The luckiest biologists of their generations will be landed at monitoring stations. Remote sensors will be maintained, camera lenses cleaned. A little crisis intervention might be allowed at first: aerial tankers putting out a fire about to destroy the last known stand of some special plant. But as far as humanly possible, the biologists would keep their hands off, acting only as passive receptors. Nature would be the protagonist and the star. A living Earth regenerating from the ruins. The miracle that struggles to happen in every vacant lost happening everywhere. All with appropriate inspirational music, of course.

Conflict for a story line should be easy. At the start the conflict would be over whether to leave; I could stoop to a line something like: "Gazing out into the dark—30 stories above the East River—after a day of hearing out the biologists' deputations, the Secretary-General became biologically literate." Later the conflict over whether it was time to return would grow stronger: The latter argument would not sound entirely unfamiliar to anyone who follows today's debates over multiple use versus preserving wilderness areas unsullied. A writer might suffer the temptation to inject ideological harangues into the dialogue.

In the meantime, the miracle would be fact. The biological crisis would be past. Nothing would have returned from extinction, but the several million species left would be plenty to keep the bio in biosphere. An optimist would end the movie with humans returning to live in gentle coexistence. A pessimist might have us come back to ravish the Earth all over again. Something in between seems more reasonable.

I'm completely over my head in every part of this fantasy, of course. If we flew 100,000 people off this Earth every day, it would take 125 years to move the current population. I certainly don't know if hemlocks could or would ever grow again in that boathouse parking lot.

But I like the uniting of what are now inimical factions: the high technologists who believe the future of our species lies in space, and the environmentalists who fear we would foul the rest of the solar system just as we have fouled the planet. Environmentalists might be a little humbler if the spacers save the world. I also like the idea of a species, grown out of its infancy, given a second chance at husbanding a remarkable place to live. Possibly even the only place to live.

But the strongest appeal is really the vision I started with—fish leaping in clear water, forests growing to the water's edge, swamps and marshes pulsating with life. The way things were here just five or six lifetimes ago.

To some people today, an environmentalist is a monomaniac. Worse, still, is a preservationist: an elitist unconcerned with people. Perhaps I am most unspeakable of all: a preservationist who not only wants to keep what we still have but would like to bring back what we once had. I don't feel antipeople at all. We people need the life support of the biosphere. The whole system is slowly failing, but still has the power to regenerate without any help from us. All we have to do is stand back. Now, if only that were somehow possible.

In this article Wiley poses a problem having to do with the future of the Earth's environment. He speculates about possible outcomes. His conclusions are not certain. They cannot be proven and he admits that aspects of his scenario could not happen. The exploration serves to raise a question about the nature of the planet's regenerative processes and the impact of human beings on the ecosystem.

THE REFLECTIVE FOCUS

Any work that has a reflective focus, including the so-called *New Journalism* that appeared in the 1960s and 70s, tries to maintain reader interest almost to the point of losing its objectivity. Such writing usually focuses on stories about people. Many of its techniques are similar to those used by the writer of realistic fiction. But reflective writing focuses on real people. What keeps such writing from being literary is that the writer is making an effort to explain a subject. The entertainment we derive from reading reflective writing is secondary to our interest in the subject being revealed to us. Sometimes reflective writing is called parajournalistic writing because it can be distinguished from the typical informative patterns present in traditional journalism.

Reflective writing has four characteristics.

- ❏ The thesis addresses the significance of the topic.
- ❏ A dramatic structure is used to present the evidence.
- ❏ First person or omniscient point of view is used.
- ❏ Realistic detail is used.

Significance

The topic explained in reflective writing will have some significance. The thesis will address that significance. The thesis in reflective writing may not be stated explicitly because the initial interest in the work may be created by dramatic tension.

Dramatic Structure

The writer uses a scene by scene construction. Events are reported that cast some light on the characters or place being explained.

Point of View

The writer may intrude into the narrative through a first person point of view or may appear to know what is in the mind of the characters depicted in the work through an omniscient point of view.

Critics of this kind of writing say that such uses of point of view compromise the objectivity of the report. In addition, writers who have used omniscient point of view have defended the practice by saying that they research and interview people with just that in mind, to find out what the characters being written about are thinking.

Defenders of authorial intrusion argue that objectivity is a fiction anyway and that the writer, by revealing his or her own responses to the scene or events, is simply being honest.

Realistic Detail

The details the writer uses may reveal the status of the subject being investigated. For instance, a description of an item of jewelry or a mannerism may reveal quite a lot about the character. Details also help create a setting, as in literary writing. Dialogue may be used to allow the reader to better understand the characters involved. The kinds of things characters say give important clues to their personalities.

AN EXAMPLE

James Boswell wrote an engaging biography of the life of Samuel Johnson, an eccentric and fascinating literary figure in eighteenth-century England. In this excerpt, written in 1769, we can see how Boswell uses some of the techniques of reflective writing to present Johnson to us.

Fear of Death

JAMES BOSWELL

When we were alone, I introduced the subject of death, and endeavored to maintain that the fear of it might be got over. I told him that David Hume said to me he was no more uneasy to think he should not be after this life than that he had not been before he began to exist. JOHNSON. "Sir, if he really thinks so, his perceptions are disturbed; he is mad. If he does not think so, he lies. He may tell you he holds his finger in the flame of a candle without feeling pain; would you believe him? When he dies, he at least gives up all he has." BOSWELL. "Foote, Sir, told me that when he was very ill he was not afraid to die." JOHNSON. "It is not true, Sir. Hold a pistol to Foote's breast, or to Hume's breast and threaten to kill them, and you'll see how they behave." BOSWELL. "But may we not fortify our mind for the approach of death?" Here I am sensible I was in the wrong, to bring before his view what he ever looked upon with horror; for although when in a celestial frame, in his "Vanity of Human Wishes," he has supposed death to be "kind nature's signal for retreat," from this state of being to "a happier seat," his thoughts upon this awful change were in general full of dismal apprehensions. His mind resembled the vast amphitheater, the coliseum at Rome. In the center stood his judgment, which, like a mighty gladiator, combated those apprehensions that, like the wild beasts of the arena, were all around in cells, ready to be let out upon him. After a conflict, he drives them back into their dens; but not killing them, they were still assailing him. To my question, whether we might not fortify our minds for the approach of death, he answered in a passion, "No, Sir, let alone. It matters not how a man dies, but how he lives. The act of dying is not of importance; it lasts so short a time." He added, with an earnest look, "A man knows it must be so, and submits. It will do him no good to whine."

I attempted to continue the conversation. He was so provoked that he said, "Give us no more of this," and was thrown into such a state of agitation that he expressed himself in a way that alarmed and distressed me; showed an impatience that I should leave him, and when I was going away, called to me sternly, "Don't let us meet tomorrow."

I went home exceedingly uneasy. All the harsh observations which I had ever heard made upon his character crowded into my mind; and I seemed to myself like the man who had put his head into the lion's mouth a great many times with perfect safety, but a last had it bit off.

Next morning I sent him a note stating that I might have been in the wrong, but it was not intentionally; he was therefore, I could not help thinking, too severe upon me. That notwithstanding our agreement not to meet that day, I would call on him in my way to the city, and stay five minutes to my watch. "You are," said I, "in my mind, since last night, surrounded with cloud and storm. Let me have a glimpse of sunshine and go about my affairs in serenity and cheerfulness."

Upon entering his study, I was glad that he was not alone, which would have made our meeting more awkward. There were with him, Mr. Stevens and Mr. Tyers, both of whom I now saw for the first time. My note had, on his own reflection, softened him, for he received me very complacently; so that I unexpectedly found myself at ease, and joined in the conversation. . . .

Johnson spoke unfavorably of a certain pretty voluminous author, saying, "He used to write anonymous books, and then other books commending those books, in which there was something of rascality."

I whispered him, "Well, Sir, you are now in good humor." JOHNSON. "Yes, Sir." I was going to leave him, and had got as far as the staircase. He stopped me, and smiling, said, "Get you gone *in*"; a curious mode of inviting me to stay, which I accordingly did for some time longer.

This little incidental quarrel and reconciliation, which perhaps, I may be thought to have detailed too minutely, must be esteemed as one of many proofs which his friends had, that though he might be charged with bad humor at times, he was always a good-natured man; and I have heard Sir Joshua Reynolds, a nice and delicate observer of manners, particularly remark that when upon any occasion Johnson had been rough to any person in company, he took the first opportunity of reconciliation, by drinking to him or addressing his discourse to him; but if he found his dignified indirect overtures sullenly neglected, he was quite indifferent, and considered himself as having done all that he ought to do, and the other as now in the wrong.

Boswell presents Johnson's character by letting us listen to him speak and by allowing us to see him in a dramatic situation. He presents the episode in two scenes: the quarrel and the reconciliation. The dialogue in both instances allows us to see Johnson's reactions to the conflict. Boswell uses the

first person point of view. In addition, he speculates about what is in Johnson's mind. At the end of the piece Boswell sums up this aspect of Johnson's
character by citing the observations of another friend.

COMBINATIONS

Obviously, informative elements appear in other kinds of referential writing. It
is what the writer does with the information presented that distinguishes one
form of referential writing from another. Interpretive elements may appear
in exploratory writing and exploration provides the basis of much scientific
research.

WRITING STRATEGIES

All referential writing starts with facts. A referential purpose reflects an attempt on the part of the writer to explain some subject to the reader. Even
though you may feel that you don't know enough to write an extended
referential paper on anything, you know quite a lot about many subjects.
Search your experiences. You can also gain information through reading and
research.

Remember that accuracy and clarity are central to referential writing.
Topics which, for you, are laden with emotion or which involve debatable issues that can't be proved with certainty will be developed in expressive and
persuasive writing rather than in referential writing.

A clearly stated thesis is usually the key to a well-developed referential
paper. Consider the following thesis: *Endangered species is a difficult problem to
solve.* Such a statement is too vague to be a good starting point for a paper
about endangered species. A better thesis statement would be this one: *Habitat destruction threatens many species of animals and plants with extinction.* This
thesis provides more focus for the paper and suggests the kind of evidence
that would be needed to support the thesis. A paper with such a thesis would
probably include studies of the changes in the numbers of threatened species
of animals and plants in areas where natural habitat had been destroyed.

Consider the following questions as you develop your ideas for a referential paper:

- ❏ Is your thesis clearly stated?
- ❏ What evidence relates to your thesis?
- ❏ Is all the evidence available to you?
- ❏ Can you draw any conclusions from the evidence you have?
- ❏ Do your conclusions account for all the evidence?
- ❏ Is the validity of the evidence apparent?
- ❏ Is the conclusion supported by most of the evidence?

PART 2

Pattern

Classification

Description

Narration

Evaluation

Classification

We seem to use classification almost automatically to organize the enormous amount of information we deal with everyday. Examples of classification are all around us. For instance, we are able to find products in a supermarket because they are in a particular place along with other products of the same *kind*. Produce is in one place, meat in another, and dairy products in still another. This arrangement of products in a supermarket is based on a system of classification. We know where to look for a book in a library because it has been put in a place with other books of the same *type*. Psychology books are in one place; English books, in another; and books about automotive repair, in yet another. Again the principle of arrangement is based on a classification system, putting books of the same *category* together.

The tendency to classify seems to be a human preoccupation. Films are rated G, PG, PG-13, R, and NC-17. Vitamins are labeled A, B, C, etc. Singers are classified as sopranos, altos, tenors, and basses. Musical instruments are grouped into strings, woodwinds, brasses, and percussion.

We can call this use of classification formal classification. Two other variations of the use of classification are 1) comparison and contrast and 2) definition. Comparison and contrast involves two elements in a classification system while definition involves just one.

FORMAL CLASSIFICATION

When we classify, we arrange information into groups and then name the groups. These groups, or classes, are related to each other categorically. In other words, we put similar things into categories together. We are concerned with groups of things, rather than with individuals. We are interested in showing how groups are related to each other, how something is like others of its class, and what all members of the class have in common.

Using a system of classification to organize a paper is an effective method of explaining a topic clearly. Almost any topic can be organized by using a system of classification. All it takes is asking the question, "What kinds of _____ are there?" The answer to the question is a system of classification that tells us how to arrange the details of the topic. If we ask a question like, "What kinds of alternate energy sources are there?" the answer will suggest a system of classification, a way of organizing a paper about alternate energy sources. The classification system for alternate energy sources might look something like this:

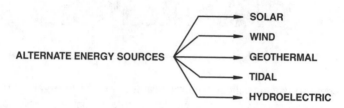

Alternative energy sources is the general category. It includes the subclasses of solar, wind, geothermal, tidal, and hydroelectric. These sub-classes are related to each other categorically because they are members of the same class, alternative energy sources. You can develop almost any topic by using classification, but you will need to keep in mind three considerations: the scope of the topic, the basis of classification, and the hierarchical relationships.

As a general rule, for papers written in school, the number of categories will need to be limited. In the example above, kinds of alternative energy sources, we can see that the topic limited itself naturally to five categories. Not all topics, however, are quite so easy. For some topics, the structure of the system must be altered in order to get the kind of narrowing of the topic needed.

Classification systems, although they are logical, are arbitrary. For most topics, classification systems can be changed by changing the basis of the classification. For example, for the topic *household appliances*, we could create a classification system based on the manufacturer of the appliance. The following list illustrates this principle: Admiral, Amana, AMC, Brothers, Caloric, Emerson, Frigidaire, Gaffers/Sattler, Gibson, GE/Hotpoint, Jenn-Air, Kelvinator, Kenmore, Kitchen-Aid, Litton, Magic Chef, Maytag, Modern Maid, Norse, Quasar, Roper, Scotsman, Sears, Speed Queen, Sub-Zero, Tappan, Thermador, U Line, Wards, Westinghouse, and Whirlpool. Obviously, a paper with that many categories would be unmanageable. The categories would have to be limited in some way, but selecting just three or four brands to discuss would not be adequate, especially if the purpose of the explanation was referential. A referential paper with an informative focus creates the expectation of comprehensiveness on the part of the reader.

Changing the *basis of classification* would create a new way of looking at the topic. If the basis of classification were changed to the location of the appliance in the house, the system would look like this.

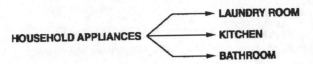

This classification system has three categories. By selecting one of the locations, say the kitchen, another classification system could be created, as shown in the following tree diagram.

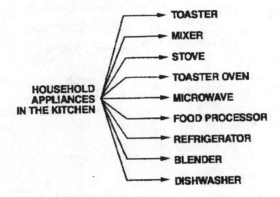

This system could be limited further by narrowing the scope of the category.

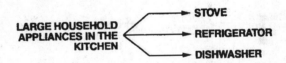

or

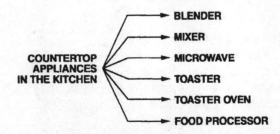

With a basis of classification other than manufacturer or location, such as the use or the function of the appliance, a classification system would look like this.

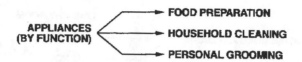

Of course, that system could be narrowed as we did before with the other bases of classification.

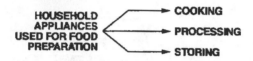

Classification involves not only the relationships among the categories of the system, but also a hierarchical relationship from general to specific. In the tree diagrams used to represent classification systems, each category is more specific than the one to the left of it. The following diagram illustrates this concept.

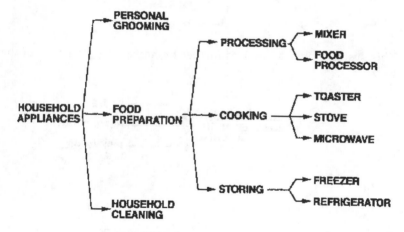

In the preceding diagram, the category *stove* is more specific than the category *cooking*, which is more specific than the category *food preparation*. The same kind of relationship between specific and general exists in all classification systems. The categories for personal grooming and household cleaning could be completed in a similar way.

AN EXAMPLE

In the following essay we discover how formal classification is used to explain a complex body of medical research on addiction.

'Behavioral' Addictions: Do They Exist?

CONSTANCE HOLDEN

Aided by brain imaging advances, scientists are looking for evidence that compulsive nondrug behaviors lead to long-term changes in reward circuitry.

People toss around the term "addiction" to describe someone's relationship to a job, a boyfriend, or a computer. But scientists have traditionally confined their use of the term to substances—namely alcohol and other drugs—that clearly foster physical dependence in the user.

That's changing, however. New knowledge about the brain's reward system, much gained by superrefined brain scan technology, suggests that as far as the brain is concerned, a reward's a reward, regardless of whether it comes from a chemical or an experience. And where there's a reward, there's the risk of the vulnerable brain getting trapped in a compulsion.

"Over the past 6 months, more and more people have been thinking that, contrary to earlier views, there is commonality between substance addictions and other compulsions," says Alan Leshner, head of the National Institute on Drug Abuse (NIDA) and incoming executive officer of the American Association for the Advancement of Science, publisher of Science.

Just where to draw the line is not yet clear. The unsettled state of definitions is reflected in psychiatry's bible, the Diagnostic and Statistical Manual IV. Addictions, obsessions, and compulsions—all related to loss of voluntary control and getting trapped in repetitious, self-defeating behavior—are scattered around under "substance-related disorders," "eating disorders," "sexual and gender identity disorders," "anxiety disorders," and "impulse-control disorders not elsewhere classified." In that last grab-bag are compulsive gambling, kleptomania, fire-setting, hair-pulling, and "intermittent explosive disorder."

Addiction used to be defined as dependence on a drug as evidenced by craving, increased tolerance, and withdrawal. But even some seemingly classical addictions don't follow that pattern. Cocaine, for example, is highly addictive but causes little withdrawal. And a person who gets hooked on morphine while in the hospital may stop taking the drug without developing an obsession with it.

Now many researchers are moving toward a definition of addiction based more on behavior, and they are starting to look at whether brain activity and biochemistry are affected the same way in "behavioral" addictions as they are by substance abuse. One who endorses this perspective is psychologist Howard Shaffer, who heads the Division on Addictions at Harvard. "I had great difficulty with my own colleagues when I suggested that a lot of addiction is the result of experience . . . repetitive, high-emotion, high-frequency experience," he says. But it's become clear that neuroadaptation—that is, changes in neural circuitry that help perpetuate the behavior—occurs even in the absence of drug-taking, he says.

The experts are fond of saying that addiction occurs when a habit "hijacks" brain circuits that evolved to reward survival-enhancing behavior such as eating and sex. "It stands to reason if you can derange these circuits with pharmacology, you can do it with natural rewards too," observes Stanford University psychologist Brian Knutson. Thus, drugs are no longer at the heart of the matter. "What is coming up fast as being the central core issue . . . is continued engagement in self-destructive behavior despite adverse consequences," says Steven Grant of NIDA.

Not everybody is on board with this open-ended definition. For one thing, says longtime addiction researcher Roy Wise of NIDA, drugs are far more powerful than any "natural" pleasure when it comes to the amounts of dopamine released. Nonetheless, behavioral resemblances to addiction are getting increasing notice.

Gambling

In a class of its own as the disorder that most resembles drug addiction is pathological gambling. Compulsive gamblers live from fix to fix, throwing away the rest of their lives for another roll of the dice—and deluding themselves that luck will soon smile on them. Their subjective cravings can be as intense as those of drug abusers; they show tolerance through their need to increase betting; and they experience highs rivaling that of a drug high. Up to half of pathological gamblers "show withdrawal symptoms looking like a mild form of drug withdrawal," says Shaffer—including churning guts, sleep disturbance, sweating, irritability, and craving. And like drug addicts, they are at risk of sudden relapse even after many years of abstinence.

Furthermore, what's going on inside gamblers' heads looks like what goes on in addicts' heads. Yale psychiatrist Marc Potenza finds that when pathological gamblers are exposed to videos of people gambling and talking about gambling, they show activity changes in some of the same frontal and limbic brain regions as do cocaine addicts exposed to images that stir up drug craving, as assessed by functional magnetic resonance imaging (fMRI). And a positron emission tomography study of pathological gamblers playing blackjack, conducted by psychiatrist Eric Hollander of Mount Sinai School of Medicine in New York City, showed significant changes in cortical arousal depending on whether they were just playing cards or betting with a $100 stake. He says it resembles another study showing alcoholics' brain reactions to looking at a bottle of Coke versus a bottle of whiskey.

Like addicts, gamblers also respond to drugs that block drug highs. Suck Won Kim, a psychiatrist at the University of Minnesota Medical School in Minneapolis, has tried naltrexone, an opiate antagonist, on a variety of compulsive behaviors including gambling. In an 11-week trial on 45 gamblers, naltrexone inhibited both the urge to gamble and the high from it in 75% of the group—compared with 24% of a comparable group on placebo—suggesting that drugs and gambling stimulate some of the same biochemical pathways.

And finally, there's cognitive evidence: Gamblers, like drug addicts, do badly at a "gambling task," success at which requires the ability to perceive that delayed gains will be larger than immediate ones.

Food

Can food be said to be an addiction? Overeaters Anonymous—which, like Gamblers Anonymous, is patterned on Alcoholics Anonymous—says yes. The experts, however, say it depends on the disorder.

Compulsive overeating certainly has the look of an addiction that can dominate a person's life. There's also biochemical evidence suggesting a kinship. Psychiatrist Nora Volkow of Brookhaven National Laboratory in Upton, New York, and colleagues found that in a group of compulsive overeaters, dopamine receptor availability was lower, an anomaly also seen in drug addicts. "Dopamine deficiency in obese individuals may perpetuate pathological eating as a means to compensate for decreased activation of these circuits," Volkow's team suggests.

Bulimia, which is characterized by bingeing and vomiting, also looks a lot like an addiction, Hollander notes. Unlike anorexia, which involves rigidly controlled behavior and no high, "bulimia and binge eating have an impulsive component—pleasure and arousal followed by guilt and remorse."

Patricia Faris, a gastrointestinal physiologist at the University of Minnesota, Minneapolis, believes that as with drug addictions, bulimic behavior is initially voluntary but is transformed into a compulsion because of changes that it wreaks on the nervous system. Bulimia clearly affects reward centers: Faris says patients become increasingly depressed and anxious before episodes; immediately following, they uniformly report a pleasant "afterglow."

Faris has come up with a novel hypothesis: that bulimia disregulates the vagal nerve, which regulates heart and lungs as well as the vomiting impulse. She suspects that a binge-purge episode then brings the vagal nerve back to its normal role. This retraining of the vagal nerve also has long-term effects on the brain's reward circuitry, she believes, as suggested by the fact that bulimics have a high relapse rate and are very hard to help once they've been at it for a few years. Kim says that although the theory is speculative, he believes Faris is on the right track in approaching the problem "from neural system concepts" as opposed to a more traditional emphasis on biochemistry.

Sex

There's not much research on sex as an addiction, and some researchers are dubious about whether such a basic function can have that distinction. Sex is really a distinct subject because it's "wired separately," in the opinion of Kim of Minnesota. He notes, for example, that the opioid antagonist naltrexone "really doesn't affect sexual desire that much," so it doesn't follow the same pathways as, say, gambling.

Yet so-called sex addicts do display behaviors characteristic of addiction: They obsess about whatever their favorite practice is, never get enough, feel out of control, and experience serious disruption of their lives because of it. That leads Shaffer to conclude that some behaviors qualify as sex addictions: "I think those things that are robust and reliable shifters of subjective experience all hold the potential for addiction." To be sure, he adds, sex trails behind drugs or gambling, being "relatively robust but unreliable" in delivering satisfaction.

Anna Rose Childress, who does brain imaging studies at the University of Pennsylvania in Philadelphia, says sex addicts resemble cocaine addicts and probably share with them a defect in "inhibitory circuitry." In both instances, "people say when they're in this big 'go' state they feel as though there is override [of inhibition] . . . a feeling of being unable to stop," says Childress.

Scientists are just beginning to use imaging to try to determine whether there's a tangible basis to these feelings. Childress has been comparing the circuits activated by cocaine in addicts and sexual desire in normal subjects in hope of identifying the "stop!" circuitry. And psychiatrist Peter Martin at Vanderbilt University in Nashville, Tennessee, says a preliminary study with normal subjects indicates that brain activity associated with sexual arousal looks like that accompanying drug consumption. He plans to do further comparisons using self-described sex addicts.

Shopping, running, clicking . . .

Although there is no shortage of therapies for every imaginable addiction, there is little or no published research on other disorders. One problem that afflicts a great many women, in particular, is compulsive shopping, says Kim. Compulsive shoppers typically end up with huge debts and their houses stuffed with unused merchandise. Shopping binges are very often precipitated by feelings of depression and anxiety, Shaffer says; the shopping itself can generate temporary druglike highs before the shopper—like a cocaine addict—crashes into depression, guilt, anxiety, and fatigue.

Some have no doubt this is an addiction. "In my clinical experience, [compulsive shoppers] have a similar kind of withdrawal," says Shaffer. Kim agrees: "These people can't control it. We think it's essentially the same thing as gambling." Kim thinks compulsive shoplifting (kleptomania) is also closely related and, in fact, has published the first formal study trying doses of naltrexone with kleptomania; 9 of 10 patients, he says, were much improved after 11 weeks of treatment.

Then there's Internet abuse, the country's fastest growing "addiction." But whether any such phenomenon exists is something about which scientists—if not therapists—are cautious. There are indeed people who neglect the rest of their lives as they spend every waking moment at the monitor. But is it the technology or the behavior that the technology enables that people are really hooked on? The things people are addicted to on the Net are the same things people get hooked on without it: gambling (including day trading), pornography, and shopping, notes Marc Pratarelli of the University of Southern Colorado in Pueblo. His group is doing factor analysis of questionnaire responses by computer users to get at the "core issues" and to determine "if it is in fact just one more fancy tool" to enable a primary habit.

And what about "positive addictions"? Some years ago jogging was touted as one that raised endorphin levels (which in turn stoke up the dopamine) and resulted in a "natural high." Although human behavioral addictions are difficult if not impossible to model in animals, Stefan Brené of the Karolinska Institute in Stockholm, Sweden, thinks he has done it with running. He says rats that have been bred to be addiction-prone spend much more time on the running wheel than other rats do. Furthermore, biochemical tests indicate the impulses both to run and to consume cocaine are governed by "similar biochemical adaptations." He also says the work— most of it as yet unpublished—shows that in an addiction-prone rat, running can increase preference for ethanol—"indicating that a natural, nontoxic . . . addiction can under some instances potentiate the preference for a drug."

The above by no means exhausts the list of behaviors that some scientists see as addictive. And it seems to be true across the board that having one addiction lowers the threshold for developing another, says Walter Kaye, who does research on eating disorders at the University of Pittsburgh Medical Center. Just what form addictions take has a lot to do with one's sex, says Pratarelli. Men are overwhelmingly represented among sex "addicts" and outnumber women by about 2 to 1 in gambling and substance abuse; women are prone to what psychiatrist Susan McElroy of the University of Cincinnati College of Medicine calls the "mall disorders"—eating, shopping, and kleptomania. (Kim says the ratio of females to males in kleptomania is 2 or 3 to 1; perhaps 90% of compulsive shoppers are women.)

To cast more light on the mechanisms of addiction, scientists have taken a growing interest in behavior of the brain's reward circuitry in normal subjects. In a much-cited paper in last May's issue of Neuron, Hans Breiter of Massachusetts General Hospital in Boston and his colleagues used fMRI to map the responses of normal males in a roulette-type game of chance. Blood flow in dopamine-rich areas, the scientists found, indicated that "the same neural circuitry is involved in the highs and lows of winning money, abusing drugs, or anticipating a gastronomical treat." Other research has been showing that many types of rewards besides money—including chocolate, music, and beauty—affects those reward circuits.

Shaffer and others in his camp believe that if such a reward is powerful enough, it can retrain those circuits in a vulnerable person. Not everyone, however, buys the idea that nondrug stimuli really can be potent enough to generate what has been traditionally thought of as addiction. "Many people believe that [only] addictive drugs alter the circuitry in some critical way," says Wise of NIDA. And, he says, drugs are far more powerful than "natural" rewards, increasing dopamine "two to five times more strongly." Kaye also warns that the fact that certain disorders share the same pathways does not necessarily prove they're closely linked. After all, he notes, "stroke and Parkinson's also involve the same pathway."

Despite the uncertainties, addiction research is "going beyond the earlier conceptual framework," says neuroscientist Read Montague of Baylor College of Medicine in Houston. "Historically, these definitions have come out of animal behavior literature," and addiction has been defined in terms of rats frenziedly pressing levers for cocaine. Now, he says, "we need a better theory of how the brain processes rewarding events," one that involves discovering the "algorithms" people follow that lead them into and then keep them trapped in their disastrous behaviors.

In this work we can see clearly how classification enables the writer to present information clearly and coherently. Each category is addressed in sequence. This arrangement allows the reader to see the relationships that exist within the classification system.

VARIATIONS IN FORMAL CLASSIFICATION

The discussion of classification so far has focused on its use in referential writing. When classification is used as a pattern of organization for one of the other kinds of writing (expressive, literary, or persuasive), the structure explained above may change in some ways. For instance, the need for comprehensiveness is associated with informative writing. However, expressive, literary, and persuasive classifications don't necessarily require that the writer include all possible categories for a topic. In addition, in non-referential writing, categories may overlap and different bases of classification may appear in the system.

EXPRESSIVE CLASSIFICATION

Although formal classification with an expressive purpose is not very common, sometimes it does appear. When it is used in expressive writing, formal classification will appear more frequently in works that have either an autobiographical or a ritual perspective because those forms of expressive writing are less spontaneous than either personal or interpersonal forms are.

AN EXAMPLE

The following example from *The Autobiography of Bertrand Russell* illustrates how classification can be used to reveal the identity of the writer.

Three Passions

BERTRAND RUSSELL

Three passions, simple but overwhelmingly strong, have governed my life: the longing for love, the search for knowledge, and unbearable pity for the suffering of mankind. These passions, like great winds, have blown me hither and thither, in a wayward course, over a deep ocean of anguish, reaching to the very verge of despair.

I have sought love, first, because it brings ecstasy—ecstasy so great that I would often have sacrificed all the rest of life for a few hours of this joy. I have sought it, next because it relieves loneliness—that terrible loneliness in which one shivering consciousness looks over the rim of the world into the cold unfathomable lifeless abyss. I have sought it, finally, because in the union of love I have seen, in a mystic miniature, the prefiguring vision of the heaven that saints and poets have imagined. This is what I sought, and though it might seem too good for human life, this is what—at last—I have found.

With equal passion I have sought knowledge. I have wished to understand the hearts of men. I have wished to know why the stars shine. And I have tried to apprehend the Pythagorean power by which number holds sway above the flux. A little of this, but not much, I have achieved.

Love and knowledge, so far as they were possible, led upward toward the heavens. But always pity brought me back to earth. Echoes of cries of pain reverberate in my heart. Children in famine, victims tortured by oppressors, helpless old people a hated burden to their sons, and the whole world of loneliness, poverty, and pain make a mockery of what human life should be. I long to alleviate the evil, but I cannot, and I too suffer.

This has been my life. I have found it worth living, and would gladly live it again if the chance were offered me.

Bertrand Russell, a distinguished philosopher, reveals his analytical mind in this excerpt. In his carefully considered analysis of his own inner emotional responses and his values, he defines himself and allows us to share in his vision of himself.

He organizes the writing by putting his passions into three categories: love, knowledge, and pity. Each category is then developed by adding details, examples, and, in the case of knowledge, further classification.

LITERARY CLASSIFICATION

Formal classification, when it appears as an organizing principle for writing with a literary purpose, is usually not a work of fiction because fiction, both long and short, is typically organized by a combination of narration and description. Consequently, literary works that organize with classification will usually be non-fiction.

AN EXAMPLE

The following example is taken from an article in the eighteenth-century periodical entitled the *Spectator*, an influential paper written by Joseph Addison and Sir Richard Steele. This excerpt is from an article written by Addison for the *Spectator* on Monday, March 12, 1711. In it Addison identifies the different kinds of audiences he intends the *Spectator* to affect.

The Aims of the Spectator

JOSEPH ADDISON

It is with much satisfaction that I hear this great city inquiring day by day after my papers, and receiving my morning lectures with a becoming seriousness and attention. My publisher tells me that there are already three thousand of them distributed every day. So that if I allow twenty readers to every paper, which I look upon as a modest computation, I may reckon about three-score thousand disciples in London and Westminster, who I hope will take care to distinguish themselves from the thoughtless herd of their ignorant and unattentive brethren. Since I have raised myself so great an audience, I shall spare no pains to make their instruction agreeable, and their diversion useful. For which reasons I shall endeavor to enliven morality with wit, and to temper wit with morality, that my readers may, if possible, both ways find their account in the speculation of the day. And to the end that their virtue and discretion may not be short, transient, intermitting starts of thought, I have resolved to refresh their memories from day to day, till I have recovered them out of that desperate state of vice and folly into which the age is fallen. The mind that lies fallow but a single day sprouts up in follies that are only to be killed by a constant and assiduous culture. It was said of Socrates that he brought philosophy down from heaven, to inhabit among men; and I shall be ambitious to have it said of me that I have brought philosophy out of closets and libraries, schools and colleges, to dwell in clubs and assemblies, at tea tables and in coffeehouses.

I would therefore in a very particular manner recommend these my speculations to all well-regulated families that set apart an hour in every morning for tea and bread and butter; and would earnestly advise them for their good to order this paper to be punctually served up, and to be looked upon as part of the tea equipage.

Sir Francis Bacon observes that a well-written book, compared with its rivals and antagonists, is like Moses' serpent, that immediately swallowed up and devoured those of the Egyptians. I shall not be so vain as to think that where *The Spectator* appears the other public prints will vanish; but shall leave it to my reader's consideration whether is it not much better to be let into the knowledge of one's self, than to hear what passes in Muscovy or Poland; and to amuse ourselves with such writings as tend to the wearing out of ignorance, passion, and prejudice, than such as naturally conduce to inflame hatreds, and make enmities irreconcilable?

In the next place, I would recommend this paper to the daily perusal of those gentlemen whom I cannot but consider as my good brothers and allies, I mean the fraternity of spectators, who live in the world without having anything to do in it; and either by the affluence of their fortunes or laziness of their dispositions have no other business with the rest of mankind but to look upon them. Under this class of men are comprehended all contemplative tradesmen, titular physicians, fellows of the Royal Society, Templars that are not given to be contentious, and statesmen that are out of business; in short, everyone that considers the world as a theater, and desires to form a right judgment of those who are the actors on it.

There is another set of men that I must likewise lay a claim to, whom I have lately called the blanks of society, as being altogether unfurnished with ideas, till the business and conversation of the day has supplied them. I have often considered these poor souls with an eye of great commiseration, when I have heard them asking the first man they have met with, whether there was any news stirring? and by that means gathering together materials for thinking. These needy persons do not know what to talk of till about twelve o'clock in the morning; for by that time they are pretty good judges of the weather, know which way the wind sits, and whether the Dutch mail be come in. As they lie at the mercy of the first man they meet, and are grave or impertinent all the day long, according to the notions which they have imbibed in the morning, I would earnestly entreat them not to stir out of their chambers till they have read this paper, and do promise them that I will daily instil into them such sound and wholesome sentiments as shall have a good effect on their conversation for the ensuing twelve hours.

In this excerpt we are made aware of three groups of readers: well-regulated families, the fraternity of spectators, and blanks of society. As you can see, the literary purpose of the essay is especially apparent in Addison's humorous characterization of the "blanks of society."

Persuasive Classification

The categories developed in persuasive classifications can be used to create an appeal to the audience.

An Example

John F. Kennedy, the charismatic thirty-fifth President of the United States, illustrates in his "Inaugural Address" how classification can be used to persuade an audience.

Inaugural Address

JOHN F. KENNEDY

We observe today not a victory of party but a celebration of freedom, symbolizing an end as well as a beginning, signifying renewal as well as change. For I have sworn before you and Almighty God the same solemn oath our forebears prescribed nearly a century and three-quarters ago.

The world is very different now. For man holds in his mortal hands the power to abolish all forms of human poverty and all forms of human life. And yet the same revolutionary belief for which our forebears fought is still at issue around the globe, the belief that the rights of man come not from generosity of the state but from the hand of God.

We dare not forget today that we are the heirs of the first revolution. Let the word go forth from this time and place, to friend and foe alike, that the torch has been passed to a new generation of Americans, born in this century, tempered by war, disciplined by a hard and bitter peace, proud of our ancient heritage, and unwilling to witness or permit the slow undoing of those human rights to which this nation has always been committed, and to which we are committed today at home and around the world.

Let every nation know, whether it wishes us well or ill, that we shall pay any price, bear any burden, meet any hardship, support any friend, oppose any foe to assure the survival and the success of liberty.

This much we pledge—and more.

To those allies whose cultural and spiritual origins we share, we pledge the loyalty of faithful friends. United, there is little we cannot do in a host of co-operative ventures. Divided, there is little we can do, for we dare not meet a powerful challenge at odds and split asunder.

To those new states whom we welcome to the ranks of the free, we pledge our word that one form of colonial control shall not have passed away merely to be replaced by a far more iron tyranny. We shall not always hope to find them strongly supporting their own freedom, and to remember that, in the past, those who foolishly sought power by riding the back of the tiger ended up inside.

To those people in the huts and villages of half the globe struggling to break the bonds of mass misery, we pledge our best efforts to help them help themselves, for whatever period is required, not because the communists may be doing it, not because we seek their votes, but because it is right. If a free society cannot help the many who are poor, it cannot save the few who are rich.

To our sister republics south of the border, we offer a special pledge: to convert our good words into good deeds, in a new alliance for progress, to assist free men and free governments in casting off the chains of poverty. But this peaceful revolution of hope cannot become the prey of hostile powers. Let all our neighbors know that we shall join with them to oppose aggression or subversion anywhere in the Americas. And let every other power know that this hemisphere intends to remain the master of its own house.

To that world assembly of sovereign states, the United Nations, our last best hope in an age where the instruments of war have far outpaced the instruments of peace, we renew our pledge of support: to prevent it from becoming merely a forum for invective, to strengthen its shield of the new and the weak, and to enlarge the area in which its writ may run.

Finally, to those nations who would make themselves our adversary, we offer not a pledge but a request: that both sides begin anew the quest for peace, before the dark powers of destruction unleashed by science engulf all humanity in planned or accidental self-destruction.

We dare not tempt them with weakness. For only when our arms are sufficient beyond doubt can we be certain beyond doubt that they will never be employed.

But neither can two great and powerful groups of nations take comfort from our present course—both sides over-burdened by the cost of modern weapons, both rightly alarmed by the steady spread of the deadly atom, yet both racing to alter that uncertain balance of terror that stays the hand of mankind's final war.

So let us begin anew, remembering on both sides that civility is not a sign of weakness, and sincerity is always subject to proof. Let us never negotiate out of fear, but let us never fear to negotiate.

Let both sides explore what problems unite us instead of belaboring those problems which divide us.

Let both sides seek to invoke the wonders of science instead of its terrors. Together let us explore the stars, conquer the deserts, eradicate disease, tap the ocean depths and encourage the arts and commerce.

Let both sides unite to heed in all corners of the earth the commands of Isaiah to "undo the heavy burdens . . . [and] let the oppressed go free."

And if a beachhead of co-operation may push back the jungle of suspicion, let both sides join in creating a new endeavor, not a new balance of power, but a new world of law, where the strong are just and the weak secure and the peace preserved.

All this will not be finished in the first one hundred days. Nor will it be finished in the first one thousand days, nor in the life of this Administration, nor even perhaps in our lifetime on this planet. But let us begin.

In your hands, my fellow citizens, more than mine, will rest the final success or failure of our course. Since this country was founded, each generation of Americans has been summoned to give testimony to its national loyalty. The graves of young Americans who answered the call to service surround the globe.

Now the trumpet summons us again—not as a call to bear arms, though arms we need; not as a call to battle, though embattled we are; but a call to bear the burden of a long twilight struggle, year in and year out, "rejoicing in hope, patient in tribulation," a struggle against the common enemies of men: tyranny, poverty, disease and war itself.

> Can we forge against these enemies a grand and global alliance, North and South, East and West, that can assure a more fruitful life for all mankind? Will you join in that historic effort?
>
> In the long history of the world, only a few generations have been granted the role of defending freedom in its hour of maximum danger. I do not shrink from this responsibility; I welcome it. I do not believe that any of us would exchange places with any other people or any other generation. The energy, the faith, the devotion which we bring to this endeavor will light our country and all who serve it, and the glow from that fire can truly light the world.
>
> And so, my fellow Americans, ask not what your country can do for you; ask what you can do for your country.
>
> My fellow citizens of the world, ask not what America will do for you, but what together we can do for the freedom of man.
>
> Finally, whether you are citizens of America or citizens of the world, ask of us here the same high standards of strength and sacrifice which we ask of you. With a good conscience our only sure reward, with history the final judge of our deeds, let us go forth to lead the land we love, asking His blessing and His help, but knowing that here on earth God's work must truly be our own.

Kennedy's speech uses classification to identify the various kinds of audiences he is addressing. Since the speech is persuasive rather than referential, the categories are arranged for rhetorical effect rather than for logical coherence. Some categories overlap and some are not parallel to the others. For example, the categories "allies," "new states," "sister republics south of the border," and "nations that would make themselves our adversary" are all included in the category "world assembly of sovereign states." The category "people in the huts and villages of half the globe struggling to break the bonds of mass misery" is not parallel to the other categories.

REFERENTIAL CLASSIFICATION

Classification is used frequently to organize information in referential writing. It has the advantage of allowing the writer to organize a large amount of information and present it to the reader in a meaningful way.

AN EXAMPLE

In his book *The Naked Ape* (1967), Desmond Morris explains the close relationship between animal behavior and human behavior. In this excerpt he uses classification to explain the development of some aspects of human language.

Four Kinds of Talking

DESMOND MORRIS

The behaviour pattern of talking evolved originally out of the increased need for the cooperative exchange of information. It grew out of the common and widespread animal phenomenon of nonverbal mood vocalization. From the typical, inborn mammalian repertoire of grunts and squeals there developed a more complex series of learnt sound signals. These vocal units and their combinations and recombinations became the basis of what we can call *information talking*. Unlike the more primitive nonverbal mood signals, this new method of communication enabled our ancestors to refer to objects in the environment and also to the past and the future as well as to the present. To this day, information talking has remained the most important form of vocal communication for our species. But, having evolved, it did not stop there. It acquired additional functions. One of these took the form of *mood talking*. Strictly speaking, this was unnecessary, because the nonverbal mood signals were not lost. We still can and do convey our emotional states by giving vent to ancient primate screams and grunts, but we augment these messages with verbal confirmation of our feelings. A yelp of pain is closely followed by a verbal signal that "I am hurt." A roar of anger is accompanied by the message "I am furious." Sometimes the nonverbal signal is not performed in its pure state but instead finds expression as a tone of voice. The words "I am hurt" are whined or screamed. The words "I am furious" are roared or bellowed. The tone of voice in such cases is so unmodified by learning and so close to the ancient nonverbal mammalian signaling system that even a dog can understand the message, let alone a foreigner from another race of our own species. The actual words used in such instances are almost superfluous. (Try snarling "good dog," or cooing "bad dog" at your pet, and you will see what I mean.) At its crudest and most intense level, mood talking is little more than a "spilling over" of verbalized sound signaling into an area of communication that is already taken care of. Its value lies in the increased possibilities it provides for more subtle and sensitive mood signaling.

A third form of verbalization is *exploratory talking*. This is talking for talking's sake, aesthetic talking, or, if you like, play talking. Just as that other form of information-transmission, picture-making, became used as a medium tor aesthetic exploration, so did talking. The poet paralleled the painter. But it is the fourth type of verbalization that we are concerned with in this chapter, the kind that has aptly been described recently as *grooming talking*. This is the meaningless, polite chatter of social occasions. The "nice weather we are having" or "have you read any good books lately" form of talking. It is not concerned with the exchange of important ideas or information, nor does it reveal the true mood of the speaker, nor is it aesthetically pleasing. Its function is to reinforce the greeting smile and to maintain the social togetherness. It is our substitute for the social grooming of other primates. By providing us with a nonaggressive social preoccupation, it enables us to expose ourselves communally to one another over comparatively long periods, in this way enabling valuable group bonds and friendships to grow and become strengthened.

Morris creates four categories. He develops the categories by explaining the processes that occur and by giving examples that illustrate the concepts.

WRITING STRATEGIES

If you are using classification to organize your paper, consider the following questions.

- ❑ What "kinds" of your topic are there? (List them)
- ❑ What principle of classification accounts for how you generated your categories?
- ❑ If you have generated more than five categories, how can you limit the number?
- ❑ What details will you include in each category?
- ❑ What other patterns of organization will you use to develop the categories?

COMPARISON AND CONTRAST

Comparison and contrast is a method of organization derived from classification that shows how two closely related things are similar and/or different. For example, we can compare and contrast two people, two cars, two cats, or two of just about anything. But we can make meaningful comparisons and contrasts only if there is a categorical relationship between the two things being compared and contrasted. Although a comparison and contrast between an oak tree and house is possible, it probably would not be very meaningful. (The discussion of *analogy* in the next section of this chapter shows that there are circumstances when the comparison of an oak tree and a house could be made.) In most cases, the similarities and differences are meaningful only if they are derived from a classification system. We recognize similarities and differences when we create a classification system. For example, a marine biologist might classify whales, which are members of the same species, by noting the differences in the kind of food they eat. The potential for comparison and contrast is always present in a classification system.

PATTERNS OF COMPARISON AND CONTRAST

There are two types of organization used in comparison and contrast. Comparison and contrast can be structured by presenting the similarities and then the differences, a pattern called *separation of detail*, or by alternating between the similarities and differences of each aspect of the subject, a pattern called *alternation of detail*.

As with other decisions about the appropriate organizational pattern, whether to use alternation or separation of detail depends on the purpose, the audience, and the situational context. The length of the work may be a factor as well.

SEPARATION OF DETAIL

Separation of detail can be used effectively if there are only a few points to be considered. If the two things being compared and contrasted are complicated with a great many details to consider, the reader may be overburdened in trying to make the connections between them. The conclusion is especially important when separation of detail is used.

AN EXAMPLE

In this classic study of culture in *Patterns of Culture* (1934), anthropologist Ruth Benedict compares two kinds of Native American culture.

The Pueblos of New Mexico

RUTH BENEDICT

The Pueblos are a ceremonious people. But that is not the essential fashion in which they are set off from the other peoples of North America and Mexico. It goes much deeper than any difference in degree in the amount of ritual that is current among them. The Aztec civilization of Mexico was as ritualistic as the Pueblo, and even the Plains Indians with their sun dance and their men's societies, their tobacco orders and their war rituals, had a rich ceremonialism.

The basic contrast between the Pueblos and the other cultures of North America is the contrast that is named and described by Nietzsche in his studies of Greek tragedy. He discusses two diametrically opposed ways of arriving at the value of existence. The Dionysian pursues them through 'the annihilation of the ordinary bounds and limits of existence'; he seeks to attain in his most valued moments escape from the boundaries imposed upon him by his five senses, to break through into another order of experience. The desire of the Dionysian, in personal experience or in ritual, is to press through it toward a certain psychological state, to achieve excess. The closest analogy to the emotions he seeks is drunkenness, and he values the illuminations of frenzy. With Blake, he believes 'the path of excess leads to the palace of wisdom.' The Apollonian distrusts all this, and has often little idea of the nature of such experiences. He finds means to outlaw them from his conscious life. He 'knows but one law, measure in the Hellenic sense.' He keeps the middle of the road, stays within the known map, does not meddle with disruptive psychological states. In Nietzsche's fine phrase, even in the exaltation of the dance he 'remains what he is, and retains his civic name.'

The Southwest Pueblos are Apollonian. Not all of Nietzsche's discussion of the contrast between Apollonian and Dionysian applies to the contrast between the Pueblos and the surrounding peoples. The fragments I have quoted are faithful descriptions, but there were refinements of the types in Greece that do not occur among the Indians of the Southwest, and among these latter, again, there are refinements that did not occur in Greece. It is with no thought of equating the civilization of Greece with that of aboriginal America that I use, in describing the cultural configurations of the latter, terms borrowed from the culture of Greece. I use them because they are categories that bring clearly to the fore the major qualities that differentiate Pueblo culture from those of other American Indians, not because all the attitudes that are found in Greece are found also in aboriginal America.

Apollonian institutions have been carried much further in the pueblos than in Greece. Greece was by no means single-minded. In particular, Greece did not carry out as the Pueblos have the distrust of individualism that the Apollonian way of life implies, but which in Greece was scanted because of forces with which it came in conflict. Zuñi ideals and institutions on the other hand are rigorous on this point. The known map, the middle of the road, to any Apollonian is embodied in the common tradition of his people. To stay always within it is to commit himself to precedent, to tradition. Therefore those influences that are powerful against tradition are uncongenial and minimized in their institutions, and the greatest of these is individualism. It is disruptive, according to Apollonian philosophy in the Southwest, even when it refines upon and enlarges the tradition itself. That is not to say that the Pueblos prevent this. No culture can protect itself from additions and changes. But the process by which these come is suspect and cloaked, and institutions that would give individuals a free hand are outlawed.

It is not possible to understand Pueblo attitudes toward life without some knowledge of the culture from which they have detached themselves: that of the rest of North America. It is by the force of the contrast that we can calculate the strength of their opposite drive and the resistances that have kept out of the Pueblos the most characteristic traits of the American aborigines. For the American Indians as a whole, and including those of Mexico, were passionately Dionysian. They valued all violent experience, all means by which human beings may break through the usual sensory routine, and to all such experiences they attributed the highest value.

The Indians of North America outside the Pueblos have, of course, anything but uniform culture. They contrast violently at almost every point, and there are eight of them that it is convenient to differentiate as separate culture areas. But throughout them all, in one or another guise, there run certain fundamental Dionysian practices. The most conspicuous of these is probably their practice of obtaining supernatural power in a dream or vision, of which we have already spoken. On the western plains men sought these visions with hideous tortures. They cut strips from the skin of their arms, they struck off fingers, they swung themselves from tall poles by straps inserted under the muscles of their shoulders. They went without food and water for extreme periods. They sought in every way to achieve an order of experience set apart from daily living. It was grown men, on the plains, who went out after visions. Sometimes they stood motionless, their hands tied behind them, or they staked out a tiny spot from which they could not move till they had received their blessing. Sometimes, in other tribes, they wandered over distant regions, far out into dangerous country. Some tribes chose precipices and places especially associated with danger. At all events a man went alone, or, if he was seeking his vision by torture and some had to go out with him to tie him to the pole from which he was to swing till he had his supernatural experience, his helper did his part and left him alone for his ordeal.

1934

Benedict's comparison of two cultures is organized by separation of detail. She contrasts Pueblo cultures to other North American cultures by using the categories described by Nietzsche in his study of Greek tragedy.

ALTERNATION OF DETAIL

Alternation of detail makes it easier to maintain a balanced treatment of the topic and allows the reader to follow the comparison and contrast without confusion. However, if there are a great number of points to compare or contrast, alternation of detail can become somewhat tedious.

AN EXAMPLE

Mathew Arnold gives a point by point comparison and contrast of two major influences on Western culture.

Hebraism and Hellenism

MATTHEW ARNOLD

Hebraism and Hellenism,—between these two points of influence moves our world. At one time it feels more powerfully the attraction of one of them, at another time of the other; and it ought to be, though it never is, evenly and happily balanced between them.

The final aim of both Hellenism and Hebraism, as of all great spiritual disciplines, is no doubt the same: man's perfection or salvation. The very language which they both of them use in schooling us to reach this aim is often identical. Even when their language indicates by variation,—sometimes a broad variation, often a but slight and subtle variation,—the different courses of thought which are uppermost in each discipline, even then the unity of the final end and aim is still apparent. To employ the actual words of that discipline with which we ourselves are all of us most familiar, and the words of which, therefore, come most home to us, that final end and aim is "that we might be partakers of the divine nature." These are the words of a Hebrew apostle, but of Hellenism and Hebraism alike this is, I say, the aim. When the two are confronted, as they very often are confronted, it is nearly always with what I may call a rhetorical purpose; the speaker's whole design is to exalt and enthrone one of the two, and he uses the other only as a foil and to enable him the better to give effect to his purpose. Obviously, with us, it is usually Hellenism which is thus reduced to minister to the triumph of Hebraism. There is a sermon on Greece and the Greek spirit by a man never to be mentioned without interest and respect, Frederick Robertson, in which this rhetorical use of Greece and the Greek spirit, and the inadequate exhibition of them necessarily consequent upon this, is almost ludicrous, and would be censurable if it were not to be explained by the exigencies of a sermon. On the other hand, Heinrich Heine, and other writers of his sort, give us the spectacle of the table completely turned, and of Hebraism brought in just as a foil and contrast to Hellenism, and to make the superiority of Hellenism more manifest. In both these cases there is injustice and misrepresentation. The aim and end of both Hebraism and Hellenism is, as I have said, one and the same, and this aim and end is august and admirable.

Still, they purse this aim by very different courses. The uppermost idea with Hellenism is to see things as they really are; the uppermost idea with Hebraism is conduct and obedience. Nothing can do away with this ineffaceable difference. The Greek quarrel with the body and its desires is, that they hinder right thinking; the Hebrew quarrel with them is, that they hinder right acting. "He that keepeth the law, happy is he"; "Blessed is the man that feareth the Eternal, that delighteth greatly in his commandments"; that is the Hebrew notion of felicity; and, pursued with passion and tenacity, this notion would not let the Hebrew rest till, as is well known, he had at last got out of the law a network of prescriptions to enwrap his whole life, to govern every moment of it, every impulse, every action. The Greek notion of felicity, on the other hand, is perfectly conveyed in these words of a great French moralist: "*C'est le bonheur des hommes,*"—when? when they abhor that which is evil?—no; when they exercise themselves in the law of the Lord day and night?—no; when they die daily?—no; when they walk about the New Jerusalem with palms in their hand?—no; but when they think aright, when their thought hits: "*quand ils pensent juste.*" At the bottom of both the Greek and the Hebrew notion is the desire, native in man, for reason and the will of God, the feeling after the universal order,—in a word, the love of God. But, while Hebraism seizes upon certain plain, capital intimations of the universal order, and rivets itself, one may say, with unequalled grandeur of earnestness and intensity on the study and observance of them, the bent of Hellenism is to follow, with flexible activity, the whole play of the universal order, to be apprehensive of missing any part of

it, of sacrificing one part to another, to slip away from resting in this or that intimation of it, however capital. An unclouded clearness of mind, an unimpeded
play of thought, is what this bent drives at. The governing idea of Hellenism is
spontaneity of consciousness; that of Hebraism, *strictness of conscience*.

1869

Arnold's comparison and contrast of Hebraism and Hellenism is organized by alternation of detail. He moves from detail to detail on each aspect of
the comparison. Throughout the essay, within each paragraph Arnold treats
first one concept and then the other, explaining different aspects of each.

ANALOGY

An analogy is a comparison between two things that may be similar in some
ways, but come from different classification systems. Similes and metaphors
(discussed in Chapter 2) are analogies. When we use the term analogy, however, we usually associate it with a comparison more elaborate than a simile
or a metaphor. An analogy could be thought of as an *extended* metaphor. In
referential writing and persuasion, an analogy is used to explain something
that is unfamiliar by comparing it with something that is familiar. For instance, the structure of the human eye, something unfamiliar to most of us,
can be explained by comparing it to a camera; or the human circulatory system can be explained by comparing it to a plumbing system.

AN EXAMPLE

In his book *On Human Nature* (1978), Edward O. Wilson explains the difference between nature and nurture by using an analogy.

The Development of Human Behavior

EDWARD O. WILSON

Thus even in the relatively simple categories of behavior we inherit a *capacity*
for certain traits, and a bias to learn one or another of those available. Scientists as diverse in their philosophies as Konrad Lorenz, Robert A. Hinde, and B.
F. Skinner have often stressed that no sharp boundary exists between the inherited and the acquired. It has become apparent that we need new descriptive
techniques to replace the archaic distinction between nature and nurture. One
of the most promising is based on the imagery invented by Conrad H. Waddington, the great geneticist who died in 1975. Waddington said that develop-

ment is something like a landscape that descends from highlands to the shore. Development of a trait—eye color, handedness, schizophrenia, or whatever—resembles the rolling of a ball down the slopes. Each trait traverses a different part of the landscape, each is guided by a different pattern of ridges and valleys. In the case of eye color, given a starting set of genes for blue or some other iris pigment, the topography is a single, deep channel. The ball rolls inexorably to one destination: once the egg has been joined by a sperm, only one eye color is possible. The developmental landscape of the mosquito can be similarly envisioned as a parallel series of deep, unbranching valleys, one leading to the sexual attraction of the wingbeat's sound, another to automatic bloodsucking, and so on through a repertory of ten or so discrete responses. The valleys form a precise, unyielding series of biochemical steps that proceed from the DNA in the fertilized egg to the neuromuscular actions mediated by the mosquito's brain.

The developmental topography of human behavior is enormously broader and more complicated, but it is still a topography. In some cases the valleys divide once or twice. An individual can end up either right- or left-handed. If he starts with the genes or other early physiological influences that predispose him to the left hand, that branch of the developmental channel can be viewed as cutting the more deeply. If no social pressure is exerted the ball will in most cases roll on down into the channel for left-handedness. But if parents train the child to use the right hand, the ball can be nudged into the shallower channel for right-handedness. The landscape for schizophrenia is a broader network of anastomosing channels, more difficult to trace, and the ball's course is only statistically predictable.

The landscape is just a metaphor, and it is certainly inadequate for the most complex phenomena, but it focuses on a critical truth about human social behavior. If we are to gain full understanding of its determination, each behavior must be treated separately and traced to some extent, as a developmental process leading from the genes to the final product.

Wilson compares the interaction between genetic and environmental influences on the development of human behavior to a ball rolling through a landscape from highlands to the shore. The analogy does not prove the validity of Wilson's account of the development of human behavior. It simply explains a difficult scientific process in terms that most readers would understand.

VARIATIONS IN COMPARISON AND CONTRAST

The structure of the comparison/contrast will be affected by what the purpose of the paper is. For instance, more emphasis may be given to one of the two things being compared if the argument involves an issue and the purpose of the argument is to convince the audience of the rightness of the writer's position. On the other hand, in a referential comparison/contrast, the writer would try to maintain a balanced treatment of the two topics.

EXPRESSIVE COMPARISON AND CONTRAST

Expressive comparisons are controlled by the values and emotional responses of the writer. One of the two things being compared and contrasted may be preferred over the other.

AN EXAMPLE

Mark Twain reveals in this expressive contrast, how his views changed as he became more familiar with the river.

Two Ways of Viewing the River

MARK TWAIN

Now when I had mastered the language of this water, and had come to know every trifling feature that bordered the great river as familiarly as I knew the letters of the alphabet, I had made a valuable acquisition. But I had lost something, too. I had lost something which could never be restored to me while I lived. All the grace, the beauty, the poetry, had gone out of the majestic river! I still keep in mind a certain wonderful sunset which I witnessed when steamboating was new to me. A broad expanse of the river was turned to blood; in the middle distance the red hue brightened into gold, through which a solitary log came floating black and conspicuous; in one place a long, slanting mark lay sparkling upon the water; in another the surface was broken by boiling, tumbling rings, that were as many-tinted as an opal; where the ruddy flush was faintest, was a smooth spot that was covered with graceful circles and radiating lines, ever so delicately traced; the shore on our left was densely wooded, and the somber shadow that fell from this forest was broken in one place by a long, ruffled trail that shone like silver; and high above the forest wall a clean-stemmed dead tree waved a single leafy bough that glowed like a flame in the unobstructed splendor that was flowing from the sun. There were graceful curves, reflected images, woody heights, soft distances; and over the whole scene, far and near, the dissolving lights drifted steadily, enriching it every passing moment with new marvels of coloring.

I stood like one bewitched. I drank it in, in a speechless rapture. The world was new to me, and I had never seen anything like this at home. But as I have said, a day came when I began to cease from noting the glories and the charms which the moon and the sun and the twilight wrought upon the river's face; another day came when I ceased altogether to note them. Then, if that sunset scene had been repeated, I should have looked upon it without rapture, and should have commented upon it, inwardly, after this fashion: "This sun means that we are going to have wind to-morrow; that floating log means that the river is rising, small thanks to it; that slanting mark on the water refers to a bluff reef which is going to kill somebody's steamboat one of these nights, if it keeps on stretching out like that; those tumbling 'boils' show a dissolving bar and a changing channel there; the lines and circles in the slick water over yonder are a warning that that troublesome place is shoaling up dangerously; that silver streak in the shadow of the forest is the 'break' from a new snag, and he has located himself in the very best place he could have found to fish for steamboats; that tall dead tree, with a single living branch, is not going to last long, and then how is a body ever going to get through this blind place at night without the friendly old landmark?"

No, the romance and beauty were all gone from the river. All the value any feature of it had for me now was the amount of usefulness it could furnish toward compassing the safe piloting of a steamboat. Since those days, I have pitied doctors from my heart. What does the lovely flush in a beauty's cheek mean to a doctor but a "break" that ripples above some deadly disease? Are not all her visible charms sown thick with what are to him the signs and symbols of hidden decay? Does he ever see her beauty at all, or doesn't he simply view her professionally, and comment upon her unwholesome condition all to himself? And doesn't he sometimes wonder whether he has gained most or lost most by learning his trade?

Mark Twain's use of comparison and contrast reveals his changing perceptions. He makes emotional responses when he reflects on the beauty of his initial contact with the river. He says that he "stood like one bewitched." Twain reveals his value system when he expresses regret about his loss of the sense of "romance and beauty" he first felt.

Literary Comparison and Contrast

Literary comparisons are often analogies. They may use many of the devices of language characteristic of literature: graphic images, figurative images, and personification.

An Example

Samuel Johnson uses analogy to present Shakespeare to us. He makes use of a great many graphic images and figures of speech to express his admiration for Shakespeare's abilities as a writer.

On Shakespeare

SAMUEL JOHNSON

The work of a correct and regular writer is a garden accurately formed and diligently planted, varied with shades, and scented with flowers; the composition of Shakespeare is a forest, in which oaks extend their branches, and pines tower in the air, interspersed sometimes with weeds and brambles, and sometimes giving shelter to myrtles and to roses; filling the eye with awful pomp and gratifying the mind with endless diversity. Other poets display cabinets of precious rarities, minutely finished, wrought into shape, and polished into brightness. Shakespeare opens a mine which contains gold and diamonds in unexhaustible plenty, though clouded by incrustations, debased by impurities, and mingled with a mass of meaner minerals.

Johnson uses four analogies in this brief commentary on Shakespeare's work. He compares the work of regular writers to a garden "accurately formed" and "diligently planted." He compares Shakespeare's writing to a forest that, although it sometimes has "weeds and brambles," also offers majesty and "endless diversity." The work of other poets he compares to carefully wrought jewelry in "display cabinets." On the other hand, he compares Shakespeare's work to a mine that, even though mixed with impurities, is an inexhaustible source of "gold and diamonds." The vivid, graphic images Johnson uses create an appealing picture of Shakespeare's work.

PERSUASIVE COMPARISON AND CONTRAST

A writer may use comparison and contrast to convince us to favor one thing over another. Presenting one topic in relation to another allows for the selection of details that favor the preferred position and cast the other in a less favorable light.

AN EXAMPLE

In this selection the noted feminist Gloria Steinem uses comparison and contrast to support a persuasive claim.

Erotica and Pornography

GLORIA STEINEM

Human beings are the only animals that experience the same sex drive at times when we can—and cannot—conceive.

Just as we developed uniquely human capacities for language, planning, memory, and invention along our evolutionary path, we also developed sexuality as a form of expression; a way of communicating that is separable from our need for sex as a way of perpetuating ourselves. For humans alone, sexuality can be and often is primarily a way of bonding, of giving and receiving pleasure, bridging differentness, discovering sameness, and communicating emotion.

We developed this and other human gifts through our ability to change our environment, adapt physically, and in the long run, to affect our own evolution. But as an emotional result of this spiraling path away from other animals, we seem to alternate between periods of exploring our unique abilities to change new boundaries, and feelings of loneliness in the unknown that we ourselves have created; a fear that sometimes sends us back to the comfort of the animal world by encouraging us to exaggerate our sameness.

The separation of "play" from "work," for instance, is a problem only in the human world. So is the difference between art and nature, or an intellectual accomplishment and a physical one. As a result, we celebrate play, art, and invention as leaps into the unknown; but any imbalance can send us back to nostalgia for our primate past and the conviction that the basics of work, nature, and physical labor are somehow more worthwhile or even moral.

In the same way, we have explored our sexuality as separable from conception: a pleasurable, empathetic bridge to strangers of the same species. We have even invented contraception—a skill that has probably existed in some form since our ancestors figured out the process of birth—in order to extend this uniquely human difference. Yet we also have times of atavistic suspicion that sex is not complete—or even legal or intended-by-god—if it cannot end in conception.

No wonder the concepts of "erotica" and "pornography" can be so crucially different, and yet so confused. Both assume that sexuality can be separated from conception, and therefore can be used to carry a personal message. That's a major reason why, even in our current culture, both may be called equally "shocking" or legally "obscene," a word whose Latin derivative means "dirty, containing filth." This gross condemnation of all sexuality that isn't harnessed to childbirth and marriage has been increased by the current backlash against women's progress. Out of fear that the whole patriarchal structure might be upset if women really had the autonomous power to decide our reproductive futures (that is, if we controlled the most basic means of production), right-wing groups are not only denouncing prochoice abortion literature as "pornographic," but are trying to stop the sending of all contraceptive information through the mails by invoking obscenity laws. In fact, Phyllis Schlafly recently denounced the entire Women's Movement as "obscene."

Not surprisingly, this religious, visceral backlash has a secular, intellectual counterpart that relies heavily on applying the "natural" behavior of the animal world to humans. That is questionable in itself, but these Lionel Tiger-ish studies make their political purpose even more clear in the particular animals they select and the habits they choose to emphasize. The message is that females should accept their "destiny" of being sexually dependent and devote themselves to bearing and rearing their young.

Defending against such reaction in turn leads to another temptation: to merely reverse the terms, and declare that *all* nonprocreative sex is good. In fact, however, this human activity can be as constructive as destructive, moral or immoral, as any other. Sex as communication can send messages as different as life and death; even the origins of "erotica" and "pornography" reflect that fact. After all, "erotica" is rooted in *eros* or passionate love, and thus in the idea of positive choice, free will, the yearning for a particular person. (Interestingly, the definition of erotica leaves open the question of gender.) "Pornography" begins with a root meaning "prostitution" or "female captives," thus letting us know that the subject is not mutual love, or love at all, but domination and violence against women. (Though, of course, homosexual pornography may imitate this violence by putting a man in the "feminine" role of victim.) It ends with a root meaning "writing about" or "description of" which puts still more distance between subject and object, and replaces a spontaneous yearning for closeness with objectification and a voyeur.

The difference is clear in the words. It becomes even more so by example.

Look at any photo or film of people making love; really making love. The images may be diverse, but there is usually a sensuality and touch and warmth, an acceptance of bodies and nerve endings. There is always a spontaneous sense of people who are there because they *want* to be, out of shared pleasure.

Now look at any depiction of sex in which there is clear force, or an unequal power that spells coercion. It may be very blatant, with weapons of torture or bondage, wounds and bruises, some clear humiliation, or an adult's sexual power being used over a child. It may be much more subtle: a physical attitude of conqueror and victim, the use of race or class difference to imply the same thing, perhaps a very unequal nudity, with one person exposed and vulnerable while the other is clothed. In either case, there no sense of equal choice or equal power.

The first is erotic: a mutually pleasurable, sexual expression between people who have enough power to be there by positive choice. It may or may not strike a sense-memory in the viewer, or be creative enough to make the unknown seem real; but it doesn't require us to identify with a conqueror or a victim. It is truly sensuous, and may give us a contagion of pleasure.

The second is pornographic: its message is violence, dominance, and conquest. It is sex being used to reinforce some inequality, or to create one, or to tell us the lie that pain and humiliation (ours or someone else's) are really the same as pleasure. If we are to feel anything, we must identify with conqueror or victim. That means we can only experience pleasure through the adoption of some degree of sadism or masochism. It also means that we may feel diminished by the role of conqueror, or enraged, humiliated, and vengeful by sharing identity with the victim.

Perhaps one could simply say that erotica is about sexuality, but pornography is about power and sex-as-weapon—in the same way we have come to understand that rape is about violence, and not really about sexuality at all.

Yes, it's true that there are women who have been forced by violent families and dominating men to confuse love with pain; so much so that they have become masochists. (A fact that in no way excuses those who administer such pain.) But the truth is that, for most women—and or men with enough humanity to imagine themselves into the predicament of women—true pornography could serve as aversion therapy for sex.

Of course, there will always be personal differences about what is and is not erotic, and there may be cultural differences for a long time to come. Many women feel that sex makes them vulnerable and therefore may continue to need more sense of personal connection and safety before allowing any erotic feelings. We now find competence and expertise erotic in men, but that may pass as we develop those qualities in ourselves. Men, on the other hand, may continue to feel less vulnerable, and therefore more open to such potential danger as sex with strangers. As some men replace the need for submission from childlike women with the pleasure of cooperation from equals, they may find a partner's competence to be erotic, too.

Such group changes plus individual differences will continue to be reflected in sexual love between people of the same gender, as well as between women and men. The point is not to dictate sameness, but to discover ourselves and each other through sexuality that is an exploring, pleasurable, empathetic part of our lives; a human sexuality that is unchained both from unwanted pregnancies and from violence.

But that is a hope, not a reality. At the moment, fear of change is increasing both the indiscriminate repression of all nonprocreative sex in the religious and "conservative" male world, and the pornographic vengeance against women's sexuality in the secular world of "liberal" and "radical" men. It's almost futuristic to debate what is and is not truly erotic, when many women are again being forced into compulsory motherhood, and the number of pornographic murders, tortures, and woman-hating images are on the increase in both popular culture and real life.

It's a familiar division: wife or whore, "good" woman who is constantly vulnerable to pregnancy or "bad" woman who is unprotected from violence. *Both* roles would be upset if we were to control our own sexuality. And that's exactly what we must do.

In spite of all our atavistic suspicions and training for the "natural" role of motherhood, we took up the complicated battle for reproductive freedom. Our bodies had borne that health burden of endless births and poor abortions, and we had a greater motive for separating sexuality and conception.

Now we have to take up the equally complex burden of explaining that all nonprocreative sex is *not* alike. We have a motive: our right to a uniquely human sexuality, and sometimes even to survival. As it is, our bodies have too rarely been enough our own to develop erotica in our own lives, much less in art and literature. And our bodies have too often been the objects of pornography and the woman-hating, violent practice that it preaches. Consider also our spirits that break a little each time we see ourselves in chains or full labial display for the conquering male viewer, bruised or on our knees, screaming a real or pretended pain to delight the sadist, pretending to enjoy what we don't enjoy, to be blind to the images of our sisters that really haunt us—humiliated often enough ourselves by the truly obscene idea that sex and the domination of women must be combined.

Sexuality *is* human, free, separate—and so are we.

But until we untangle the lethal confusion of sex with violence, there will be more pornography and less erotica. There will be little murders in our beds—and very little love.

Steinem's claim that women should control their own sexuality is supported by her comparison and contrast of erotica and pornography. Through this comparison and contrast, she argues further that pornography results from the confusion of sex with violence and presents women as objects to be dominated.

REFERENTIAL COMPARISON AND CONTRAST

Referential comparison and contrast gives an accurate and clear explanation of the two things. The author makes an effort to balance the presentation and present an unbiased view.

AN EXAMPLE

In the following excerpt from his book *Landscape and Memory*, art historian Simon Schama uses comparison and contrast to explain the meaning of two nineteenth-century German paintings.

The Track through the Woods

SIMON SCHAMA

The Kerstings [paintings by Georg Friedrich Kersting] were shown in an exhibition of patriotic painting at Dresden in 1814 alongside a painting that became the most enduring of all the icons of the *Freiheitskrieg*: Caspar David Friedrich's *"Chasseur" in the Forest*. Contemporary critics had no difficulty in recognizing the heavy load of patriotic symbols carried by the painting: the raven, perched on the felled fir stumps (signifying martyred soldiers), singing its song of death to the isolated *French chasseur*. But Friedrich's composition was much more than a mechanical inventory of such inspirational emblems. It might almost be considered as a bookend to the Altdorfer *St. George*. Both panels are dominated by a forbidding screen of foliage that sharply encloses the space within which their histories may be read. In both cases, too, the forest itself acts German, but there the similarities end. For while the leaves of Altdorfer's *Silva Hercynia* are lit with the illumination of a sacred triumph, in Friedrich's fir forest they are edged with the snow of death. The Christian-German warrior George is seen in heroic profile, whereas the French soldier, serving Napoleon—the new emperor and, by virtue of his conquests, the king of Italy, too—is seen from the rear, as if to emphasize his vulnerability. Whereas the woodland solitude seems to be the ally of St. George, it is evidently the adversary of the new "Latin" invader. Even his helmet, accurately described from the French military, seems strangely Roman, as if borrowed from one of Varus's lost centurions. Perhaps there were even echoes in their respective weapons, for while the ancient Germans carried javelins and spears not much different from the lance that pierces the dragon, the Romans used swords, represented in Friedrich's paintings by the weapon trailing clumsily beneath the *chasseur's* cape. And while St. George is set parallel to the plane of the forest, as if in consort with it, the hapless *chasseur* faces it dead-on, pulled into its interior by the relentlessly commanding path leading nowhere good. For where, in the Altdorfer, the vegetation is pierced by light, exposing a space beyond, in the Friedrich there is only blackness. Like Varus's centurions, the *chasseur* is surrounded and dwarfed by the impenetrable line of evergreens, the massed troops of the reborn Germania.

Schama's comparison and contrast of the two paintings gives us a better understanding of both of them. He begins with the point of similarity between the paintings—the forest. Then he explains the elements that create the contrast: the Christian-German St. George and the French Chasseur, their weapons, and finally their position in relation to the forest. In pointing out these contrasting elements, Schama reveals the difference between the Germanic and Latin attitudes toward the forest.

WRITING STRATEGIES

If you are using comparison and contrast to organize your work, consider the following questions:

- ❏ How are the two subjects similar?
- ❏ How are the two subjects different?
- ❏ What details should be included?
- ❏ How should those details be arranged?

DEFINITION

A definition is a statement of the meaning of a word, a phrase, or a term. When we define, we typically use the principles of classification. Instead of presenting an entire classification system, however, we consider only a single category.

KINDS OF DEFINITIONS

Definitions can be either simple or extended. A simple definition will give a concise meaning of the term. An extended definition will give an elaborated explanation of a complicated concept.

Simple Definitions

Three commonly used methods of giving simple definitions are to put the term we are defining in its class, to give a synonym for it, or to give an example of it. If we defined a desk as a piece of furniture, we would be putting it in a general category or class. Defining it as a writing table would be defining by synonym. Saying that an example of a desk is the oak roll-top in the library would be defining the term by example.

Simple definitions are used not to develop an entire essay, but rather to clarify and explain terms that the reader may not understand. This function of definition is often important in interpretive writing when technical language is used.

Extended Definitions

As the term implies, an extended definition is an elaborate explanation of a concept. Such a definition will go into some detail and will structure an entire essay or even an entire book. Extended definitions usually make use of other patterns of organization to explain the term or concept being defined.

AN EXAMPLE

Rybczynski gives an extended definition of comfort. Note that he makes extensive use of examples to develop his definition.

A Definition of "Comfort"

WITOLD RYBCZYNSKI

What is comfort? Perhaps the question should have been asked earlier, but without a review of the long evolution of this complex and profound subject the answer would almost certainly have been wrong, or at least incomplete. The simplest response would be that comfort concerns only human physiology—feeling good. Nothing mysterious about that. But this would not explain why, although the human body has not changed, our idea of what is comfortable differs from that of a hundred years ago. Nor is the answer that comfort is a subjective experience of satisfaction. If comfort were subjective, one would expect a greater variety of attitudes toward it; instead, at any particular historical period there has always been a demonstrable consensus about what is comfortable and what is not. Although comfort is experienced personally, the individual judges comfort according to broader norms, indicating that comfort may be an objective experience.

If comfort is objective, it should be possible to measure it. This is more difficult than it sounds. It is easier to know when we are comfortable than why, or to what degree. It would be possible to identify comfort by recording the personal reactions of large numbers of people, but this would be more like a marketing or opinion survey than a scientific study; a scientist prefers to study things one at a time, and especially to measure them. It turns out that in practice it is much easier to measure *discomfort* than comfort. To establish a thermal "comfort zone," for example, one ascertains at which temperatures most people are either too cold or too hot, and whatever is in between automatically becomes "comfortable." Or if one is trying to identify the appropriate angle for the back of a chair, one can subject people to angles that are too steep and too flat, and between the points where they express discomfort lies the "correct" angle. Similar experiments have been carried out concerning the intensity of lighting and noise, the size of room dimensions, the hardness and softness of sitting and lying furniture, and so on. In all these cases, the range of comfort is discovered by measuring the limits at which people begin to experience discomfort. When the interior of the Space Shuttle was being designed, a cardboard mock-up of the cabin was built. The astronauts were required to move around in this full-size model, miming their daily activities, and every time they knocked against a corner or a projection, a technician would cut away the offending piece. At the end of the process, when there were no more obstructions left, the cabin was judged to be "comfortable." The scientific definition of comfort would be something like "Comfort is that condition in which discomfort has been avoided."

Most of the scientific research that has been carried out on terrestrial comfort has concerned the workplace, since it has been found that comfortable surroundings will affect the morale, and hence the productivity, of workers. Just how much comfort can affect economic performance is indicated by a recent estimate that backaches—the result of poor working posture—account for over ninety-three million lost workdays, a loss of nine billion dollars to the American economy. The modern office interior reflects the scientific definition of comfort. Lighting levels have been carefully controlled to fall within an acceptable level for optimal reading convenience. The finishes of walls and floors are restful; there are no garish or gaudy colors. Desks and chairs are planned to avoid fatigue.

But how comfortable do the people feel who work in such surroundings? As part of an effort to improve its facilities, one large pharmaceutical corporation, Merck & Company, surveyed two thousand of its office staff regarding their attitudes to their place of work—an attractive modern commercial interior. The survey team prepared a questionnaire that listed various aspects of the workplace. These included factors affecting appearance, safety, work efficiency, convenience, comfort, and so on. Employees were asked to express their satisfaction, or dissatisfaction, with different aspects, and also to indicate those aspects that they personally considered to be the most important. The majority distinguished between the visual qualities of their surroundings—decoration, color scheme, carpeting, wall covering, desk appearance—and the physical aspects—lighting, ventilation, privacy, and chair comfort. The latter group were all included in a list of the ten most important factors, together with size of work area, safety, and personal storage space. Interestingly, none of the purely visual factors was felt to be of major importance, indicating just how mistaken is the notion that comfort is solely a function of appearance or style.

What is most revealing is that the Merck employees expressed some degree of dissatisfaction with *two-thirds* of the almost thirty different aspects of the workplace. Among those about which there was the strongest negative feelings were the lack of conversational privacy, the air quality, the lack of visual privacy, and the level of lighting. When they were asked what aspects of the office interior they would like to have individual control over, most people identified room temperature, degree of privacy, choice of chair and desk, and lighting intensity. Control over decor was accorded the lowest priority. This would seem to indicate that although there is wide agreement about the importance of lighting or temperature, there is a good deal of difference of opinion about exactly how much light or heat feels comfortable to different individuals; comfort is obviously both objective and subjective.

The Merck offices had been designed to eliminate discomfort, yet the survey showed that many of the employees did not experience well-being in their workplace—an inability to concentrate was the common complaint. Despite the restful colors and the attractive furnishings (which everyone appreciated), something was missing. The scientific approach assumes that if background noises are muffled and direct view controlled, the office worker will feel comfortable. But working comfort depends on many more factors than these. There must also be a sense of intimacy and privacy, which is produced by a balance between isolation and publicness; too much of one or the other will produce discomfort. A group of architects in California recently identified as many as nine different aspects of workplace enclosure that must be met in order to create this feeling. These included the presence of walls behind and beside the worker, the amount of open space in front of the desk, the area of the workspace, the amount of enclosure, a view to the outside, the distance to the nearest person, the number of people in the immediate vicinity, and the level and type of noise. Since most office layouts do not address these concerns directly, it is not surprising that people have difficulty concentrating on their work.

The fallacy of the scientific definition of comfort is that it considers only those aspects of comfort that are measurable, and with not untypical arrogance denies the existence of the rest—many behavioral scientists have concluded that because people experience only discomfort, comfort as a physical phenomenon does not really exist at all. It is hardly surprising that genuine intimacy, which is impossible to measure, is absent in most planned office environments. Intimacy in the office, or in the home, is not unusual in this respect; there are many complicated experiences that resist measurement. It is impossible, for example, to describe scientifically what distinguishes a great wine from a mediocre one, although a group of wine experts would have no difficulty establishing which was which. The wine industry, like manufacturers of tea and coffee, continues to rely on nontechnical testing—the "nose" of an experienced taster—rather than on objective standards alone. It might be possible to measure a threshold below which wine would taste "bad"—acidity, alcohol content, sweetness, and so on—but no one would suggest that simply avoiding these deficiencies would result in a good wine. A room may feel uncomfortable—it may be too bright for intimate conversations, or too dark for reading—but avoiding such irritations will not automatically produce a feeling of well-being. Dullness is not annoying enough to be disturbing, but it is not stimulating either. On the other hand, when we open a door and think, "What a comfortable room," we are reacting positively to something special, or rather to a series of special things.

Here are two descriptions of comfort. The first is by a well-known interior decorator, Billy Baldwin: "Comfort to me is a room that works for you and your guests. It's deep upholstered furniture. It's having a table handy to put down a drink or a book. It's also knowing that if someone pulls up a chair for a talk, the whole room doesn't fall apart. I'm tired of contrived decorating." The second is by an architect, Christopher Alexander: "Imagine yourself on a winter afternoon with a pot of tea, a book, a reading light, and two or three huge pillows to lean back against. Now make yourself comfortable. Not in some way which you can show to other people, and say how much you like it. I mean so that you *really* like it, for *yourself*. You put the tea where you can reach it: but in a place where you can't possibly knock it over. You pull the light down, to shine on the book, but not too brightly, and so that you can't see the naked bulb. You put the cushions behind you, and place them, carefully, one by one, just where you want them, to support your back, your neck, your arm: so that you are supported just comfortably, just as you want to sip your tea, and read, and dream." Baldwin's description was the result of sixty years of decorating fashionable homes; Alexander's was based on the observation of ordinary people and ordinary places. Yet they both seem to have converged in the depiction of a domestic atmosphere that is instantly recognizable for its ordinary, human qualities.

These qualities are something that science has failed to come to grips with, although to the layman a picture, or a written description, is evidence enough. "Comfort is simply a verbal invention," writes one engineer despairingly. Of course, that is precisely what comfort is. It is an invention—a cultural artifice. Like all cultural ideas—childhood, family, gender—it has a past, and it cannot be understood without reference to its specific history. One-dimensional, technical definitions of comfort, which ignore history, are bound to be unsatisfactory. How rich, by comparison, are Baldwin's and Alexander's descriptions of comfort. They include convenience (a handy table), efficiency (a modulated light source), domesticity (a cup of tea), physical ease (deep chairs and cushions), and privacy (reading a book, having a talk). Intimacy is also present in these descriptions. All these characteristics together contribute to the atmosphere of interior calm that is a part of comfort.

This is the problem with understanding comfort and with finding a simple definition. It is like trying to describe an onion. It appears simple on the outside, just a spheroidal shape. But this is deceptive, for an onion also has many layers. If we cut it apart, we are left with a pile of onion skins, but the original form has disappeared; if we describe each layer separately, we lose sight of the whole. To complicate matters further, the layers are transparent, so that when we look at the whole onion we see not just the surface but also something of the interior. Similarly, comfort is both something simple and complicated. It incorporates many transparent layers of meaning—privacy, ease, convenience—some of which are buried deeper than others.

The onion simile suggests not only that comfort has several layers of meaning, but also that the idea of comfort has developed historically. It is an idea that has meant different things at different times. In the seventeenth century, comfort meant privacy, which lead to intimacy and, in turn, to domesticity. The eighteenth century shifted the emphasis to leisure and ease, the nineteenth to mechanically aided comforts—light, heat, and ventilation. The twentieth-century domestic engineers stressed efficiency and convenience. At various times, and in response to various outside forces—social, economic, and technological—the idea of comfort has changed, sometimes drastically. There was nothing foreordained or inevitable about the changes. If seventeenth-century Holland had been less egalitarian and its women less independent, domesticity would have arrived later than it did. If eighteenth-century England had been aristocratic rather than bourgeois, comfort would have taken a different turn. If servants had not been scarce in our century, it is unlikely that anyone would have listened to Beecher and Frederick. But what is striking is that the idea of comfort, even as it has changed, has preserved most of its earlier meanings. The evolution of comfort should not be confused with the evolution of technology. New technical devices usually—not always—rendered older ones obsolete. The electric lamp replaced the gasolier, which replaced the oil lamp, which replaced candles, and so on. But new ideas about how to achieve comfort did not displace fundamental notions of domestic well-being. Each new meaning added a layer to the previous meanings, which were preserved beneath. At any particular time, comfort consists of all the layers, not only the most recent.

So there it is, the Onion Theory of Comfort—hardly a definition at all, but a more precise explanation may be unnecessary. It may be enough to realize that domestic comfort involves a range of attributes—convenience, efficiency, leisure, ease, pleasure, domesticity, intimacy, and privacy—all of which contribute to the experience; common sense will do the rest. Most people—"I may not know why I like it, but I know what I like"—recognize comfort when they experience it. This recognition involves a combination of sensations—many of them subconscious—and not only physical, but also emotional as well as intellectual, which makes comfort difficult to explain and impossible to measure. But it does not make it any less real. We should resist the inadequate definitions that engineers and architects have offered us. Domestic well-being is too important to be left to experts; it is, as it has always been, the business of the family and the individual. We must rediscover for ourselves the mystery of comfort, for without it, our dwellings will indeed be machines instead of homes.

Rybczynski explores the complexities of defining a simple term. He uses narration and analogy to develop the definition.

WRITING STRATEGIES

If your work involves the use of definition, consider the following questions:

- ❑ What general class is your subject a member of?
- ❑ What is a synonym for the thing being defined?
- ❑ What are its characteristics?
- ❑ What details should be included in the definition?
- ❑ What is an example of the thing being defined?

6

Description

When we organize with description, we attempt to give the reader an impression of a person, a place, a thing, or a concept. Description focuses on the uniqueness of the thing depicted, how it is different from those that may be in the same class. Instead of looking at general features that would be found in other members of its class, as we do when we organize by classification, we look at specific features that differentiate that one thing from all others. We ask what makes the thing we are describing unique. For instance, if you wanted to describe a particular building, you would focus on those characteristics that make it different from all other buildings.

There are three different ways of using description: to depict a physical appearance, to divide a subject into its component parts, and to analyze a concept. In all three of these variations of description we are dealing with an organizing principle based on a relationship between the whole and its parts. With description, we show how the various parts of the thing we are depicting fit together to form the whole. If you were describing a building, you would tell where the doors and windows were, what the roof was like, what the walls were made of, and what other significant design features were apparent. You would show how each part was related to the other parts and situated in relation to the whole.

PHYSICAL DESCRIPTION

When we try to give an impression of what a person, place, or thing is like, we are creating physical descriptions. These descriptions reveal the physical characteristics of whatever it is we are describing. We may start by giving an overall impression (the whole) and then include relevant details (the parts). The selection and ordering of the details of the description reflect the point of view the writer has in relation to the thing being described.

DESCRIBING A PERSON

The problem we face when we describe people is how much detail to include in the description. We don't have to include some details because everybody knows in general what a person looks like. We assume that the reader will know that the person has the same physical characteristics as other people—a head, hair, a nose, and hands. Only if some physical characteristic is different, will we make note of it and indicate that "he is tall" or that "she has purple hair."

Frequently in descriptions of people we include other details besides physical characteristics. Such descriptions are called character sketches. In addition to recording observations about physical characteristics, the character sketch will give impressions of personality traits and mannerisms.

AN EXAMPLE

In the following example, Thomas Carlyle, an English essayist, gives us an impression of what the English poet Alfred, Lord Tennyson was like at the age of thirty-four. This excerpt is from a letter to the American philosopher Ralph Waldo Emerson, August 5, 1844.

Tennyson

THOMAS CARLYLE

Alfred is one of the few British or Foreign Figures (a not increasing number I think!) who are and remain beautiful to me;—a true human soul, or some authentic approximation thereto, to whom your own soul can say, Brother!—However, I doubt he will not come; he often skips me, in these brief visits to Town; skips everybody indeed; being a man solitary and sad, as certain men are dwelling in an element of gloom,—carrying a bit of Chaos about him, in short, which he is manufacturing into Cosmos!

Alfred is the son of a Lincolnshire Gentleman Farmer, I think; indeed, you see in his verses that he is a native of "moated granges," and green, fat pastures, not of mountains and their torrents and storms. He had his breeding at Cambridge, as if for the Law or Church; being master of a small annuity on his Father's decease, he preferred clubbing with his Mother and some Sisters, to live unpromoted and write Poems. In this way he lives still, now here, now there; the family always within reach of London, never in it; he himself making rare and brief visits, lodging in some old comrade's rooms. I think he must be under forty, not much under it. One of the finest-looking men in the world. A great shock of rough dusty-dark hair; bright-laughing hazel eyes; massive aquiline face, most massive yet delicate; of sallow-brown complexion, almost Indian-looking; clothes cynically loose, free-and-easy;—smokes infinite tobacco.

His voice is musical metallic,—fit for loud laughter and piercing wail, and all that may lie between; speech and speculation free and plenteous: I do not meet, in these late decades, such company over a pipe!—We shall see what he will grow to. He is often unwell; very chaotic,—his way is through Chaos and the Bottomless and Pathless; not handy for making out many miles upon.

Carlyle describes Tennyson in terms of both his physical appearance and his behavior. Notice that Carlyle focuses on Tennyson's outstanding physical characteristics: his "great shock of rough dusty-dark hair," his "hazel eyes," his "massive aquiline face," and his "sallow-brown complexion." These distinguishing physical features make Tennyson unique. Carlyle also includes a description of his voice—"musical metallic"—his clothing—"cynically loose" —and his characteristic behavior—"smokes infinite tobacco." Taken together these details give us a memorable portrait of Tennyson.

DESCRIBING A PLACE

As with the description of people, it is impossible to include every single detail in a description of a place. The point of view of the observer is especially important in descriptions of places.

AN EXAMPLE

Peter Matthiessen, in *The Tree Where Man Was Born* (1972), records his travels through East Africa in 1969. The following excerpt gives us a striking description of a river valley.

The Tree Where Man Was Born

PETER MATTHIESSEN

Winds of the southeast monsoon blew up from the hot nyika, and a haze of desert dust obscured the mountains. But the Uaso Nyiro flows all year, and along its green banks the seasons are the same. A dark lioness with a shining coat lay on a rise, intent on the place where game came down to water. At a shady bend, on sunlit sandbars, baboon and elephant consorted, and a small crocodile, gray-green and gleaming at the edge of the thick river, evoked a childhood dream of darkest Africa. Alone on the plain, waiting for his time to come full circle, stood an ancient elephant, tusks broken and worn, hairs fallen from his tail; over his monumental brow, poised for the insects started up by the great trunk, a lilac-breasted roller hung suspended, spinning turquoise lights in the dry air.

On a plateau that climbs in steps from the south bank of the river, three stone pools in a grove of doum palms form an oasis in the elephant-twisted thorn scrub and dry stone. The lower spring, where the water spreads into a swampy stream, has a margin of high reeds and sedge; here the birds and animals come to water. One afternoon I swam in the steep-sided middle pool, which had been, in winter, as clear as the desert wind; now the huge gangs building the road north to Ethiopia were washing here with detergent soaps that bred a heavy film, and I soon got out, letting the sun dry me. A turtle's shadow vanished between ledges of the pool, and dragonflies, one fire-colored and the other cobalt blue, zipped dry-winged through the heat. Despite the wind, there was stillness in the air, expectancy: at the lower spring a pair of spurwing plover stood immobile, watching man grow older.

In the dusty flat west of the spring, ears alert, oryx and zebra waited. Perhaps one had been killed the night before, for jackals came and went in their hangdog way east of the springs and vultures sat like huge galls in the trees. With a shift in the wind, a cloud across the sun, the rush of fronds in the dry palms took on an imminence. Beyond the springs oryx were moving at full run, kicking up dust as they streamed onto the upper plateau. Nagged by the wind, I put my clothes on and set off for camp.

Matthiessen begins his description of the Kenyan landscape by creating an overall impression of the scene—the wind, the haze of desert dust, and the green banks of a river. He adds details showing the specific features of the place and including references to various animals: "a dark lioness" lying on a rise, "baboon and elephant" on sand bars, and "a small crocodile, gray-green and gleaming at the edge of the thick river." Intertwined with the description is a narrative of Matthiessen swimming in a pool, drying in the sun, returning to camp. Other images, like references to dragonflies, "one fire-colored and the other cobalt blue," add depth to the description.

DESCRIBING A THING

Describing a thing often begins by putting it into a class. Then the various individual features of the thing are identified and elaborated on.

AN EXAMPLE

In his award-winning book *Arctic Dreams* (1986), Barry Lopez creates a masterful description of the narwhal.

The Narwhals

BARRY LOPEZ

Scientists can speak with precision only about the physical animal, not the ecology or behavior of this social and gregarious small whale. (It is the latter, not the former, unfortunately, that is most crucial to an understanding of how industrial development might affect narwhals.) Adult males, 16 feet long and weighing upwards of 3300 pounds, are about a quarter again as large as adult females. Males are also distinguished by an ivory tusk that pierces the upper lip on the left side and extends forward as much as 10 feet. Rarely, a female is found with a tusk, and, more rarely still, males and females with tusks on both sides of the upper jaw.

From the side, compared with the rest of its body, the narwhal's head seems small and blunt. It is dominated by a high, rounded forehead filled with bioacoustical lipids—special fats that allow the narwhal to use sound waves to communicate with other whales and to locate itself and other objects in its three-dimensional world. Its short front flippers function as little more than diving planes. The cone-shaped body tapers from just behind these flippers—where its girth is greatest, as much as eight feet—to a vertical ellipse at the tail. In place of a dorsal fin, a low dorsal ridge about five feet long extends in an irregular crenulation down the back. The tail flukes are unique. Seen from above, they appear heart-shaped, like a ginkgo leaf, with a deep-notched center and trailing edges that curve far forward.

Viewed from the front, the head seems somewhat squarish and asymmetrical, and oddly small against the deep chest. The mouth, too, seems small for such a large animal, with the upper lip just covering the edge of a short, wedge-shaped jaw. The eyes are located just above and behind the upturned corners of the mouth, which give the animal a bemused expression. (The evolutionary loss of facial muscles, naturalist Peter Warshall has noted, means no quizzical wrinkling of the forehead, no raised eyebrow of disbelief, no pursed lip of determination.) A single, crescent-shaped blowhole on top of the head is in a transverse line with the eyes.

Narwhal calves are almost uniformly gray. Young adults show spreading patches and streaks of white on the belly and marbling on the flanks. Adults are dark gray across the top of the head and down the back. Lighter grays predominate on top of the flippers and flukes, whites and light yellow-whites underneath. The back and flanks are marbled with blackish grays. Older animals, especially males, may be almost entirely white. Females, say some, are always lighter-colored on their flanks.

The marbled quality of the skin, which feels like smooth, oiled stone, is mesmerizing. On the flukes especially, where curvilinear streaks of dark gray overlap whitish-gray tones, the effect could not be more painterly. Elsewhere on the body, spots dominate. "These spots," writes William Scoresby, "are of a roundish or oblong form: on the back, where they seldom exceed two inches in diameter, they are the darkest and most crowded together, yet with intervals of pure white among them. On the side the spots are fainter, smaller, and more open. On the belly, they become extremely faint and few, and in considerable surfaces are not to be seen." These patterns completely penetrate the skin, which is a half-inch thick.

In the water, depending on sunlight and the color of the water itself, narwhals, according to British whaling historian Basil Lubbock, take on "many hues, from deep sea green to even an intense lake [blue] colour."

Narwhals are strong swimmers, with the ability to alter the contours of their body very slightly to reduce turbulence. Their speed and maneuverability are sufficient to hunt down swift prey—arctic cod, Greenland halibut, redfish—and to avoid their enemies, the orca and the Greenland shark.

Narwhals live in close association with ice margins and are sometimes found far inside heavy pack ice, miles from open water. (How they determine whether the lead systems they follow into the ice will stay open behind them, ensuring their safe return, is not known.) They manage to survive in areas of strong currents and wind where the movement of ice on the surface is violent and where leads open and close, or freeze over, very quickly. (Like sea-birds, they seem to have an uncanny sense of when a particular lead is going to close in on them, and they leave.) That they are not infallible in anticipating the movement and formation of ice, which seals them off from the open air and oxygen, is attested to by a relatively unusual and often fatal event called a savssat.

Savssats are most commonly observed on the west coast of Greenland. Late in the fall, while narwhals are still feeding deep in a coastal fiord, a band of ice may form in calm water across the fiord's mouth. The ice sheet may then expand toward the head of the fiord. At some point the distance from its landward to its seaward edge exceeds the distance a narwhal can travel on a single breath. By this time, too, shorefast ice may have formed at the head of the fiord, and it may grow out to meet the sea ice. The narwhals are thus crowded into a smaller and smaller patch of open water. Their bellowing and gurgling, their bovinelike moans and the plosive screech of their breathing, can sometimes be heard at a great distance.

The Danish scientist Christian Vibe visited a savssat on March 36, 1943, on the west coast of central Greenland. Hundreds of narwhals and belukhas were trapped in an opening less than 20 feet square. The black surface of the water was utterly "calm and still," writes Vibe. "Then the smooth surface was suddenly broken by black shadows and white animals which in elegant curves came up and disappeared—narwhals and white whales by the score. Side by side they emerged so close to each other that some of them would be lifted on the backs of the others and turn a somersault with the handsome tail waving in the air. First rows of narwhal, then white whales and then again narwhals—each species separately. It seethed, bobbed, and splashed in the opening. With a hollow, whistling sound they inhaled the air as if sucking it in through long iron tubes. The water was greatly disturbed . . . and the waves washed far in over the ice." The splashed water froze to the rim of the breathing hole, as did the moisture from their exhalations, further reducing the size of the savssat. In spite of the frenzy, not a single animal that Vibe saw was wounded by the huge tusks of the narwhal.

Lopez' description gives us an idea of what the narwhal looks like. The details he includes give us an accurate picture of the bodies of the animals. He gives us information about shape, distinguishing features, and color.

VARIATIONS IN PHYSICAL DESCRIPTION

A change of purpose will alter the nature of a physical description. The way the details are presented, which details are selected, and what pattern of presentation is used will be determined by the purpose.

EXPRESSIVE DESCRIPTION

Expressive descriptions may be disjointed and fragmented. They may also be layered with emotional responses.

AN EXAMPLE

Two days after the death of his six-year-old son Waldo, Ralph Waldo Emerson made the following entry in his journal dated January 30, 1842. In this entry we find various descriptions that reflect his feelings about the death of his son.

Journal

RALPH WALDO EMERSON

What he looked upon is better, what he looked not upon is insignificant. The morning of Friday I woke at 3 oclock, & every cock in every barnyard was shrilling with the most unnecessary noise. The sun went up the morning sky with all his light, but the landscape was dishonored by this loss. For this boy in whose remembrance I have both slept & awaked so oft, decorated for me the morning star, & the evening cloud, how much more all the particulars of daily economy; for he had touched with his lively curiosity every trivial fact & circumstance in the household, the hard coal & the soft coal which I put into my stove; the wood of which he brought his little quota for grandmother's fire, the hammer, the pincers, & file, he was so eager to use; the microscope, the magnet, the little globe, & every trinket and instrument in the study; the loads of gravel on the meadow, the nests in the henhouse and many & many a little visit to the doghouse and to the barn—For every thing he had his own name & way of thinking, his own pronunciation & manner. And every word came mended from that tongue. A boy of early wisdom, of a grave & even majestic deportment, of a perfect gentleness.

Every tramper that ever tramped is abroad but the little feet are still.
He gave up his little innocent breath like a bird.

> He dictated a letter to his cousin Willie on Monday night to thank him for the Magic Lantern which he had sent him, and said I wish you would tell Cousin Willie that I have so many presents that I do not need that he should send me any more unless he wishes to very much.
>
> The boy had his full swing in this world. Never I think did a child enjoy more. He had been thoroughly respected by his parents & those around him & not interfered with; and he had been the most fortunate in respect to the influences near him for his Aunt Elizabeth had adopted him from his infancy & treated him ever with that plain & wise love which belongs to her and, as she boasted, had never given him sugar plums. So he was won to her & always signalized her arrival as a visit to him & left playmates playthings & all to go to her. Then Mary Russell had been his friend & teacher for two summers with true love & wisdom. Then Henry Thoreau had been one of the family for the last year, & charmed Waldo by the variety of toys whistles boats popguns & all kinds of instruments which he could make & mend; & possessed his love & respect by the gentle firmness with which he always treated him. Margaret Fuller & Caroline had also marked the boy & caressed & conversed with him whenever they were here. Meantime every day his Grandmother gave him his reading lesson & had by patience taught him to read & spell; by patience & love for she loved him dearly.
>
> Sorrow makes us all children again, destroys all differences of intellect. The wisest knows nothing.

The places Emerson describes in this entry take on new meaning in light of his son's death. The details he selects are controlled by his emotional responses to that event. He includes many things that were important to Waldo.

LITERARY DESCRIPTION

Literary descriptions must fit into the design for an overall aesthetic effect. Graphic, vivid images enhance the aesthetic appeal of such descriptions for the reader.

AN EXAMPLE

Walter Pater offers an interesting description of the *Mona Lisa*, obviously created to please the reader.

Mona Lisa

WALTER PATER

Hers is the head upon which all "the ends of the world are come," and the eyelids are a little weary. It is a beauty wrought out from within upon the flesh, the deposit, little cell by cell of strange thoughts and fantastic reveries and exquisite passions. Set it for a moment beside one of those White Greek goddesses or beautiful women of antiquity, and how would they be troubled by this beauty, into which the soul with all its maladies has passed!

All the thoughts and experiences of the world have etched and moulded there, in that which they have of power to refine and make expressive the outward form, the animalism of Greece, the lust of Rome, the mysticism of the middle age with its spiritual ambition and imaginative lovers, the return of the Pagan world, the sins of the Borgias.

She is older than the rocks among which she sits; like the vampire, she has been dead many times, and learned the secrets of the grave; and has been a diver in deep seas, and keeps their fallen day about her; and trafficked for strange webs with Eastern merchants, and, as Leda was the mother of Helen of Troy, and, as Saint Anne, the mother of Mary; and all this has been to her but as the sound of lyres and flutes, and lives only in the delicacy with which it has moulded the changing lineaments, and tinged the eyelids and the hands.

In his description Pater uses graphic literal images ("tinged the eyelids a and the hands"), figures of speech ("like the vampire, she has been dead many times"), and allusions to classical literature ("as Leda was the mother of Helen of Troy") to make the reader's response to Mona Lisa more aesthetically appealing.

PERSUASIVE DESCRIPTION

A persuasive description will try to give the reader an enticing portrayal of the person, place, or thing being described.

AN EXAMPLE

This description, taken from *The Territory Ahead* catalogue, is designed to motivate the reader to buy the product. Notice how the detail included is intended to make the reader associate the product with a notable cultural icon from film history.

Women's Europa Jacket

The writer's selection of detail is controlled by the persuasive purpose. Notice that the details such as "broken in look and feel" and "feminine, slightly shaped silhouette" suggest a kind of worldly femininity. The ad is obviously designed to persuade the reader that wearing the leather jacket will make her as alluring and mysterious as the character created by Ingrid Bergman in *Casablanca*.

REFERENTIAL DESCRIPTION

Referential descriptions focus on accuracy. They support the clear explanation of a topic by adding details that allow the reader to picture the thing described as it really is (or at least a close approximation).

AN EXAMPLE

The famous novelist Henry James offers this rather objective description of Chartres Cathedral.

Chartres Cathedral

HENRY JAMES

I spent a long time looking at Chartres Cathedral. I revolved around it, like a moth around a candle; I went away and I came back; I chose twenty different standpoints; I observed it during the different hours of the day, and saw it in the moonlight as well as the sunshine. I gained, in a word, a certain sense of familiarity with it; and yet I despair of giving any coherent account of it. Like most French Cathedrals, it rises straight out of the street, and is without that setting of turf and trees and deaneries and canonries which contribute so largely to the impressiveness of the great English churches. Thirty years ago a row of old houses was glued to its base and made their back walls of its sculptured sides. These have been plucked away, and, relatively speaking, the church is fairly isolated. But the little square that surrounds it is regretfully narrow, and you flatten your back against the opposite houses in the vain attempt to stand off and survey the towers. The proper way to look at the towers would be to go up in a balloon and hang poised, face to face with them, in the blue air. There is, however, perhaps an advantage in being forced to stand so directly under them, for this position gives you an overwhelming impression of their height. I have seen, I suppose, churches as beautiful as this one, but I do not remember ever to have been so touched and fascinated by architectural beauty. The endless upward reach of the great west front, the clear, silvery tone of its surface, the way a few magnificent features are made to occupy its vast serene expanse, its simplicity, majesty, and dignity—these things crowd upon one's sense with a force that makes the act of vision seem for the moment almost all of life. The impressions produced by architecture lend themselves as little to interpretation by another medium as those produced by music. Certainly there is something of the beauty of music in the sublime proportions of the facade of Chartres.

The doors are rather low, as those of the English cathedral are apt to be, but (standing three together) are set in a deep framework of sculpture—rows of arching grooves, filled with admirable little images, standing with their heels on each other's heads. The church, as it now exists, except the northern tower, are full of the grotesqueness of the period. Above the triple portals is a vast round-topped window, in three divisions, of the grandest dimensions and the stateliest effect. Above the window is a circular aperture, of huge circumference, with a double row of sculptured spokes radiating from its centre and looking on its lofty field of stone as expansive and symbolic as if it were the wheel of Time itself. Higher still is a little gallery with a delicate balustrade, supported on a beautiful cornice and stretching across the front from tower to tower; and above this is a range of niched statues of kings—fifteen, I believe, in number. Above the statues is a gable, with an image of the Virgin and Child on its front, and another of Christ on its apex. In the relation of all these parts there is such a spaciousness and harmony that while on the one side the eye rests on a great many broad stretches of naked stone there is no approach on the other to over profusion of detail.

The arrangement of detail is from the perspective of a tourist. Notice how James places one detail in relation to others with such words as "above," "centre," and "across the front." This placement allows the observer to picture how the details are situated in the whole structure.

WRITING STRATEGIES

When you write descriptions, you will go through a process of selecting which details should be included in the description and then arranging them into an effective pattern. Consider these questions to help you get started when you are writing a physical description.

- ❏ What are you describing?
- ❏ What is its shape?
- ❏ What color is it?
- ❏ What does it taste like?
- ❏ What does it smell like?
- ❏ What does it feel like when you touch it?
- ❏ What does it sound like?
- ❏ What are its unique characteristics?
- ❏ What does it remind you of?
- ❏ What is its overall appearance?

DIVISION

Like physical descriptions, organization by division shows the relationship between the various parts that make up a whole. Although division has some features similar to classification, it deals not with classes, but with parts. Division answers the question, what are its component parts? Classification answers the questions, what kinds of the topic are there? If we wanted to explain the parts of a school building, we could list and define the parts that make up the whole: classrooms, offices, hallways, rest rooms, auditoriums, and laboratories. This division details the parts of a school building. If we discussed *kinds* of buildings—like office buildings, schools, factories, shopping centers—we would be classifying buildings by categories, and thereby arranging into groups.

The Structure of Division

With division we are interested not so much in the overall impression of the thing being considered as we are in the individual parts that make up the whole. The parts of the whole are separated and examined in some detail.

AN EXAMPLE

In the following essay, we can see clearly that a subject, music, has been divided into its parts.

The Five Basic Elements of Music

DAVID RANDOLPH

There is nothing mysterious about the appreciation of music. Proof of your own potential ability to appreciate it lies in the very fact that you are reading these lines. If it were not for the existence of *something* in music that appeals to you, you would not have chosen to read a book on the subject.

As we proceed to consider the various elements in music that attract you, you may find yourself surprised by the degree of appreciation that you already have. These days, when so many of the world's great symphonies, operas, concertos, songs, and instrumental pieces are readily available on records, in radio broadcasts, and at concerts, anyone with the slightest liking for music must of necessity have listened to some of the most sophisticated musical works ever created. Merely to "like" or to be "attracted to" one of the symphonies of Beethoven or Tchaikovsky implies a complexity of response that would amaze you, if you were to take note of all the factors involved. These symphonies are not simple works, and even what we might regard as only a slight degree of appreciation of them—merely a vague sense of pleasure upon hearing them—bespeaks an ability to respond to music at many levels.

Let us see what it is that you respond to in music.

Do you find something appealing about the famous tune from Schubert's *Unfinished Symphony?* If so, then you are responding to one of the most important elements of music—*melody.*

Do you find that you feel like tapping your foot during the march movement of Tchaikovsky's *Pathétique Symphony?* If so, then you are responding to another extremely important element—*rhythm.*

Yet observe that rhythm is present in the melody of Schubert's *Unfinished* (just tap out the melody on a table with your finger, without singing, and you will isolate the rhythm), and that melody is present in even the most rhythmic portion of the Tchaikovsky march. Therefore, in the process of merely "liking" one of these works, you are actually appreciating *two* musical elements at once. While this example may not impress you by its profundity, the *principle*—being aware of what it is that you respond to—is at the root of all genuine music appreciation.

Now imagine how much less satisfying Schubert's melody would be if it were buzzed through a tissue-papered comb, instead of being played by the entire cello section of an orchestra. The melody and the rhythm would still be present as before; the difference would lie only in the quality of the sound that reached your ears. Therefore, when you enjoy the richness of the sound of the massed cellos playing the melody, you are responding to another of the basic elements—*tone color*. Your appreciation, then, really involves *three* elements.

Now, let us suppose that a pianist is playing one of your favorite songs—the melody in the right hand, the accompanying chords in the left. Suppose that his finger slips as he plays one of the chords, causing him to play a sour note. Your immediate awareness of the wrong note comes from your response to another of the basic elements—*harmony*.

Let us briefly consider the more positive implications of harmony. Whether you are attracted by barbershop-quartet singing, or by an atmospheric work by Debussy, or by the powerful, forthright ending of Beethoven's *Fifth Symphony*, *part* of your reaction stems from your response to the harmony, which may be defined as the simultaneous sounding of two or more notes (usually more than two, as in these three examples). Thus we have found a *fourth* element in your appreciation.

Do you have a sense of completeness at the conclusion of a performance of (we will use only one of countless possible examples) Beethoven's *Ninth Symphony*? Are you left with a feeling of satisfaction as well as of elation? If so, part of that sense of satisfaction—of completion—comes from your feeling for *form,* which is the last of the five basic elements of music.

Perhaps you will feel that you have not been consciously aware of the music's form as such. You may argue that your feelings of satisfaction and elation stem merely from the fact that the symphony ends with the full chorus and orchestra singing and playing loud and fast (by which argument, incidentally, you are acknowledging your appreciation of the work's melody, rhythm, harmony, and tone color).

In that case, imagine that you have just turned on your radio, and the first thing you hear is the final few seconds of Beethoven's Ninth. In spite of the fact that you are hearing a large chorus and orchestra singing and playing at full tilt, your reaction to the sudden outburst of sound would not be the same as it might have been had you experienced the cumulative effect of all the music that preceded it.

True, you would be hearing a climactic moment, but—as a climax to *what?* What would be the motivation—the "reason"—for that tremendous sound, from either the intellectual or the emotional viewpoint? To the extent that you found such an experience unsatisfying, it would be your sense of musical *form* that would be left unsatisfied. Whether or not you have ever thought of it consciously, you demand of music a certain sense of continuity, a "hanging together," a feeling of one passage or mood leading logically to another.

We see, in the light of all this, that you are drawn to music through an appreciation of its basic elements: its melody, rhythm, tone color, harmony, and form. At every moment in which you are listening to music, all five of them are at work to some degree, although their relative importance may change quickly, both in the music itself and in our conscious and unconscious responses to it. As you turn on your radio at random, a song or a popular ballad will emphasize melody, while a jazz orchestra will place greater emphasis upon rhythm, although, to be sure, the other elements will also be present. A work for piano will be limited, of course, to the tone color of the piano, but it will have its full measure of all the other elements. On the other hand, a work for full orchestra by a late nineteenth-century romantic composer is likely to abound in contrasting instrumental colors.

Harmony of one kind or another will be present in any music that you happen upon, unless it be a rare work for, let us say, an unaccompanied flute or perhaps for unaccompanied voice, of which Gregorian chant would be the most likely example. Even in music of this sort, consisting of a single unaccompanied melody, you may feel a certain effect of harmony, an *implied* harmony.

Though form, too, will be present in all the music you hear, it will often be one of the more elusive elements. In a popular song or a folk song, the form is usually quite simple and obvious. In an extended orchestral work, such as one of the tone poems of Richard Strauss or Tchaikovsky's Overture-Fantasy *Romeo and Juliet,* the form will be quite complex and less easy to follow.

By way of this intentional oversimplification, we now come to an extremely important point. It is the fact that music can affect our *feelings.* While it would be impossible to catalogue all the varying emotional responses that we may derive from music, let us at least begin by seeing how we respond to the basic elements. Melody goes hand in hand with rhythm; change the *rhythm* of the melody of Schubert's *Unfinished* and you have changed the melody. Hum it to yourself, giving each note the same even time value, and notice that it becomes difficult to recognize, as well as dull in feeling. Play only the rhythm of the most exciting march, without the melody, and the music loses most of its appeal. If all the notes of Beethoven's Fifth Symphony, without a single alteration of the melody, rhythm, harmony, or form, were to be played by an orchestra of harmonicas or mandolins, we would hear a radically different tonal effect from the one intended by Beethoven—and the emotional impact would be completely changed.

Just as all music, therefore, is a composite of basic elements, in which each one affects all the others, so our response to music at any given moment is the total of our reactions to all the elements.

At this point, it would be beneficial for the reader to explore these five basic elements by means of listening. Choose a piece that you have heard before—preferably a short one—and listen to it several times. With each hearing, try to concentrate on one or the other of the elements.

As you listen for melody—the "subject matter" of the music—take note of the *kinds* of melodies that are presented: their lengths, their contrasting characters, their reappearances, the way they may reappear in fragmentary form or in combination with one another.

The best way to concentrate upon the rhythm—the physical aspect of the music—is to beat the time in some fashion, whether it is by "conducting," moving your head, or tapping your foot. To the extent that the rhythm may at times be hard to follow, you will in this way be gaining an insight into the composer's rhythmic imagination and originality.

> As you listen for the tone color—the sensuous aspect of the music—
> be alert for the contrasts in *kinds* of sounds that are offered, for the different
> feelings that a melody will arouse when it is played by different instruments,
> and for the excitement created by a great number of instruments playing
> together.
>
> It might be unwise to attempt to discern the form at the beginning stages
> of listening. It is nevertheless a fact that each recognition of the reappearance
> of a melody will increase your awareness of form—the "ground plan" of the
> music.
>
> If we wanted to be rigid about definitions, we could say that music con-
> sists of nothing but the manipulation of the five elements. The statement is
> correct in that there is no music in the world, regardless of the time or place
> of its origin, that can be based upon anything other than some combination of
> these five elements. Thus, to offer the most extreme contrast possible, what
> we may imagine as the ritual stamping on the ground by the savage appealing
> to his gods partakes of some of the same basic elements as does Bach's *Pas-
> sion According to St. Matthew*, notably rhythm and tone color, and certainly, to
> a degree, form.

The five basic elements of music are explained in this essay. Each of the
elements that makes up a piece of music is explained. The division of the
topic answers the following question: What are the elements of music?

WRITING STRATEGIES

Consider the following questions when you are using division to organize
your writing.

❑ What are the parts?
❑ What is each part like?
❑ How are the parts arranged?

ANALYSIS

Like division, analysis divides a subject into its component parts, but it goes
beyond simple division. Analytical organization allows us to examine a concept in some detail and so come to understand not only how the parts are
interrelated, but also why they exist.

THE STRUCTURE OF ANALYSIS

An analysis will have a structure that allows the writer to make clear to the reader complex concepts and subjects. The parts are identified and defined. The relationships among the various parts are explained. Finally the interactions among the parts are described.

AN EXAMPLE

In this example, we can see how a scientific analysis of the physical features of certain animals answers the question of why there is an optimum size for every type of animal.

On Being the Right Size

J. B. S. HALDANE

The most obvious differences between different animals are differences of size, but for some reason the zoologists have paid singularly little attention to them. In a large textbook of zoology before me I find no indication that the eagle is larger than the sparrow, or the hippopotamus bigger than the hare, though some grudging admissions are made in the case of the mouse and the whale. But yet it is easy to show that a hare could not be as large as a hippopotamus, or a whale as small as a herring. For every type of animal there is a most convenient size, and a large change in size inevitably carries with it a change of form.

Let us take the most obvious of possible cases, and consider a giant man sixty feet high—about the height of Giant Pope and Giant Pagan in the illustrated *Pilgrim's Progress* of my childhood. These monsters were not only ten times as high as Christian, but ten times as wide and ten times as thick, so that their total weight was a thousand times his, or about eighty to ninety tons. Unfortunately the cross sections of their bones were only a hundred times those of Christian, so that every square inch of giant bone had to support ten times the weight borne by a square inch of human bone. As the human thighbone breaks under about ten times the human weight, Pope and Pagan would have broken their thighs every time they took a step. This was doubtless why they were sitting down in the picture I remember. But it lessens one's respect for Christian and Jack the Giant Killer.

Turn to zoology, suppose that a gazelle, a graceful little creature with long thin legs, is to become large, it will break its bones unless it does one of two things. It may make its legs short and thick, like the rhinoceros, so that every pound of weight still about the same area bone to support it. Or it can compress its body and stretch out its legs obliquely to gain stability, like the giraffe. I mention these two beasts because they happen to belong to the same order as the gazelle, and both are quite successful mechanically, being remarkably fast runners.

Gravity, a mere nuisance to Christian, was a terror to Pope, Pagan, and Despair. To the mouse and any smaller animal it presents practically no dangers. You can drop a mouse down a thousand-yard mine shaft; and, on arriving at the bottom, it gets a slight shock and walks away, provided that the ground is fairly soft. A rat is killed, a man is broken, a horse splashes. For the resistance presented to movement by the air is proportional to the surface of the moving object. Divide an animal's length, breadth, and height each by ten; its weight is reduced to a thousandth, but its surface only to a hundredth. So the resistance to falling in the case of the small animal is relatively ten times greater than the driving force.

An insect therefore, is not afraid of gravity; it can fall without danger, and can cling to the ceiling with remarkably little trouble. It can go in for elegant and fantastic forms of support like that of the daddy-longlegs. But there is a force which is as formidable to an insect as gravitation to a mammal. This is surface tension. A man coming out of a bath carries with him a film of water of about one-fiftieth of an inch in thickness. This weighs roughly a pound. A wet mouse has to carry about its own weight of water. A wet fly has to lift many times its own weight and, as everyone knows, a fly once wetted by water or any other liquid is in a very serious position indeed. An insect going for a drink is in as great danger as a man leaning out over a precipice in search of food. If it once falls into the grip of the surface tension of the water—that is to say, gets wet—it is likely to remain so until it drowns. A few insects, such as water-beetles, contrive to be unwettable; the majority keep well away from their drink by means of a long proboscis.

Of course tall land animals have other difficulties. They have to pump their blood to greater heights than a man, and therefore, require a larger blood pressure and tougher blood-vessels. A great many men die from burst arteries, especially in the brain, and this danger is presumably still greater for an elephant or a giraffe. But animals of all kinds find difficulties in size for the following reason. A typical small animal, say a microscopic worm or rotifer, has a smooth skin through which all the oxygen it requires can soak in, a straight gut with sufficient surface to absorb its food, and a single kidney. Increase its dimensions tenfold in every direction, and its weight is increased a thousand times, so that if it is to use its muscles as efficiently as its miniature counterpart, it will need a thousand times as much food and oxygen per day and will excrete a thousand times as much of waste products.

Now if its shape is unaltered its surface will be increased only a hundredfold, and ten times as much oxygen must enter per minute through each square millimetre of skin, ten times as much food through each square niil-limetre of intestine. When a limit is reached to their absorptive powers their surface has to be increased by some special device. For example, a part of the skin may be drawn out into tufts to make gills or pushed in to make lungs, thus increasing the oxygen-absorbing surface in proportion to the animal's bulk. A man, for example, has a hundred square yards of lung. Similarly, the gut, instead of being smooth and straight, becomes coiled and develops a velvety surface, and other organs increase in complication. The higher animals are not larger than the lower because they are more complicated. They are more complicated because they are larger. Just the same is true of plants. The simplest plants, such as the green algae growing in stagnant water or on the bark of trees, are mere round cells. The higher plants increase their surface by putting out leaves and roots. Comparative anatomy is largely the story of the struggle to increase surface in proportion to volume.

Some of the methods of increasing the surface are useful up to a point, but not capable of a very wide adaptation. For example, while vertebrates carry the oxygen from the gills or lungs all over the body in the blood, insects take air directly to every part of their body by tiny blind tubes called tracheae which open to the surface at many different points. Now, although by their breathing movements they can renew the air in the outer part of the tracheal system, the oxygen has to penetrate the finer branches by means of diffusion. Gases can diffuse easily through very small distances, not many times larger than the average length travelled by a gas molecule between collisions with other molecules. But when such vast journeys—from the point of view of a molecule—as a quarter of an inch have to be made, the process becomes slow. So the portions of an insect's body more than a quarter of an inch from the air would always be short of oxygen. In consequence hardly any insects are much more than half an inch thick. Land crabs are built on the same general plan as insects, but are much clumsier. Yet like ourselves they carry oxygen around in their blood, and are therefore able to grow far larger than any insects. If the insects had hit on a plan for driving air through their tissues instead of letting it soak in, they might well have become as large as lobsters, though other considerations would have prevented them from becoming as large as man.

Exactly the same difficulties attach to flying. It is an elementary principle of aeronautics that the minimum speed needed to keep an aeroplane of a given shape in the air varies as the square root of its length. If its linear dimensions are increased four times, it must fly twice as fast. Now the power needed for the minimum speed increases more rapidly than the weight of the machine. So the larger aeroplane, which weighs sixty-four times as much as the smaller, needs one hundred and twenty-eight times its horsepower to keep up. Applying the same principle to the birds, we find that the limit to their size is soon reached. An angel whose muscles developed no more power weight for weight than those of an eagle or a pigeon would require a breast projecting for about four feet to house the muscles engaged in working its wings, while to economize in weight, its legs would have to be reduced to mere stilts. Actually a large bird such as an eagle or kite does not keep in the air mainly by moving its wings. It is generally to be seen soaring, that is to say balanced on a rising column of air. And even soaring becomes more and more difficult with increasing size. Were this not the case eagles might be as large as tigers and as formidable to man as hostile aeroplanes.

But it is time that we pass to some of the advantages of size. One of the most obvious is that it enables one to keep warm. All warm-blooded animals at rest lose the same amount of heat from a unit area of skin, for which purpose they need a food-supply proportional to their surface and not to their weight. Five thousand mice weigh as much as a man. Their combined surface and food or oxygen consumption are about seventeen times a man's. In fact a mouse eats about one quarter its own weight of food every day, which is mainly used in keeping it warm. For the same reason small animals cannot live in cold countries. In the arctic regions there are no reptiles or amphibians, and no small mammals. The smallest mammal in Spitzbergen is the fox. The small birds fly away in winter, while the insects die, though their eggs can survive six months or more of frost. The most successful mammals are bears, seals, and walruses.

Similarly, the eye is a rather inefficient organ until it reaches a large size. The back of the human eye on which an image of the outside world is thrown, and which corresponds to the film of a camera, is composed of a mosaic of "rods and cones" whose diameter is little more than a length of an average light wave. Each eye has about a half a million, and for two objects to be distinguishable their images must fall on separate rods or cones. It is obvious that with fewer but larger rods and cones we should see less distinctly. If they were twice as broad two points would have to be twice as far apart before we could distinguish them at a given distance. But if their size were diminished and their number increased we should see no better. For it is impossible to form a definite image smaller than a wavelength of light. Hence a mouse's eye is not a small-scale model of a human eye. Its rods and cones are not much smaller than ours, and therefore there are far fewer of them. A mouse could not distinguish one human face from another six feet away. In order that they should be of any use at all the eyes of small animals have to be much larger in proportion to their bodies than our own. Large animals on the other hand only require relatively small eyes, and those of the whale and elephant are little larger than our own.

For rather more recondite reasons the same general principle holds true of the brain. If we compare the brain-weights of a set of very similar animals such as the cat, cheetah, leopard, and tiger, we find that as we quadruple the body-weight the brain-weight is only doubled. The larger animal with proportionately larger bones can economize on brain, eyes, and certain other organs.

Such are a very few of the considerations which show that for every type of animal there is an optimum size. Yet although Galileo demonstrated the contrary more than three hundred years ago, people still believe that if a flea were as large as a man it could jump a thousand feet into the air. As a matter of fact the height to which an animal can jump is more nearly independent of its size than proportional to it. A flea can jump about two feet, a man about five. To jump a given height, if we neglect the resistance of the air, requires an expenditure of energy proportional to the jumper's weight. But if the jumping muscles form a constant fraction of the animal's body, the energy developed per ounce of muscle is independent of the size, provided it can be developed quickly enough in the small animal. As a matter of fact an insect's muscles, although they can contract more quickly than our own, appear to be less efficient; as otherwise a flea or grasshopper could rise six feet into the air.

This analysis is not simply a division of a subject into parts; it shows the relationship of physical size to such factors as gravity, the surface tension of water, and the resistance of air. By explaining these physical relationships, Haldane reveals the dynamic connections that are at work in determining restrictions on size.

CRITICAL ANALYSIS OF WRITING

We have looked at the basic structure of analysis and have seen that an analysis of a subject works on the assumption that the whole is composed of parts. With an analysis the writer not only presents elements that make up the concept being analyzed, but also explains the interrelations among the elements. In this section we briefly look at critical analysis of writing, a kind of analysis used in a great many areas of academic work. The ability to read and analyze a written work is an essential skill in most academic fields. Researchers in the physical and behavioral sciences must be able to read and analyze the writings of other researchers in their disciplines.

Critical analyses of writing function in the same way other analyses do. The parts of the written texts are examined in some detail. Typically such analyses will summarize the content of the work and then examine the meaning, the structure, and the style of the writing.

Five student essays analyzing five essays (each with a different purpose) are included in the Student Writing section.

The structure of each analysis is based on the concepts presented in the first eight chapters of this book. The following is a suggested pattern that you may find helpful in structuring your analysis of a written work.

In the first sentence of the first paragraph identify the author and the title of the work being analyzed. In addition, in the first paragraph summarize the content and identify the purpose and the overall pattern of organization.

In the second paragraph analyze the purpose with quotations taken from the work that illustrate the characteristics you are examining. Use the quotations as evidence to support your interpretive thesis about the meaning of the work.

In the third paragraph analyze the pattern that organizes the entire piece of writing and any other patterns that are present. Support this analysis with quotations taken from the work. As with the analysis of purpose, these quotations need to support your interpretation and analysis.

In the fourth paragraph give a conclusion that sums up the essence of the analysis, restating the major points of your interpretation. In addition, you may want to offer some evaluative comment on the effectiveness of the work.

WRITING STRATEGIES

For Analysis

❑ How are the parts related to each other?
❑ How do the parts affect each other?

For Critical Analysis

Since critical analysis involves distinguishing and explaining the various parts of a written text, you must begin the process of critical analysis by reading the text. As you are reading, you may find it helpful to identify words and phrases that you think might be important to your analysis of the work you are analyzing. These words and phrases can be used to support the interpretation you give to what you have read.

The following questions may help you organize your work on a critical analysis:

❑ What features does the selection have that identify it as expressive, literary, persuasive, or referential?
❑ What organizational patterns are used?
❑ What examples from the selection support your interpretation?
❑ How do all the features you have found work together help the writer achieve the purpose?

Narration

When we create details that take place in time, we organize them by narration. The organizing principle of narration is the relationship between events in time. We present one event or occurrence after another so that they create a coherent sequence. Each event is connected causally to each event that precedes it and each event that follows it. Narrations of all kinds are dynamic; that is, they change over time. The story is the most familiar form of narration, but narration can also be used to explain a process or to examine causes and effects.

NARRATION OF EVENT

A narration of an event is a record of a sequence of actions that has occurred only once. Those events have never happened before and they will never happen again. A historian, for instance, writing about what happened at the Battle of Little Bighorn when the Sioux defeated Custer would be narrating a series of events that obviously took place only once.

THE STAGES OF A NARRATION OF EVENT

A complete narration of an event has a number of specific stages. First a potential for action must exist. Then something, an inciting event, creates a disturbance that causes the action to move forward and become complicated. This complication, produced by conflict and an interaction of forces, moves the action to a crisis that must be resolved. When the resolution occurs, the narration ends. Imagine the surface of a pond, clear and unmoving. If a stone were thrown into it, ripples would form and move out until they dissipated at the bank. That is the way a narration of an event works. The surface of the pond represents the potential for action. The stone being thrown into the water corresponds to the inciting event that causes an interaction of forces to create the ripples, just as conflict moves the action of a plot to crisis and eventual resolution.

The stages of a narration of an event can be seen in the following diagram.

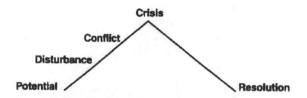

PARTIAL NARRATIVES

Not all narrations of event are complete. Some narratives, like epic poems, begin in the middle of the action. The earlier events are filled in by flashback to previous events, or they may already be known if the plot of the narrative is based on some well-known myth or legend. A number of Classical Greek dramas were based on myths that would have been known by the contemporary audiences that attended the performances. Many of Shakespeare's history plays were adaptations of actual historical events that his audiences would have been well acquainted with. Some narrations end before the resolution occurs. These narratives are said to have indeterminate endings. Modern short story writers often end their stories before the resolution to suggest a universal human condition and to allow the audience to participate in the action of the plot. Because we know the stages of the complete narrative intuitively, we tend to want to fill in the beginning or the end with our imaginations.

It is possible to have a narrative devoted to each one of the stages of narration. A narration devoted to the potential for action is called a *field narrative*. It involves quite a lot of description and only suggests that action may be possible. A *disturbance narrative* focuses on the moment of transition when potential becomes action. A *conflict narrative* centers on those events leading to crisis. A *crisis narrative* looks only at the action associated with the crisis and does not dwell on events building up to that crisis or on the events leading to its resolution. A *resolution narrative* would focus on the conclusion of the action.

THE NARRATOR

The narrator is the person who is telling the story. That person can be a first-person narrator who is actually involved in the events of the narration and who uses first-person personal pronouns (*I, me, my, mine*). The narrator may also be a third-person narrator who is telling the story from a vantage point outside the action of the narrative and who uses third-person pronouns (*he, she, it, they, them*).

AN EXAMPLE

In this excerpt from Owen Wister's novel *The Virginian* we see an episode that, although brief, does illustrate the different stages of the narration of event as told by a first-person narrator.

The Virginian Does Some Roping

OWEN WISTER

Some notable sight was drawing the passengers, both men and women to the window; and therefore I rose and crossed the car to see what it was. I saw near the track an enclosure, and round it some laughing men, and inside it some whirling dust, and amid the dust some horses, plunging, huddling, and dodging. There were cow ponies in a corral, and one of them would not be caught, no matter who threw the rope. We had plenty of time to watch this sport, for our train had stopped that the engine might take water at the tank before it pulled us up beside the station platform of Medicine Bow. We were also six hours late, and starving for entertainment. The pony in the corral was wise, and rapid of limb. Have you seen a skillful boxer watch his antagonist with a quiet, incessant eye? Such an eye as this did the pony keep upon whatever man took the rope. The man might pretend to look at the weather, which was fine; or he might affect earnest conversation with a bystander; it was bootless. The pony saw through it. No feint hoodwinked him. This animal was thoroughly a man of the world. His undistracted eye stayed fixed upon the dissembling foe, and the gravity of his horse expression made the matter one of high comedy. The rope would sail out at him, but he was already elsewhere; and if horses laugh, gayety must have abounded in that corral. Sometimes the pony took a turn alone; next he had slid in a flash among his brothers, and the whole of them like a school of playful fish whipped round the corral, kicking up the fine dust, and (I take it) roaring with laughter. Through the window-glass of our Pullman the thud of their mischievous hoofs reached us, and the strong, humorous curses of the cowboys. Then for the first time I noticed a man who sat on the high gate of the corral, looking on. For he now climbed down with lithe undulations of a tiger, smooth and easy, as if his muscles flowed beneath his skin. The others had all visibly whirled the rope, some of them even shoulder high. I did not see his arm lift or move. He appeared to hold the rope down, low, by his leg. But like a sudden snake I saw the noose go out its length and fall true; and the thing was done. As the captured pony walked in with a sweet, church-door expression, our train moved slowly on to the station, and a passenger remarked, "That man knows his business."

In this narrative the potential for action is the corral full of horses. The inciting event is the horse evading the rope. The complication and conflict increases between the frustrated ropers and the cagey pony. When the Virginian moves onto the scene, the narration approaches crisis which is resolved when the Virginian ultimately ropes the horse.

VARIATIONS IN NARRATION OF EVENT

The presentation of the events in the narrative will be altered depending on the writer's purpose. For example, some writers may alter the simple chronological sequence of presentation and tell some of the earlier events in flashback sequences (after the plot has already begun). This technique creates a dramatic effect and is frequently used in literary and expressive narratives.

EXPRESSIVE NARRATION OF EVENT

An expressive narrative will be episodic. The events of the narrative may be broken up and told in smaller units (episodes) that are all connected by the associations in the mind of the writer. Sometimes the reader can understand the associative connections and sometimes not.

AN EXAMPLE

This excerpt from Billie Holiday's autobiography illustrates how the subjective nature of expressive writing affects the narrative.

My Big Dream

BILLIE HOLIDAY

I've been told that nobody sings the word "hunger" like I do. Or the word "love."

Maybe I remember what those words are all about. Maybe I'm proud enough to *want* to remember Baltimore and Welfare Island, the Catholic institution and the Jefferson Market Court, the sheriff in front of our place in Harlem and the towns from coast to coast where I got my lumps and my scars, Philly and Alderson, Hollywood and San Francisco—every damn bit of it.

All the Cadillacs and minks in the world—and I've had a few—can't make it up or make me forget it. All I've learned in all those places from all those people is wrapped up in those two words. You've got to have something to eat and a little love in your life before you can hold still for any damn body's sermon on how to behave.

Everything I am and everything I want out of life goes smack back to that.

Look at my big dream! It's always been to have a big place of my own out in the country someplace where I could take care of stray dogs and orphan kids, kids that didn't ask to be born; kids that didn't ask to be black, blue, or green or something in between.

I'd only want to be sure of one thing—that nobody in the world wanted these kids. Then I would take them. They'd have to be illegit, no mama, no papa.

I'd have room for twenty-five or thirty, with three or four big buxom women just like my mom to take care of them, feed them, see to it the little bastards go to school; knock them in the head when they're wrong, but love them whether they're good or bad.

We'd have a crazy big kitchen with a chartreuse stove and refrigerator to match, and I'd supervise the cooking and baking. We might have a doctor and a nurse and a couple of tutors. But I'd always be around to teach them my kind of teaching—not the kind that tells them how to spell Mississippi, but how to be glad to be who you are and what you are.

When they grow up enough to go out and do babysitting and take little jobs or start on their own, away they'd go. And then there would always be more.

Grownups can make it some kind of way. They might have a little more or a little less to eat than the next guy—a little more or a little less love, and it isn't fatal.

But kids? Take me, I didn't ask Clarence Holiday and Sadie Fagan to get together in that Baltimore hallway and have me and then have to leave me to get pushed around and hassle with life on my own. Sure, my old lady took care of me the best she could and she was the greatest. But she was just a young kid trying to raise a young kid.

Anyway, that's my dream and there is another dream too.

All my life I've wanted my own club. A small place where I can walk in, have my own piano, drums, and a swinging guitar. I'd want it to be crowded if there were one hundred and twenty-five people there—that's how intimate I want it.

I've fought all my life to be able to sing what I wanted the way I wanted to sing it. Before I die I want a place of my own where nobody can tell me *when* to go on. I might go on at nine, or four in the morning; I might sing forty-nine songs or one song. I might even get up and stop the band in the middle of a number and sing something I felt like singing.

But it would be a place where my friends could come and really relax and enjoy themselves—sleep if they wanted to sleep, and eat if they wanted to eat.

And I'd run that kitchen myself. I might not actually cook everything, but I'd oversee it and taste it and see that it's my kind of cooking and that it's straight. I used to laugh when Mom talked about having her own place, but look at me now.

I could have had a dozen clubs in my time, but I'd always have been fronting for something else. Even today there are promoters willing to get behind a club of mine. But I wouldn't take somebody else's money even if they were fool enough to give it me. I'd always be scared someone would come in and plant some stuff in my place, have me raided and busted.

Besides, it would have to be proven to me that it was mine, all mine, before the law would let me sing in it. And I would have to know it was mine before I could sing in it anyway.

Although people sometimes act like they think so, a singer is not like a saxophone. If you don't sound right, you can't go out and get some new reeds, split them just right. A singer is only a voice and a voice is completely dependent on the body God gave you. When you walk out there and open your mouth, you never know what's going to happen.

I'm not supposed to get a toothache, I'm not supposed to get nervous; I can't throw up or get sick to my stomach; I'm not supposed to get the flu or have a sore throat. I'm supposed to go out there and look pretty and sing good and smile and I'd just better.

Why? Because I'm Billie Holiday and I've been in trouble.

Louis and I have made plenty of miles together, by train, plane, every kind of way. But I'll never forget one night when we were coming in by plane from the Coast.

When we took our seats in this big fancy air liner I knew the man next to me was going to cause a scene. I could just smell him. He started fidgeting and peeking and staring at me and Louis. He made it perfectly clear he wished he'd taken the train where he wouldn't have had to sit next to no damn Negroes.

I didn't pay any attention. This has happened to me too many times. But it bothered Louis.

We hadn't been out thirty minutes, when one of the engines caught fire. Before long the whole wing was blazing and everybody thought we'd had it.

You should have seen this dicty neighbour of ours. He got religion in a hurry. He wanted to hold Louis' hand. He wanted to be nice. He even wanted to say he hadn't meant to be nasty, he was sorry and couldn't we all pray together?

Louis had been a preacher when he was fifteen and he was ready to go along. I flipped.

"This man didn't even want to sit next to me until he thought he was going to die," I told Louis.

"You die in your seat, mister," I told him, "and we'll die in ours."

We rode out the fire someway and made the airport.

When we got on the ground, the man was so ashamed of himself he cut right on by Louis without even speaking.

"Mr. McKay," I told him, "you've had your lesson today. Some people is and some people ain't, and this man ain't."

That's the way I've found it, and that's still the way it is.

Holiday's expressive narration is episodic. She recounts a number of different events, short episodes that are pieced together and connected by the associations she makes from one idea to another.

LITERARY NARRATION OF EVENT

The narrative is perhaps the most frequently used pattern for literary works. Literary narratives focus on the conflict and crisis inherent in the narrative structure. They also typically include descriptions that present the setting and characters to the reader.

AN EXAMPLE

In the following story written by Mark Twain, we find a narrative based on the experiences of a traveler on the prairie.

Coyote

MARK TWAIN

Another night of alternate tranquility and turmoil. But morning came, by and by. It was another glad awakening to fresh breezes, vast expanses of level greensward, bright sunlight, an impressive solitude utterly without visible human beings or human habitations, and an atmosphere of such amazing magnifying properties that trees that seemed close at hand were more than three miles away. We resumed undress uniform, climbed atop of the flying coach, dangled our legs over the side, shouted occasionally at our frantic mules, merely to see them lay their ears back and scamper faster, tied our hats on to keep our hair from blowing away, and leveled an outlook over the world-wide carpet about us for things new and strange to gaze at. Even at this day it thrills me through and through to think of the life, the gladness and the wild sense of freedom that used to make the blood dance in my veins on those fine overland mornings!

Along about an hour after breakfast we saw the first prairie-dog villages, the first antelope, and the first wolf. If I remember rightly, this latter was the regular coyote (pronounced ky-o-te) of the farther deserts. And if it was, he was not a pretty creature, or respectable either, for I got well acquainted with his race afterward, and can speak with confidence. The coyote is a long, slim, sick and sorry-looking skeleton, with a gray wolf-skin stretched over it, a tolerably bushy tail that forever sags down with a despairing expression of forsakenness and misery, a furtive and evil eye, and a long, sharp face, with slightly lifted lip and exposed teeth. He has a general slinking expression all over. The coyote is a living, breathing allegory of Want. He is always hungry. He is always poor, out of luck and friendless. The meanest creatures despise him, and even the fleas would desert him for a velocipede. He is so spiritless and cowardly that even while his exposed teeth are pretending a threat, the rest of his face is apologizing for it. And he is so homely!—so scrawny, and ribby, and coarse-haired, and pitiful. When he sees you he lifts his lips and lets a flash of his teeth out, and then turns a little out of the course he was pursuing, depresses his head a bit, and strikes a long, soft-footed trot through the sage-brush, glancing over his shoulder at you, from time to time, till he is about out of easy pistol range, and then he stops and takes a deliberate survey of you; he will trot fifty yards and stop again—another fifty and stop again; and finally the gray of his gliding body blends with the gray of the sage-brush, and he disappears. All this is when you make no demonstration against him; but if you do, he develops a livelier interest in his journey, and instantly electrifies his heels and puts such a deal of real estate between himself and your weapon, that by the time you have raised the hammer you see that you need a mini rifle, and by the time you have got him in line you need a rifled cannon, and by the time you have "drawn a bead" on him you see well enough that nothing but an unusually long-winded streak of lightning could reach him where he is now. But if you start a swift-footed dog after him, you will enjoy it ever so much—especially if it is a dog that has a good opinion of himself, and has been brought up to think he knows something about speed. The coyote will go swinging gently off on that deceitful trot of his, and every little while he will smile a fraudful smile over his shoulder that will fill that dog entirely full of encouragement and worldly ambition, and make him lay his head still lower to the ground, and stretch his neck further to the front, and pant more fiercely, and stick his tail out straighter behind, and move his furious legs with a yet wilder frenzy, and leave a broader and broader, and higher and denser cloud of desert sand smoking behind, and marking his long wake across the level plain! And all this time the dog is only a short twenty feet behind the coyote, and to save the soul of him he cannot understand why it is that he cannot get perceptibly closer; and he begins to get aggravated, and it makes him madder and madder to see how gently the coyote glides along and never pants or sweats or ceases to smile; and he grows still more and more incensed to see how shamefully he has been taken in by an entire stranger, and what an ignoble swindle that long, calm, soft-footed trot is; and next he notices that he is getting fagged, and that the coyote actually has to slacken speed a little to keep from running away from him—and then that town-dog is mad in earnest, and he begins to strain and weep and swear, and paw the sand higher than ever, and reach for the coyote with concentrated and desperate energy. This "spurt" finds him six feet behind his gliding enemy, and two miles from his friends. And then, in the instant that a wild new hope is lighting up his face, the coyote turns and smiles blandly upon him once more, and with a something about it which seems to say: "Well, I shall have to tear myself away from you, bub—business is business, and it will not do for me to be fooling along this way all day"—and forthwith there is a rushing sound, and the sudden splitting of a long crack through the atmosphere, and behold that dog is solitary and alone in the midst of a vast solitude!

It makes his head swim. He stops, and looks all around; climbs the nearest sand-mound, and gazes into the distance; shakes his head reflectively, and then, without a word, he turns and jogs along back to his train, and takes up a humble position under the hindmost wagon, and feels unspeakable mean, and

> looks ashamed, and hangs his tail at half-mast for a week. And for as much as a year after that, whenever there is a great hue and cry after a coyote, that dog will merely glance in that direction without emotion, and apparently observe to himself, "I believe I do not wish any of the pie."
>
> 1872

The descriptions of the setting and the animals create verisimilitude. The conflict between the coyote and the dog creates tension. In addition, Twain uses a number of figurative images, notably personification, to develop his descriptions.

PERSUASIVE NARRATION OF EVENT

A narration in persuasion will likely function as an example, which is a commonly used type of rational appeal. If the narrative is in the first person and reflects the experiences of the narrator, then the example would be a personal appeal included in an effort to enhance the credibility of the author.

AN EXAMPLE

This first-person narrative of a personal experience by Benjamin Franklin addresses the issue of what kind of approach should be used to defeat an opponent, in this case a political opponent. Franklin presents a surprising claim.

Seducing an Enemy

BENJAMIN FRANKLIN

I therefore did not like the opposition of this new member, who was a gentleman of fortune and education with talents that were likely to give him in time great influence in the House, which indeed, afterwards happened. I did not, however, aim at gaining his favour by paying any servile respect to him, but after some time took this other method. Having heard that he had in his library a certain scarce and curious book, I wrote a note to him expressing my desire of perusing that book and requesting he would do me the favour of lending it to me for a few days. He sent it immediately; and I returned it in about a week with another note expressing strongly my sense of the favour. When we next met in the House, he spoke to me (which he had never done before), and with great civility. And he ever afterwards manifested a readiness to serve me on all occasions, so that we became great friends, and our friendship continued to his death. This is another instance of the truth of an old maxim I had learned, which says, "He that has once done you a kindness will be more ready to do you another than he whom you yourself have obliged." And it shows how much more profitable it is prudently to remove, than to resent, return and continue inimical proceedings.

Franklin addresses the issue of what kind of behavior is best in confronting an adversary. His claim is that instead of trying to curry favor from an opponent by doing that person favors, you should rather ask the opponent to do you a favor. In addition to telling his personal experience (both a personal and a rational appeal), Franklin quotes a maxim, which is another rational appeal.

REFERENTIAL NARRATION OF EVENT

Referential narratives give an orderly, clear presentation of the events. They present evidence to support a thesis.

AN EXAMPLE

This report of the earthquake that occurred on April 18, 1906 in San Francisco was originally published in *Collier's* magazine. Jack London, noted for his novels and short stories depicting life in harsh environments, records his impressions of the devastating events surrounding the earthquake. He selects events that reveal the extent of the destruction.

The San Francisco Earthquake

JACK LONDON

The earthquake shook down in San Francisco hundreds of thousands of dollars' worth of walls and chimneys. But the conflagration that followed burned up hundreds of millions of dollars worth of property. There is no estimating within hundreds of millions the actual damage wrought. Not in history has a modern imperial city been so completely destroyed. San Francisco is gone. Nothing remains of it but memories and a fringe of dwelling-houses on its outskirts. Its industrial section is wiped out. Its business section is wiped out. The factories and warehouses, the great stores and newspaper buildings, the hotels and the palaces of the nabobs, are all gone. Remains only the fringe of dwelling-houses on the outskirts of what was once San Francisco.

Within an hour after the earthquake shock the smoke of San Francisco's burning was a lurid tower visible a hundred miles away. And for three days and nights this lurid tower swayed in the sky, reddening the sun, darkening the day, and filling the land with smoke.

On Wednesday morning at a quarter past five came the earthquake. A minute later the flames were leaping upward. In a dozen different quarters south of Market Street, in the working-class ghetto, and in the factories, fires started. There was no opposing the flames. There was no organization, no communication. All the cunning adjustments of a twentieth century city had been smashed by the earthquake. The streets were humped into ridges and depressions, and piled with the debris of fallen walls. The steel rails were twisted into perpendicular and horizontal angles. The telephone and telegraph systems were disrupted. And the great water-mains had burst. All the shrewd contrivances and safe-guards of man had been thrown out of gear by thirty seconds' twitching of the earth-crust.

The Fire Made Its Own Draft

By Wednesday afternoon, inside of twelve hours, half the heart of the city was gone. At that time I watched the vast conflagration from out on the bay. It was dead calm. Not a flicker of wind stirred. Yet from every side wind was pouring in upon the city. East, west, north, and south, strong winds were blowing upon the doomed city. The heated air rising made an enormous suck. Thus did the fire of itself build its own colossal chimney through the atmosphere. Day and night this dead calm continued, and yet, near to the flames, the wind was often half a gale, so mighty was the suck.

Wednesday night saw the destruction of the very heart of the city. Dynamite was lavishly used, and many of San Francisco's proudest structures were crumbled by man himself into ruins, but there was no withstanding the onrush of the flames. Time and again successful stands were made by the fire-fighters, and every time the flames flanked around on either side, or came up from the rear, and turned to defeat the hard-won victory.

An enumeration of the buildings destroyed would be a directory of San Francisco. An enumeration of the buildings undestroyed would be a line and several addresses. An enumeration of the deeds of heroism would stock a library and bankrupt the Carnegie Medal fund. An enumeration of the dead will never be made. All vestiges of them were destroyed by the flames. The number of victims of the earthquake will never be known. South of Market Street, where the loss of life was particularly heavy, was the first to catch fire.

Remarkable as it may seem, Wednesday night, while the whole city crashed and roared into ruin, was a quiet night. There were no crowds. There was no shouting and yelling. There was no hysteria, no disorder. I passed Wednesday night in the path of the advancing flames, and in all those terrible hours I saw not one woman who wept, not one man who was excited, not one person who was in the slightest degree panic-stricken.

Before the flames, throughout the night, fled tens of thousands of homeless ones. Some were wrapped in blankets. Others carried bundles of bedding and dear household treasures. Sometimes a whole family was harnessed to a carriage or delivery wagon that was weighted down with their possessions. Baby buggies, toy wagons, and go-carts were used as trucks, while every other person was dragging a trunk. Yet everybody was gracious. The most perfect courtesy obtained. Never, in all San Francisco's history, were her people so kind and courteous as on this night of terror.

A Caravan of Trunks

All night these tens of thousands fled before the flames. Many of them, the poor people from the labor ghetto, had fled all day as well. They had left their homes burdened with possessions. Now and again they lightened up, flinging out upon the street clothing and treasures they had dragged for miles.

They held on longest to their trunks, and over these trunks many a strong man broke his heart that night. The hills of San Francisco are steep, and up these hills, mile after mile, were the trunks dragged. Everywhere were trunks, with across them lying their exhausted owners, men and women. Before the march of the flames were flung picket lines of soldiers. And a block at a time, as the flames advanced, these pickets retreated. One of their tasks was to keep the trunk-pullers moving. The exhausted creatures, stirred on by the menace of bayonets, would arise and struggle up the steep pavements, pausing from weakness every five or ten feet.

Often, after surmounting a heart-breaking hill, they would find another wall of flame advancing upon them at right angles and be compelled to change anew the line of their retreat. In the end, completely played out, after toiling for a dozen hours like giants, thousands of them were compelled to abandon their trunks. Here the shopkeepers and soft members of the middle class were at a disadvantage. But the working men dug holes in vacant lots and backyards and buried their trunks.

The Doomed City

At nine o'clock Wednesday evening I walked down through the very heart of the city. I walked through miles and miles of magnificent buildings and towering skyscrapers. Here was no fire. All was in perfect order. The police patrolled the streets. Every building had its watchman at the door. And yet it was doomed, all of it. There was no water. The dynamite was giving out. And at right angles two different conflagrations were sweeping down upon it.

At one o'clock in the morning I walked down through the same section. Everything still stood intact. There was no fire. And yet there was a change. A rain of ashes was falling. The watchmen at the doors were gone. The police had been withdrawn. There were no firemen, no fire engines, no men fighting with dynamite. The district had been absolutely abandoned. I stood at the corner of Kearney and Market, in the very innermost heart of San Francisco. Kearney Street was deserted. Half a dozen blocks away it was burning on both sides. The street was a wall of flame, and against this wall of flame, silhouetted sharply, were two United States cavalrymen sitting their horses, calmly watching. That was all. Not another person was in sight. In the intact heart of the city two troopers sat their horses and watched.

Spread of the Conflagration

Surrender was complete. There was no water. The sewers had long since been pumped dry. There was no dynamite. Another fire had broken out further uptown, and now from three sides conflagrations were sweeping down. The fourth side had been burned earlier in the day. In that direction stood the tottering walls of the Examiner building, the burned-out Call building, the smoldering ruins of the Grand Hotel, and the gutted, devastated, dynamited Palace Hotel.

The following will illustrate the sweep of the flames and the inability of men to calculate their spread. At eight o'clock Wednesday evening I passed through Union Square. It was packed with refugees. Thousands of them had gone to bed on the grass. Government tents had been set up, supper was being cooked, and the refugees were lining up for free meals.

At half-past one in the morning three sides of Union Square were in flames. The fourth side, where stood the great St. Francis Hotel, was still holding out. An hour later, ignited from top and sides, the St. Francis was flaming heavenward. Union Square, heaped high with mountains of trunks, was deserted. Troops, refugees, and all had retreated.

A Fortune for a Horse!

It was at Union Square that I saw a man offering a thousand dollars for a team of horses. He was in charge of a truck piled high with trunks for some hotel. It had been hauled here into what was considered safety, and the horses had been taken out. The flames were on three sides of the Square, and there were no horses.

Also, at this time, standing beside the truck, I urged a man to seek safety in flight. He was all but hemmed in by several conflagrations. He was an old man and he was on crutches. Said he, "Today is my birthday. Last night I was worth thirty thousand dollars. I bought five bottles of wine, some delicate fish, and other things for my birthday dinner. I have had no dinner, and all I own are these crutches."

I convinced him of his danger and started him limping on his way. An hour later, from a distance, I saw the truckload of trunks burning merrily in the middle of the street.

On Thursday morning, at a quarter past five, just twenty-four hours after the earthquake, I sat on the steps of a small residence on Nob Hill. With me sat Japanese, Italians, Chinese, and Negroes—a bit of the cosmopolitan flotsam of the wreck of the city. All about were the palaces of the nabob pioneers of Forty-nine. To the east and south, at right angles, were advancing two mighty walls of flame.

I went inside with the owner of the house on the steps of which I sat. He was cool and cheerful and hospitable. "Yesterday morning," he said, "I was worth six hundred thousand dollars. This morning this house is all I have left. It will go in fifteen minutes." He pointed to a large cabinet "That is my wife's collection of china. This rug upon which we stand is a present. It cost fifteen hundred dollars. Try that piano. Listen to its tone. There are few like it. There are no horses. The flames will be here in fifteen minutes."

Outside, the old Mark Hopkins residence, a palace, was just catching fire. The troops were falling back and driving the refugees before them. From every side came the roaring of flames, the crashing of walls, and the detonations of dynamite.

The Dawn of the Second Day

I passed out of the house. Day was trying to dawn through the smoke-pall. A sickly light was creeping over the face of things. Once only the sun broke through the smoke-pall, blood-red, and showing quarter its usual size. The smoke-pall itself, viewed from beneath, was a rose color that pulsed and fluttered with lavender shades. Then it turned to mauve and yellow and dun. There was no sun. And so dawned the second day on stricken San Francisco.

An hour later I was creeping past the shattered dome of the City Hall. Than it there was no better exhibit of the destructive forces of the earthquake. Most of the stone had been shaken from the great dome, leaving standing the naked frame-work of steel. Market Street was piled high with wreckage, and across the wreckage lay the overthrown pillars of the City Hall shattered into short crosswise sections.

This section of the city, with the exception of the Mint and the Post-Office, was already a waste of smoking ruins. Here and there through the smoke, creeping warily under the shadows of tottering walls, emerged occasional men and women. It was like the meeting of the handful of survivors after the day of the end of the world.

Beeves Slaughtered and Roasted

On Mission Street lay a dozen steers, in a neat row stretching across the street, just as they had been struck down by the flying ruins of the earthquake. The fire had passed through afterward and roasted them. The human dead had been carried away before the fire came. At another place on Mission Street I saw a milk wagon. A steel telegraph pole had smashed down sheer through the driver's seat and crushed the front wheels. The milkcans lay scattered around.

All day Thursday and all Thursday night, all day Friday and Friday night, the flames still raged.

Friday night saw the flames finally conquered, though not until Russian Hill and Telegraph Hill had been swept and three-quarters of a mile of wharves and docks had been licked up.

The Last Stand

The great stand of the fire-fighters was made Thursday night on Van Ness Avenue. Had they failed here, the comparatively few remaining houses of the city would have been swept. Here were the magnificent residences of the second generation of San Francisco nabobs, and these, in a solid zone, were dynamited down across the path of the fire. Here and there the flames leaped the zone, but these fires were beaten out, principally by the use of wet blankets and rugs.

San Francisco, at the present time, is like the crater of a volcano, around which are camped tens of thousands of refugees. At the Presidio alone are at least twenty thousand. All the surrounding cities and towns are jammed with the homeless ones, where they are being cared for by the relief committees. The refugees were carried free by the railroads to any point they wished to go, and it is estimated that over one hundred thousand people have left the peninsula on which San Francisco stood. The Government has the situation in hand, and, thanks to the immediate relief given by the whole United States, there is not the slightest possibility of a famine. The bankers and business men have already set about making preparations to rebuild San Francisco.

This report covers a specific time frame, Wednesday through Friday. Note that the introductory and concluding paragraphs provide a context for the events. Along with the major events of the narrative, London also includes descriptions that help the reader visualize the events he is recounting.

WRITING STRATEGIES

When you begin writing a narrative, think about the events as an interconnected series. You may find the following questions to be helpful.

- ❏ What are the events in your narrative?
- ❏ How do the forces interact?
- ❏ What is the crisis?
- ❏ How is the conflict resolved?
- ❏ Where does the narrative take place?
- ❏ Who is the narrator?

NARRATION OF PROCESS

A narration of process does not have the five stages that a narration of event has. All events in a narration of process are of equal importance. There is no point of crisis. The resolution is simply the last event. As a result, tension is not increased as the series of events is presented to the reader.

Most narrations of process are written in the present tense. This feature gives the presentation a sense of immediacy and reinforces the reader's impression that the process can be repeated over and over.

INSTRUCTIONAL PROCESS

Some narrations of process tell "how to" do something. They are written in the second person (you) and the imperative mood (commands). A set of instructions is an instructional process. It gives steps that must be completed to perform the activity.

AN EXAMPLE

In his book *The Relaxation Response* (1975), Herbert Benson, a medical doctor and an Associate Professor at The Harvard Medical School, explains how to elicit the Relaxation Response.

The Relaxation Response

HERBERT BENSON

It is important to remember that there is not a single method that is unique in eliciting the Relaxation Response. For example, Transcendental Meditation is one of the many techniques that incorporate these components. However, we believe it is not necessary to use the specific method and specific *secret*, personal sound taught by Transcendental Meditation. *Tests at the Thorndike Memorial Laboratory of Harvard have shown that a similar technique used with any sound or phrase or prayer or mantra brings forth the same physiologic changes noted during Transcendental Meditation:* decreased oxygen consumption; decreased carbon-dioxide elimination; decreased rate of breathing. In other words using the basic necessary components, any one of the age-old or the newly derived techniques produces the same physiological results regardless of the mental device used. The following set of instructions, used to elicit the Relaxation Response, was developed by our group at Harvard's Thorndike Memorial Laboratory and was found to produce the same physiologic changes we had observed during the practice of Transcendental Meditation. This technique is now being used to lower blood pressure in certain patients. A noncultic technique, it is drawn with little embellishment from the four basic components found in the myriad of historical methods. We claim no innovation but simply a scientific validation of age-old wisdom. The technique is our current method of eliciting the Relaxation Response in our continuing studies at the Beth Israel Hospital of Boston.

(1) *Sit quietly in a comfortable position.*
(2) *Close your eyes.*
(3) *Deeply relax all your muscles, beginning at your feet and progressing up to your face. Keep them relaxed.*
(4) *Breathe through your nose. Become aware of your breathing. As you breathe out, say the word, "ONE," silently to yourself. For example,*

breathe IN . . . OUT, "ONE"; IN . . . OUT, "ONE"; etc. Breathe easily and naturally.

(5) Continue for 10 to 20 minutes. You may open your eyes to check the time, but do not use an alarm. When you finish, sit quietly for several minutes, at first with your eyes closed and later with your eyes opened. Do not stand up for a few minutes.

(6) Do not worry about whether you are successful in achieving a deep level of relaxation. Maintain a passive attitude and permit relaxation to occur at its own pace. When distracting thoughts occur, try to ignore them by not dwelling upon them and return to repeating "ONE." With practice, the response should come with little effort. Practice the technique once or twice daily, but not within two hours after any meal, since the digestive processes seem to interfere with the elicitation of the Relaxation Response.

The subjective feelings that accompany the elicitation of the Relaxation Response vary among individuals. The majority of people feel a sense of calm and feel very relaxed. A small percentage of people immediately experience ecstatic feelings. Other descriptions that have been related to us involve feelings of pleasure, refreshment, and well-being. Still others have noted relatively little change on a subjective level. Regardless of the subjective feelings described by our subjects, we have found that the physiologic changes such as decreased oxygen consumption are taking place.

There is no educational requirement or aptitude necessary to experience the Relaxation Response. Just as each of us experiences anger, contentment, and excitement, each has the capacity to experience the Relaxation Response. It is an innate response within us. Again, there are many ways in which people bring forth the Relaxation Response, and your own individual considerations may be applied to the four components involved. You may wish to use the technique we have presented but with a different mental device. You may use a syllable or phrase that may be easily repeated and sounds natural to you.

Another technique you may wish to use is a prayer from your religious tradition. Choose a prayer that incorporates the four elements necessary to bring forth the Relaxation Response. As we have shown in Chapter 5, we believe every religion has such prayers. We would reemphasize that we do not view religion in a mechanistic fashion simply because a religious prayer brings forth this desired physiologic response. Rather, we believe, as did William James, that these age-old prayers are one way to remedy an inner incompleteness and to reduce inner discord. Obviously, there are many other aspects to religious beliefs and practices which have little to do with the Relaxation Response. However, there is little reason not to make use of an appropriate prayer within the framework of your own beliefs if you are most comfortable with it.

> Your individual considerations of a particular technique may place different emphasis upon the components necessary to elicit the Relaxation Response and also may incorporate various practices into the use of the technique. For example, for some a quiet environment with little distraction is crucial. However, others prefer to practice the Relaxation Response in subways or trains. Some people choose always to practice the Relaxation Response in the same place and at a regular time.

This instructional process tells the reader how to experience the relaxation response. Obviously, following the directions will enable the reader to reproduce the effects explained by Benson.

INFORMATIONAL PROCESS

An informational process is written in the third person. It tells how something is done, not how to do something.

AN EXAMPLE

In his book *The Relaxation Response* (1975), Herbert Benson explains physiological response called "the fight-or-flight response."

The Fight-or-Flight Response

HERBERT BENSON

The stressful consequences of living in our modern, Western society—constant insecurity in a job, inability to make deadlines because of the sheer weight of obligations, or the shift in social rules once binding and now inappropriate—will be described here in a manner that clearly explains how they lead to the ravaging diseases such as hypertension which are prevalent today and which are likely to become more widespread in the years ahead. We are all too familiar with the stresses we encounter. However, we are less knowledgeable about the consequences of these stresses, not only psychological but physiologic. Humans, like other animals, react in a predictable way to acute and chronic stressful situations, which trigger an inborn response that has been part of our physiologic makeup for perhaps millions of years. This has been popularly labeled the "fight-or-flight" response. When we are faced with situations that require adjustment of our behavior, an involuntary response increases our blood pressure, heart rate, rate of breathing, blood flow to the muscles, and metabolism, preparing us for conflict or escape.

This innate fight-or-flight reaction is well recognized in animals. A frightened cat standing with arched back and hair on end, ready to run or fight; an enraged dog with dilated pupils, snarling at its adversary; an African gazelle running from a predator; all are responding by activation of the fight-or-flight response. Because we tend to think of man in Cartesian terms, as essentially a rational being, we have lost sight of his origins and of his Darwinian struggle for survival where the successful use of the fight-or-flight response was a matter of life or death.

Man's ancestors with the most highly developed fight-or-flight reactions had an increased chance of surviving long enough to reproduce. Natural selection favored the continuation of the response. As progeny of ancestors who developed the response over millions of years, modern man almost certainly still possesses it.

In fact, the fight-or-flight response, with its bodily changes of increased blood pressure, rate of breathing, muscle blood flow, metabolism, and heart rate, has been measured in man. Situations that demand that we adjust our behavior elicit this response. It is observed, for example, among athletes prior to a competitive event. But the response is not used as it was intended—that is, in preparation for running or fighting with an enemy. Today, it is often brought on by situations that require behavioral adjustments, and *when not used appropriately, which is most of the time, the fight-or-flight response repeatedly elicited may ultimately lead to the dire diseases of heart attack and stroke.*

Benson's informational process outlines the processes associated with the inborn fight-or-flight response. He explains the physiological mechanisms involved.

VARIATIONS IN NARRATION OF PROCESS

When the purpose of a narration of process changes, elements consistent with that purpose are introduced. In general, although the events recorded in all kinds of narration of process will receive equal emphasis, the number of events included will vary when the purpose is different.

EXPRESSIVE NARRATION OF PROCESS

Obviously, expressive narration of process will be in the first person. The writer is explaining how he or she usually completes some task. As a result, the events in the process will be unique to that person and will probably be different from the way other people might complete the same task.

AN EXAMPLE

Henry David Thoreau, in an excerpt from his journal in 1852, tells how he keeps a journal.

On Keeping a Journal

HENRY DAVID THOREAU

To set down such choice experiences that my own writings may inspire me and at last I may make wholes of parts. Certainly it is a distinct profession to rescue from oblivion and to fix the sentiments and thoughts which visit all men more or less generally, that the contemplation of the unfinished picture may suggest its harmonious completion. Associate reverently and as much as you can with your loftiest thoughts. Each thought that is welcomed and recorded is a nest egg, by the side of which more will be laid. Thoughts accidentally thrown together become a frame in which more may be developed and exhibited. Perhaps this is the main value of a habit of writing, of keeping a journal—that so we remember our best hours and stimulate ourselves. My thoughts are my company. They have a certain individuality and separate existence, aye, personality. Having by chance recorded a few disconnected thoughts and then brought them into juxtaposition, they suggest a whole new field in which it was possible to labor and to think. Thought begat thought.

Thoreau's journal entry illustrates how an expressive purpose can affect a narration of process. He tells how he keeps a journal, but the presentation shifts from first person to third person to second person. The explanation is not an orderly account; rather it touches on those features of journal writing that Thoreau sees as most important and most valuable.

LITERARY NARRATION OF PROCESS

A narration of process with a literary purpose will include elements that are intended to entertain the reader. In fact, the process itself may be an imaginary creation with little or no correspondence to anything anybody would ever actually do.

AN EXAMPLE

In the following excerpt, the humorist Robert Benchley offers a delightful account of how he goes about writing a novel.

How I Create

ROBERT BENCHLEY

In an article on How Authors Create, in which the writing methods of various masters of English prose like Conrad, Shaw, and Barrie are explained (with photographs of them in knickerbockers plaguing dogs and pushing against sundials), I discover that I have been doing the whole thing wrong all these years. The interviewer in this case hasn't got around to asking me yet—doubtless because I have been up in my room with the door shut and not answering the bell—but I am going to take a chance anyway and tell him how I do my creative work and just how much comes from inspiration and how much from hashish and other perfumes. I may even loosen up and tell him what my favorite hot weather dishes are.

When I am writing a novel I must actually live the lives of my characters. If, for instance, my hero is a gambler on the French Riviera, I make myself pack up and go to Cannes or Nice, willynilly, and there throw myself into the gay life of the gambling set until I really feel that I *am* Paul De Lacroix, or Ed Whelan, or whatever my hero's name is. Of course this runs into money, and I am quite likely to have to change my ideas about my hero entirely and make him a bum on a tramp steamer working his way back to America, or a young college boy out of funds who lives by his wits until his friends at home send him a hundred and ten dollars.

One of my heroes (Dick Markwell in "Love's How-do-you-do"), after starting out as a man-about-town in New York who "never showed his liquor" and was "an apparently indestructible machine devoted to pleasure," had to be changed into a patient in the Trembly Ward of a local institution, whose old friends didn't recognize him and furthermore didn't want to.

But, as you doubtless remember, it was a corking yarn.

This actually living the lives of my characters takes up quite a lot of time and makes it a little difficult to write anything. It was not until I decided to tell stories about old men who just sit in their rooms and shell walnuts that I ever got around to doing any work. It doesn't make for very interesting novels, but at any rate the wordage is there and there is something to show the publishers for their advance royalties. (Publishers are crotchety that way. They want copy, copy, copy all the time, just because they happen to have advanced a measly three hundred dollars a couple of years before. You would think that printing words on paper was their business.)

And now you ask me how I do my work, how my inspiration comes? I will tell you, Little Father. Draw up your chair and let me put my feet on it. Ah, that's better! Now you may go out and play!

Very often I must wait weeks and weeks for what you call "inspiration." In the meantime I must sit with my quill pen poised in air over a sheet of foolscap, in case the divine spark should come like a lightning bolt and knock me off my chair on to my head. (This has happened more than once.) While I am waiting I mull over in my mind what I am going to do with my characters.

Shall I have Mildred marry Lester, or shall Lester marry Evelyn? ("Who is Evelyn?" I often say to myself, never having heard of her before.) Should the French proletariat win the Revolution, or should Louis XVI come back suddenly and establish a Coalition Cabinet? Can I afford to let Etta clean up those dishes in the sink and get them biscuits baked, or would it be better to keep her there for another year, standing first on one foot and then on the other?

You have no idea how many problems an author has to face during those feverish days when he is building a novel, and you have no idea how he solves them. Neither has he.

Sometimes, while in the throes of creative work, I get out of bed in the morning, look at my writing desk piled high with old bills, odd gloves, and empty gingerale bottles, and go right back to bed again. The next thing I know it is night once more, and time for the Sand Man to come around. (We have a Sand Man who comes twice a day, which makes it very convenient. We give him five dollars at Christmas.)

Even if I do get up and put on a part of my clothes—I do all my work in a Hawaiian straw skirt and a bow tie of some neutral shade—I often can think of nothing to do but pile the books which are on one end of my desk very neatly on the other end and then kick them one by one off on to the floor with my free foot.

But all the while my brain is work, work, working, and my plot is taking shape. Sometimes it is the shape of a honeydew melon and sometimes a shape which I have never been quite able to figure out. It is a sort of amorphous thing with two heads but no face. When this shape presents itself, I get right back in bed again. I'm no fool.

I find that, while working, a pipe is a great source of inspiration. A pipe can be placed diagonally across the keys of a typewriter so that they will not function, or it can be made to give out such a cloud of smoke that I cannot see the paper. Then, there is the process of lighting it. I can make lighting a pipe a ritual which has not been equaled for elaborateness since the five-day festival to the God of the Harvest. (See my book on Rituals: the Man.)

In the first place, owing to twenty-six years of constant smoking without once calling in a plumber, the space left for tobacco in the bowl of my pipe is now the size of a medium body pore. Once the match has been applied to the tobacco therein, the smoke is over. This necessitates refilling, relighting, and reknocking. The knocking out of a pipe can be made almost as important as the smoking of it, especially if there are nervous people in the room. A good, smart knock of a pipe against a tin wastebasket and you will have a neurasthenic out of his chair and into the window sash in no time.

The matches, too, have their place in the construction of modern literature. With a pipe like mine, the supply of burnt matches in one day could be floated down the St. Lawrence River with two men jumping them. . . .

When the novel is finished, it is shipped to the Cutting and Binding Room, where native girls roll it into large sheets and stamp on it with their bare feet. This accounts for the funny look of some of my novels. It is then taken back to the Drying Room, where it is rewritten by a boy whom I engage for the purpose, and sent to the publishers. It is then sent back to me.

And so you see now how we creative artists work. It really isn't like any other kind of work, for it must come from a great emotional upheaval in the soul of the writer himself; and if that emotional upheaval is not present, it must come from the works of any other writers which happen to be handy and easily imitated.

Benchley, in this humorous narration of process, exaggerates most of the events he includes in the essay. His creation of absurd situations is designed to make light of a process most people think of as a very serious activity. He distorts some actions, like the account of his ritual of smoking a pipe, in order to entertain. The events included in the process are selected for the humorous effect they have, rather than for their accuracy and comprehensiveness.

PERSUASIVE NARRATION OF PROCESS

A persuasive narration of process will support a claim advising the reader that an action should be performed in a certain way. In essence, the process is a set of rules for right behavior.

AN EXAMPLE

Ben Jonson (1572–1637), a contemporary of William Shakespeare, gives sound advice about writing well.

On Style

BEN JONSON

For a man to write well there are required three necessities: to read the best authors, observe the best speakers, and much exercise of his own style. In style, to consider what ought to be written, and after what manner, he must first think and excogitate his matter, then choose his words, and examine the weight of either. Then take care, in placing and ranking both matter and words, that the composition be comely, and to do this with diligence and often. No matter how slow the style be at first, so it be labored and accurate; seek the best, and be not glad of the forward conceits, or first words, that offer themselves to us; but judge of what we invent, and order what we approve. Repeat often what we have formerly written; which beside that it helps the consequence and make the juncture better, it quickens the heat of the imagination, that often cools in the time of setting down, and gives new strength, as if it grew lustier by the going back. As we see in the contention of leaping, they jump farthest that fetch their race largest; or, as in throwing a dart or javelin, we force back our arms to make our loose the stronger. Yet if we have a fair gale of wind, I forbid not the steering out of our sail, so the favor of the gale deceive us not. For all that we invent does please us in the conception or birth, else we would never set it down. But the safest is to return to our judgment and handle over again those things the easiness of which might make them justly suspected. So did the best writers in their beginnings; they imposed upon themselves care and industry; they did nothing rashly: they obtained first to write well, and then custom made it easy and a habit. By little and little their matter showed itself to them more plentifully; their words answered; their composition followed; and all, as in a well-ordered family, presented itself in the place. So that the sum of all is, ready writing makes not good writing; but good writing brings on ready writing: yet, when we think we have got the faculty, it is even then good to resist it; as to give a horse a check sometimes with a bit, which doth not so much stop his course, as stirs his mettle. Again, whither a man's genius is best able to reach thither, it should more and more contend, lift, and dilate itself, as men of low stature raise themselves on their toes, and so ofttimes get even, if not eminent. Besides, as it is fit for grown and able writers to stand of themselves and work with their own strength, to trust and endeavor by their faculties: so it is fit for the beginner and learner to study others and the best. For the mind and memory are more sharply exercised in comprehending another man's things than our own; and such as accustom themselves, and are familiar with the best authors, shall never and anon find somewhat of them in themselves, and in the expression of their minds, even when they feel it not, be able to utter something like theirs, which hath an authority above their own. Nay, sometimes it is the reward of a man's study, the praise of quoting another man fitly: and though a man be more prone and able for one kind of writing than another, yet he must exercise all. For as in an instrument, so in style, there must be a harmony and consent of parts.

Jonson gives a number of steps that someone wanting to write well should follow. He especially addresses the matter of style and supports an implied claim that those wanting to improve their ability should practice writing and follow his advice. The elaboration of the process supports the claim. He addresses the reader directly using the imperative mood. His also uses analogy as rational and stylistic appeal.

REFERENTIAL NARRATION OF PROCESS

As we have seen previously, referential narration of process will include all the steps in the process so that the reader can either perform the process (instructional process) or understand it completely (informational).

AN EXAMPLE

This work explains the complex process of counting populations of animals.

How Do They Count Populations of Animals?

CAROLINE SUTTON

Humans are the only beasts who use telephones or permanent addresses, or fill out census forms. How are the other animals counted? How can anyone tell that the timber wolf and the California condor are rare and "endangered"? How do we know how many robins chirp every spring? The task of taking a census of wild animals is one of the most difficult in biology.

The methods of enumeration scientists use vary with the species; its size, behavior, and habitat make certain ways more practical than others. The best way to count ducks, whistling swans, elephants, antelope, caribou, and timber wolves is to fly over them in a helicopter or bush plane and count them one by one, taking photographs to verify the number. This is obviously not a good method for counting field mice; they are too small to be seen from the air, are too well camouflaged by the color of their fur, and spend too much time in their burrows. The only way to determine the number of mice living in a field is by "saturation trapping"—catching every single mouse until no more are left and counting them.

Lizards are counted by the "capture, recapture" method. To find the population in a certain area, a herpetologist (one who studies reptiles and amphibians) might catch 50 lizards, mark them all with a harmless paint or metal tag, and set them free again. After a few weeks, the marked lizards have dispersed back into the general population. The scientist then captures another 50 lizards and finds that some of this batch are creatures he marked in his first catch, and some are unmarked—meaning they were *not* in the first batch. The herpetologist's next step is to make assumptions for the purpose of his census. He assumes that the new batch of 50 marked and unmarked lizards is a representative sample—a microcosm—of the population as a whole. He assumes that after he marked the first 50 lizards and released them, they distributed themselves at random throughout the population. Thus, when he catches the second 50 and finds that he earlier marked, say, 10 of them—or 20 percent—he assumes that 20 percent of the *entire lizard population* is marked. He knows that he originally marked 50 lizards; concluding from the second sample that 20 percent were marked, he assumes that 50 is 20 percent of the total population. Since $5 \times 20\% = 100\%$, 5 times 50 lizards is the whole population: 250 lizards.

Fish are counted a similar way. Experimenters put a knockout solution in the water, which does the fish no permanent harm but makes them float to the surface belly-up. They then collect the fish, count them, mark them with dye or tags, and revive and release them. The same number are later recaptured, the marked ones counted, and the total figured as for lizards.

How about animals that are harder to grab, such as songbirds? Ornithologists often use a grid system in a wooded area to get an approximate number. They mark evenly spaced, parallel straight trails through the region that interests them. People carrying pads and pens walk down the trails in a phalanx, each member keeping another in sight to the left and right, counting every bird they see or hear. Each member only counts birds observed a certain distance to either side of him, so that two people don't count the same bird. This ritual is performed several times and the results averaged.

How does one count things as small as the microscopic plankton that live in the ocean? A sample of ocean water is whipped around in a centrifuge, so that all the solids collect at one end, including the tiny plankton. This residue is slid under a microscope bit by bit and the plankton counted. That gives the plankton per unit volume of ocean water.

As you can see, different methods are needed to keep track of animals living in different niches or habitats. To get an idea of the total number of a species in an entire region or country (or planet), scientists determine the size of the habitat available to the species, instead of counting individuals, and multiply by the number of individuals that usually live in a given area of habitat. It is in the nature of living things that they fill any habitat with as many individuals as the food and space in the area will allow.

Knowing the number of acres of woodland, mountain, prairie, and city in the United States, we can arrive at a ballpark estimate of 6 billion land birds of all kinds in the country. By contrast, some water birds such as the whooping crane are not nearly so adaptable; whoopers can live only in certain areas of Texas marshland, where about 100 nest each year.

Other forms of life build on a minuscule scale and fit vast numbers of individuals into their ecological niches. Insects have adapted through evolution to live in an incredible variety of conditions. The world population of insects in their many habitats is estimated to total a *billion billion*, or 10 to the 18th power (10^{18})—the number 1 followed by 18 zeroes. That's roughly a billion times the world's human population; if the world insect population were represented by a bucketful of sand, the human population would be a single grain of sand in that bucket. More amazing still, if we look closely at the bodies of those insects, we find as many as a hundred thousand one-celled animals called protozoa living in the digestive tract of *each insect*, eating what the insect is unable to digest. There are therefore about 10^{23} of these digestive protozoa living in the world's insects. That number is greater than the number of stars in the universe.

As Jonathan Swift wrote after the invention of the microscope, which revealed for the first time the existence of protozoa, animals smaller than the naked eye could see:

> *Big fleas have little fleas*
> *Upon their backs to bite'em;*
> *And little fleas have lesser fleas,*
> *And so* ad infinitum.

This narration of process is in fact an explanation of a series of processes. Each one of the explanations is complete in itself, but taken together they reveal the complexity of counting animals.

WRITING STRATEGIES

Consider the following questions as you write a narration of process.

- ❑ What type of process are you narrating?
- ❑ What are the steps?
- ❑ Are they in the proper sequence?
- ❑ What is the goal of the process?
- ❑ Have you given the audience enough information?

CAUSE AND EFFECT

As with narration of event and narration of process when we organize with cause and effect, we arrange events as they occur in time. When organizing with cause and effect, however, we are interested in telling not only what happened, but also *why* it happened.

Causes and effects are implicit in all narrations. When we organize with cause and effect, we make them explicit. For example, a story about an automobile accident (that a car going through an intersection failed to stop and hit another car, critically injuring both drivers) would be a narration of an event. An explanation of why the accident happened (because the driver's brakes failed) and what the results of the accident were (the cars were totalled and the drivers were taken to the hospital) would have a cause and effect organization.

THE STRUCTURE

The structure of cause and effect narratives reflects not only the time order that all narratives have, but also two levels of causation—immediate and ultimate. In the previous example, attributing the immediate cause of the accident (that the driver's brakes failed) to the driver's failure to perform preventive maintenance on the car would be giving an ultimate cause. Similarly, going beyond the immediate effect (the drivers' being hospitalized) to explain some long-term disability (that they were confined to wheelchairs) would be explaining an ultimate effect.

Extensive analyses of both immediate and ultimate causes and effects are frequently used in historical writing. Explaining causes and effects allows scholars to support interpretations of events studied in their disciplines.

An Example

In the following essay, which first appeared in *The Immense Journey* (1957), Loren Eisley explains the causal relationship between the emergence of flowers and the development of mammals and birds.

How Flowers Changed the World

LOREN EISELEY

If it had been possible to observe the Earth from the far side of the solar system over the long course of geological epochs, the watchers might have been able to discern a subtle change in the light emanating from our planet. That world of long ago would, like the red deserts of Mars, have reflected light from vast drifts of stone and gravel, the sands of wandering wastes, the blackness of naked basalt, the yellow of dust of endlessly moving storms. Only the ceaseless marching of the clouds and the intermittent flashes from the restless surface of the sea would have told a different story, but still essentially a barren one. Then, as the millennia rolled away and age followed age, a new and greener light would, by degrees, have come to twinkle across those endless miles.

This is the only difference those far watchers, by use of subtle instruments, might have perceived in the whole history of the planet Earth, Yet that slowly growing green twinkle would have contained the epic march of life from the tidal oozes upward across the raw and unclothed continents. Out of the vast chemical bath of the sea—not from the deeps, but from the element-rich, light-exposed platforms of the continental shelves—wandering fingers of green had crept upward along the meanderings of river systems and fringed the gravels of forgotten lakes.

In those first ages plants clung of necessity to swamps and watercourses. Their reproductive processes demanded direct access to water. Beyond the primitive ferns and mosses that enclosed the borders of swamps and streams the rocks still lay vast and bare, the winds still swirled the dust of a naked planet. The grass cover that holds our world secure in place was still millions of years in the future. The green marchers had gained a soggy foothold upon the land but that was all. They did not reproduce by seeds but by microscopic swimming sperm that had to wriggle their way through water to fertilize the female cell. Such plants in their higher forms had clever adaptations for the use of rain water in their sexual phases, and survived with increasing success in a wet land environment. They now seem part of man's normal environment. The truth is, however, that there is nothing very "normal" about nature. Once upon a time there were no flowers at all.

A little while ago—about one hundred million years, as the geologist estimates time in the history of our four-billion-year-old planet—flowers were not to be found anywhere on the five continents. Wherever one might have looked, from the poles to the equator, one would have seen only the cold dark monotonous green of a world whose plant life possessed no other color.

Somewhere, just a short time before the close of the Age of Reptiles, there occurred a soundless, violent explosion. It lasted millions of years, but it was an explosion, nevertheless. It marked the emergence of the angiosperms —the flowering plants. Even the great evolutionist, Charles Darwin, called them "an abominable mystery," because they appeared so suddenly and spread so fast.

Flowers changed the face of the planet. Without them, the world we know—even man himself—would never have existed. Francis Thompson, the English poet, once wrote that one could not pluck a flower without troubling a star. Intuitively he had sensed like a naturalist the enormous interlinked complexity of life. Today we know that the appearance of the flowers contained also the equally mystifying emergence of man.

If we were to go back into the Age of Reptiles, its drowned swamps and birdless forest would reveal to us a warmer but, on the whole, a sleepier world than that of today. Here and there, it is true, the serpent heads of bottom-feeding dinosaurs might be upreared in suspicion of their huge flesh-eating compatriots. Tyrannosaurs, enormous bipedal caricatures of men, would stalk mindlessly across the sites of future cities and go their slow way down into the dark of geologic time.

In all that world of living things nothing saw save with the intense concentration of the hunt, nothing moved except with the grave sleepwalking intentness of the instinct-driven brain. Judged by modern standards, it as a world in slow motion, a cold-blooded world whose occupants were most active at noonday but torpid on chill nights, their brains damped by a slower metabolism than any known to even the most primitive of warm-blooded animals today.

A high metabolic rate and the maintenance of a constant body temperature are supreme achievements in the evolution of life. They enable an animal to escape, within broad limits, from the overheating or the chilling of its immediate surroundings, and at the same time to maintain a peak mental efficiency. Creatures without a high metabolic rate are slaves to weather. Insects in the first frosts of autumn all run down like little clocks. Yet if you pick one up and breathe warmly upon it, it will begin to move about once more.

In a sheltered spot such creatures may sleep away the winter, but they are hopelessly immobilized. Though a few warm-blooded mammals, such as the woodchuck of our day, have evolved a way of reducing their metabolic rate in order to undergo winter hibernation, it is a survival mechanism with drawbacks, for it leaves the animal helplessly exposed if enemies discover him during his period of suspended animation. Thus bear or woodchuck, big animal or small, must seek, in this time of descending sleep, a safe refuge in some hidden den or burrow. Hibernation is, therefore, primarily a winter refuge of small, easily concealed animals rather than of large ones.

A high metabolic rate, however, means a heavy intake of energy in order to sustain body warmth and efficiency. It is for this reason that even some of these later warm-blooded mammals existing in our day have learned to descend into a slower, unconscious rate of living during the winter months when food may be difficult to obtain. On a slightly higher plane they are following the procedure of the cold-blooded frog sleeping in the mud at the bottom of a frozen pond.

The agile brain of the warm-blooded birds and mammals demands a high oxygen consumption and food in concentrated forms, or the creatures cannot long sustain themselves. It was the rise of flowering plants that provided that energy and changed the nature of the living world. Their appearance parallels in a quite surprising manner the rise of the birds and mammals.

Slowly, toward the dawn of the Age of Reptiles, something over two hundred and fifty million years ago, the little naked sperm cells wriggling their way through dew and raindrops had given way to a kind of pollen carried by the wind. Our present-day pine forests represent plants of a pollen-disseminating variety. Once fertilization was no longer dependent on exterior water, the march over drier regions could be extended. Instead of spores simple primitive seeds carrying some nourishment for the young plants had developed, but true flowers were still scores of millions of years away. After a long period of hesitant evolutionary groping, they exploded upon the world with truly revolutionary violence.

The event occurred in Cretaceous times in the close of the Age of Reptiles. Before the coming of the flowering plants our own ancestral stock, the warm-blooded mammals, consisted of a few mousy little creatures hidden in trees and underbrush. A few lizard-like birds with carnivorous teeth flapped awkwardly on ill-aimed flights among archiac shubbery. None of these insignificant creatures gave evidence of any remarkable talents. The mammals in particular had been around for some millions of years, but had remained well lost in the shadow of the mighty reptiles. Truth to tell, man was still, like the genie in the bottle, encased in the body of a creature about the size of a rat.

As for the birds, their reptilian cousins the Pterodactyls, flew farther and better. There was just one thing about the birds that paralleled the physiology of the mammals. They, too, had evolved warm blood and its accompanying temperature control. Nevertheless, if one had been seen stripped of its feathers, he would still have seemed a slightly uncanny and unsightly lizard.

Neither the birds nor the mammals, however, were quite what they seemed. They were waiting for the Age of Flowers. They were waiting for what flowers, and with them the true encased seed, would bring. Fish-eating, gigantic leather-winged reptiles, twenty-eight feet from wing tip to wing tip, hovered over the coasts that one day would be swarming with gulls.

Inland the monotonous green of the pine and spruce forests with their primitive wooden cone flowers stretched everywhere. No grass hindered the fall of the naked seeds to earth. Great sequoias towered to the skies. The world of that time has a certain appeal but it is a giant's world, a world moving slowly like the reptiles who stalked magnificently among the boles of its trees.

The trees themselves are ancient, slow-growing, and immense, like the redwood groves that have survived to our day on the California coast. All is stiff, formal, upright and green, monotonously green. There is no grass as yet; there are no wide plains rolling in the sun, no tiny daisies dotting the meadows underfoot. There is little versatility about this scene; it is, in truth, a giant's world.

A few nights ago it was brought home vividly to me that the world has changed since that far epoch. I was awakened out of a sleep by an unknown sound in my living room. Not a small sound—not a creaking timber or a mouse's scurry—but a sharp, rending explosion as though an unwary foot had been put down upon a wine glass. I had come instantly out of sleep and lay tense, unbreathing. I listened for another step. There was none.

Unable to stand the suspense any longer, I turned on the light and passed from room to room glancing uneasily behind chairs and into closets. Nothing seemed disturbed, and I stood puzzled in the center of the living room floor. Then a small button-shaped object upon the rug caught my eye. It was hard and polished and glistening. Scattered over the length of the room were several more shining up at me like wary little eyes. A pine cone that had been lying in a dish had been blown the length of the coffee table. The dish itself could hardly have been the source of the explosion. Beside it I found two ribbon-like strips of velvety-green. I tried to place the two strips together to make a pod. They twisted resolutely away from each other and would no longer fit.

I relaxed in a chair, then, for I had reached a solution of the midnight disturbance. The twisted strips were wisteria pods that I had brought in a day or two previously and placed in the dish. They had chosen midnight to explode and distribute their multiplying fund of life down the length of the room. A plant, a fixed, rooted thing, immobolized in a single pod, had devised a way of propelling its offspring across open space. Immediately there passed before my eyes the million airy troopers of the milkweed pod and the clutching hooks of the sandburs. Seeds on the coyote's tail, seeds on the hunter's coat, thistledown mounting on the winds—all were somehow triumphing over life's limitations. Yet the ability to do this had not been with them at the beginning. It was the product of endless effort and experiment,

The seeds on my carpet were not going to lie stiffly where they had dropped like their antiquated cousins, the naked seeds on the pine-cone scales. They were travelers. Struck by the thought, I went out the next day and collected several other varieties. I line them up now in a row on my desk—so many little capsules of life, winged, hooked or spiked. Every one is an angiosperm, a product of the true flowering plants. Contained in these little boxes is the secret of that far-off Cretaceous explosion of a hundred million years ago that changed the face of the planet. And somewhere in here, I think, as I spoke seriously at one particularly resistant seedcase of a wild grass, was once man himself.

Eisley explains the series of causes that began with the development the angiosperms at the end of the Age of Reptiles. He shows how the explosion of flowering plants created an environment where mammals and birds could thrive. At the end of the essay, his example of the explosion of some seedpods he had left in his living room graphically illustrates the power of flowering plants.

VARIATIONS IN CAUSE AND EFFECT

When the purpose of the writing changes, the author will alter the use of cause and effect accordingly. Both causes and effects will be treated in light of the demands of the purpose.

EXPRESSIVE CAUSE AND EFFECT

In expressive cause and effect writers will often look at events that have shaped identity and values and have had an impact on subsequent events.

AN EXAMPLE

Eldridge Cleaver examines forces that caused him to leave the country in light of his identity and his value system.

Why I Left the U.S. and Why I Am Returning

ELDRIDGE CLEAVER

I am often asked why I want to return to the United States. This question never fails to bowl me over, and I find it impossible to answer. I also feel that it is an improper question. In fact, most people who ask are not really interested in that question. What they actually want to know is what will I do if they allow me to return.

I always take the opportunity to explain why I left in the first place. Lots of people believe I left because I preferred to go live in a Communist country, and that now, several years and many Communist countries later, I find the grass not greener on the Communist side of the fence. So now, here I stand, locked outside the gates of the paradise I once scorned, begging to be let back in. Let me clarify.

On April 6, 1968, two days after Dr. Martin Luther King, Jr., was assassinated, there was a gun battle between members of the Black Panther Party and the Oakland Police Department. Bobby Hutton was killed. Warren Wells and I received gunshot wounds. Two policemen were wounded. Eight party members, myself included, were arrested in the area of the gunfight.

After I received emergency treatment, guards from the California Department of Corrections transported me directly to San Quentin State Prison, in the spirit of "Oh, boy, we got you now!" It seemed obvious to them that I had violated my parole. I, along with the others, was indicted by an Alameda County Grand Jury. And although bail was set on all of us, the Corrections Department refused to allow me to go free on bail, claiming jurisdiction over me as a parole violator.

I pleaded not guilty. Without a trial or hearing of any sort, the prison authorities were prejudging my case, declaring me guilty, and, in effect, sentencing me to prison. My attorneys filed a petition for a writ of habeas corpus. A hearing was held before Chief Judge Raymond J. Sherwin of the Solano County Superior Court.

Judge Sherwin ordered me free on bail. I quote . . . from his decision:

> The record here is that though the petitioner was arrested and his parole cancelled more than two months ago, hearings before the Adult Authority [the state parole board for male felons] have not even been scheduled.
>
> There is nothing to indicate why it was deemed necessary to cancel his parole before his trial on the pending criminal charges of which he is presumed innocent.
>
> It has to be stressed that the uncontradicted evidence presented to this Court indicated that the petitioner had been a model parolee. The peril to his parole status stemmed from no failure of personal rehabilitation, but from his undue eloquence in pursuing political goals, goals which were offensive to many of his contemporaries.
>
> Not only was there absence of cause for the cancellation of parole, it was the product of a type of pressure unbecoming, to say the least, to the law enforcement paraphernalia of this state.

Judge Sherwin's decision exploded like a bomb inside California legal, political and police circles, because it missed the whole point: From Governor Ronald Reagan down, the politicians wanted me silenced, and here Judge Sherwin was talking about due process of law!

People who supported my fight for my rights posted $50,000 bail, and I was free.

The law-enforcement paraphernalia was not stopped by Judge Sherwin's condemnation, and the Adult Authority moved swiftly to have his ruling reversed in the Appellate Court. The court refused to examine the facts at issue in the case and instead simply affirmed the arbitrary power of the Adult Authority to revoke parole. Because of a technicality in court procedure, the ruling ordering me returned to prison could not become effective for sixty days. I was due to surrender on November 27. That day, I was in Montreal. That was seven years ago.

History shows that when the American political system is blocked and significant segments of the population are unable to have their will brought to bear on the decision-making process, you can count upon the American people to revolt, to take it out into the streets, in the spirit of the Boston Tea Party.

During the 1960's, the chips were down in a fateful way, uniting the upsurge of black Americans against the oppressive features of the system, and the gargantuan popular opposition to the Indochina wars. It was left to the Nixon Administration to bring the issues to a head. In the end, the system rejected President Nixon and reaffirmed its own basic principles.

A fabulous new era of progress is opening up to the world, and coping with all of the problems unleashed by Watergate has opened up a creative era for American democracy. I believe that every American, regardless of his politics, has a duty to reexamine some of his beliefs.

This is particularly true of those active at both extremes of the political spectrum. Those of us who developed a psychology of opposition must take a pause and sum up our experiences. We must recognize that in a sense we are playing in a brand new ball game. The slogans of yesterday will not get us through the tasks at hand. I believe that for America to deal with problems posed on the world level, a fundamental reorientation in the relationship between the American people is absolutely necessary.

We can not afford to refight battles that have already been either won or lost. If Richard Nixon and his friends had accepted the verdict of the people in 1960, rejecting him at the polls, the nation would have been spared the debacle of Watergate. But the truth is that nations do get the leaders they deserve.

With all of its faults, the American political system is the freest and most democratic in the world. The system needs to be improved, with democracy spread to all areas of life, particularly the economic. All of these changes must be conducted through our established institutions, and people with grievances must find political methods for obtaining redress.

Each generation subjects the world it inherits to severe criticism. I think that my generation has been more critical than most, and for good reason. At the same time, at the end of the critical process, we should arrive at some conclusions. We should have discovered which values are worth conserving. It is the beginning of another fight, the fight to defend those values from the blind excesses of our fellows who are still caught up in the critical process. It is my hope to make a positive contribution in this regard.

1975

In this essay Cleaver uses cause and effect to justify his actions and defend his beliefs. His reaction to the influences on his life are shaped by his values and his self-definition.

LITERARY CAUSE AND EFFECT

In literary works, we are usually more interested in the narrative itself than we are in the causes and effects that are embedded in the structure of the plots. But causes and effects are sometimes explored by writers who are influenced by a theory of naturalism. In stories by such writers, we become aware of the underlying causes that motivate and control characters.

An Example

Katherine Anne Porter explores the causes that motivate her characters in this story.

The Necessary Enemy

KATHERINE ANNE PORTER

She is a frank, charming, fresh-hearted young woman who married for love. She and her husband are one of those gay, good-looking young pairs who ornament this modern scene rather more in profusion perhaps than ever before in our history. They are handsome, with a talent for finding their way in their world, they work at things that interest them, their tastes agree and their hopes. They intend in all good faith to spend their lives together, to have children and do well by them and each other—to be happy, in fact, which for them is the whole point of their marriage. And all in stride, keeping their wits about them. Nothing romantic, mind you; their feet are on the ground.

Unless they were this sort of person, there would be not much point to what I wish to say; for they would seem to be an example of the high-spirited, right-minded young whom the critics are always invoking to come forth and do their duty and practice all those sterling old-fashioned virtues which in every generation seem to be falling into disrepair. As for virtues, these young people are more or less on their own, like most of their kind; they get very little moral or other aid from their society; but after three years of marriage this very contemporary young woman finds herself facing the oldest and ugliest dilemma of marriage.

She is dismayed, horrified, full of guilt and forebodings because she is finding out little by little that she is capable of hating her husband, whom she loves faithfully. She can hate him at times as fiercely and mysteriously, indeed in terribly much the same way, as often she hated her parents, her brothers and sisters, whom she loves, when she was a child. Even then it had seemed to her a kind of black treacherousness in her, her private wickedness that, just the same, gave her her only private life. That was one thing her parents never knew about her, never seemed to suspect. For it was never given a name. They did and said hateful things to her and to each other as if by right, as if in them it was a kind of virtue. But when they said to her, "Control your feelings," it was never when she was amiable and obedient, only in the black times of her hate. So it was her secret, a shameful one. When they punished her, sometimes for the strangest reasons, it was, they said, only because they loved her—it was for her good. She did not believe this, but she thought herself guilty of something worse than ever they had punished her for. None of this really frightened her: the real fright came when she discovered that at times her father and mother hated each other; this was like standing on the doorsill of a familiar room and seeing in a lightning flash that the floor was gone, you were on the edge of a bottomless pit. Sometimes she felt that both of them hated her, but that passed, it was simply not a thing to be thought of, much less believed. She thought she had outgrown all this, but here it was again, an element in her own nature she could not control, or feared she could not. She would have to hide from her husband, if she could, the same spot in her feelings she had hidden from her parents, and for the same no doubt disreputable, selfish reason: she wants to keep his love.

Above all, she wants him to be absolutely confident that she loves him, for that is the real truth, no matter how unreasonable it sounds, and no matter how her own feelings betray them both at times. She depends recklessly on his love; yet while she is hating him, he might very well be hating her as much or even more, and it would serve her right. But she does not want to be served right, she wants to be loved and forgiven—that is, to be sure he would forgive her anything, if he had any notion of what she had done. But best of all she would like not to have anything in her love that should ask forgiveness. She doesn't mean about their quarrels—they are not so bad. Her feelings are out of proportion, perhaps. She knows it is perfectly natural for people to disagree, have fits of temper, fight it out; they learn quite a lot about each other that way, and not all of it disappointing either. When it passes, her hatred seems quite unreal. It always did.

Love. We are early taught to say it. I love you. We are trained to the thought of it as if there were nothing else, or nothing else worth having without it, or nothing worth having which it could not bring with it. Love is taught, always by precept, sometimes by example. Then hate, which no one meant to teach us, comes of itself. It is true that if we say I love you, it may be received with doubt, for there are times when it is hard to believe. Say I hate you, and the one spoken to believes it instantly once for all.

Say I love you a thousand times to that person afterward and mean it every time, and still it does not change the fact that once we said I hate you, and meant that too. It leaves a mark on that surface love had worn so smooth with its eternal caresses. Love must be learned, and learned again and again; there is no end to it. Hate needs no instruction, but waits only to be provoked . . . hate, the unspoken word, the unacknowledged presence in the house, that faint smell of brimstone among the roses, that invisible tongue-tripper, that unkempt finger in every pie, that sudden oh-so-curiously chilling look—could it be boredom?—on your dear one's features, making them quite ugly. Be careful: love, perfect love, is in danger.

If it is not perfect, it is not love, and if it is not love, it is bound to be hate sooner or later. This is perhaps a not too exaggerated statement of the extreme position of Romantic Love, more especially in America, where we are all brought up on it, whether we know it or not. Romantic Love is changeless, faithful, passionate, and its sole end is to render the two lovers happy. It has no obstacles save those provided by the hazards of fate (that is to say, society), and such sufferings as the lovers may cause each other are only another word for delight: exciting jealousies, thrilling uncertainties, the ritual dance of courtship within the charmed closed circle of their secret alliance; all real troubles come from without, they face them unitedly in perfect confidence. Marriage is not the end but only the beginning of true happiness, cloudless, changeless to the end. That the candidates for this blissful condition have never seen an example of it, nor ever knew anyone who had, makes no difference. That is the ideal and they will achieve it.

How did Romantic Love manage to get into marriage at last, where it was most certainly never intended to be? At its highest it was tragic: the love of Héloise and Abélard. At its most graceful, it was the homage of the trouvère for his lady. In its most popular form, the adulterous strayings of solidly married couples who meant to stray for their own good reasons, but at the same time do nothing to upset the property settlements or the line of legitimacy; at its most trivial, the pretty trifling of shepherd and shepherdess.

This was generally condemned by church and state and a word of fear to honest wives whose mortal enemy it was. Love within the sober, sacred realities of marriage was a matter of personal luck, but in any case, private feelings were strictly a private affair having, at least in theory, no bearing whatever on the fixed practice of the rules of an institution never intended as a recreation ground for either sex. If the couple discharged their religious and social obligations, furnished forth a copious progeny, kept their troubles to themselves, maintained public civility and died under the same roof, even if not always on speaking terms, it was rightly regarded as a successful marriage. Apparently this testing ground was too severe for all but the stoutest spirits; it too was based on an ideal, as impossible in its way as the ideal Romantic Love. One good thing to be said for it is that society took responsibility for the conditions of marriage, and the sufferers within its bounds could always blame the system, not themselves. But Romantic Love crept into the marriage bed, very stealthily, by centuries, bringing its absurd notions about love as eternal springtime and marriage as a personal adventure meant to provide personal happiness. To a Western romantic such as I, though my views have been much modified by painful experience, it still seems to me a charming work of the human imagination, and it is a pity its central notion has been taken too literally and has hardened into a convention as cramping and enslaving as the older one. The refusal to acknowledge the evils in ourselves which therefore are implicit in any human situation is as extreme and unworkable a proposition as the doctrine of total depravity; but somewhere between them, or maybe beyond them, there does exist a possibility for reconciliation between our desires for impossible satisfactions and the simple unalterable fact that we also desire to be unhappy and that we create our own suffering; and out of these sufferings we salvage our fragments of happiness.

Our young woman who has been taught that an important part of her human nature is not real because it makes trouble and interferes with her peace of mind and shakes her self-love, has been very badly taught; but she has arrived at a most important stage of her re-education. She is afraid her marriage is going to fail because she has not love enough to face its difficulties; and this because at times she feels a painful hostility toward her husband, and cannot admit its reality because such an admission would damage in her own eyes her view of what love should be, an absurd view, based on her vanity of power. Her hatred is real as her love is real, but her hatred has the advantage at present because it works on a blind instinctual level, it is lawless; and her love is subjected to a code of ideal conditions, impossible by their very nature of fulfill-ment, which prevents its free growth and deprives it of its right to recognize its human limitations and come to grips with them. Hatred is natural in a sense that love, as she conceives it, a young person brought up in the tradition of Romantic Love, is not natural at all. Yet it did not come by hazard, it is the very imperfect expression of the need of the human imagination to create beauty and harmony out of chaos, no matter how mistaken its notion of these things may be, nor how clumsy its methods. It has conjured love out of the air, and seeks to preserve it by incantations; when she spoke a vow to love and honor her husband until death, she did a very reckless thing, for it is not possible by an act of the will to fulfill such an engagement. But it was the necessary act of faith performed in defense of a mode of feelings, the statement of honorable intention to practice as well as she is able the noble, acquired faculty of love, that very mysterious overtone to sex which is the best thing in it. Her hatred is part of it, the necessary enemy and ally.

1948

Porter explores the effects of Romantic Love on a young woman in a mar-riage. She also reveals how the attitudes of the characters in her narrative are shaped by social and culture forces.

PERSUASIVE CAUSE AND EFFECT

Cause and effect can provide a powerful argument for a persuasive claim. If a writer is able to convince the reader that a disaster will occur because of a certain cause, then an argument will have some force.

AN EXAMPLE

Joseph Wood Krutch argues that humans must learn to share the earth with other creatures.

Conservation Is Not Enough

JOSEPH WOOD KRUTCH

Moralists often blame races and nations because they have never learned how to live and let live. In our time we seem to have been increasingly aware how persistently and brutally groups of men undertake to eliminate one another. But it is not only the members of his own kind that man seems to want to push off the earth. When he moves in, nearly everything else suffers from his intrusion—sometimes because he wants the space they occupy and the food they eat, but often simply because when he sees a creature not of his kind or a man not of his race his first impulse is "kill it."

Hence it is that even in the desert, where space is cheaper than in most places, the wild life grows scarcer and more secretive as the human population grows. The coyote howls further and further off. The deer seek closer and closer cover. To almost everything except man the smell of humanity is the most repulsive of all odors, the sight of man the most terrifying of all sights. Biologists call some animals "cryptozoic," that is to say "leading hidden lives." But as the human population increases most animals develop, as the deer has been developing, cryptozoic habits. Even now there are more of them around than we realize. They see us when we do not see them—because they have seen us first. Albert Schweitzer remarks somewhere that we owe kindness even to an insect when we can afford to show it, just because we ought to do something to make up for all the cruelties, necessary as well as unnecessary, which we have inflicted upon almost the whole of animate creation.

Probably not one man in ten is capable of understanding such moral and aesthetic considerations, much less of permitting his conduct to be guided by them. But perhaps twice as many, though still far from a majority, are beginning to realize that the reckless laying waste of the earth has practical consequences. They are at least beginning to hear about "conservation," though they are not even dimly aware of any connection between it and a large morality and are very unlikely to suppose that "conservation" does or could mean anything more than looking after their own welfare.

Hardly more than two generations ago Americans first woke up to the fact that their land was not inexhaustible. Every year since then more and more has been said, and at least a little more has been done about "conserving resources," about "rational use" and about such reconstruction as seemed possible. Scientists have studied the problem, public works have been undertaken, laws passed. Yet everybody knows that the using up still goes on, perhaps not so fast nor so recklessly as once it did, but unmistakably nevertheless. And there is nowhere that it goes on more nakedly, more persistently or with a fuller realization of what is happening than in the desert regions where the margin to be used up is narrower.

First, more and more cattle were set to grazing and overgrazing the land from which the scanty rainfall now ran off even more rapidly than before. More outrageously still, large areas of desert shrub were rooted up to make way for cotton and other crops watered by wells tapping underground pools of water which are demonstrably shrinking fast. These pools represent years of accumulation not now being replenished and are exhaustible exactly as an oil well is exhaustible. Everyone knows that they will give out before long, very soon, in fact, if the number of wells continues to increase as it has been increasing. Soon dust bowls will be where was once a sparse but healthy desert, and man, having uprooted, slaughtered or driven away everything which lived healthily and normally there, will himself either abandon the country or die. There are places where the creosote bush is a more useful plant than cotton.

To the question why men will do or are permitted to do such things there are many answers. Some speak of population pressures, some more brutally of unconquerable human greed. Some despair; some hope that more education and more public works will, in the long run, prove effective. But is there, perhaps, something more, something different, which is indispensable? Is there some missing link in the chain of education, law and public works? Is there not something lacking without which none of these is sufficient?

After a lifetime spent in forestry, wild-life management and conservation of one kind or another, after such a lifetime during which he nevertheless saw his country slip two steps backward for every one it took forward, the late Aldo Leopold pondered the question and came up with an unusual answer which many people would dismiss as "sentimental" and be surprised to hear from a "practical" scientific man. He published his article originally in the *Journal of Forestry* and it was reprinted in the posthumous volume, *A Sand County Almanac*, where it was given the seemingly neutral but actually very significant title "The Land Ethic."

This is a subtle and original essay full of ideas never so clearly expressed before and seminal in the sense that each might easily grow into a separate treatise. Yet the conclusion reached can be simply stated. Something *is* lacking and because of that lack education, law and public works fail to accomplish what they hope to accomplish. Without that something, the high-minded impulse to educate, to legislate and to manage become as sounding brass and tinkling cymbals. And the thing which is missing is love, some feeling for, as well as some understanding of, the inclusive community of rocks and soils, plants and animals, of which we are a part.

It is not, to put Mr. Leopold's thoughts in different words, enough to be enlightenedly selfish in our dealings with the land. That means, of course, that it is not enough for the farmer to want to get the most out of his farm and the lumberer to get the most out of his forest without considering agriculture and wood production as a whole both now and in the future. But it also means more than that. In the first place enlightened selfishness cannot be enough because enlightened selfishness cannot possibly be extended to include remote posterity. It may include the children, perhaps, and grandchildren, possibly, but it cannot be extended much beyond that because the very idea of "self" cannot be stretched much further. Some purely ethical considerations must operate, if anything does. Yet even that is not all. The wisest, the most enlightened, the most remotely long-seeing exploitation of resources is not enough, for the simple reason that the whole concept of exploitation is so false and so limited that in the end it will defeat itself and the earth will have been plundered no matter how scientifically and farseeingly the plundering has been done.

To live healthily and successfully on the land we must also live with it. We must be part not only of the human community, but of the whole community; we must acknowledge some sort of oneness not only with our neighbors, our countrymen and our civilization but also some respect for the natural as well as for the man-made community. Ours is not only "one world" in the sense usually implied by that term. It is also "one earth." Without some acknowledgment of that fact, men can no more live successfully than they can if they refuse to admit the political and economic interdependency of the various sections of the civilized world. It is not a sentimental but a grimly literal fact that unless we share this terrestrial globe with creatures other than ourselves, we shall not be able to live on it for long.

You may, if you like, think of this as a moral law. But if you are skeptical about moral laws, you cannot escape the fact that it has its factual, scientific aspect. Every day the science of ecology is making clearer the factual aspect as it demonstrates those more and more remote interdependencies which, no matter how remote they are, are crucial even for us.

Before even the most obvious aspects of the balance of nature had been recognized, a greedy, self-centered mankind naïvely divided plants into the useful and the useless. In the same way it divided animals into those which were either domestic on the one hand or "game" on the other, and the "vermin" which ought to be destroyed. That was the day when extermination of whole species was taken as a matter of course and random introductions which usually proved to be either complete failures or all too successful were everywhere being made. Soon, however, it became evident enough that to rid the world of vermin and to stock it with nothing but useful organisms was at least not a simple task—if you assume that "useful" means simply "immediately useful to man."

Yet even to this day the *ideal* remains the same for most people. They may know, or at least they may have been told, that what looks like the useless is often remotely but demonstrably essential. Out in this desert country they may see the land being rendered useless by overuse. They may even have heard how, when the mountain lion is killed off, the deer multiply; how, when the deer multiply, the new growth of trees and shrubs is eaten away; and how, when the hills are denuded, a farm or a section of grazing land many miles away is washed into gulleys and made incapable of supporting either man or any other of the large animals. They may even have heard how the wonderful new insecticides proved so effective that fish and birds died of starvation; how on at least one Pacific island insects had to be reintroduced to pollinate the crops; how when you kill off almost completely a destructive pest, you run the risk of starving out everything which preys upon it and thus run the risk that the pest itself will stage an overwhelming comeback because its natural enemies are no more. Yet, knowing all this and much more, their dream is still the dream that an earth for man's use only can be created if only we learn more and scheme more effectively. They still hope that nature's scheme of checks and balances which provides for a varied population, which stubbornly refuses to scheme only from man's point of view and cherishes the weeds and "vermin" as persistently as she cherishes him, can be replaced by a scheme of his own devising. Ultimately they hope they can beat the game. But the more the ecologist learns, the less likely it seems that man can in the long run do anything of the sort.

Krutch uses cause and effect to suggest that the actions of human beings are having a disastrous effect on the earth and that we should change our behavior and learn to live with the land.

REFERENTIAL CAUSE AND EFFECT

In many academic disciplines, but especially in the social sciences and the natural sciences, analysis of cause and effect is fundamental. To understand ourselves and our world, we rely on studies that tell us why phenomena of all kinds occur.

AN EXAMPLE

In the following essay, Lewis Thomas discusses the effects of science.

On the True Nature of Science

LEWIS THOMAS

The transformation of human society by science is probably only at its beginning, and nobody can guess at how it will all turn out. At the moment, the most obvious and visible effects on our lives are those resulting from the technology that derives from science, for better or worse, and much of today's public argument over whether science is good or bad is really an argument about the value of the technology, not about science.

Walking around on the moon was a feat of world-class engineering, made possible by two centuries of classical physics, most of it accomplished by physicists with no faintest notion of walking on the moon.

Penicillin was a form of technology made feasible by sixty years of fundamental research in bacteriology. You had to have streptococci and staphylococci in hand, and you had to know their names as well as their habits, before you could begin thinking of such things as antibiotics.

Nuclear bombs, nuclear power plants, and radioisotopes for the study of human disease symbolize the range of society's choices for the application of mid-twentieth-century science, as were in their day the light bulb, the automobile, and the dial telephone.

But technology is only one aspect of science, perhaps in the very long run the least important. Quite apart from the instruments it has made available for our survival, comfort, entertainment, or annihilation, science affects the way we think together.

The effects on human thought tend to come at us gradually, often subtly, and sometimes subconsciously. Because of new information, we change the ways in which we view the world. We are not so much the center of things anymore, because of science. We feel lost, or at least not yet found.

We are not as informed about our role in the universe as we thought we were a few centuries ago, and despite our vast population we live more in loneliness and, at many times, dismay. Science is said to be the one human endeavor above all others that we should rely on for making predictions (after all, prediction is a central business of science), yet, for all the fact that we live in the Age of Science, we feel less able to foretell the future than ever before in our history.

This is, to date, the most wrenching of all the transformations that science has imposed on human consciousness—in the Western world, anyway. We have learned that we do not really understand nature at all, and the more information we receive, the more strange and mystifying is the picture before us.

There was a time, just a few centuries back, when it was not so. We thought then that we could comprehend almost all important matters: the earth was the centerpiece of the universe, we humans were the centerpiece of the earth, God was in his heaven just beyond what we have now identified as a narrow layer of ozone, and all was essentially right with the world; we were in full charge, for better or worse.

Now, we know different, or think we do. There is no center holding anywhere, as far as we can see, and we can see great distances. What we thought to be the great laws of physics turn out to be local ordinances, subject to revision any day. Time is an imaginary space.

We live in a very small spot, and for all we know, there may be millions of other small spots like ours in the millions of other galaxies; in theory, the universe can sprout life any old time it feels like it, anywhere, even though the other parts of our own tiny solar system have turned out to be appallingly, depressingly dead. The near views we have had of Mars, and what we have seen of the surfaces of Jupiter and Venus, are a new cause of sadness in our culture; humans have never before seen, close up, so vast a lifelessness. It is, when you give it a thought, shocking.

It is sometimes made to seem that the sciences have already come most of their allotted distance and we have learned most of what we will ever know. Lord Kelvin is reported to have concluded as much for physics, near the turn of this century, with an announcement that physics was a finished, perfected discipline with only a few odds and ends needing tidying up; soon thereafter came X rays, quantum theory, and relativity—and physics was back at the beginning again.

I believe this is the true nature of science, and I can imagine no terminal point of human inquiry into nature, ever.

Thomas tells us that science has effects not only on technology, but also on human thought. He further discusses some of the implications of the continuing effect of science on our perceptions and attitudes.

WRITING STRATEGIES

You may want to consider the following questions if you are writing about causes and effects.

❑   What important events occurred?
❑   What are the immediate causes of each event?
❑   What are the ultimate causes?

Evaluation

When we organize with evaluation, we show a relationship between values and judgments. Evaluation involves saying whether the subject of evaluation is good or bad or something in between. The words *good* and *bad* or synonyms of relative degrees of goodness and badness appear in evaluations. Most of us make evaluations every day. Someone who said that a meal was *delicious* or that a movie was *terrible* would be making an evaluation.

VALUES

Values are those principles that tell us that something is worthwhile and desirable. Values tell us what we want and what we need. For instance, those possessions that we acquire and keep are usually what we consider to be valuable. Those possessions that we throw away or reject are what we consider to be worthless, without value.

THE STRUCTURE OF EVALUATION

Evaluation when used to organize any piece of writing will have a structure controlled by three elements: the presentation of the subject to be evaluated, the judgment, and the criteria.

The Subject Presented

Whatever we are evaluating must be presented to the reader in some way. That presentation will depend on another pattern of organization: narration, description, or classification. What details we use to present the subject (narrative, descriptive, or classificatory) will affect how the audience perceives the evaluation and, to a certain extent, how we apply the criteria we are using.

THE JUDGMENT

The judgment is the outcome of our evaluation of the subject. The judgment may be positive, negative, or mixed depending on how the subject is viewed in relation to the criteria. Whatever the judgment is, it will reflect the connections we have made between the subject and the values that are controlling the evaluation.

THE CRITERIA

Criteria are the standards by which we make judgments. They are derived from the system of values relevant to the evaluation. These standards may be stated or unstated in the evaluation. But regardless, they are essential to making a judgment. A judgment cannot be made without criteria.

These standards are stated in such a way that they could be applied to other things that are in the same category as the subject being evaluated. In evaluating a particular community college, Austin Community College for instance, we might generate the criteria that a community college is good if it has

> qualified teachers,
> convenient locations,
> adequate library resources,
> low tuition, and
> a broad curriculum.

(Of course, other criteria are possible, but these illustrate the kinds of standards that would be considered in an evaluation.) Notice that these criteria could be used to evaluate another community college, that is, any member of the group that Austin Community College belongs to.

THE EVALUATION POSTULATE

Evaluation can be reduced to a single statement called an evaluation postulate. That statement is a kind of formula that includes those elements essential for any evaluation. Evaluations are usually not reduced to such brief terms, but the evaluation postulate does allow us to see clearly the essential elements of an evaluation. Sometimes it can be helpful to think about an evaluation in terms of its basic structure.

The following pattern can be used to create an evaluation postulate of any evaluation.

If something (the subject) has certain characteristics (the criteria), then it is good or bad (the judgment).

An Example

In 1862 Nathaniel Hawthorne, the author of *The Scarlet Letter*, wrote this evaluation of Abraham Lincoln.

Lincoln

NATHANIEL HAWTHORNE

Of course, there was one other personage, in the class of statesmen, whom I should have been truly mortified to leave Washington without seeing; since (temporarily, at least, and by force of circumstances) he was the man of men. But a private grief had built up a barrier about him, impeding the customary free intercourse of Americans with their chief magistrate; so that I might have come away without a glimpse of his very remarkable physiognomy, save for a semi-official opportunity of which I was glad to take advantage. The fact is, we were invited to annex ourselves, as supernumeraries, to a deputation that was about to wait upon the President, from a Massachusetts whip factory, with a present of a splendid whip.

Our immediate party consisted only of four or five (including Major Ben Perley Poore, with his note-book and pencil), but we were joined by several other persons, who seemed to have been lounging about the precincts of the White House, under the spacious porch, or within the hall, and who swarmed in with us to take the chances of a presentation. Nine o'clock had been appointed as the time for receiving the deputation, and we were punctual to the moment; but not so the President, who sent us word that he was eating breakfast, and would come as soon as he could. His appetite, we were glad to think, must have been a pretty fair one; for we waited about half an hour in one of the ante-chambers, and then were ushered into a reception-room, in one corner of which sat the Secretaries of War and the Treasury, expecting, like ourselves, the termination of the Presidential breakfast. During this interval there were several new additions to our group, one or two of whom were in a working-garb, so that we formed a very miscellaneous collection of people, mostly unknown to each other, and without any common sponsor, but all with an equal right to look our head servant in the face.

By and by there was a little stir on the staircase and in the passageway, and in lounged a tall, loose-jointed figure, of an exaggerated Yankee port and de- meanor, whom (as being about the homeliest man I ever saw, yet by no means repulsive or disagreeable) it was impossible not to recognize as Uncle Abe.

Unquestionably, Western man though he be, and Kentuckian by birth, President Lincoln is the essential representative of all Yankees, and the veri- table specimen, physically, of what the world seems determined to regard as our characteristic qualities. It is the strangest and yet the fittest thing in the jumble of human vicissitudes, that he, out of so many millions, unlooked for, un- selected by any intelligible process that could be based upon his genuine quali- ties, unknown to those who chose him, unsuspected of what endowments may adapt him for his tremendous responsibility, should have found the way open for him to fling his lank personality into the chair of state—where, I presume, it was his first impulse to throw his legs on the council-table, and tell the Cabinet Ministers a story. There is no describing his lengthy awkwardness, nor the uncouthness of his movement; and yet it seemed as if I had been in the habit of seeing him daily, and had shaken hands with him a thousand times in some village street; so true was he to the aspect of the pattern American, though with a certain extravagance which, possibly, I exaggerated still further by the delighted eagerness with which I took it in. If put to guess his calling and livelihood, I should have taken him for a country school-master as soon as anything else. He was dressed in a rusty black frock coat and pantaloons, unbrushed, and worn so faithfully that the suit had adapted itself to the curves and angularities of his figure, and had grown to be an outer skin of the man. His hair was black, still unmixed with gray, stiff, somewhat bushy, and had apparently been acquainted with neither brush nor comb that morning, after the disarrangement of the pillow; and as to a nightcap, Uncle Abe probably knows nothing of such effeminacies. His complexion is dark and sallow, betokening, I fear, an insalubrious atmosphere around the White House; he has thick black eyebrows and an impending brow; his nose is large, and the lines around his mouth are very strongly defined.

The whole physiognomy is as coarse a one as you would meet anywhere in the length and breadth of the States; but, withal, it is redeemed, illuminated, softened, and brightened by a kindly though serious look out of his eyes, and an expression of homely sagacity, that seems weighted with rich results of village experience. A great deal of native sense; no bookish cultivation, no refinement; honest at heart, and thoroughly so, and yet, in some sort, sly—at least, endowed with a sort of tact and wisdom that are akin to craft, and would impel him, I think, to take an antagonist in flank, rather than to make a bull-run at him right in front. But, on the whole, I like this sallow, queer, sagacious visage, with the homely human sympathies that warmed it; and, for my small share in the matter, would as lief have Uncle Abe for a ruler as any man whom it would have been practicable to put in his place.

Immediately on his entrance the President accosted our member of Congress, who had us in charge, and, with a comical twist of his face made some jocular remark about the length of his breakfast. He then greeted us all round, not waiting for an introduction, but shaking and squeezing everybody's hand with the utmost cordiality, whether the individual's name was announced to him or not. His manner towards us was wholly without pretence, but yet had a kind of natural dignity, quite sufficient to keep the forwardest of us from clapping him on the shoulder and asking him for a story. A mutual acquaintance being established, our leader took the whip out of its case, and began to read the address of presentation. The whip was an exceedingly long one, its handle wrought in ivory (by some artist in the Massachusetts State Prison, I believe), and ornamented with a medallion of the President, and other equally beautiful devices; and along its whole length there was a succession of golden bands and ferrules. The address was shorter than the whip, but equally well made, consisting chiefly of an explanatory description of these artistic designs, and closing with a hint that the gift was a suggestive and emblematic one, and that the President would recognize the use to which such an instrument should be put.

This suggestion gave Uncle Abe rather a delicate task in his reply, because, slight as the matter seemed, it apparently called for some declaration, or intimation, or faint foreshadowing of policy in reference to the conduct of the war, and the final treatment of the Rebels. But the President's Yankee aptness and not-to-be-caughtness stood him in good stead, and he jerked or wiggled himself out of the dilemma with an uncouth dexterity that was entirely in character; although, without his gesticulation of eye and mouth—and especially the flourish of the whip, with which he imagined himself touching a pair of fat horses—I doubt whether his words would be worth recording, even if I could remember them. The gist of the reply was, that he accepted the whip as an emblem of peace, not punishment; and, this great affair over, we retired out of the presence in high good humor, only regretting that we could not have seen the President sit down and fold up his legs (which is said to be a most extraordinary spectacle), or have heard him tell one of those delectable stories for which he is so celebrated. A good many of them are afloat upon the common talk of Washington, and are certainly the aptest, pithiest, and funniest little things imaginable; though, to be sure, they smack of the frontier freedom, and would not always bear repetition in a drawing-room, or on the immaculate page of the *Atlantic*.

Good Heavens! what liberties have I been taking with one of the potentates of the earth, and the man on whose conduct more important consequences depend than on that of any other historical personage of the century! But with whom is an American citizen entitled to take a liberty, if not with his own chief magistrate? However, lest the above allusions to President Lincoln's little peculiarities (already well known to the country and to the world) should be misinterpreted, I deem it proper to say a word or two in regard to him, of unfeigned respect and measurable confidence. He is evidently a man of keen faculties, and, what is still more to the purpose, of powerful character. As to his integrity, the people have that intuition of it which is never deceived. Before he actually entered upon his great office, and for a considerable time afterwards, there is no reason to suppose that he adequately estimated the gigantic task about to be imposed on him, or, at least, had any distinct idea how it was to be managed; and I presume there may have been more than one veteran politician who proposed to himself to take the power out of President Lincoln's hands into his own, leaving our honest friend only the public responsibility for the good or ill success of the career. The extremely imperfect development of his statesmanly qualities, at that period, may have justified such designs. But the President is teachable by events, and has now spent a year in a very arduous course of education; he has a flexible mind, capable of much expansion, and convertible towards far loftier studies and activities than those of his early life; and if he came to Washington a backwoods humorist, he has already transformed himself into as good a statesman (to speak moderately) as his prime minister.

Hawthorne's evaluation presents his subject Abraham Lincoln in several different ways, using several different patterns of organization. He describes Lincoln as "a tall, loose-jointed figure" and as "the homeliest man" he as ever seen. He talks further about his "awkwardness" and "the uncouthness of his movement." Finally Hawthorne makes the physical description even more detailed when he refers to Lincoln's hair, "black, still unmixed with gray, stiff, somewhat bushy," to his "thick black eyebrows," and to his large nose. Overall he regards Lincoln's appearance as "coarse." In contrast to those rather negative features, Hawthorne says that he has a "serious look," "an expression of homely sagacity," and a "great deal of native sense." In addition, to the physical descriptions, Hawthorne narrates the events surrounding his meeting the president. When Lincoln is presented with the gift of a whip from a Massachusetts whip factory, we discover that he is quick witted and diplomatic.

Toward the end of the evaluation, Hawthorne makes his judgment of Lincoln and reveals his "unfeigned respect" for and "confidence" in the president, remarking on Lincoln's "powerful character" and "his integrity." Finally, he observes that the president had become a "good statesman." These judgments are based on criteria that most people would agree are valid for measuring the performance of a political leader.

VARIATIONS IN EVALUATION

A change of purpose will create a different evaluation. As we saw in Chapter 1, expressive writing involves an articulation of a value system, so the potential for evaluation is always there. Persuasion, too, often involves using social and cultural values to convince the reader of the validity of a claim.

EXPRESSIVE EVALUATION

In expressive evaluations the criteria are often unstated. Because the writer of self-expression is defining the self at least partially in terms of a value system, the statement of values is usually inextricably intertwined with the identity of the writer.

AN EXAMPLE

After surrendering to U.S. troops in 1832, Black Hawk, chief of the Sauk tribe in the Midwest, delivered this speech. He evaluates himself, the Indians, and white men.

Black Hawk's Farewell Address

BLACK HAWK

You have taken me prisoner with all my warriors. I am much grieved, for I expected, if I did not defeat you, to hold out much longer, and give you more trouble before I surrendered. I tried hard to bring you into ambush, but your last general understands Indian fighting. The first one was not so wise. When I saw that I could not beat you by Indian fighting, I determined to rush on you, and fight you face to face. I fought hard. But your guns were well aimed. The bullets flew like birds in the air, and whizzed by our ears like the wind through the trees in the winter. My warriors fell around me; it began to look dismal. I saw my evil day at hand. The sun rose dim on us in the morning, and at night it sunk in a dark cloud, and looked like a ball of fire. That was the last sun that shone on Black Hawk. His heart is dead, and no longer beats quick in his bosom. He is now a prisoner to the white men; they will do with him as they wish. But he can stand torture, and is not afraid of death. He is no coward. Black Hawk is an Indian.

He has done nothing for which an Indian ought to be ashamed. He has fought for his countrymen, the squaws and papooses, against white men, who came, year after year, to cheat them and take away their lands. You know the cause of our making war. It is known to all white men. They ought to be ashamed of it. The white men despise the Indians, and drive them from their homes. But the Indians are not deceitful. The white men speak bad of the Indian, and look at him spitefully. But the Indian does not tell lies; Indians do not steal.

An Indian who is as bad as the white men could not live in our nation; he would be put to death, and eaten up by the wolves. The white men are bad schoolmasters; they carry false looks, and deal in false actions; they smile in the face of the poor Indian to cheat him; they shake them by the hand to gain their confidence, to make them drunk, to deceive them, and to ruin our wives. We told them to let us alone, and keep away from us; but they followed on, and beset our paths, and they coiled themselves among us, like the snake. They poisoned us by their touch. We were not safe. We lived in danger. We were becoming like them, hypocrites and liars, adulterers, lazy drones, all talkers, and no workers.

We looked up to the Great Spirit. We went to our great father. We were encouraged. His great council gave us fair words and big promises; but we got no satisfaction. Things were growing worse. There were no deer in the forest. The opossum and beaver were fled; the springs were drying up, and our squaws and papooses without victuals to keep them from starving; we called a great council, and built a large fire. The spirit of our fathers arose and spoke to us to avenge our wrongs and die. We all spoke before the council fire. It was warm and pleasant. We set up the war-whoop, and dug up the tomahawk; our knives were ready, and the heart of Black Hawk swelled high in his bosom when he led his warriors to his duty. His father will meet him there, and commend him.

> Black Hawk is a true Indian, and disdains to cry like a woman. He feels for his wife, his children, and his friends. But he does not care for himself. The white men do not scalp the head; but they do worse—they poison the heart; it is not pure with them. His countrymen will not be scalped, but they will, in a few years, become like the white men, so that you can't trust them, and there must be, as in the white settlements, nearly as many officers as men, to take care of them and keep them in order.
>
> Farewell, my nation! Black Hawk tried to save you, and avenge your wrongs. He drank the blood of some of the whites. He has been taken prisoner, and his plans stopped. He can do no more. He is near his end. His sun is setting, and he will rise no more. Farewell to Black Hawk.

This speech illustrates what evaluation looks like with an expressive purpose. Based on the criteria that people are good if they are honest, brave, and hard working, Black Hawk makes judgments about white men and Indians. He says that "the Indian does not tell lies; Indians do not steal," and that any "Indian who is as bad as the white men could not live in our nation. . . ." Further he calls white men "bad schoolmasters" who "carry false looks," "deal in false actions," and "cheat" the Indian. He evaluates himself and gives a self-definition when he says, "Black Hawk is a true Indian. . . ." In this speech the self-expression is achieved through an evaluation of white and Indian culture.

LITERARY EVALUATION

The writer of literary evaluation tends to engage in satire and humor and often has a persuasive intent as well.

AN EXAMPLE

Twain creates a humorous parody of the advice adults frequently offer to young people.

Advice to Youth

MARK TWAIN

Being told I would be expected to talk here, I inquired what sort of a talk I ought to make. They said it should be something suitable to youth—something didactic, instructive, or something in the nature of good advice. Very well. I have a few things in my mind which I have often longed to say for the instruction of the young, for it is in one's tender early years that such things will best take root and be most enduring and most valuable. First, then, I will say to you, my young friends—and I say it beseechingly, urgingly—

Always obey your parents, when they are present. This is the best policy in the long run, because if you don't they will make you. Most parents think they know better than you do, and you can generally make more by humoring that superstition than you can by acting on your own better judgment.

Be respectful to your superiors, if you have any, also to strangers, and sometimes to others. If a person offend you, and you are in doubt as to whether it was intentional or not, do not resort to extreme measures; simply watch your chance and hit him with a brick. That will be sufficient. If you shall find that he had not intended any offense, come out frankly and confess yourself in the wrong when you struck him; acknowledge it like a man and say you didn't mean to. Yes, always avoid violence; in this age of charity and kindliness, the time has gone by for such things. Leave dynamite to the low unrefined.

Go to bed early, get up early—this is wise. Some authorities say get up with the sun; some others say get up with one thing, some with another. But a lark is really the best thing to get up with. It gives you a splendid reputation with everybody to know that you get up with the lark; and if you get the right kind of a lark, and work at him right, you easily train him to get up at half past nine, every time—it is no trick at all.

Now as to the matter of lying. You want to be very careful about lying; otherwise you are nearly sure to get caught. Once caught, you can never again be, in the eyes of the good and the pure, what you were before. Many a young person has injured himself permanently through a single clumsy and illfinished lie, the result of carelessness born of incomplete training. Some authorities hold that the young ought not to lie at all. That, of course, is putting it rather stronger than necessary; still, while I cannot go quite so far as that, I do maintain, and I believe I am right, that the young ought to be temperate in the use of this great art until practice and experience shall give them that confidence, elegance, and precision which alone can make the accomplishment graceful and profitable. Patience, diligence, painstaking attention to detail—these are the requirements; these, in time, will make the student perfect; upon these, and upon these only, may he rely as the sure foundation for future eminence. Think what tedious years of study, thought, practice, experience, went to the equipment of that peerless old master who was able to impose upon the whole world the lofty and sounding maxim that "truth is mighty and will prevail"—the most majestic compound fracture of fact which any of woman born has yet achieved. For the history of our race, and each individual's experience, are sown thick with evidence that a truth is not hard to kill and that a lie told well is immortal. There is in Boston a monument of the man who discovered anaesthesia; many people are aware, in these latter days, that that man didn't discover it at all, but stole the discovery from another man. Is this truth mighty, and will it prevail? Ah no, my hearers, the monument is made of hardy material, but the lie it tells will outlast it a million years. An awkward, feeble, leaky lie is a thing which you ought to make it your unceasing study to avoid; such a lie as that has no more real permanence than an average truth. Why, you might as well tell the truth at once and be done with it. A feeble, stupid, preposterous lie will not live two years—except it be a slander upon somebody. It is indestructible, then, of course, but that is no merit of yours. A final word: begin your practice of this gracious and beautiful art early—begin it now. If I had begun earlier, I could have learned how.

Never handle firearms carelessly. The sorrow and suffering that have been caused through the innocent but heedless handling of firearms by the young! Only four days ago, right in the next farmhouse to the one where I am spending the summer, a grandmother, old and gray and sweet, one of the loveliest spirits in the land, was sitting at her work, when her young grandson crept in and got down an old, battered, rusty gun which had not been touched for many years and was supposed not to be loaded, and pointed it at her, laughing and threatening to shoot. In her fright she ran screaming and pleading toward the door on the other side of the room; but as she passed him he placed the gun almost against her very breast and pulled the trigger! He had supposed it was not loaded. And he was right—it wasn't. So there wasn't any harm done. It is the only case of that kind I ever heard of. Therefore, just the same, don't you meddle with old unloaded firearms; they are the most deadly and unerring things that have ever been created by man. You don't have to take any pains at all with them; you don't have to have a rest, you don't have to have any sights on the gun, you don't have to take aim, even. No, you just pick out a relative and bang away, and you are sure to get him. A youth who can't hit a cathedral at thirty yards with a Gatling gun in three-quarters of an hour, can take up on old empty musket and bag his grandmother every time, at a hundred. Think what Waterloo would have been if one of the armies had been boys armed with old muskets supposed not to be loaded, and the other army had been composed of their female relations. The very thought of it makes one shudder.

There are many sorts of books; but good ones are the sort for the young to read. Remember that. They are a great, an inestimable, an unspeakable means of improvement. Therefore be careful in your selection, my young friends; be very careful; confine yourselves exclusively to Robertson's Sermons, Baxter's *Saint's Rest, The Innocents Abroad*, and works of that kind.

But I have said enough. I hope you will treasure up the instructions which I have given you, and make them a guide to your feet and a light to your understanding. Build your character thoughtfully and painstakingly upon these precepts, and by and by, when you have got it built, you will be surprised and gratified to see how nicely and sharply it resembles everybody else's.

Mark Twain, in this literary evaluation, entertains the reader by offering unexpected bits of advice. The style of the writing is didactic and at first seems to contain the kind of advice we might expect an adult to give to a young person. But as we read, we discover that every moral truism we anticipate is contradicted. In this way Twain delights us with humorous, outlandish twists on the expected. He reveals the true subject of the evaluation at the end of the essay. Rather than evaluating the behavior of young people, as he maintains at the beginning, he is really evaluating the behavior of everyone else. He makes this clear in the last sentence when he suggests that if young people will follow his contradictory advice, then they will "be surprised and gratified to see how nicely and sharply" their behavior "resembles everybody else's." At this point we become aware of a secondary persuasive purpose at work, a satire on human behavior.

PERSUASIVE EVALUATION

Evaluations tend toward persuasion, so persuasion is often a part of an evaluation no matter what other purpose the writer has. Any evaluation will become persuasive if an imperative is added, as in the following statement: this thing (subject) is good (judgment), so you should try it (persuasive assertion).

AN EXAMPLE

The following student essay offers a persuasive evaluation of a restaurant.

A Rare Find

CHRIS WOFFENDEN

Living in Texas, it's never hard to find a Tex-Mex restaurant around. You run into them on just about every other street corner it seems. I have eaten at many Tex-Mex joints, and I'll say that most of them have been decent. *Decent.* It's very rare that you come across a restaurant that captures the taste of Mom's home cooking, whether it's Mexican food, Chinese, or just a plain ol' steak house. It was only by chance that I found this perfect Tex-Mex restaurant. It's the closest thing to my mother's cooking I have ever tasted. It's a little pink house on East Seventh Street, just east of the Interstate, across from the downtown area. Angie's Mexican Restaurant delivers a combination of service, taste, and atmosphere like no other restaurant I have ever set foot in. Let me tell you about the magic that is Angie's.

The service is superb. As soon as you walk through the door, you are greeted with a smile by one of about five or six servers who work there. Having such a small wait staff all but eliminates the possibility of getting bad service. I know each one of them and have always been treated like a special guest. Barring weekday lunch hours, it never takes more than about five minutes to get a table. The staff is fast and friendly and does a wonderful job of keeping your glass full and a smile on your face with pleasant conversation. Even the busboy there is a delight to talk to. Each time I eat there, he comes out from the back room and says hello and chats with me a bit, usually about cars or football. I have never been to a restaurant with a staff that, as a whole, is as friendly as Angie's. They make you feel as if you are a long-lost cousin visiting from a distant city. They are open every day from 7 a.m. to 4 p.m. and are closed on Tuesday. They are just as happy to see you at ten 'til 4 as they are at opening time.

Once you are seated, you'll get started with chips and salsa, a custom at just about any Mexican restaurant. But this is not your average salsa. Oh, no. It is a perfect blend of tomatoes, jalapenos, and onions that'll set your mouth on fire. After munching on the appetizer and sipping your iced tea for a short time, you get to the real good stuff. There are a number of platters to choose from including tacos, chalupas, and enchiladas. Any of these delicious dishes come with corn tortillas that are made right in the back of the restaurant every day. If you choose the enchilada or taco platter, you have a choice of beef or chicken, either of which are perfectly seasoned with salt, ground cominos, and diced bell pepper. The chalupas are pretty messy, but definitely worth the wash your hands will need afterward. All platters are served with beans, rice, and two hot flour tortillas. My personal favorite is the beef enchilada platter. When the plate comes, it is steaming hot, and the cheese melts in with the chili sauce to form an enchilada base that has no equal. For dessert you can choose from any of the common goodies they serve like cobbler, pecan pie, etc. But if you want to finish the meal off right, have a bowl of homemade flan. It's a custard-like dessert topped with a vanilla liqueur. Simply delicious! By the way, anything on the menu is all available for take-out if you are in a rush, and you can pay by check or credit card if you are short on cash.

As you sit, savoring each bite of this authentic Mexican food, you will also be treated to traditional Mexican surroundings. The limited space of Angie's always gives me a feeling that I'm back home eating freshly cooked food at my mom's small kitchen table. The tables are situated fairly close together giving it a very intimate setting. The building is an old house that was converted into a restaurant, so it's got a very homey feel. It's not fancy, but it is very clean and attractive. And if, for some reason, you do not care for the interior of Angie's, you can request outdoor seating which is situated right under a cluster of nice shade trees. They always have beautiful Mexican music playing, ' and the sound of accordion and Spanish guitar fill the room. There is nothing quite like feasting on a tasty Mexican meal and listening to Ana Gabriel while you enjoy every last morsel. On one of the walls in the restaurant there is a mural of the skyline of Austin that was painted by an employee there. Looking out the west window, you have a beautiful view of the real Austin skyline. On the ceiling, there are paintings of the constellations, which may sound a bit strange. But all these things combine to put forth a very unpretentious setting that is very relaxing.

A few days ago, some friends of mine came into town and were in the mood for some good Mexican cooking. Since my mother lives in Abilene, the choice was clear. Without disagreement, we decided on Angie's not only for the excellent food, but also for the stellar service and comfortable setting. So, if you are ever in the mood for authentic Mexican food and you're in the downtown area, give Angie's a try. Heck, even if you aren't downtown, make the trip. You won't be disappointed.

Chris Woffenden's evaluation supports his persuasive claim that the reader should "give Angie's a try." The evaluation, based on three criteria (service, taste, and atmosphere), develops the persuasive argument. The descriptive and narrative details show how the restaurant meets the criteria. In addition, those details create both rational and emotional appeals. The writer's account of his own experiences in the restaurant creates a personal appeal.

REFERENTIAL EVALUATION

Criteria in referential evaluations are derived by objective means. Writers of referential evaluations will need to consider the necessity of validating the criteria they use or at least making sure that there is a general agreement about the validity of the criteria used.

AN EXAMPLE

This essay evaluates one of the classic novels in American literature.

Why "Huckleberry Finn" is a Great World Novel

LAURIAT LANE, JR.

Of all forms of literature, the novel is in many ways the hardest to describe with any precision. Its relative newness as a form and its varied and complex nature combine to make this so. Whenever we try to view such a full and living book as *The Adventures of Huckleberry Finn*, some of it always escapes our gaze. In fact, apart from its mere physical presence, paper, ink, glue, covers, and so forth, it is often easiest to assume that the novel does not exist at all, but only the experience of reading it. Each time we read *Huckleberry Finn* we read a certain book, and each time we read it we read a different book. No one of these books is the real *Huckleberry Finn*; in a sense, they all are.

At the heart of *Huckleberry Finn* lies a story about real human figures with genuine moral and ethical problems and decisions, figures placed in a society which we recognize as having everywhere in it the flavor of authenticity—the whole combination treated, for the most part, as directly and realistically as possible. I would like to move beyond this primary description or definition of *Huckleberry Finn*, however, and suggest that the novel may contain other elements equally important to a full appreciation. I would like to extend the novel in three directions, in space, in time, and in degree: in space, by considering some of the ways in which the book extends beyond its position as one of the masterworks of American fiction and becomes, if the term be allowed, a world novel; in time, by considering how much *Huckleberry Finn* resembles a literary form much older than the novel, the epic poem; and in degree, by considering just how much *Huckleberry Finn* transcends its position as a realistic novel and takes on the forms and qualities of allegory.

I

A world novel may be defined as that kind of novel whose importance in its own literature is so great, and whose impact on its readers is so profound and far-reaching, that it has achieved world-wide distinction. In the total picture of world literature, such a novel stands out as a work always to be reckoned with. The world novel, however, achieves its position not only through its importance but also because of its essential nature. And in discussing *Huckleberry Finn* as a world novel I shall deal not so much with this importance, as measured by permanent popularity and influence, as with the special qualities *Huckleberry Finn* has in common with certain other world novels.

The first real novel and the first world novel is, by almost universal consent, Cervantes' *The Adventures of Don Quixote*. The most important thing which *Don Quixote* has bequeathed to the novels after it (apart of course from the all-important fact of there being such a thing as a novel at all) is the theme which is central to *Don Quixote* and to almost every great novel since, the theme of appearance versus reality. This theme is also central to *Huckleberry Finn*.

Even on the simplest plot level the world of *Huckleberry Finn* is one of deception. The very existence of Huck at all is a continual deception—he is supposed to be dead. This falseness in his relations with the world at large merely reflects the difference between his standards and those of the outside world. Huck's truth and the truth of the world are diametrically opposed. Throughout the novel his truth is always cutting through the surfaces of the world's appearance and learning the contrary reality beneath. At the climax Huck tells himself, "You can't pray a lie—I found that out." That is to say, the lie of appearance is always far different from the truth of reality, and to the truly heroic and individual conscience no amount of self-delusion can ever bridge the gap lying between.

In the final section of the book, the theme of appearance versus reality reaches almost philosophical proportions. Both because of the way in which

Jim's escape is carried out and because of the underlying fact of there being no need for him to escape at all, the situation is one of total dramatic and moral irony. At the end, however, Twain relaxes the tone, straightens out the plot complications, and lets the moral issue fade away. He avoids, in fact, the logical conclusion to the kind of disorder he has introduced into his world-in-fiction, a world in which the distinction between appearance and reality has, from the reader's point of view, been lost forever. For if we cannot tell appearance from reality, if the two do become totally confused and impossible to distinguish, the only answer can be the one Twain eventually came to in his most pessimistic work, *The Mysterious Stranger*; that all is illusion, and nothing really exists. In *Huckleberry Finn*, Twain does not yet reach this point of despair. By centering his action within the essentially balanced mind of the boy, Huck, he keeps his hold on reality and manages to convey his hold to the reader. But the main issue of the novel, between the way things seem and the way they are, is nevertheless one that trembles in the balance almost up to the final page.

Huckleberry Finn also gains its place as a world novel by its treatment of one of the most important events of life, the passage from youth into maturity. The novel is a novel of education. Its school is the school of life rather than of books, but Huck's education is all the more complete for that reason. Huck, like so many other great heroes of fiction—Candide, Tom Jones, Stephen Dedalus, to mention only a few—goes forth into life that he may learn. One of the central patterns of the novel is the progress of his learning.

Yet another theme which *Huckleberry Finn* shares with most of the world's great novels is that of man's obsession with the symbols of material wealth. The book opens with an account of the six thousand dollars Huck got from the robber's hoard and ends on the same note. Throughout the intervening pages gold is shown to be not only the mainspring of most human action, but usually the only remedy mankind can offer to atone for the many hurts they are forever inflicting on one another. And as Mr. Lionel Trilling has remarked, in a certain sense all fiction is ultimately about money.

The world novel may also convey a total vision of the nation or people from which it takes its origin. It not only addresses the world in a language which is uniquely the language of that nation or people, but it brings before the view of the world at large many character types which are especially national. In *Huckleberry Finn* we recognize in Jim, in the Duke and the Dauphin, in Aunt Sally, and in Huck himself, typically American figures whom Twain has presented for inspection by the world's eye. *Huckleberry Finn* gains much of its justification as a world novel from the fact that it is an intensely American novel as well.

II

In his essay on "The Poetic Principle" Poe remarks that "no very long poem will ever be popular again." In part, no doubt, Poe bases this remark on his own special definition of poetry. But he is also recognizing that during the eighteenth and nineteenth centuries the epic poem was gradually dying out as a literary form. Or, to be more precise, it was gradually merging with another form, the novel. Much of the poetic form of the epic came from the requirements of oral rendition; with the invention of printing, these requirements vanished. More and more writers gradually turned to prose fiction as the appropriate form to accomplish what had once been accomplished in the epic poem. Some novelists, such as Fielding or Scott, drew quite consciously on epic tradition; other novelists and novels, by a more indirect drawing on tradition, took over some of the qualities originally associated with epic poetry.

One quality of the epic poem is simply scope. Some novels confine themselves to treating exhaustively and analytically a limited segment of life. But others seem to be constantly trying to gather all life into their pages and to say, within a single story, all the important things that need to be said. Such novels derive much of their strength from the epic tradition, and *Huckleberry Finn* is such a novel. It has geographical scope. It ranges down the length of the great river and cuts through the center of a whole nation. As it does so, it gains further scope by embracing all levels of society, from the lowest to the highest. And it has the added scope of its own varying qualities, ranging from high comedy to low farce, from the poetic tranquility of life on the raft to the mob violence and human depravity always waiting on the shore.

Epic poetry gives literary form to the national destiny of the people for whom it is written. *Huckleberry Finn* gives literary form to many aspects of the national destiny of the American people. The theme of travel and adventure is characteristically American, and in Twain's day it was still a reality of everyday life. The country was still very much on the move, and during the novel Huck is moving with it. Huck's movements also embody a desire to escape from the constrictions of civilized society. Such a desire is of course not uniquely American, but during the nineteenth century Americans took it and made it their own. The American of that time could always say, as did Huck at the very end of the story, "I reckon I got to light out for the territory ahead of the rest, because Aunt Sally she's going to adopt me and sivilize me, and I can't stand it. I been there before."

The epic hero is usually an embodiment of some virtue or virtues valued highly by the society from which he has sprung. Huck has many such virtues. He holds a vast store of practical knowledge which makes itself felt everywhere in the story. He knows the river and how to deal with it; and he knows mankind and how to deal with it. And he has the supreme American virtue of never being at a loss for words. In fact Huck, though he still keeps some of the innocence and naiveté of youth, has much in common with one of the greatest epic heroes, Odysseus, the practical man. Jim also has some of the qualities of an epic hero. He has strength and courage, and he possesses the supreme virtue of epic poetry, loyalty. It is part of Twain's irony that in Huck and Jim we have, in one sense, the two halves of an epic hero. In Huck, the skill and canniness; in Jim, the strength and simple loyalty.

In the society along the shore we see traces of other epic values, values which have survived from a more primitive world. The Grangerford-Shepherdson feud strikes the modern reader as a senseless mess, but as Huck says, "There ain't a coward amongst them Shepherdsons—not a one. And there ain't no cowards amongst the Grangerfords either." Huck sees the essential folly behind this courage, but the reader, one degree further removed from the harsh reality, is allowed the luxury of a double vision. Similarly, Colonel Sherburn, destroying a lynching mob merely by the courage of his presence, illustrates another epic theme, the bravery of one against many.

One final quality which *Huckleberry Finn* derives from its epic ancestry is its poetry. The novel is full of poetry. Not just the passages of lyric description, which mark a pause between the main actions and give a heightened and more literary tone just as they often did in the traditional epic, but also the many similes and turns of speech Huck uses, which, if they are not quite Homeric, are certainly unforgettable. And much of the exaggerated language of the frontier world, one not far removed in kind from that of the primitive migrations, is also a natural part of the epic style.

III

Allegory may be defined simply as the representation of one thing in the form of another. A second definition, more germane to literature, is that allegory is a process by which the spiritual is embodied in the physical. To go one step further, the main purpose of allegory is somehow to embody a spiritual action in a physical action. By making a suitable physical object stand for some metaphysical one, or at least for one which cannot be contained in the terms of normal, everyday life, the writer carries out one of the main purposes of all art, which is to bring to its audience, through the representation of real objects, an awareness and knowledge which transcend the limitations of such reality. Allegory, that is, deals primarily with matters of the spirit.

This assumption helps to explain why the great allegories deal either with a physical journey or a physical conflict or both. For a spiritual change, when embodied allegorically, will take the form of a meaningful physical journey through symbolic space. And a spiritual conflict, when embodied allegorically, will take the form of a real physical conflict between significant forces, each of them representing some metaphysical quality.

Although all novels are in a certain sense descended from *Don Quixote*, it is also true that in another sense all novels, and especially English ones, are descended from Bunyan's *Pilgrim's Progress*. The main difference between the allegorical novel as we know it today and Bunyan's narrative of the human soul is that whereas *Pilgrim's Progress* we have an allegory that tends to turn into a novel, in most modern instances we have a novel that tends to turn into an allegory. As the author, whether he be Melville or Mann or Twain, develops and elaborates his original materials, he may become aware of certain meaningful connections which are tending to establish themselves between the physical objects and the physical narrative he is describing and the related spiritual values and conflicts. Drawing on a tradition which has existed for a long time in literature and which is a natural part of the artistic process in any form, the author finds himself writing allegory. And this is what happened to Mark Twain. Writing as he was a great novel, his masterpiece in fact, he organized and related certain physical materials to certain metaphysical conditions so that their relationship became meaningful in a special way—became, in short, allegory.

Huckleberry Finn is the story of a journey, a real journey. If we are to find any meaning in Huck's journey beyond the literal level, we must seek it first in the medium through which Huck journeys, in the great river down which he drifts during much of the story. And Huck's movements take on at least the external form of a basic symbolic pattern, one seen in such poems as Shelley's *Alastor*, Arnold's *The Future*, and Rimbaud's *Bateau Ivre*, a pattern stated most directly in *Prometheus Unbound*, "My soul is an enchanted boat." Implicit in this pattern is the suggestion that the river journey can have a distinctly metaphysical quality, that it can be, in fact, a journey of the soul as well as of the body. This suggestion is not at all arbitrary. Of all forms of physical progression, that of drifting downstream in a boat, or on a raft, is the most passive one possible. The mind under such conditions is lulled, as Huck's mind is, into the illusion that it has lost all contact with reality and is drifting bodilessly through a world of sleep and of dreams. Thus the nakedness of Huck and Jim when they are alone on the raft becomes a symbol of how they have shucked off the excrescences of the real world, their clothes, and have come as close as possible to the world of the spirit.

All journeys, even allegorical ones, must have a goal. What is the goal of Huck's journey? We find the answer in what happens while Huck and Jim float down the river. The pattern is, very simply, one of an ever-increasing engagement of the world of the raft, of the spirit, with the world of the shore, of reality. As the book progresses, more and more Huck tells about events that take place on the banks, and less and less he tells about those that take place out on the river. No matter how hard Huck and Jim try to escape, the real world is always drawing them back into it. Finally, in the Duke and the Dauphin, themselves fleeing for the moment from the harsh reality of the river's shores, the real world invades the world of the raft, and the latter loses forever the dream-like and idyllic quality it has often had for the two voyagers. The climax of Huck's lyric praise of the river comes significantly just before this mood is shattered forever by the arrival of the Duke and Dauphin.

Parallel to this pattern of the ever-increasing engagement of the world of the shore with that of the raft is a pattern which begins with Huck's pretended death, a death which is actual to all the world but Huck and Jim. The symbolic fact of his death accomplished, Huck must find an identity with which he can face the real world. His assumptions of various such identities forms a significant pattern. The various masks he assumes, starting with that of a girl, as far removed from the reality as possible, gradually draw back nearer the truth. Huck's final disguise, as Tom Sawyer, is only slightly removed from his real self.

> When he is about to reveal this real self and is instead taken for Tom, Huck almost recognizes the meaning of his journey. For he says to himself, "But if they was joyful, it warn't nothing to what I was; for it was like being born again, I was so glad to find out who I was."
>
> This, then, is the allegory of *Huckleberry Finn*. Dying symbolically almost at the opening of the novel, Huck journeys through the world of the spirit, ever working out a pattern of increasing involvement with the world of reality and with his own self, both cast aside at the beginning of the journey. Only when he is finally forced to assume this real self in the eyes of the world, through the sudden arrival of Aunt Polly, is he allowed to learn the all-important truth Jim has kept from him throughout the novel, that his Pap, "ain't comin back no mo." We cannot say that Huck has undergone a total initiation and is now fully prepared to take on adulthood, but neither can we doubt that he has undergone a knowledgeful and maturing experience. And at the end of the story he is about to undertake another journey, this time to the west, in search of further experience and further knowledge.

In this essay, Lane evaluates *Huckleberry Finn* by examining it according to several clearly stated criteria: the significance of its themes, its scope, and its allegorical pattern. By analyzing the novel according to these criteria, the author is able to show us why the novel is a great one.

WRITING STRATEGIES

Part of writing an evaluation is choosing words that accurately communicate the judgment you are making. Creating a list of possible words to use to make the judgment can be helpful. Write down the subject of the evaluation and use free association (putting down on paper whatever comes to mind) to create a list of words that express your judgment.

Consider these questions as you create an evaluation.

❏ How is the subject to be evaluated presented to the reader? (What other patterns of organization are used?)
❏ What judgment or judgments are you making about the subject?
❏ What criteria are you using to make the judgment?
❏ How can you defend the criteria?
❏ How does your presentation fit the characteristics of your primary purpose?

PART **3**

Process

Ideas

Details

Focus

Refinement

Ideas

The writing process usually begins before you actually start putting words down. Before you can do anything else, you must have an idea. Depending on the occasion that has prompted your writing, your idea may take one of two different forms: it may be rather vague and undefined, or it may be fairly well focused on a general subject or even on a specific topic. Your use of the techniques suggested in this chapter will vary depending on how far along you are in shaping your topic. If your idea is vague and undefined, you will probably need to use a number of the strategies suggested in this chapter to define the subject a little more clearly. These strategies include using techniques of free association, working with your journal, and doing background research.

If you have already decided on a general subject, you will need to narrow the the scope of the subject so that it is a manageable topic. As your topic becomes more clearly defined, you may still use the techniques suggested in this chapter, but in more definitive way. For instance, you would probably start a free association activity with an explicit focus in mind. Similarly, research, rather than being concerned with general background information, would become more precise in its focus.

FREE ASSOCIATION

One of the most straightforward ways to get ideas is by using one of several different free association activities. These activities allow you to gain access to the creative flow of ideas in your mind.

BRAINSTORMING

Brainstorming is the most unstructured of all free association activities. It can be done individually or in a group. (Group brainstorming has the advantage of bringing a broad range of perspectives to bear on a topic.) Anything goes in brainstorming. You may jot down words and phrases or even draw pictures and doodle. No possible avenue of exploration should be rejected. Brainstorming will open up your mind to whatever resources you have available.

After you have made some notes (10 minutes is usually enough), you can go back and restructure, or you can start over again and explore the subject from a different perspective.

LISTING

Listing is a bit more structured than brainstorming. The advantage is that you can generate quite a lot of relevant information quickly. The list can be totally random, or it can begin from a general subject, of even a specific topic.

An Example of Listing on the Topic of Bird Watching

colors
feathers
shapes of birds—pelicans, woodpeckers . . .
drab colored birds
camouflage
brightly colored birds
mating
feathers for flight
feathers for warmth
structure of the body
how they fly
songs
identifying birds—by songs, by shape, by flight
field guides
notebooks
observing—how to observe, what to look for
habitat—trees, water, ground
habits—breeding, migration, nesting
ecology—range
distribution of birds over the world
classification of birds
evolution

MAPPING

Mapping (also called clustering) allows you to explore your ideas graphically. You simply put an idea down in the middle of a page and then begin to put down associated ideas around it. You can show a number of relationships between the ideas on the page by drawing lines to show connections.

An Example of Mapping on the Topic of Bird Watching

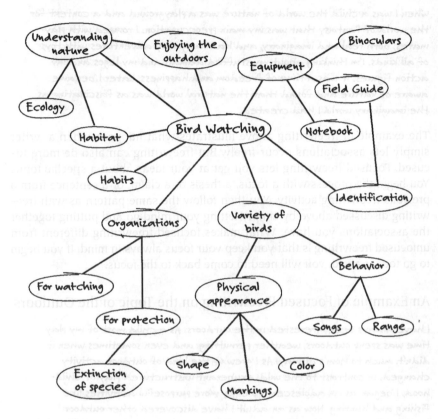

FREEWRITING

Freewriting is, in effect, "talking on paper." It is an attempt to capture in written form the natural, spontaneous flow of conversation. As with other forms of free association, you follow wherever the associations take you, but freewriting is in sentence form. Often, freewriting can open you up to the flow of ideas as no other technique can because freewriting stimulates thinking in terms that can be translated immediately into writing. It can also be a kind of "warmup" to prepare you for writing a draft, or it may even be a part of the initial draft itself. Freewriting is such a versatile technique that you can use it anytime you get stuck and need to start the flow of words again.

An Example of Freewriting

When I was a child the world of nature was a playground and a context for the world of fantasy that was my main preoccupation. I romped with playmates, both real and imaginary, and had imaginary adventures with toys of all kinds. I'm thinking about my stuffed animals and my legos and my action figures. It was a time of freedom and happiness. Later I became aware of nature and found that the natural world was as fascinating as the imaginary world I had created.

The example of freewriting above illustrates what happens when a writer simply lets associations occur freely. But freewriting can also be more focused. Focused freewriting lets you get at your ideas about a specific topic. You begin the process with a focus, a thesis or a claim, or a sentence from a previous freewriting activity. You then follow the same pattern as with freewriting discussed above by simply letting your mind go and putting together the associations you have. What makes focused freewriting different from unfocused freewriting is that you keep your focus always in mind. If you begin to go too far afield, you will need to come back to the focus.

An Example of Focused Freewriting on the Topic of the Outdoors

I have always been interested in the outdoors. As a child most of my play time was spent outdoors, weather permitting, and even sometimes when it didn't, much to Mom's dismay. As I grew up the kind of outdoor activity changed. In contrast to the wild, exuberant unstructured play of childhood, I began as an adolescent to enjoy more purposeful activities like fishing and hunting. Now as an adult I have discovered other outdoor pastimes, less aggressive. These turn out to be both physical and intellectual. Like, last year I took up bird watching. I have found that bird watching fulfills my desire for enjoying the world of nature, while, at the same time allowing me to assemble a body of knowledge about that world.

Focused freewriting can be repeated again and again by *looping* back to another focus. Simply identify a new focus and begin again. The following is an example of a focused freewriting activity that begins with the sentence *last year I took up bird watching* taken from the previous exercise.

Last year I took up bird watching. I guess I have always been a bird watcher to some degree. It is something children do naturally. When we were children, we didn't find it necessary to label ourselves as much as we do when we are adults. I find it necessary to call myself a bird watcher, perhaps as a way of committing to the activity and justifying myself in doing it. If you buy binoculars and a field guide and tramp around in the woods looking for birds, then you must be a bird watcher. I mean, I kind of feel guilty spending all this time and money—so I better have a good reason—like being a bird watcher. But the activity itself should, and does for most people who do it, come from an abiding interest in and a curiosity about the natural environment. Finding and identifying birds in some ways is an excuse for indulging an interest in natural science. For some people it is a hobby; for others, a sport; and for still others, almost a religion. Like Bill who's making a pilgrimage to Alaska to see a bird he's never seen. But bird watchers all share a common bond—a fascination with the working of nature, and birds are perhaps the most fascinating of the earth's fauna: after all, they can actually fly.

You could keep going with this kind of activity by identifying a phrase in the previous exercise and using it as the focus of a new freewriting activity.

THE JOURNAL

Another source of ideas is the journal. Many writers keep personal journals in which they record reactions to what is happening to them, ideas of interest, and explorations of the self. The section on the personal perspective of expressive writing in Chapter 1 explains the characteristics of the journal.

Keeping a personal journal will allow you to experiment with style, explore ideas for your writing assignments, and become more comfortable with writing. Even if your writing instructor doesn't require you to keep a journal, you should consider doing it on your own. You may be surprised at what you discover.

RESEARCH

If you are searching for ideas, casual exploration can help you uncover things that interest you and help you shape your ideas. Watching television, reading the newspaper, surfing the net, or simply talking with friends can all be sources of material to include in your writing projects. This kind of background research can be used as a stimulus for free association or for journal writing. It may help you remember things that you had forgotten. So even if your topic is personal in nature, some background research may be beneficial.

If you already have a subject or a topic in mind, your research will be more focused than it would be if you were doing background research. Gathering information through focused research enables you to explore ideas systematically that are relevant to your topic. Some general sources, like encyclopedias and almanacs, may give you an initial overview of your topic, but chances are you will need to consult other sources, like books on the topic and articles in periodicals.

Research may simply help you understand your topic better, or it may become an integral part of your composition. How you use research information will, of course, depend on your topic, your purpose, and your audience.

NARROWING A SUBJECT

When you first get an idea, you may have a subject that is too broad. You will need to narrow it to a topic that is manageable. Usually, this means making the topic more specific and concrete. You may discover ways to narrow your topic while you are doing free association activities, as you are doing research, or while you are writing in your journal.

Creating a ladder can help you narrow a subject that is too general. Begin with the general subject and list below it more specific and concrete topics.

An Example

> The Environment
> Pollution
> Air Pollution
> Sources of Air Pollution

Each related idea above is more specific than the one above it. *The environment* is a broad concept that suggests related ideas like the general subject *pollution*. *Air pollution* is more specific than *pollution* and more general than *sources of pollution*.

10

Details

nce you have a manageable topic, you will need to add details to it. You may not always know in advance that the topic is manageable until you begin working with it by generating detail. If it is still too broad, you may need to go back and try to narrow it more.

In this part of the writing process, you will be interested in translating your ideas into words. You may have already begun to do that if you used freewriting and journal entries as a way of exploring a topic that were discussed in the previous chapter. Other techniques discussed in this chapter such as asking questions and using specific kinds of elaboration are also helpful techniques that will enable you to generate details.

QUESTIONS

In one sense, writing is answering questions that arise naturally in relation to the topic you are considering. Journalists' questions and logical questions can help you create content for your paper. Your response to questions will determine in part the pattern of organization you will use.

JOURNALISTIC QUESTIONS

In putting together news stories, journalists often rely on a questioning technique to make sure that they have all the facts necessary. They ask who? what? when? where? how? and why?

These questions are especially helpful when your topic is an informative narrative because they will help you achieve the comprehensiveness usually required in informative writing. In other words, if you answer these six questions, you can be sure that all essential information will be included in your paper.

LOGICAL QUESTIONS

Logical questions are those that grow naturally out of the topic. You will notice that the questions in the following lists suggest a number of the patterns of organization discussed in Chapters 5–8.

A Person (e.g., a relative or a celebrity)
What does he or she look like?
What does he or she do?
How does he or she behave?
What is his or her personality like?
What is unusual or notable about him or her?

A Place (e.g., a city or a landmark)
Where is it?
What are its characteristics?
What is it similar to?
How is it unusual?
How old is it?

A Thing (e.g., a car or a painting)
What is it made of?
What are its parts?
How is it used?
What is it similar to?
Where did it come from?

An Event (e.g., an athletic event or the French Revolution)
Where did it happen?
When did it happen?
What happened before and after it?
What caused it?
What is its significance?

A Process (e.g., cooking or working out)
What are its steps?
What is it similar to?
How difficult is it?
What causes it to happen?
What are its consequences?

An Abstraction (e.g., freedom or justice)
What is its definition?
What is its significance?
What is it similar to?

What forms does it take?
What is it related to?

A Problem (e.g., overpopulation or drug abuse)
What causes it?
Why does it occur?
Who or what does it affect?
What are some related problems?
What are some possible solutions?

Questions about Categories

Classification allows you to explore a topic by asking questions about the categories related to your topic. By shifting the basis of classification, you can very often come up with other patterns of classification that you may not have considered initially.

Tree diagrams are useful tools for exploring topics that are organized by classification. The three diagrams that follow are interconnected and illustrate how classification can be used to explore a topic. Look at them and study the connections among them.

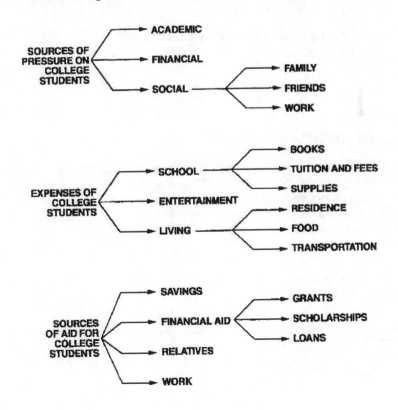

THE OUTLINE

The outline is a common way of representing classification systems. For example, the topic "Kinds of Post-Secondary Education" could be represented by the following tree diagram.

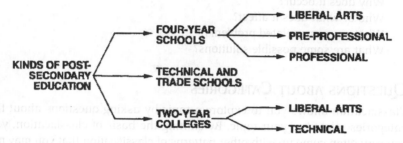

Or the same information could be presented as an outline.

  I.   Universities and Colleges

   A. Liberal Arts

   B. Pre-Professional

   C. Professional

 II.   Business, Industrial, Technical, and Trade Schools

III.   Two-Year Colleges

   A. Liberal Arts

   B. Technical

THE CLASSICAL TOPICS

Greek and Roman philosophers developed the topics as a way to have ready access to arguments. This way of looking at a topic can be useful for persuasive arguments because it enables you to come up with content that is frequently used as support in persuasion. The topics are grouped into five categories with several subcategories for each.

Topic of Definition
Definition by Classification
Definition by Division

Topic of Comparison
Comparison by Similarity
Comparison by Difference
Comparison by Degree

Topic of Relationship
Relationship of Cause and Effect
Relationship of Antecedent and Consequent
Relationship of Contraries and Contradictories

Topic of Circumstance
Circumstance--the Possible and Impossible
Circumstance--Past Fact and Future Fact

Topic of Evidence
Evidence of Authority
Evidence of Testimonial
Evidence of Statistics
Evidence of Maxims and Proverbs
Evidence of Law
Evidence of Precedent

You will notice that a number of the categories are discussed as patterns of organization, particularly classification (Chapter 5), division (Chapter 6), comparison and contrast (Chapter 5), and cause and effect (Chapter 7). Other categories, like maxims and proverbs, are discussed in the Chapter 3, Persuasive Writing.

ELABORATION

Elaboration means that you need to make sure that you have said enough about the topic. There are four ways that you can add depth to any given piece of writing: reiteration, generalization, contrast, and exemplification.

Consider the following sentence:

Air pollution adversely affects almost everybody.

Any sentence that follows it will elaborate in one of four ways mentioned above.

The following sentence is a reiteration or restatement of the same idea:

It creates a problem for our society.

Notice that this sentence is at roughly the same level of generality as the first one. It simply restates in other words, the same idea. This kind of elaboration will not produce the kind of detail that you need in most situations, so it has limitations.

Another way to elaborate on the idea in the first sentence is by generalization:

All environmental problems create problems for our society.

This sentence is more general than the first one, but it too has limitations as a method of elaboration. Usually the most general statement in a paragraph or in a paper will be the main idea and, as a result, will need to be developed by statements that follow it. General statements like this frequently appear at the beginning of a paper as part of the introduction or perhaps at the end as part of the conclusion.

A third way to elaborate on an idea is by contrast, as in the following sentence:

However, the problem is usually worse in large cities.

Developing by contrast takes the ideas off in a different direction.

The fourth way to elaborate on an idea is by exemplification, as in this sentence:

On days when the levels are high, especially in the summer, some people cannot engage in outdoor activities.

This sentence is more specific than the first one. It gives a specific example of the idea in the first sentence. Exemplification is the most common method of elaborating detail. Writing that moves back and forth between general and specific statements is usually easier for the reader to follow.

RESEARCH

At this stage in the process if your paper includes research, you will need to identify specific sources that you intend to use in your paper. You will also need to look for information in those sources that you can incorporate into your paper. Identifying possible quotations and paraphrases will help you decide if you need to do additional research, identify more sources, and collect more information. At this point the process is still quite fluid and you can still change directions if the initial draft proves to be unmanageable.

THE INITIAL DRAFT

An initial draft is a first attempt to put ideas into words in a way that roughly approximates what the final paper will be like. It may begin as a freewriting activity, but will probably be a bit more unified.

As you write the rough draft, you will become aware of an emerging main idea. Depending on the purpose, the main idea will be a self-definition (expressive writing), a theme (literary writing), a claim (persuasive writing), or a thesis (referential writing). (See the discussion of purpose in the introductory chapter.) If the main idea is actually stated in the paper, it will be in the form of a generalization.

The nature of an initial draft will vary from person to person and from paper to paper for the same writer. At times an initial draft will be more highly developed than at others depending on how familiar the writer is with the topic and under what circumstances the paper is being produced.

An Example

Take a look at the following passage:

> Look at the problems with the environment. Like air pollution. Air pollution adversely affects almost everybody. Just look at the smog that covers our cities like a blanket. It's stifling. Smoke stacks are belching out toxic wastes. On bad smog days, I can hardly breath. Fish are dying in the oceans. We should really try to do something about it before it destroys the earth. I mean, this is a serious problem that many people aren't even aware of. Acid rain kills trees in the forests.

This passage from an initial draft represents the writer's effort to get something down in writing. The writer reflects some personal experiences by saying, "I can hardly breath," as well as showing values by saying, "I mean, this is a serious problem." These examples reflect the writer's initial conception of purpose. The style is natural and conversational, and so we might assume that the writing is going to be controlled by an expressive purpose. However, a persuasive intent has caused the writer to characterize the issue as a "problem" and to make an appeal to "do something about it." An awareness of the potential audience is revealed by the sentence, "Air pollution adversely affects almost everybody."

11

Focus

Although you may engage in focusing activities at all stages of of the writing process, usually you will do more of it in the intermediate drafts. After all, you can't really focus ideas, structure details, and clarify points if you don't have something to work with. This focusing can be explained by three concepts: clarity, unity, and coherence.

CLARITY

Clarity means that the individual sentences and the ideas presented are clear to the reader. As you are drafting, especially the initial draft, you may create sentences that are not as clear as they could be. As you are revising your work, you will need to be sensitive so that all sentences are clear to the reader.

Although a great many things can go wrong with a sentence, and you may need to consult a handbook of writing for some of them, often unclear sentences can be corrected by simply reading your work aloud. Sometimes we fall into traps by trying to impress the reader with words and phrases we may not feel comfortable with. Try first to communicate your ideas clearly and simply. Save stylistic niceties for later drafts once you have said what you want to say.

UNITY

Unity means that everything included in a piece of writing relates to the main idea (the self-definition in expressive writing, the theme in literary writing, the claim in persuasive writing, or the thesis in referential writing). Any sentence that isn't related to the main idea in some way will distract the reader.

In addition, each paragraph in a piece of writing will have a main idea, sometimes called a topic sentence. Each sentence in the paragraph should be related to that topic sentence.

Notice how the writer of the following passage maintains unity:

That sandwich man I'd replaced had little chance of getting his job back. I went bellowing up and down those train aisles. I sold sandwiches, coffee, candy, cake, and ice cream as fast as the railroad's commissary department could supply them. It didn't take me a week to learn that all you had to do was give white people a show and they'd buy anything you offered them. It was like popping your shoeshine rag. The dining car waiters and Pullman porters knew it too, and they faked their Uncle Tomming to get bigger tips. We were in that world of Negroes who are both servants and psychologists, aware that white people are so obsessed with their own importance that they will pay liberally, even dearly, for the impression of being catered to and entertained.

—Malcolm X, with the assistance of Alex Haley,
The Autobiography of Malcolm X

The first six sentences in this passage lead up to and contribute to our understanding of the paragraph's main idea stated in the last sentence.

COHERENCE

Coherence means that the sentences are connected to each other in a natural way and that the movement from one sentence to the next is smooth and easy for the reader to follow. Coherence can be increased in three ways: by using transitional words and phrases, by using pronouns, and by repeating key words and phrases.

TRANSITIONS

Transitional words and phrases show relationships between sentences and ideas. Typically, they appear at the beginning of a sentence and indicate what kind of relationship it has to sentences that preceded it. Some commonly used transitions and their functions follow:

To indicate an addition: *again, and, also, finally, furthermore, in addition, likewise, moreover, next, second, similarly, then*

To introduce a contrast: *but, conversely, however, instead, or, nevertheless, nor, on the contrary, on the other hand, still*

To mark a conclusion: *accordingly, as a result, consequently, in conclusion, in other words, then, therefore, thus*

To introduce an example: *for example, for instance, in other words, namely, that is, thus*

Notice how transitions are used in the following example:

In all our literary experience there are two kinds of response. There is the direct experience of the work itself, while we're reading a book or seeing a play, especially for the first time. The experience is uncritical, or rather pre-critical, so it's not infallible. If our experience is limited, we can be roused to enthusiasm or carried away by something that we can later see to have been second-rate or even phony. Then there is the conscious, critical response we make after we've finished reading or left the theatre, where we compare what we've experienced with other things of the same kind, and form a judgment of value and proportion on it. This critical response, with practice, gradually makes our pre-critical responses more sensitive and accurate, or improves our taste, as we say. But behind our responses to individual works, there's a bigger response to our literary experience as a whole, as a total possession.
—Northrop Frye, *The Educated Imagination*

Frye has used three transitions (*so*, *then*, and *but*) to help maintain coherence. Especially important is his use of the word *then* to mark the second of the two kinds of response.

Pronouns

Pronouns will help you achieve coherence in papers because they tie together the pronouns and the words they refer back to.

Notice how pronouns are used to create coherence in the following passage:

No matter how far-ranging some of the mental probes that man has philosophically devised, by his own created nature he is forced to hold the specious and emerging present and transform it into words. The words are startling in their immediate effectiveness, but at the same time they are always finally imprisoning because man has constituted himself a prison keeper. He does so out of no conscious intention, but because for immediate purposes he has created an unnatural world of his own, which he calls the cultural world, and in which he feels at home. It defines his needs and allows him to lay a small immobilizing spell upon the nearer portions of his universe. Nevertheless, it transforms that universe into a cosmic prison house which is no sooner mapped than man feels its inadequacy and his own.

—Loren Eiseley, *The Invisible Pyramid*

In this passage Eiseley uses twelve personal pronouns to refer to the word *man*. He uses the word *it* three times, once to refer to the word *present* and twice to refer to the word *world*. Finally, he uses the words *they* and *their* to refer to the word *words*.

REPETITION

Although the repetition of words can be monotonous if used clumsily, when it is used skillfully, it can help achieve coherence.

Notice how repetition is used in the following passage:

Our lives are completely dominated by the fundamental rhythms. My breathing, my pulse, my unconscious processes of diges-tion, my hearing, my eyesight, my sense of touch, my speech, my thought—all are matters of rhythm. Life is governed by the rhythms. The female animal has rhythmic periods of fertility. The sex act of fertilization is rhythmic. Birth is accomplished in rhythmic labor. And all the rhythmic processes in us, pulse to speech, are a part of growth, maturity, life's continuation. When they cease, a unit of life has come to its physical end. When my pulse stops, I die. But my progeny, in whom the rhythm continues, live on, the next step, the next beat, in the rhythm of life.

—Hal Borland, *What We Save Now*

Borland uses the repetition of forms of the word *rhythm* nine times. In this passage it does not seem to be excessive, but rather allows the reader to see the connections more clearly.

AN EXAMPLE

Notice how the following passage illustrates all three techniques of achieving coherence:

The good educator is very serious but also very sensible. And somewhere in his soul there is a saving lightness. He understands, to begin with, the meaning of a recent remark: "Not everything can be learned." Some things are never taught; they are simply known. Other things cannot in the nature of things be known, either by student or by teacher. And then there is that endless series of know-able things only a few of which can be bestowed upon the student during the fragment of his life he spends in school.

—Mark Van Doren, *Liberal Education*

The personal pronouns *his* and *he* refer back to the word *educator*. The phrases *some things* and *other things* are a repetition of *everything*. In addition, Van Doren uses the transitions *and* and *and then* to show relationships between his ideas.

RESEARCH

At this point in the writing process, you will be ready to include some quotations and paraphrases in your drafts.

The information given below should be used as a guideline when using longer direct quotations and indirect quotations in your essays. The following passage from Lauriat Lane, Jr.'s "Why Huckleberry Finn's a Great World Novel," which can be found in Chapter 8 of this book, will be used as an example to demonstrate different methods for quoting and paraphrasing:

> Allegory may be defined simply as the representation of one thing in the form of another. A second definition, more germane to literature, is that allegory is a process by which the spiritual is embodied in the physical. To go one step further, the main purpose of allegory is somehow to embody a spiritual action in a physical action. By making a suitable physical object stand for some metaphysical one, or at least for one which cannot be contained in the terms of normal everyday life, the writer carries out one of the main purposes of all art, which is to bring to its audience, through the representation of real objects, an awareness and knowledge which transcend the limitations of such reality. Allegory, that is, deals primarily with matters of the spirit.

Embed the Quote: When using quotations, you must try to incorporate the source material smoothly and elegantly into your own sentences. One way to ensure that your quotation is integrated nicely into your writing is to embed the quotation between an introductory phrase and an interpretation. Failing to properly introduce and interpret the quotation will make your writing seem choppy and unclear.

Begin by introducing the quotation with a "signal phrase." The signal phrase provides context for the quote and also indicates to the reader that a quotation is forthcoming. After writing the signal phrase, enclose the quote within quotation marks making sure to cite the page number in parentheses at the end of the sentence. Next, interpret the quotation to justify your rationale for using this piece of evidence from the text.

AN EXAMPLE

> In his essay, Lauriat Lane, Jr. provides an explanation for the allegory's role in the world of literature: "the main purpose of allegory is somehow to embody a spiritual action in a physical action" (223). He asserts that the real function of the allegory is to convey abstract truths through the use of the commonplace and the familiar.

If you can make your point by using just the signal phrase and the quotation, then you do not need to follow up with an interpretation.

Use Short Quotations: Integrate short quotations directly into your sentences. You can embed the phrase between an introduction and follow-up phrase. Your voice guiding us to an author's opinion can be quite effective, as long as you do not distort the original thought. You must then cite the page number in parentheses at the end of your sentence.

AN EXAMPLE

> Lane suggests that the allegory addresses "matters of the spirit" through its use of the familiar and the commonplace (223).

Use of Long Quotations: Quotations longer than four lines should start on a new line and be indented 10 spaces. You do not use quotation marks when setting off longer indented quotations. Avoid using too many long quotations as a way of filling space in your paper. On occasion, however, longer quotations are necessary to present an author's complex point.

AN EXAMPLE

In his essay, "Why Huckleberry Finn's a Great World Novel" Lauriat Lane, Jr. addresses how allegories are used by writers to convey larger, more abstract truths about the human experience:

> By making a suitable physical object stand for some metaphysical one, or at least for one which cannot be contained in the terms of normal everyday life, the writer carries out one of the main purposes of all art, which is to bring to its audience, through the representation of real objects, an awareness and knowledge which transcend the limitations of such reality. Allegory, that is, deals primarily with matters of the spirit. (223)

Altering and Condensing Long Quotations: Sometimes long quotations can be edited and condensed. Doing this can actually make your writing more concise and elegant. The original quote can be altered as long as you correctly indicate to the reader the changes you have made to the actual quotation.

The two common techniques used by writers to alter quotations are through the use of square brackets and ellipses. Square brackets can be used to insert your own words and letters into the original quote. You can do this in order to preserve grammatical correctness when you integrate the quotation directly into your sentence. You can also condense a long quote by using ellipses to indicate that words were deleted from the original quotation. You must ensure, however, that your edited version is grammatically correct.

An Example

In his essay, Lauriat Lane, Jr. asserts that the true function of the allegory is the use of common everyday objects to convey to the reader larger and more abstract concerns: "By making a suitable physical object stand for some metaphysical one...the writer... bring[s] to [his or her] audience...an awareness and knowledge which transcend the limitations of such reality" (223).

Paraphrasing: Paraphrasing is the method where you rewrite the source material in your own words. This is a very effective way to combine both the original evidence and your interpretation of the material into your own writing. Use this technique if you find that the source material cannot be quoted in a concise manner and if the longer indented quotation seems excessive and unnecessary. If you do paraphrase, however, you must cite the page number and include the author's name if you have not indicated it in a signal phrase.

An Example

Lauriat Lane Jr. in his essay, "Why Huckleberry Finn's a Great World Novel" tackles the idea that the allegory functions as a way for the writer to convey the larger, more abstract truths about the human experience. He begins by defining the allegory as simply a symbol, but then expands this definition into the realm of literature, where he characterizes the allegorical as a physical representation of a spiritual, more abstract notion. Lane sees the writer as fulfilling in the allegory one of the primary purposes of art: the ability to let the audience experience the profound in ordinary, commonplace objects and actions. Allegory, he emphasizes, broaches the metaphysical through the depiction of the materialistic (223).

INTERMEDIATE DRAFTS

Intermediate drafts, and there may be several of them, can be thought of as the essential building blocks that create the final product. Each time you do an intermediate draft, you will no doubt add something essential to the work, change what you have already written, or delete material altogether.

In intermediate drafts you may still be creating ideas and generating details as well as focusing what you have already done. If you do generate detail at this stage, it will probably take on a character different from the previously produced work in that it will in some way be related to that original material and will serve to make the work clearer, more unified, or more coherent.

An Example

Consider this revision of the previous draft in Chapter 10:

> Never before have we had such problems with the quality of our environment. Air pollution in particular affects all of us. For example, just look at the smog that covers cities like a blanket. It's stifling. Smoke stacks and exhaust pipes are belching out toxic wastes. On bad smog days, I can hardly breath. We should really try to do something about it before it destroys the earth. I mean, this is a serious problem that many people aren't even aware of. We should enact some laws that restrict the use of fossil fuels.

You will notice that this draft, in contrast to the one in Chapter 10, is more unified and more coherent. The ideas have been arranged into a more understandable pattern and the main idea, "We should enact some laws that restrict the use of fossil fuels" has been added to clarify the meaning. Because the main idea reflects a persuasive intent, the purpose has been made clearer by this more explicit statement. The phrase "exhaust pipes" has been added to make the statement about emissions more complete and more understandable. The second sentence was created by combining two sentences, thus giving more power and clarity to the idea that air pollution affects everybody. The addition of the phrase "for example" in the third sentence makes the passage more coherent. Two sentences from the previous draft that were not relevant to the topic, "Fish are dying in the oceans" and "Acid rain is killing trees in the forests," have been deleted. Leaving them in this part of paper would have distracted the reader from the main idea, which addresses air pollution only.

12

Refinement

U sually toward the end of the drafting process, but not exclusively, you will begin to refine the work. That is, you will begin to be more concerned about stylistic details than you were in earlier drafts. In this final revision of your work, you will make fewer changes in content. Rather you do a kind of fine tuning, making adjustments in the way you say what you have already decided you are going to say.

In some cases you will streamline what you have said by making the language used more economical. In other cases you will embellish by adding variety to sentence structure. Finally, you will need to be attentive to the requirements of mechanics, grammar, and usage that are appropriate to your writing project.

STYLE

When writers give special attention to language itself, regardless of the primary purpose of the writing, we often refer to that feature as style. For example, articles in newspapers and news magazines are usually more stylistically sophisticated than information that comes from a wire service reporting the basic facts of a story. Similarly, events recorded in expressive works like autobiographies or memoirs usually show more attention to stylistic considerations than do the same events reported in a journal or a diary. This attention to style results in writing that is more interesting and generally more pleasing to read than a collection of bare facts or random observations would be.

The discussions of economy and variety that follow will enable you to make some stylistic decisions about your work as you revise. Although that kind of refinement often comes at the end of the writing process, you may find that you will make use of some of these principles while you are working on initial drafts.

ECONOMY

Sometimes you say too much in the early drafts and the extraneous material will need to be cut away. In a sense, this process is the opposite of elaboration. You may have already done some deleting in the intermediate drafts, but in the final draft, it becomes even more important.

Some words communicate very little information and so should be cut. You will want to become sensitive to words that take up space but contribute little to either the meaning or the readability of what you have written. The following suggestions will help you make your work more concise.

NOUNS

❑ You should try to figure out ways to eliminate vague nouns like these: *area, aspect, concept, condition, consideration, factor, indication, infrastructure, parameter, phase,* and *situation.*

❑ You will make your work more readable if you eliminate nouns created from verbs. When these nouns create wordy verb phrases, replace them with the original verbs.

> *give consideration to: consider*
> *give encouragement to: encourage*
> *is reflective of: reflects*
> *is representative of: represents*
> *make adjustments: adjust*
> *make an approximation of: approximate*

MODIFIERS

❑ Other wordy phrases can also be replaced by single words.

> *at the present time: now*
> *due to the fact that: because*
> *during the course of: during*
> *for the simple reason that: because*
> *in a very real sense: truly*
> *in spite of the fact: although*
> *in view of the fact: since*
> *on the part of: by*
> *owing to the fact that: because*

❑ Some modifiers that carry very little meaning can usually be eliminated from your drafts: *absolutely, basically, certainly, definitely, incredibly, intensely, just, of course, perfectly, positively, quite, really, simply,* and *very.*

❑ A cliché is an overused expression. They were once original metaphors, but they have now lost that freshness. They should be eliminated from your drafts. Some examples follow: *quick as a cat, strong as an ox, sly as a fox,* and *green as grass.*

Verbs

When you revise, you will find that in some cases simply changing verbs can make a real difference in the impact of sentences. In particular, you should pay attention to forms of the verb *to be* (*be, been, being, am, is, are, was,* and *were*). *To be* verbs create passive voice, linking constructions, and the progressive tense. These three forms have legitimate uses and certainly writers use them all the time. But, as a general rule, eliminating *to be* verbs will make your writing more effective.

> The following sentence is written in the passive voice:
> Stress can be reduced by exercise.

> The more straightforward active voice is probably better:
> Exercise can reduce stress.

Occasionally, the passive may be preferable if, for example, the receiver of the action is more important than the doer of the action, as in the following sentence:
> The house has just been remodeled.

The passive may also be preferable if the action itself is more important than the doer of the action, as in this sentence:
> Talking is not allowed during the performance.

Look carefully at each *to be* verb as you proofread. If you don't have a specific reason for keeping it, you will probably improve the sentence by changing it.

VARIETY

A monotonous presentation will make any piece of writing more difficult for the reader, so it is important to for you to consider ways of creating variety. You can accomplish this in two ways, by varying sentence length and by varying sentence structure.

Length

Readers can begin to lose track of the content if the sentences in a paragraph are all the same length.

> Notice the following paragraph:

> Pollution is a problem. It seems to be getting worse. Cars are a major source of air pollution. There are many cars in the world. They are increasing

in number. They emit carbon dioxide. Carbon dioxide is a greenhouse gas. Greenhouse gases contribute to the greenhouse effect. The greenhouse effect causes global warming.

Obviously, this is not an effectively written paragraph. Try your hand at rewriting it. Simply combining a few sentences will make a noticeable difference in readability.

Similarly, if all sentences are long, information can become obscured. Using a variety of sentence lengths helps the reader focus on important ideas more easily.

SENTENCE STRUCTURE

By paying attention to the structure of sentences, you can make your writing more interesting and more accurate. With more highly structured sentences, it is possible to show relationships between ideas that would be impossible in simple sentences.

Notice how the following base sentence can be changed by the addition of a variety of sentence elements.

The bridge collapsed.

Adjective
The **ancient** bridge collapsed.

Adverb
The bridge collapsed **violently**.

Prepositional Phrases
After the snow, the bridge collapsed **in a heap**.

Participial Phrases
Weakened by time, the bridge collapsed, **tumbling into the chasm**.

Absolute Phrase
Metal twisting and snapping, the bridge collapsed.

Adverbial Clause
Because time and the elements had weakened the supporting structures, the bridge collapsed.

Adjective Clause
The bridge, **which spans a wild river**, collapsed.

MECHANICS, GRAMMAR, AND USAGE

The following discussions will help you proofread your drafts more effectively. As you proofread your final draft, you may need to pay attention to some of the following problems that often plague first-year college writers.

SENTENCES

A sentence expresses a complete thought.

It rained all night.

The streets were flooded.

I wasn't able to go to school.

The rain continued throughout the night, flooding streets all over the city, so that most commuters found it impossible to get anywhere the next morning.

Each of the preceding sentences expresses a complete thought. Occasionally, you may create a sentence that creates problems for the reader because it doesn't express a complete thought. When you are proofreading, you should be able to find those sentences and rewrite them.

FUSED SENTENCES

Consider the following sentence.

It rained all night I was not able to go to school the next morning.

The preceding sentence is a fused sentence. Two independent clauses (complete thoughts) are fused together without any punctuation. Such sentences can be corrected in a number of different ways. You can simply divide it into two sentences.

It rained all night. I was not able to go to school the next morning.

You could create a complex sentence by subordinating one clause to the other.

Because it rained all night, I was not able to go to school the next morning.

You could create a compound sentence by inserting a semicolon or a coordinating conjunction between the two independent clauses.

It rained all night; I was not able to go to school the next morning.

It rained all night, and I was not able to go to school the next morning.

It rained all night, so I was not able to go to school the next morning.

If you use a comma without a conjunction, you will have created a comma splice. See below.

COMMA SPLICES

It rained all night, I was not able to go to school the next morning.

In the sentence above, the two independent clauses have been connected by a comma; a comma splice results. A comma splice can be corrected in a number of different ways. You can simply make two separate sentences.

It rained all night. I was not able to go to school the next morning.

You could create a complex sentence by subordinating one clause to the other.

Because it rained all night, I was not able to go to school the next morning.

You could create a compound sentence by inserting a semicolon or a coordinating conjunction between the two independent clauses.

It rained all night; I was not able to go to school the next morning.

It rained all night, and I was not able to go to school the next morning.

It rained all night, so I was not able to go to school the next morning.

FRAGMENTS

Fragments are incomplete sentences. Look at the following:

Running through the woods. He tripped over a root.

He fell down. Because he tripped over a root.

You

Trying to figure out when to use the pronoun *you* can be perplexing when you are proofreading your papers. In general in referential forms of writing you should use the third person, *he, she,* or *they*—someone other than the writer, *I,* or the reader, *you*—or you can use nouns like *students, professors,* or *employees* and proper nouns like *John, Mary,* or *Americans.* In persuasive writing when the writer is addressing the reader directly, obviously the word *you* must be used. Even in some referential forms like informative narration of process the second person is mandatory. Consider the following imperative sentence: Put the red wire in the red slot. There is an implied *you:* (You) put the red wire in the red slot. Obviously you must use the second person when you are giving directions.

We tend to use *you* so extensively in conversation that we may be tempted to use *you* without thinking about it when we write. The difficulty arises with the so-called indefinite *you,* that is, using *you* to refer to "anybody." Consider the following sentence: During the Puritan rule in England, you could not go to the theater. The "you" in that sentence cannot possibly be the reader. To correct that sentence, you would simply substitute a word like *people* for the word *you.* Some uses of the indefinite *you* are less obvious. Consider this sentence: Because mystics report experiences that are completely subjective, you have no way to validate their assertions.

VERB ENDINGS

An –ed ending creates the past tense and an –s ending creates the present tense. In the drafting process, occasionally you may fail to put an ending on a verb. When you are proofreading and revising your work, make sure to check the verb endings.

They are suppos<u>ed</u> to go with us.

He ask<u>ed</u> about the assignment.

He feel<u>s</u> he should make an effort to catch up.

She hope<u>s</u> she can make it to the meeting.

The dog want<u>s</u> to go for a walk.

MODIFIERS

A modifier is a word or phrase that qualifies, limits, or describes other words.

This is a **nice** house.

When the word modifies a noun or a pronoun, it is called an adjective.

There goes a **powerful** motorcycle.

An adverb modifies a verb, an adjective, or another adverb.

Jerry jumps **higher** than anyone else.

Modifiers serve the same purpose as the single word adjective or adverb even when they are phrases or clauses.

The Chevrolet **with the silver fins** is still in good shape.

Placement of the modifier in the sentence is critical. You should always make it clear to the reader what the modifier refers to. Sometimes the modifier is misplaced and confusion results. In the following examples the misplaced modifiers are obvious because they are comical.

My sister dated a man with a Buick named Fred.

I once bought a piano from a woman with mahogany legs.

When a modifier, usually a participle, has nothing to modify, it is said to be dangling. Consider the following sentence.

Running through the woods, a root tripped him. [The root is not running.]

The sentence should be reworded so that that participle, functioning as an adjective, is close to the word it should be modifying.

Running thorough the woods, he tripped over a root.

POSSESSIVES

Possessives are formed by adding an apostrophe *s* to singular nouns (or plural nouns not ending in *s*) and by adding an apostrophe after the *s* to plural nouns ending in *s*.

It is not clear how we are supposed to read the following sentence.

The boys room was a mess.

There are two options for creating an appropriate possessive.

The boy's room was a mess. [This sentence shows that the room belongs to one boy.]

The boys' room was a mess. [This sentence shows that the room belongs to more than one boy.]

When you proofread, make sure that you have checked to see that you have used apostrophes in an appropriate way.

MISSPELLINGS

A spell checker will catch most misspellings, but occasionally when you have used the wrong word correctly spelled, you will end up with a spelling error without realizing it. Check troublesome words like the following.

Accept/Except
The two words sound alike, but they have very different meanings.

Accept is a verb that means "to receive."
Sallie accepted her gift with gratitude.

Except is a preposition that means "with the exclusion of."
Everyone was there except Charles.

Affect/Effect
These two words are frequently confused. Part of the problem is that both words can be used as both a noun and a verb. The confusion can be overcome if you remember that *affect* is generally used as a verb and *effect* is generally used as a noun.

We have been greatly affected by the oil embargo.
[Here it is used as a verb.]

The oil embargo had a great effect on the economy.
[Here it is used as a noun.]

Effect can be used as a verb when it means to cause a change: The dean will effect a change in the operation of the college.

Affect is used as a noun only as a technical term in psychology: The affect involves the entire range of emotions.

Its/It's
Its is the possessive form of *it*.
It's is a contraction meaning *it is*.

Loose/Lose
Loose means "not fastened or free."
Lose means "to be unable to find or mislay."

Their/There/They're
Their is the possessive form of *they*.

There is a pronoun that indicates a place, or it can be used as an expletive to hold a place in the sentence, as in the following: There were three birds sitting on the post.

They're is a contraction meaning *they are*.

Your/You're
Your is the possessive form of *you*.
You're is a contraction meaning *you are*.

RESEARCH

If you have used sources in your paper and have included parenthetical citations, make sure that you have a list of works cited at the end of the paper. The following is a sample list of works cited. Note: Your list of works cited should be put in alphabetical order without the headings. The headings are included here as information only and should not appear in a list of works cited.

WORKS CITED

BOOK

Plath, Sylvia. *The Bell Jar*. New York: Harper Perennial, 2005. Print.

PERIODICAL ARTICLE

Smith, Jennie Erin. "A State of Nature." *The New Yorker* 22 Apr. 2013 58–63.
  Print.

ARTICLE IN AN ONLINE MAGAZINE

Rosenberg, David. "What Does Your Kitchen Say About You." Slate.com. The
  Slate Group, 30 Apr. 2013. Web. 1 May, 2013.

SELECTION IN AN ANTHOLOGY

Lane Jr., Lauriat. "Why Huckleberry Finn's a Great World Novel." *Purpose,
  Pattern, and Process*. 9th. Lennis Polnac, Ed. Kendall Hunt, 2011. 219–225.
  Print.

ADVERTISEMENT

Love You, Skinny Cow by Nestlé. Advertisement. *Cooking Light* Mar. 2011: 61.
  Print.

FILM

Django Unchained. Dir. Quentin Tarantino. Perf. Jaime Fox, Christof Waltz, and
  Leonardo DiCaprio. The Weinstein Company, 2012. Film.

PART 4

Additional Readings and Student Writing

Additional Readings

The readings in this chapter are grouped by cultural themes and offer a variety of writing assignments related to those topics.

SOCIAL PROCESSES AND RELATIONSHIPS
The Hands of Poverty

JANE ADDAMS

Jane Addams was a social activist and reformer in late nineteenth century America. She founded Hull House in the slums of Chicago in 1889 to help those in poverty, especially newly arrived immigrants. She was the first American woman to receive the Nobel Peace Prize. This excerpt taken from Chapter 4 of her book Twenty Years at Hull-House, *published in 1912, recounts a visit to London, England where she observes appalling conditions of poverty in the East End. Notice in particular her use of descriptive detail.*

One of the most poignant of these experiences, which occurred during the first few months after our landing upon the other side of the Atlantic, was on a Saturday night, when I received an ineradicable impression of the wretchedness of East London, and also saw for the first time the overcrowded quarters of a great city at midnight. A small party of tourists were taken to the East End by a city missionary to witness the Saturday night sale of decaying vegetables and fruit, which, owing to the Sunday laws in London, could not be sold until Monday, and, as they were beyond safe keeping, were disposed of at auction as late as possible on Saturday night. On Mile End Road, from the top of an omnibus which paused at the end of a dingy street lighted by only occasional flares of gas, we saw two huge masses of ill-clad people clamoring around two hucksters' carts. They were bidding their farthings and ha'pennies for a vegetable held up by the auctioneer, which he at last scornfully flung, with a gibe for its cheapness, to the successful bidder. In the momentary pause only one man detached himself from the groups. He had bidden on a cabbage, and when it struck his hand, he instantly sat down on the curb, tore it with his teeth, and hastily devoured it, unwashed and uncooked as it was. He and his fellows were types of the "submerged tenth," as our missionary guide told us, with some little satisfaction in the then new phrase, and he further added that so many of them could scarcely be seen in one spot save at this Saturday night auction, the desire for cheap food being apparently the one thing which could move them simultaneously. They were huddled into ill-fitting, cast-off clothing, the ragged finery which one sees only in East London. Their pale faces were dominated by that most unlovely of human expressions, the cunning and shrewdness of the bargain-hunter who starves if he cannot make a successful trade, and yet the final impression was not of ragged, tawdry clothing nor of pinched and sallow faces, but of myriads of hands, empty, pathetic, nerveless and workworn, showing white in the uncertain light of the street, and clutching forward for food which was already unfit to eat.

Perhaps nothing is so fraught with significance as the human hand, this oldest tool with which man has dug his way from savagery, and with which he is constantly groping forward. I have never since been able to see a number of hands held upward, even when they are moving rhythmically in a calisthenic exercise, or when they belong to a class of chubby children who wave them in eager response to a teacher's query, without a certain revival of this memory, a clutching at the heart reminiscent of the despair and resentment which seized me then.

For the following weeks I went about London almost furtively, afraid to look down narrow streets and alleys lest they disclose again this hideous human need and suffering. I carried with me for days at a time that curious surprise we experience when we first come back into the streets after days given over to sorrow and death; we are bewildered that the world should be going on as usual and unable to determine which is real, the inner pang or the outward seeming. In time all huge London came to seem unreal save the poverty in its East End.

1910

WRITING ASSIGNMENTS

PERSONAL. Tell about an example of poverty (may include homelessness) that you have seen.

RESEARCH. In a documented paper discuss the kinds of assistance available to people in the United States whose income is below poverty level.

PERSUASIVE. In a persuasive paper argue that government should provide more (or less) assistance to people in poverty than it currently does.

ANALYTICAL. Write a paper analyzing Addams' use of description.

INVESTIGATIVE. Conduct a study of the attitudes of people about receiving assistance from the government or from charities.

The Rights of Women

MARY WOLLSTONECRAFT

The mother of Mary Shelley (the author of Frankenstein*), Mary Wollstonecraft was an early voice advocating equality for women. This excerpt is from the Introduction to* A Vindication of the Rights of Women, *published in 1792, one of the first great works of feminist literature.*

My own sex, I hope, will excuse me, if I treat them like rational creatures, instead of flattering their *fascinating* graces, and viewing them as if they were in a state of perpetual childhood, unable to stand alone. I earnestly wish to point out in what true dignity and human happiness consists—I wish to persuade women to endeavour and acquire strength, both of mind and body, and to convince them that the soft phrases, susceptibility of heart, delicacy of sentiment, and refinement of taste, are almost synonymous with epithets of weakness, and that those beings who are only the objects of pity and that kind of love, which has been termed its sister, will soon become objects of contempt.

Dismissing then those pretty feminine phrases, which the men condescendingly use to soften our slavish dependence, and despising that weak elegancy of mind, exquisite sensibility, and sweet docility of manners, supposed to be the sexual characteristics of the weaker vessel, I wish to shew that elegance is inferior to virtue, that the first object of inaudable ambition is to obtain a character as a human being, regardless of the distinction of sex; and that secondary views should be brought to this simple touchstone.

This is a rough sketch of my plan; and should I express my conviction with the energetic emotions that I feel whenever I think of the subject, the dictates of experience and reflection will be felt by some of my readers. Animated by this important object, I shall disdain to cull my phrases or polish my style;—I aim at being useful, and sincerity will render me unaffected; for, wishing rather to persuade by the force of my arguments, than dazzle by the elegance of my language, I shall not waste my time in rounding periods, or in fabricating the turgid bombast of artificial feelings, which, coming from the head, never reach the heart.—I shall be employed about things, not words!—and, anxious to render my sex more respectable members of society, I shall try to avoid that flowery diction which has slided from essays into novels, and from novels into familiar letters and conversation.

These pretty superlatives, dropping glibly from the tongue, vitiate the taste, and create a kind of sickly delicacy that turns away from simple unadorned truth; and a deluge of false sentiments and overstretched feelings stifling the natural emotions of the heart, render the domestic pleasures insipid, that ought to sweeten the exercise of those severe duties, which educate a rational and immortal being for a nobler field of action.

The education of women has, of late, been more attended to than formerly; yet they are still reckoned a frivolous sex, and ridiculed or pitied by the writers who endeavor by satire or instruction to improve them. It is acknowledged that they spend many of the first years of their lives in acquiring a smattering of accomplishments; meanwhile strength of body and mind are sacrificed to libertine notions of beauty, to the desire of establishing themselves,—the only way women can rise in the world,—by marriage. And this desire making mere animals of them, when they marry they act as such children may be expected to act:—they dress; they paint, and nickname God's creatures.—Surely these weak beings are only fit for a seraglio!—Can they be expected to govern a family with judgment, or take care of the poor babes whom they bring into the world?

If then it can be fairly deduced from the present conduct of the sex; from the prevalent fondness for pleasure which takes place of ambition and those nobler passions that open and enlarge the soul; that the instruction which women have hitherto received has only tended, with the constitution of civil society to render them insignificant objects of desire—mere propagators of fools!—if it can be proved that in aiming to accomplish them, without cultivating their understandings, they are taken out of their sphere of duties, and made ridiculous and useless when the short-lived bloom of beauty is over, I presume that *rational* men will excuse me for endeavouring to persuade them to become more masculine and respectable.

Indeed the word masculine is only a bugbear: there is little reason to fear that women will acquire too much courage or fortitude; for their apparent inferiority with respect to bodily strength, must render them, in some degree, dependent on men in the various relations of life; but why should it be increased by prejudices that give a sex to virtue, and confound simple truths with sensual reveries?

Women are, in fact so much degraded by mistaken notions of female excellence, that I do not mean to add a paradox when I assert that this artificial weakness produces a propensity to tyrannize, and gives birth to cunning, the natural opponent of strength, which leads them to play off those contemptible infantine airs that undermine esteem even whilst they excite desire. Let men become more chaste and modest, and if women do not grow wiser in the same ratio, it will be clear that they have weaker understandings. It seems scarcely necessary to say, that I now speak of the sex in general. Many individuals have more sense than their male relatives; and, as nothing preponderates where there is a constant struggle for an equilibrium, without it has naturally more gravity, some women govern their husbands without degrading themselves, because intellect will always govern.

1792

WRITING ASSIGNMENTS

Personal. Tell about any events you have witnessed when a woman's rights were violated.

Research. Write a documented paper discussing different kinds of discrimination against women.

PERSUASIVE. Write a paper advocating that women should have economic equality.

ANALYTICAL. Write a paper analyzing Wollstonecraft's use of evaluation.

INVESTIGATIVE. Find examples in the popular media (advertising and entertainment) that reinforce female stereotypes.

THE INDIVIDUAL AND IDENTITY
A Shame of Silence

MAXINE HONG KINGSTON

In this excerpt from her acclaimed memoir The Woman Warrior, *Maxine Hong Kingston reveals the complexities of adjusting to an alien culture.*

When I went to kindergarten and had to speak English for the first time, I became silent. A dumbness—a shame—still cracks my voice in two, even when I want to say "hello" casually, or ask an easy question in front of the check-out counter, or ask directions of a bus driver. I stand frozen, or I hold up the line with the complete, grammatical sentence that comes squeaking out at impossible length. "What did you say?" says the cab driver, or "Speak up," so I have to perform again, only weaker the second time. A telephone call makes my throat bleed and takes up that day's courage. It spoils my day with self-disgust when I hear my broken voice come skittering out into the open. It makes people wince to hear it. I'm getting better, though. Recently I asked the postman for special-issue stamps; I've waited since childhood for postmen to give me some of their own accord. I am making progress, a little every day.

My silence was thickest—total—during the three years that I covered my school paintings with black paint. I painted layers of black over houses and flowers and suns, and when I drew on the blackboard, I put a layer of chalk on top. I was making a stage curtain, and it was the moment before the curtain parted or rose. The teachers called my parents to school, and I saw they had been saving my pictures, curling and cracking, all alike and black. The teachers pointed to the pictures and looked serious, talked seriously too, but my parents did not understand English. ("The parents and teachers of criminals were executed," said my father.) My parents took the pictures home. I spread them out (so black and full of possibilities) and pretended the curtains were swinging open, flying up, one after another, sunlight underneath, mighty operas.

During the first silent year I spoke to no one at school, did not ask before going to the lavatory, and flunked kindergarten. My sister also said nothing for three years, silent in the playground and silent at lunch. There were other quiet Chinese girls not of our family, but most of them got over it sooner than we did. I enjoyed the silence. At first it did not occur to me I was supposed to talk or to pass kindergarten. I talked at home and to one or two of the Chinese kids in class. I made motions and even made some jokes. I drank out of a toy saucer when the water spilled out of the cup, and everybody laughed, pointing at me, so I did it some more. I didn't know that Americans don't drink out of saucers.

I liked the Negro students (Black Ghosts) best because they laughed the loudest and talked to me as if I were a daring talker too. One of the Negro girls had her mother coil braids over her ears Shanghai-style like mine; we were Shanghai twins except that she was covered with black like my paintings. Two Negro kids enrolled in Chinese school, and the teachers gave them Chinese names. Some Negro kids walked me to school and home, protecting me from the Japanese kids, who hit me and chased me and stuck gum in my ears. The Japanese kids were noisy and tough. They appeared one day in kindergarten, released from concentration camp, which was a tic-tac-toe mark, like barbed wire, on the map.

It was when I found out I had to talk that school became a misery, that the silence became a misery. I did not speak and felt bad each time that I did not speak. I read aloud in first grade, though, and heard the barest whisper with little squeaks come out of my throat. "Louder," said the teacher, who scared the voice away again. The other Chinese girls did not talk either, so I knew the silence had to do with being a Chinese girl.

Reading out loud was easier than speaking because we did not have to make up what to say, but I stopped often, and the teacher would think I'd gone quiet again. I could not understand "I." The Chinese "I" has seven strokes, intricacies. How could the American "I," assuredly wearing a hat like the Chinese, have only three strokes, the middle so straight? Was it out of politeness that this writer left off strokes the way a Chinese has to write her own name small and crooked? No, it was not politeness; "I" is a capital and "you" is lower-case. I stared at that middle line and waited so long for its black center to resolve into tight strokes and dots that I forgot to pronounce it. The other troublesome word was "here," no strong consonant to hang on to, and so flat, when "here" is two mountainous ideographs. The teacher, who had already told me every day how to read "I" and "here," put me in the low corner under the stairs again, where the noisy boys usually sat.

When my second grade class did a play, the whole class went to the auditorium except the Chinese girls. The teacher, lovely and Hawaiian, should have understood about us, but instead left us behind in the classroom. Our voices were too soft or nonexistent, and our parents never signed the permission slips anyway. They never signed anything unnecessary. We opened the door a crack and peeked out, but closed it again quickly. One of us (not me) won every spelling bee, though.

I remember telling the Hawaiian teacher, "We Chinese can't sing 'land where our fathers died.'" She argued with me about politics, while I meant because of curses. But how can I have that memory when I couldn't talk? My mother says that we, like the ghosts, have no memories.

After American school, we picked up our cigar boxes, in which we had arranged books, brushes, and an inkbox neatly, and went to Chinese school, from 5:00 to 7:30 p.m. There we chanted together, voices rising and falling, loud and soft, some boys shouting, everybody reading together, reciting together and not alone with one voice. When we had a memorization test, the teacher let each of us come to his desk and say the lesson to him privately, while the rest of the class practiced copying or tracing. Most of the teachers were men. The boys who were so well behaved in the American school played tricks on them and talked back to them. The girls were not mute. They screamed and yelled during recess, when there were no rules; they had fist-fights. Nobody was afraid of children hurting themselves or of children hurting school property. The glass doors to the red and green balconies with the gold joy symbols were left wide open so that we could run out and climb the fire escapes. We played capture-the-flag in the auditorium, where Sun Yat-sen and Chiang Kai-shek's pictures hung at the back of the stage, the Chinese flag on their left and the American flag on their right. We climbed the teak ceremonial chairs and made flying leaps off the stage. One flag headquarters was behind the glass door and the other on stage right. Our feet drummed on the hollow stage. During recess the teachers locked themselves up in their office with the shelves of books, copybooks, inks from China. They drank tea and warmed their hands at a stove. There was no play supervision. At recess we had the school to ourselves, and also we could roam as far as we could go—downtown, Chinatown stores, home—as long as we returned before the bell rang.

At exactly 7:30 the teacher again picked up the brass bell that sat on his desk and swung it over our heads, while we charged down the stairs, our cheering magnified in the stairwell. Nobody had to line up.

Not all of the children who were silent at American school found voice at Chinese school. One new teacher said each of us had to get up and recite in front of the class, who was to listen. My sister and I had memorized the lesson perfectly. We said it to each other at home, one chanting, one listening. The teacher called on my sister to recite first. It was the first time a teacher had called on the secondborn to go first. My sister was scared. She glanced at me and looked away; I looked down at my desk. I hoped that she could do it because if she could, then I would have to. She opened her mouth and a voice came out that wasn't a whisper, but it wasn't a proper voice either. I hoped that she would not cry, fear breaking up her voice like twigs underfoot. She sounded as if she were trying to sing though weeping and strangling. She did not pause or stop to end the embarrassment. She kept on going until she said the last word, and then she sat down. When it was my turn, the same voice came out, a crippled animal running on broken legs. You could hear splinters in my voice, bones rubbing jagged against one another. I was loud, though. I was glad I didn't whisper.

1975

WRITING ASSIGNMENTS

PERSONAL. Tell about an experience that has caused you to feel isolated.

RESEARCH. Write a research paper explaining the cultural forces that expedite or delay assimilation into the dominant culture. Document your sources.

PERSUASIVE. Write a paper arguing that immigrants should assimilate into the dominant culture or that they should maintain their native culture.

ANALYTICAL. Write a paper analyzing Kingston's use of narration.

INVESTIGATIVE. Create a scale to measure the degree of assimilation into the dominant culture. Interview a number of immigrants and write a paper reporting the degree of assimilation.

On Androgyny

VIRGINIA WOOLF

In this excerpt from Chapter 6 of A Room of One's Own, *Virginia Woolf muses on the dual nature of the human mind.*

Now it was bringing from one side of the street to the other diagonally a girl in patent leather boots, and then a young man in a maroon overcoat; it was also bringing a taxi-cab; and it brought all three together at a point directly beneath my window; where the taxi stopped; and the girl and the young man stopped; and they got into the taxi; and then the cab glided off as if it were swept on by the current elsewhere.

The sight was ordinary enough; what was strange was the rhythmical order with which my imagination had invested it; and the fact that the ordinary sight of two people getting into a cab had the power to communicate something of their own seeming satisfaction. The sight of two people coming down the street and meeting at the corner seems to ease the mind of some strain, I thought, watching the taxi turn and make off. Perhaps to think, as I had been thinking these two days, of one sex as distinct from the other is an effort. It interferes with the unity of the mind. Now that effort had ceased and that unity had been restored by seeing two people come together and get into a taxi-cab. The mind is certainly a very mysterious organ, I reflected, drawing my head in from the window, about which nothing whatever is known, though we depend upon it so completely. Why do I feel that there are severances and oppositions in the mind, as there are strains from obvious causes on the body? What does one mean by "the unity of the mind," I pondered, for clearly the mind has so great a power of concentrating at any point at any moment that it seems to have no single state of being. It can separate itself from the people in the street, for example, and think of itself as apart from them, at an upper window looking down on them. Or it can think with other people spontaneously, as, for instance, in a crowd waiting to hear some piece of news read out. It can think back through its fathers or through its mothers, as I have said that a woman writing thinks back through her mother. Again if one is a woman one is often surprised by a sudden splitting off of consciousness, say in walking down Whitehall, when from being the natural inheritor of that civilisation, she becomes, on the contrary, outside of it, alien and critical. Clearly the mind is always altering its focus, and bringing the world into different perspectives. But some of these states of mind seem, even if adopted spontaneously, to be less comfortable than others. In order to keep oneself continuing in them one is unconsciously holding something back, and gradually the repression becomes an effort. But there may be some state of mind in which one could continue without effort because nothing is required to be held back. And this perhaps, I thought, coming in from the window, is one of them. For certainly when I saw the couple get into the taxi-cab the mind felt as if, after being divided, it had come together again in a natural fusion. The obvious reason would be that it is natural for the sexes to co-operate. One has a profound, if irrational, instinct in favour of the theory that the union of man and woman makes for the greatest satisfaction, the most complete happiness. But the sight of the two people getting into the taxi and the satisfaction it gave me made me also ask whether there are two sexes in the mind corresponding to the two sexes in the body, and whether they also require to be united in order to get complete satisfaction and happiness. And I went on amateurishly to sketch a plan of the soul so that in each of us two powers preside, one male, one female: and in the man's brain, the man predominates over the woman, and in the woman's brain, the woman predominates over the man. The normal and comfortable state of being is that when the two live in harmony together, spiritually co-operating. If one is a man, still the woman part of the brain must have effect; and a woman also must have intercourse with the man in her. Coleridge perhaps meant this when he said that a great mind is androgynous. It is when this fusion takes place that the mind is fully fertilised and uses all its faculties.

1929

WRITING ASSIGNMENTS

PERSONAL. Tell about an experience you have had when sexual identity (in yourself or someone you know) seemed to be blurred.

RESEARCH. Find information about the manifestations of androgyny in our culture (clothing, hairstyles, etc.) and report your findings in a documented paper.

PERSUASIVE. Write a paper arguing that a rejection of the values of either sex is destructive for our culture.

ANALYTICAL. Write a paper analyzing Woolf's use of description.

INVESTIGATIVE. Collect a series of images of men and women. Survey a group of classmates and friends to determine which images are most androgynous and which are least.

EDUCATION AND HUMAN DEVELOPMENT
Higher UnEducation

ELDRIDGE CLEAVER

This excerpt from Eldridge Cleaver's controversial book Soul on Ice *gives us a disturbing look into the social turmoil of the late 1960s. A member of the Black Panthers, Cleaver reveals to us the mind of a revolutionary.*
    (written in Folsom Prison, October 9, 1965)

I'm perfectly aware that I'm in prison, that I'm, a Negro, that I've been a rapist, and that I have a Higher Uneducation. I never know what significance I'm supposed to attach to these factors. But I have a suspicion that, because of these aspects of my character, "free-normal-educated" people rather expect me to be more reserved, penitent, remorseful, and not too quick to shoot off my mouth on certain subjects. But I let them down, disappoint them, make them gape at me in a sort of stupor, as if they're thinking; "You've got your nerve! Don't you realize that you owe a debt to society?" My answer to all such thoughts lurking in their split-level heads, crouching behind their squinting bombardier eyes, is that the blood of Vietnamese peasants has paid off all my debts; that the Vietnamese people, afflicted with a rampant disease called Yankees, through their sufferings—as opposed to the "frustration" of fat-assed American geeks safe at home worrying over whether to have bacon, ham, or sausage with their grade-A eggs in the morning, while Vietnamese worry each morning whether the Yankees will gas them, burn them up, or blow away their humble pads in a hail of bombs—have canceled all my IOUs.

In beginning this letter I could just as easily have mentioned other aspects of my situation; I could have said: "I'm perfectly aware that I'm tall, that I'm skinny, that I need a shave, that I'm hard-up enough to suck my grandmother's old withered tits, and that I would dig (deeper then deeply) getting clean once more—not only in the steam-bath sense, but in getting sharp as an Esquire square with a Harlem touch—or that I would like to put on a pair of bib overalls and become a Snicker, or that I'd like to leap the whole last mile and grow a beard and don whatever threads the local nationalism might require and comrade with Che Guevara, and share his fate, blazing a new pathfinder's trail through the stymied upbeat brain of the New Left, or how I'd just love to be in Berkeley right now, to roll in that mud, to frolic in that sty of funky revolution, to breathe in its heady fumes, and look with roving eyes for a new John Brown, Eugene Debs, a blacker-meaner-keener Malcolm X, a Robert Franklin Williams with less rabbit in his hot blood, an American Lenin, Fidel, a Mao-Mao, A MAO MAO, A MAO MAO, A MAO MAO, A MAO MAO, A MAO MAO, A MAO MAO
    . . . All of which is true.

WRITING ASSIGNMENTS

PERSONAL. Tell about some public demonstration, rally, or protest you have witnessed or participated in.

RESEARCH. Write a research paper about the causes of civil unrest. Document your sources.

PERSUASIVE. Write a paper arguing that involvement in political activities is an essential part of education.

ANALYTICAL. Write a paper analyzing Cleaver's use of slang.

INVESTIGATIVE. Identify action groups (political, environmental, etc.) on your campus or in your neighborhood. Analyze the methods these groups use to gain support.

The Power of Habit

WILLIAM JAMES

William James was an American philosopher and psychologist whose writings have influenced thinkers for generations. This excerpt is taken from his The Principles of Psychology, *Chapter 4 "Habit," written in 1890.*

"Habit a second nature! Habit is ten times nature," the Duke of Wellington is said to have exclaimed; and the degree to which this is true no one can probably appreciate as well as one who is a veteran soldier himself. The daily drill and the years of discipline end by fashioning a man completely over again, as to most of the possibilities of his conduct.

"There is a story, which is credible enough, though it may not be true, of a practical joker, who, seeing a discharged veteran carrying home his dinner, suddenly called out, 'Attention!' whereupon the man instantly brought his hands down, and lost his mutton and potatoes in the gutter. The drill had been thorough, and its effects had become embodied in the man's nervous structure."

Riderless cavalry-horses, at many a battle, have been seen to come together and go through their customary evolutions at the sound of the bugle-call. Most trained domestic animals, dogs and oxen, and omnibus- and car-horses, seem to be machines almost pure and simple, undoubtingly, unhesitatingly doing from minute to minute the duties they have been taught, and giving no sign that the possibility of an alternative ever suggests itself to their mind. Men grown old in prison have asked to be readmitted after being once set free. In a railroad accident to a travelling menagerie in the United States some time in 1884, a tiger, whose cage had broken open, is said to have emerged, but presently crept back again, as if too much bewildered by his new responsibilities, so that he was without difficulty secured.

Habit is thus the enormous fly-wheel of society, its most precious conservative agent. It alone is what keeps us all within the bounds of ordinance, and saves the children of fortune from the envious uprisings of the poor. It alone prevents the hardest and most repulsive walks of life from being deserted by those brought up to tread therein. It keeps the fisherman and the deck-hand at sea through the winter; it holds the miner in his darkness, and nails the countryman to his log-cabin and his lonely farm through all the months of snow; it protects us from invasion by the natives of the desert and the frozen zone. It dooms us all to fight out the battle of life upon the lines of our nurture or our early choice, and to make the best of a pursuit that disagrees, because there is no other for which we are fitted, and it is too late to begin again. It keeps different social strata from mixing. Already at the age of twenty-five you see the professional mannerism settling down on the young commercial traveller, on the young doctor, on the young minister, on the young counsellor-at-law. You see the little lines of cleavage running through the character, the tricks of thought, the prejudices, the ways of the "shop," in a word, from which the man can by-and-by no more escape than his coat-sleeve can suddenly fall into a new set of folds. On the whole, it is best he should not escape. It is well for the world that in most of us, by the age of thirty, the character has set like plaster, and will never soften again.

If the period between twenty and thirty is the critical one in the formation of intellectual and professional habits, the period below twenty is more important still for the fixing of *personal* habits, properly so called, such as vocalization and pronunciation, gesture, motion, and address. Hardly ever is a language learned after twenty spoken without a foreign accent; hardly ever can a youth transferred to the society of his betters unlearn the nasality and other vices of speech bred in him by the associations of his growing years. Hardly ever, indeed, no matter how much money there be in his pocket, can he even learn to *dress* like a gentleman-born. The merchants offer their wares as eagerly to him as to the veriest "swell," but he simply *cannot* buy the right things. An invisible law, as strong as gravitation, keeps him within his orbit, arrayed this year as he was the last; and how his better-bred acquaintances contrive to get the things they wear will be for him a mystery till his dying day.

The great thing, then, in all education, is to *make our nervous system our ally instead of our enemy*. It is to fund and capitalize our acquisitions, and live at ease upon the interest of the fund. *For this we must make automatic and habitual, as early as possible, as many useful actions as we can*, and guard against the growing into ways that are likely to be disadvantageous to us, as we should guard against the plague. The more of the details of our daily life we can hand over to the effortless custody of automatism, the more our higher powers of mind will be set free for their own proper work. There is no more miserable human being than one in whom nothing is habitual but indecision, and for whom the lighting of every cigar, the drinking of every cup, the time of rising and going to bed every day, and the beginning of every bit of work, are subjects of express volitional deliberation. Full half the time of such a man goes to the deciding, or regretting, of matters which ought to be so ingrained in him as practically not to exist for his consciousness at all. If there be such daily duties not yet ingrained in any one of my readers, let him begin this very hour to set the matter right.

WRITING ASSIGNMENTS

PERSONAL. Write about an event in your life when you discovered that a habit was beneficial (or destructive) to you.

RESEARCH. Identify and discuss several different kinds of positive habits that can benefit a student. Document your sources.

PERSUASIVE. Identify a positive habit for a student to have and argue that it should be cultivated.

ANALYTICAL. Analyze James' use of examples.

INVESTIGATIVE. Interview or survey a number of successful students to determine the most beneficial habits for success in school. Report your findings in a paper.

HISTORY AND CULTURE
The Roots of Altruism

RENÉ DUBOS

Rene Dubos, a microbiologist by training, wrote on a wide range of topics, especially environmentalism. He often referred to these writings as his theology of life on earth.

In view of the fact that human beings evolved as hunters, it is not surprising that they have inherited a biological propensity to kill, as have all animal predators. But it is remarkable that a very large percentage of human beings find killing an extremely distasteful and painful experience. Despite the most subtle forms of propaganda, it is difficult to convince them that war is desirable. In contrast, altruism has long been practiced, often going so far as self-sacrifice. Altruism certainly has deep roots in man's biological past for the simple reason that it presents advantages for the survival of the group. However, the really human aspect of altruism is not its biological origin or its evolutionary advantages but rather the fact that humankind has now made it a virtue regardless of practical advantages or disadvantages. Since earliest recorded history altruism has become one of the absolute values by which humanity transcends animality.

The existence of altruism was recognized as far back as Neanderthal times, among the very first people who can be regarded as truly human. In the Shanidar cave of Iraq, for example, there was found a skeleton of a Neanderthalian adult male, dating from approximately 50,000 years ago. He had probably been blind, and one of his arms had been amputated above the elbow early in life. He had been killed by a collapse of the cave wall. As he was 40 years old at the time of his death and must have been incapable of fending for himself during much of his lifetime, it seems reasonable to assume that he had been cared for by the members of his clan. Several similar cases that could be interpreted as examples of "charity" have been recognized in other prehistoric sites. In fact, one of the first Neanderthalian skeletons to be discovered in Europe was that of a man approximately 50 years old who had suffered from extensive arthritis. His disease was so severe that he must have been unable to hunt or to engage in other strenuous activities. He, also, must therefore have depended for his survival upon the care of his clan.

Many prehistoric finds suggest attitudes of affection. A Stone Age tomb contains the body of a woman holding a young child in her arms. Caves in North America that were occupied some 9,000 years ago have yielded numerous sandals of different sizes: those of children's sizes are lined with rabbit fur, as if to express a special kind of loving care for the youngest members of the community.

Whether or not the words of altruism and love had equivalents in the languages of the Stone Age, the social attitudes which they denote existed. The fact that the philosophy of nonviolence was clearly formulated at the time of Jesus and Buddha suggests that it had developed at a much earlier date. The Golden Rule, "Do unto others as you would have them do unto you," exists in all religious doctrines, even in those that have reached us through the very first written documents. It must therefore have an extremely ancient origin.

WRITING ASSIGNMENTS

Personal. Tell about an experience you have had when someone acted selflessly on your behalf or when you acted selflessly on behalf of someone else.

Research. Write a research paper about kinds of charities. Document your sources.

Persuasive. Write a paper arguing that altruism should be encouraged in our society.

Analytical. Write a paper analyzing Dubos' use of inductive logic.

Investigative. Identify opportunities for charitable work in your neighborhood or hometown.

The Significance of the American Frontier

FREDERICK JACKSON TURNER

Frederick Jackson Turner, an influential historian, taught for many years at the University of Wisconsin. This excerpt is taken from Chapter 1 of Turner's book entitled The Frontier in American History *published in 1921. His "Frontier Thesis" has been much debated over the years.*

From the conditions of frontier life came intellectual traits of profound importance. The works of travelers along each frontier from colonial days onward describe certain common traits, and these traits have, while softening down, still persisted as survivals in the place of their origin, even when a higher social organization succeeded. The result is that to the frontier the American intellect owes its striking characteristics. That coarseness and strength combined with acuteness and inquisitiveness; that practical, inventive turn of mind, quick to find expedients; that masterful grasp of material things, lacking in the artistic but powerful to effect great ends; that restless, nervous energy; that dominant individualism, working for good and for evil, and withal that buoyancy and exuberance which comes with freedom—these are traits of the frontier, or traits called out elsewhere because of the existence of the frontier. Since the days when the fleet of Columbus sailed into the waters of the New World, America has been another name for opportunity, and the people of the United States have taken their tone from the incessant expansion which has not only been open but has even been forced upon them. He would be a rash prophet who should assert that the expansive character of American life has now entirely ceased. Movement has been its dominant fact, and, unless this training has no effect upon a people, the American energy will continually demand a wider field for its exercise. But never again will such gifts of free land offer themselves. For a moment, at the frontier, the bonds of custom are broken and unrestraint is triumphant. There is not *tabula rasa.* The stubborn American environment is there with its imperious summons to accept its conditions; the inherited ways of doing things are also there; and yet, in spite of environment, and in spite of custom, each frontier did indeed furnish a new field of opportunity, a gate of escape from the bondage of the past; and freshness, and confidence, and scorn of older society, impatience of its restraints and its ideas, and indifference to its lessons, have accompanied the frontier. What the Mediterranean Sea was to the Greeks, breaking the bond of custom, offering new experiences, calling out new institutions and activities, that, and more, the ever retreating frontier has been to the United States directly, and to the nations of Europe more remotely. And now, four centuries from the discovery of America, at the end of a hundred years of life under the Constitution, the frontier has gone, and with its going has closed the first period of American history.

WRITING ASSIGNMENTS

PERSONAL. Recount an event when you have seen individualism in action.

RESEARCH. Identify and discuss some of the causes of American individualism. Document your sources.

PERSUASIVE. Write a paper arguing that individualism should be encouraged or conversely that conformity to social norms should be encouraged.

ANALYTICAL. Analyze Turner's use of examples.

INVESTIGATIVE. Take a survey of students and/or friends to determine how they see themselves on a scale from individualism to conformity. Create questions that will identify those traits. Report your findings in a paper.

ECONOMICS AND BUSINESS
The Employment of Capital

ADAM SMITH

The Wealth of Nations, a book by the Scottish philosopher, Adam Smith (1723–90), was published in 1776 and is generally regarded as the classic work explaining how the free market capitalistic economy works. It also played a key role in establishing economics as an area of study in its own right. It was the first major work in the science of economics and most discussions of economic theory since its publication have been influenced by Smith's theories. This excerpt reveals some of the basic assumptions Smith makes about the way markets work.

Though all capitals are destined for the maintenance of productive labour only, yet the quantity of that labour which equal capitals are capable of putting into motion varies extremely according to the diversity of their employment; as does likewise the value which that employment adds to the annual produce of the land and labour of the country.

A capital may be employed in four different ways: either, first, in procuring the rude produce annually required for the use and consumption of the society; or, secondly, in manufacturing and preparing that rude produce for immediate use and consumption; or, thirdly, in transporting either the rude or manufactured produce from the places where they abound to those where they are wanted; or, lastly, in dividing particular portions of either into such small parcels as suit the occasional demands of those who want them. In the first way are employed the capitals of all those who undertake the improvement or cultivation of lands, mines, or fisheries; in the second, those of all master manufacturers; in the third, those of all wholesale merchants; and in the fourth, those of all retailers. It is difficult to conceive that a capital should be employed in any way which may not be classed under some one or other of those four.

Each of these four methods of employing a capital is essentially necessary either to the existence or extension of the other three, or to the general conveniency of the society.

Unless a capital was employed in furnishing rude produce to a certain degree of abundance, neither manufactures nor trade of any kind could exist.

Unless a capital was employed in manufacturing that part of the rude produce which requires a good deal of preparation before it can be fit for use and consumption, it either would never be produced, because there could be no demand for it; or if it was produced spontaneously, it would be of no value in exchange, and could add nothing to the wealth of the society.

Unless a capital was employed in transporting either the rude or manufactured produce from the places where it abounds to those where it is wanted, no more of either could be produced than was necessary for the consumption of the neighbourhood. The capital of the merchant exchanges the surplus produce of one place for that of another, and thus encourages the industry and increases the enjoyments of both.

Unless a capital was employed in breaking and dividing certain portions either of the rude or manufactured produce into such small parcels as suit the occasional demands of those who want them, every man would be obliged to purchase a greater quantity of the goods he wanted than his immediate occasions required. If there was no such trade as a butcher, for example, every man would be obliged to purchase a whole ox or a whole sheep at a time. This would generally be inconvenient to the rich, and much more so to the poor. If a poor workman was obliged to purchase a month's or six months provisions at a time, a great part of the stock which he employs as a capital in the instruments of his trade, or in the furniture of his shop, and which yields him a revenue, he would be forced to place in that part of his stock which is reserved for immediate consumption, and which yields him no revenue. Nothing can be more convenient for such a person than to be able to purchase his subsistence from day to day, or even from hour to hour, as he wants it. He is thereby enabled to employ almost his whole stock as a capital. He is thus enabled to furnish work to a greater value, and the profit, which he makes by it in this way, much more than compensates the additional price which the profit of the retailer imposes upon the goods. The prejudices of some political writers against shopkeepers and tradesmen are altogether without foundation. So far is it from being necessary either to tax them or to restrict their numbers that they can never be multiplied so as to hurt the public, though they may so as to hurt one another. The quantity of grocery goods, for example, which can be sold in a particular town is limited by the demand of that town and its neighbourhood. The capital, therefore, which can be employed in the grocery trade cannot exceed what is sufficient to purchase that quantity. If this capital is divided between two different grocers, their competition will tend to make both of them sell cheaper than if it were in the hands of one only; and if it were divided among twenty, their competition would be just so much the greater, and the chance of their combining together, in order to raise the price, just so much the less. Their competition might perhaps ruin some of themselves; but to take care of this is the business of the parties concerned, and it may safely be trusted to their dis-cretion. It can never hurt either the consumer or the producer; on the contrary, it must tend to make the retailers both sell cheaper and buy dearer than if the whole trade was monopolized by one or two persons. Some of them, perhaps, may sometimes decoy a weak customer to buy what he has no occasion for. This evil, however, is of too little importance to deserve the public attention, nor would it necessarily be prevented by restricting their numbers. It is not the multitude of ale-houses, to give the most suspicious example, that occasions a general disposition to drunkenness among the common people; but that dispo-sition arising from other causes necessarily gives employment to a multitude of ale-houses.

The persons whose capitals are employed in any of those four ways are themselves productive labourers. Their labour, when properly directed, fixes and realizes itself in the subject or vendible commodity upon which it is be-stowed, and generally adds to its price the value at least of their own mainte-nance and consumption. The profits of the farmer, of the manufacturer, of the merchant, and retailer, are all drawn from the price of the goods which the two first produce, and the two last buy and sell. Equal capitals, however, employed in each of those four different ways, will immediately put into motion very differ-ent quantities of productive labour, and augment, too, in very different propor-tions the value of the annual produce of the land and labour of the society to which they belong.

The capital of the retailer replaces, together with its profits, that of the merchant of whom he purchases goods, and thereby enables him to continue his business. The retailer himself is the only productive labourer whom it im-mediately employs. In his profits consists the whole value which its employment adds to the annual produce of the land and labour of the society.

The capital of the wholesale merchant replaces, together with their profits, the capitals of the farmers and manufacturers of whom he purchases the rude and manufactured produce which he deals in, and thereby enables them to continue their respective trades. It is by this service chiefly that he contributes indirectly to support the productive labour of the society, and to increase the value of its annual produce. His capital employs, too, the sailors and carriers who transport his goods from one place to another, and it augments the price of those goods by the value, not only of his profits, but of their wages. This is all the productive labour which it immediately puts into motion, and all the value which it immediately adds to the annual produce. Its operation in both these respects is a good deal superior to that of the capital of the retailer.

Part of the capital of the master manufacturer is employed as a fixed capital in the instruments of his trade, and replaces, together with its profits, that of some other artificer of whom he purchases them. Part of his circu-lating capital is employed in purchasing materials, and replaces, with their profits, the capitals of the farmers and miners of whom he purchases them. But a great part of it is always, either annually, or in a much shorter period, distributed among the different workmen whom he employs. It augments the value of those materials by their wages, and by their matters' profits upon the whole stock of wages, materials, and instruments of trade employed in the business. It puts immediately into motion, therefore, a much greater quantity of productive labour, and adds a much greater value to the annual produce of the land and labour of the society than an equal capital in the hands of any wholesale merchant.

No equal capital puts into motion a greater quantity of productive labour than that of the farmer. Not only his labouring servants, but his labouring cattle, are productive labourers. In agriculture, too, nature labours along with man; and though her labour costs no expence, its produce has its value, as well as that of the most expensive workmen. The most important operations of agriculture seem intended not so much to increase, though they do that too, as to direct the fertility of nature towards the production of the plants most profitable to man. A field overgrown with briars and brambles may frequently produce as great a quantity of vegetables as the best cultivated vineyard or corn field. Planting and tillage frequently regulate more than they animate the active fertility of nature; and after all their labour, a great part of the work always remains to be done by her. The labourers and labouring cattle, therefore, employed in agriculture, not only occasion, like the workmen in manufactures, the reproduction of a value equal to their own consumption, or to the capital which employs them, together with its owners' profits; but of a much greater value. Over and above the capital of the farmer and all its profits, they regularly occasion the reproduction of the rent of the landlord. This rent may be considered as the produce of those powers of nature, the use of which the landlord lends to the farmer. It is greater or smaller according to the supposed extent of those powers, or in other words, according to the supposed natural or improved fertility of the land. It is the work of nature which remains after deducting or compensating everything which can be regarded as the work of man. It is seldom less than a fourth, and frequently more than a third of the whole produce. No equal quantity of productive labour employed in manufactures can ever occasion so great a reproduction. In them nature does nothing; man does all; and the reproduction must always be in proportion to the strength of the agents that occasion it. The capital employed in agriculture, therefore, not only puts into motion a greater quantity of productive labour than any equal capital employed in manufactures, but in proportion, too, to the quantity of productive labour which it employs, it adds a much greater value to the annual produce of the land and labour of the country, to the real wealth and revenue of its inhabitants. Of all the ways in which a capital can be employed, it is by far the most advantageous to the society.

The capitals employed in the agriculture and in the retail trade of any society must always reside within that society. Their employment is confined almost to a precise spot, to the farm and to the shop of the retailer. They must generally, too, though there are some exceptions to this, belong to resident members of the society.

The capital of a wholesale merchant, on the contrary, seems to have no fixed or necessary residence anywhere, but may wander about from place to place, according as it can either buy cheap or sell dear.

The capital of the manufacturer must no doubt reside where the manufacture is carried on; but where this shall be is not always necessarily determined. It may frequently be at a great distance both from the place where the materials grow, and from that where the complete manufacture is consumed. Lyons is very distant both from the places which afford the materials of its manufactures, and from those which consume them. The people of fashion in Sicily are clothed in silks made in other countries, from the materials which their own produces. Part of the wool of Spain is manufactured in Great Britain, and some part of that cloth is afterwards sent back to Spain.

Whether the merchant whose capital exports the surplus produce of any society be a native or a foreigner is of very little importance. If he is a foreigner, the number of their productive labourers is necessarily less than if he had been a native by one man only, and the value of their annual produce by the profits of that one man. The sailors or carriers whom he employs may still belong indifferently either to his country or to their country, or to some third country, in the same manner as if he had been a native. The capital of a foreigner gives a value to their surplus produce equally with that of a native by exchanging it for something for which there is a demand at home. It as effectually replaces the capital of the person who produces that surplus, and as effectually enables him to continue his business; the service by which the capital of a wholesale merchant chiefly contributes to support the productive labour, and to augment the value of the annual produce of the society to which he belongs.

WRITING ASSIGNMENTS

Personal. Tell about a memorable experience you have had buying or selling something.

Research. Write a paper discussing the effects of a free market. Document your sources.

Persuasive. Write a paper arguing that an economy should have no controls or conversely that it should have some controls.

Analytical. Write a paper analyzing Smith's use of examples.

Investigative. Interview the owners or managers of stores in your area to find out the relationship between wholesale and retail prices and to determine how profit margins are calculated.

Conspicuous Consumption

THORSTEIN VEBLEN, 1899

Thorstein Veblen is best known for his book The Theory of the Leisure Class *(1899), from which the following excerpt is taken. The book is a devastating analysis of the causes of social pretense and snobbery. Although his work is a reflection of American society at the end of the nineteenth century, it is still relevant to contemporary society. He introduced the term "conspicuous consumption" into our vocabulary. Veblen struggled for acceptance during his lifetime, teaching at a number of different universities. Neither the university administrators nor the students were willing to accommodate his eccentric personality. Nevertheless, his contributions to an understanding of human behavior are still highly regarded.*

During the earlier stages of economic development, consumption of goods without stint, especially consumption of the better grades of goods—±ideally all consumption in excess of the subsistence minimum—pertains normally to the leisure class. This restriction tends to disappear, at least formally, after the later peaceable stage has been reached, with private ownership of goods and an industrial system based on wage labor or on the petty household economy. But during the earlier quasi-peaceable stage, when so many of the traditions through which the institution of a leisure class has affected the economic life of later times were taking form and consistency, this principle has had the force of a conventional law. It has served as the norm to which consumption has tended to conform, and any appreciable departure from it is to be regarded as an aberrant form, sure to be eliminated sooner or later in the further course of development.

The quasi-peaceable gentleman of leisure, then, not only consumes of the staff of life beyond the minimum required for subsistence and physical efficiency, but his consumption also undergoes a specialization as regards the quality of the goods consumed. He consumes freely and of the best, in food, drink, narcotics, shelter, services, ornaments, apparel, weapons and accoutrements, amusements, amulets, and idols or divinities. In the process of gradual amelioration which takes place in the articles of his consumption, the motive principle and the proximate aim of innovation is no doubt the higher efficiency of the improved and more elaborate products for personal comfort and well-being. But that does not remain the sole purpose of their consumption. The *canon* of reputability is at hand and seizes upon such innovations as are, according to its standard, fit to survive. Since the consumption of these more excellent goods is an evidence of wealth, it becomes honorific; and conversely, the failure to consume in due quantity and quality becomes a mark of inferiority and demerit.

This growth of punctilious discrimination as to qualitative excellence in eating, drinking, etc., presently affects not only the manner of life, but also the training and intellectual activity of the gentleman of leisure. He is no longer simply the successful, aggressive male—the man of strength, resource, and intrepidity. In order to avoid stultification he must also cultivate his tastes, for it now becomes incumbent on him to discriminate with some nicety between the noble and the ignoble in consumable goods. He becomes a connoisseur in creditable viands of various degrees of merit, in manly beverages and trinkets, in seemly apparel and architecture, in weapons, games, dances, and the narcotics. This cultivation of the aesthetic faculty requires time and *application*, and the demands made upon the gentleman in this direction therefore tend to change his life of leisure into a more or less arduous application to the business of learning how to live a life of ostensible leisure in a becoming way. Closely related to the requirement that the gentleman must consume freely and of the right kind of goods, there is the requirement that he must know how to consume them in a seemly manner. His life of leisure must be conducted in due form. Hence arise good manners in the way pointed out in an earlier chapter. High-bred manners and ways of living are items of conformity to the norm of conspicuous leisure and conspicuous consumption.

Conspicuous consumption of valuable goods is a means of reputability to the gentleman of leisure. As wealth accumulates on his hands, his own unaided effort will not avail to sufficiently put his opulence in evidence by this method. The aid of friends and competitors is therefore brought in by resorting to the giving of valuable presents and expensive feasts and entertainments. Presents and feasts had probably another origin than that of naive ostentation, but they acquired their utility for this purpose very early, and they have retained that character to the present; so that their utility in this respect has now long been the substantial ground on which these usages rest. Costly entertainments, such as the potlatch or the ball, are peculiarly adapted to serve this end. The competitor with whom the entertainer wishes to institute a comparison is, by this method, made to serve as a means to the end. He consumes vicariously for his host at the same time that he is a witness to the consumption of that excess of good things which his host is unable to dispose of singlehanded, and he is also made to witness his host's facility in etiquette.

In the giving of costly entertainments other motives, of a more genial kind, are of course also present. The custom of festive gatherings probably originated in motives of conviviality and religion; these motives are also present in the later development, but they do not continue to be the sole motives. The latter-day leisure-class festivities and entertainments may continue in some slight degree to serve the religious need and in a higher degree the needs of recreation and conviviality, but they also serve an invidious purpose; and they serve it none the less effectually for having a colorable non-invidious ground in these more avowable motives. But the economic effect of these social amenities is not therefore lessened, either in the vicarious consumption of goods or in the exhibition of difficult and costly achievements in etiquette.

As wealth accumulates, the leisure class develops further in function and structure, and there arises a differentiation within the class. There is a more or less elaborate system of rank and grades. This differentiation is furthered by the inheritance of wealth and the consequent inheritance of gentility. With the inheritance of gentility goes the inheritance of obligatory leisure; and gentility of a sufficient potency to entail a life of leisure may be inherited without the complement of wealth required to maintain a dignified leisure. Gentle blood may be transmitted without goods enough to afford a reputably free consumption at one's ease. Hence results a class of impecunious gentlemen of leisure, incidentally referred to already. These half-caste gentlemen of leisure fall into a system of hierarchical gradations. Those who stand near the higher and the highest grades of the wealthy leisure class, in point of birth, or in point of wealth, or both, outrank the remoter-born and the pecuniarily weaker. These lower grades, especially the impecunious, or marginal, gentlemen of leisure, affiliate themselves by a system of dependence or fealty to the great ones; by so doing they gain an increment of repute, or of the means with which to lead a life of leisure, from their patron. They become his courtiers or retainers, servants; and being fed and countenanced by their patron they are indices of his rank and vicarious consumers of his superfluous wealth. Many of these affiliated gentlemen of leisure are at the same time lesser men of substance in their own right; so that some of them are scarcely at all, others only partially, to be rated as vicarious consumers. So many of them, however, as make up the retainers and hangers-on of the patron may be classed as vicarious consumers without qualification. Many of these again, and also many of the other aristocracy of less degree, have in turn attached to their persons a more or less comprehensive group of vicarious consumers in the persons of their wives and children, their servants, retainers, etc.

Throughout this graduated scheme of vicarious leisure and vicarious consumption the rule holds that these offices must be performed in some such manner, or under some such circumstance or insignia, as shall point plainly to the master to whom this leisure or consumption pertains, and to whom therefore the resulting increment of good repute of right inures. The consumption and leisure executed by these persons for their master or patron represents an investment on his part with a view to an increase of good fame. As regards feasts and largesses this is obvious enough, and the imputation of repute to the host or patron here takes place immediately, on the ground of common notoriety. Where leisure and consumption is performed vicariously by henchmen and retainers, imputation of the resulting repute to the patron is effected by their residing ilear his person so that it may be plain to all men from what source they draw. As the group whose good esteem is to be secured in this way grows larger, more patent means are required to indicate the imputation of merit for the leisure performed, and to this end uniforms, badges, and liveries come into vogue. The wearing of uniforms or liveries implies a considerable degree of dependence, and may even be said to be a mark of servitude, real or ostensible. The wearers of uniforms and liveries may be roughly divided into two classes—the free and the servile, or the noble and the ignoble. The services performed by them are likewise divisible into noble and ignoble. Of course the distinction is not observed with strict consistency in practice; the less debasing of the base services and the less honorific of the noble functions are not infrequently merged in the same person. But the general distinction is not on that account to be overlooked. What may add some perplexity is the fact that this fundamental distinction between noble and ignoble, which rests on the nature of the ostensible service performed, is traversed by a secondary distinction into honorific and humiliating, resting on the rank of the person for whom the service is performed or whose livery is worn. So, those offices which are by right the proper employment of the leisure class are noble; such as government, fighting, hunting, the care of arms and accoutrements, and the like—in short, those which may be classed as ostensibly predatory employments. On the other hand, those employments which properly fall to the industrious class are ignoble; such as handicraft or other productive labor, menial services and the like. But a base service performed for a person of very high degree may become a very honorific office; as for instance the office of a Maid of Honor or of a Lady in Waiting to the Queen, or the King's Master of the Horse or his Keeper of the Hounds. The two offices last named suggest a principle of some general bearing. Whenever, as in these cases, the menial service in question has to do directly with the primary leisure employments of fighting and hunting, it easily acquires a reflected honorific character. In this way great honor may come to attach to an employment which in its own nature belongs to the baser sort.

In the later development of peaceable industry, the usage of employing an idle corps of uniformed men-at-arms gradually lapses. Vicarious consumption by dependents bearing the insignia of their patron or master narrows down to a corps of liveried menials. In a heightened degree, therefore, the livery comes to be a badge of servitude, or rather of servility. Something of a honorific character always attached to the livery of the armed retainer, but this honorific character disappears when the livery becomes the exclusive badge of the menial. The livery becomes obnoxious to nearly all who are required to wear it. We are yet so little removed from a state of effective slavery as still to be fully sensitive to the sting of any imputation of servility. This antipathy asserts itself even in the case of the liveries or uniforms which some corporations prescribe as the distinctive dress of their employees. In this country the aversion even goes the length of discrediting—in a mild and uncertain way—those government employments, military and civil, which require the wearing of a livery or uniform.

With the disappearance of servitude, the number of vicarious consumers attached to anyone gentleman tends, on the whole, to decrease. The like is of course true, and perhaps in a still higher degree, of the number of dependents who perform vicarious leisure for him. In a general way, though not wholly nor consistently, these two groups coincide. The dependent who was first delegated for these duties was the wife, or the chief wife; and, as would be expected, in the later development of the institution, when the number of persons by whom these duties are customarily performed gradually narrows, the wife remains the last. In the higher grades of society a large volume of both these kinds of service is required; and here the wife is of course still assisted in the work by a more or less numerous corps of menials. But as we descend the social scale, the point is presently reached where the duties of vicarious leisure and consumption devolve upon the wife alone. In the communities of the Western culture, this point is at present found among the lower middle class.

And here occurs a curious inversion. It is a fact of common observance that in this lower middle class there is no pretense of leisure on the part of the head of the household. Through force of circumstances it has fallen into disuse. But the middle-class wife still carries on the business of vicarious leisure, for the good name of the household and its master. In descending the social scale in any modern industrial community, the primary fact—the conspicuous leisure of the master of the household—disappears at a relatively high point. The head of the middle-class household has been reduced by economic circumstances to turn his hand to gaining a livelihood by occupations which often partake largely of the character of industry, as in the case of the ordinary business man of today. But the derivative fact—the vicarious leisure and consumption rendered by the wife, and the auxiliary vicarious performance of leisure by menials—remains in vogue as a conventionality which the demands of reputability will not suffer to be slighted. It is by no means an uncommon spectacle to find a man applying himself to work with the utmost assiduity, in order that his wife may in due form render for him that degree of vicarious leisure which the common sense of the time demands.

The leisure rendered by the wife in such cases is, of course, not a simple manifestation of idleness or indolence. It almost invariably occurs disguised under some form of work or household duties or social amenities, which prove on analysis to serve little or no ulterior end beyond showing that she does not occupy herself with anything that is gainful or that is of substantial use. As has already been noticed under the head of manners, the greater part of the customary round of domestic cares to which the middle-class housewife gives her time and effort is of this character. Not that the results of her attention to household matters, of a decorative and mundificatory character, are not pleasing to the sense of men trained in middle-class proprieties; but the taste to which these effects of household adornment and tidiness appeal is a taste which has been formed under the selective guidance of a canon of propriety that demands just these evidences of wasted effort. The effects are pleasing to us chiefly because we have been taught to find them pleasing. There goes into these domestic duties much solicitude for a proper combination of form and color, and for other ends that are to be classed as aesthetic in the proper sense of the term; and it is not denied that effects having some substantial aesthetic value are sometimes attained. Pretty much all that is here insisted on is that, as regards these amenities of life, the housewife's efforts are under the guidance of traditions that have been shaped by the law of conspicuously wasteful expenditure of time and substance. If beauty or comfort is achieved—and it is a more or less fortuitous circumstance if they are—they must be achieved by means and methods that commend themselves to the great economic law of wasted effort. The more reputable, "presentable" portion of middle-class household paraphernalia are, on the one hand, items of conspicuous consumption, and on the other hand, apparatus for putting in evidence the vicarious leisure rendered by the housewife.

The requirement of vicarious consumption at the hands of the wife continues in force even at a lower point in the pecuniary scale than the requirement of vicarious leisure. At a point below which little if any pretense of wasted effort, in ceremonial cleanness and the like, is observable, and where there is assuredly no conscious attempt at ostensible leisure, decency still requires the wife to consume some goods conspicuously for the reputability of the household and its head. So that, as the latter-day outcome of this evolution of an archaic institution, the wife, who was at the outset the drudge and chattel of the man, both in fact and in theory—the producer of goods for him to consume—has become the ceremonial consumer of goods which he produces. But she still quite unmistakably remains his chattel in theory; for the habitual rendering of vicarious leisure and consumption is the abiding mark of the unfree servant.

This vicarious consumption practiced by the household of the middle and lower classes can not be counted as a direct expression of the leisure-class scheme of life, since the household of this pecuniary grade does not belong within the leisure class. It is rather that the leisure-class scheme of life here comes to an expression at the second remove. The leisure class stands at the head of the social structure in point of reputability; and its manner of life and its standards of worth therefore afford the norm of reputability for the community. The observance of these standards, in some degree of approximation, becomes incumbent upon all classes lower in the scale. In modern civilized communities the lines of demarcation between social classes have grown vague and transient, and wherever this happens the norm of reputability imposed by the upper class extends its coercive influence with but slight hindrance down through the social structure to the lowest strata; The result is that the members of each stratum accept as their ideal of decency the scheme of life in vogue in the next higher stratum, and bend their energies to live up to that ideal. On pain of forfeiting their good name and their self-respect in case of failure, they must conform to the accepted code, at least in appearance.

The basis on which good repute in any highly organized industrial community ultimately rests is pecuniary strength; and the means of showing pecuniary strength, and so of gaining or retaining a good name, are leisure and a conspicuous consumption of goods. Accordingly, both of these methods are in vogue as far down the scale as it remains possible; and in the lower strata in which the two methods are employed, both offices are in great part delegated to the wife and children of the household. Lower still, where any degree of leisure, even ostensible, has become impracticable for the wife, the conspicuous consumption of goods remains and is carried on by the wife and children. The man of the household also can do something in this direction, and indeed, he commonly does; but with a still lower descent into the levels of indigence—along the margin of the slums—the man, and presently also the children, virtually cease to consume valuable goods for appearances, and the woman remains virtually the sole exponent of the household's pecuniary decency. No class of society, not even the most abjectly poor, forgoes all customary conspicuous consumption. The last items of this category of consumption are not given up except under stress of the direst necessity. Very much of squalor and discomfort will be endured before the last trinket or the last pretense of pecuniary decency is put away. There is no class and no country that has yielded so abjectly before the pressure of physical want as to deny themselves all gratification of this higher or spiritual need.

From the foregoing survey of the growth of conspicuous leisure and consumption, it appears that the utility of both alike for the purposes of reputability lies in the element of waste that is common to both. In the one case it is a waste of time and effort, in the other it is a waste of goods. Both are methods of demonstrating the possession of wealth, and the two are conventionally accepted as equivalents. The choice between them is a question of advertising expediency simply, except so far as it may be affected by other standards of propriety, springing from a different source. On grounds of expediency the preference may be given to the one or the other at different stages of the economic development. The question is, which of the two methods will most effectively reach the persons whose convictions it is desired to affect. Usage has answered this question in different ways under different circumstances.

So long as the community or social group is small enough and compact enough to be effectually reached by common notoriety alone—that is to say, so long as the human environment to which the individual is required to adapt himself in respect of reputability is comprised within his sphere of personal acquaintance and neighborhood gossip—so long the one method is about as effective as the other. Each will therefore serve about equally well during the earlier stages of social growth. But when the differentiation has gone farther and it becomes necessary to reach a wider human environment, consumption begins to hold over leisure as an ordinary means of decency. This is especially true during the later, peaceable economic stage. The means of communication and the mobility of the population now expose the individual to the observation of many persons who have no other means of judging of his reputability than the display of goods (and perhaps of breeding) which he is able to make while he is under their direct observation.

The modern organization of industry works in the same direction also by another line. The exigencies of the modern industrial system frequently place individuals and households in juxtaposition between whom there is little contact in any other sense than that of juxtaposition. One's neighbors, mechanically speaking, often are socially not one's neighbors, or even acquaintances; and still their transient good opinion has a high degree of utility. The only practicable means of impressing one's pecuniary ability on these unsympathetic observers of one's everyday life is an unremitting demonstration of ability to pay. In the modern community there is also a more frequent attendance at large gatherings of people to whom one's everyday life is unknown; in such places as churches, theaters, ballrooms, hotels, parks, shops, and the like. In order to impress these transient observers, and to retain one's self-complacency under their observation, the signature of one's pecuniary strength should be written in characters which he who runs may read. It is evident, therefore, that the present trend of the development is in the direction of heightening the utility of conspicuous consumption as compared with leisure.

It is also noticeable that the serviceability of consumption as a means of repute, as well as the insistence on it as an element of decency, is at its best in those portions of the community where the human contact of the individual is widest and the mobility of the population is greatest. Conspicuous consumption claims a relatively larger portion of the income of the urban than of the rural population, and the claim is also more imperative. The result is that, in order to keep up a decent appearance, the former habitually live hand-to-mouth to a greater extent than the latter. So it comes, for instance, that the American farmer and his wife and daughters are notoriously less modish in their dress, as well as less urbane in their manners, than the city artisan's family with an equal income. It is not that the city population is by nature much more eager for the peculiar complacency that comes of a conspicuous consumption, nor has the rural population less regard for pecuniary decency. But the provocation to this line of evidence, as well as its transient effectiveness, is more decided in the city. This method is therefore more readily resorted to, and in the struggle to outdo one another the city population push their normal standard of conspicuous consumption to a higher point, with the result that a relatively greater expenditure in this direction is required to indicate a given degree of pecuniary decency in the city. The requirement of conformity to this higher conventional standard becomes mandatory. The standard of decency is higher, class for class, and this requirement of decent appearance must be lived up to on pain of losing caste.

Consumption becomes a larger element in the standard of living in the city than in the country. Among the country population its place is to some extent taken by savings and home comforts known through the medium of neighborhood gossip sufficiently to serve the like general purpose of pecuniary repute. These home comforts and the leisure indulged in—where the indulgence is found—are of course also in great part to be classed as items of conspicuous consumption; and much the same is to be said of the savings. The smaller amount of the savings laid by the artisan class is no doubt due, in some measure, to the fact that in the case of the artisan the savings are a less effective means of advertisement, relative to the environment in which he is placed, than are the savings of the people living on farms and in the small villages. Among the latter, everybody's affairs, especially everybody's pecuniary status, are known to everybody else. Considered by itself simply—taken in the first degree—this added provocation to which the artisan and the urban laboring classes are exposed may not very seriously decrease the amount of savings; but in its cumulative action, through raising the standard of decent expenditure, its deterrent effect on the tendency to save cannot but be very great.

WRITING ASSIGNMENTS

PERSONAL. Write a paper telling about a time when you have bought something to impress your friends or neighbors.

RESEARCH. Write a research paper about different ways to spend leisure time. Document your sources.

<small>Persuasive.</small> Write a persuasive paper defending the position that people need leisure activities if they are to be successful and happy or that people should avoid wasting time.

<small>Analytical.</small> Write a paper analyzing the validity of Veblen's evidence.

<small>Investigative.</small> Identify clothes, cars, and/or other products that are designed to impress other people. How are these items marketed? Report your findings in a paper.

Politics and Law
Patriotism and Sport

G. K. Chesterton

A prolific writer, Chesterton produced a wide range of works including verse, novels, short stories, and essays. His essays cover a variety of topics addressing controversial questions about religion, politics, and cultural beliefs. This selection is taken from one of his most popular collections of essays entitled All Things Considered, *published in 1915.*

I notice that some papers, especially papers that call themselves patriotic, have fallen into quite a panic over the fact that we have been twice beaten in the world of sport, that a Frenchman has beaten us at golf, and that Belgians have beaten us at rowing. I suppose that the incidents are important to any people who ever believed in the self-satisfied English legend on this subject. I suppose that there are men who vaguely believe that we could never be beaten by a Frenchman, despite the fact that we have often been beaten by Frenchmen, and once by a Frenchwoman. In the old pictures in *Punch* you will find a recurring piece of satire. The English caricaturists always assumed that a Frenchman could not ride to hounds or enjoy English hunting. It did not seem to occur to them that all the people who founded English hunting were Frenchmen. All the Kings and nobles who originally rode to hounds spoke French. Large numbers of those Englishmen who still ride to hounds have French names. I suppose that the thing is important to any one who is ignorant of such evident matters as these. I suppose that if a man has ever believed that we English have some sacred and separate right to be athletic, such reverses do appear quite enormous and shocking. They feel as if, while the proper sun was rising in the east, some other and unexpected sun had begun to rise in the north-north-west by north. For the benefit, the moral and intellectual benefit of such people, it may be worth while to point out that the Anglo-Saxon has in these cases been defeated precisely by those competitors whom he has always regarded as being out of the running; by Latins, and by Latins of the most easy and unstrenuous type; not only by Frenchman, but by Belgians. All this, I say, is worth telling to any intelligent person who believes in the haughty theory of Anglo-Saxon superiority. But, then, no intelligent person does believe in the haughty theory of Anglo-Saxon superiority. No quite genuine Englishman ever did believe in it. And the genuine Englishman these defeats will in no respect dismay.

The genuine English patriot will know that the strength of England has never depended upon any of these things; that the glory of England has never had anything to do with them, except in the opinion of a large section of the rich and a loose section of the poor which copies the idleness of the rich. These people will, of course, think too much of our failure, just as they thought too much of our success. The typical Jingoes who have admired their countrymen too much for being conquerors will, doubtless, despise their countrymen too much for being conquered. But the Englishman with any feeling for England will know that athletic failures do not prove that England is weak, any more than athletic successes proved that England was strong. The truth is that athletics, like all other things, especially modern, are insanely individualistic. The Englishmen who win sporting prizes are exceptional among Englishmen, for the simple reason that they are exceptional even among men. English athletes represent England just about as much as Mr. Barnum's freaks represent America. There are so few of such people in the whole world that it is almost a toss-up whether they are found in this or that country.

If any one wants a simple proof of this, it is easy to find. When the great English athletes are not exceptional Englishmen they are generally not Englishmen at all. Nay, they are often representatives of races of which the average tone is specially incompatible with athletics. For instance, the English are supposed to rule the natives of India in virtue of their superior hardiness, superior activity, superior health of body and mind. The Hindus are supposed to be our subjects because they are less fond of action, less fond of openness and the open air. In a word, less fond of cricket. And, substantially, this is probably true, that the Indians are less fond of cricket. All the same, if you ask among Englishmen for the very best cricket-player, you will find that he is an Indian. Or, to take another case: it is, broadly speaking, true that the Jews are, as a race, pacific, intellectual, indifferent to war, like the Indians, or, perhaps, contemptuous of war, like the Chinese: nevertheless, of the very good prize-fighters, one or two have been Jews.

This is one of the strongest instances of the particular kind of evil that arises from our English form of the worship of athletics. It concentrates too much upon the success of individuals. It began, quite naturally and rightly, with wanting England to win. The second stage was that it wanted some Englishmen to win. The third stage was (in the ecstasy and agony of some special competition) that it wanted one particular Englishman to win. And the fourth stage was that when he had won, it discovered that he was not even an Englishman.

This is one of the points, I think, on which something might really be said for Lord Roberts and his rather vague ideas which vary between rifle clubs and conscription. Whatever may be the advantages or disadvantages otherwise of the idea, it is at least an idea of procuring equality and a sort of average in the athletic capacity of the people; it might conceivably act as a corrective to our mere tendency to see ourselves in certain exceptional athletes. As it is, there are millions of Englishmen who really think that they are a muscular race because C.B. Fry is an Englishman. And there are many of them who think vaguely that athletics must belong to England because Ranjitsinhji is an Indian.

But the real historic strength of England, physical and moral, has never had anything to do with this athletic specialism; it has been rather hindered by it. Somebody said that the Battle of Waterloo was won on Eton playing-fields. It was a particularly unfortunate remark, for the English contribution to the victory of Waterloo depended very much more than is common in victories upon the steadiness of the rank and file in an almost desperate situation. The Battle of Waterloo was won by the stubbornness of the common soldier—that is to say, it was won by the man who had never been to Eton. It was absurd to say that Waterloo was won on Eton cricket-fields. But it might have been fairly said that Waterloo was won on the village green, where clumsy boys played a very clumsy cricket. In a word, it was the average of the nation that was strong, and athletic glories do not indicate much about the average of a nation. Waterloo was not won by good cricket-players. But Waterloo was won by bad cricket-players, by a mass of men who had some minimum of athletic instincts and habits.

It is a good sign in a nation when such things are done badly. It shows that all the people are doing them. And it is a bad sign in a nation when such things are done very well, for it shows that only a few experts and eccentrics are doing them, and that the nation is merely looking on. Suppose that whenever we heard of walking in England it always meant walking forty-five miles a day without fatigue. We should be perfectly certain that only a few men were walking at all, and that all the other British subjects were being wheeled about in Bathchairs. But if when we hear of walking it means slow walking, painful walking, and frequent fatigue, then we know that the mass of the nation still is walking. We know that England is still literally on its feet.

The difficulty is therefore that the actual raising of the standard of athletics has probably been bad for national athleticism. Instead of the tournament being a healthy *melee* into which any ordinary man would rush and take his chance, it has become a fenced and guarded tilting-yard for the collision of particular champions against whom no ordinary man would pit himself or even be permitted to pit himself. If Waterloo was won on Eton cricket-fields it was because Eton cricket was probably much more careless then than it is now. As long as the game was a game, everybody wanted to join in it. When it becomes an art, every one wants to look at it. When it was frivolous it may have won Waterloo: when it was serious and efficient it lost Magersfontein.

In the Waterloo period there was a general rough-and-tumble athleticism among average Englishmen. It cannot be re-created by cricket, or by conscription, or by any artificial means. It was a thing of the soul. It came out of laughter, religion, and the spirit of the place. But it was like the modern French duel in this—that it might happen to anybody. If I were a French journalist it might really happen that Monsieur Clemenceau might challenge me to meet him with pistols. But I do not think that it is at all likely that Mr. C. B. Fry will ever challenge me to meet him with cricket-bats.

WRITING ASSIGNMENTS

PERSONAL. Write a narrative about a sporting event you have seen that had national implications.

RESEARCH. Write a paper discussing different kinds of international sporting events. Document your sources.

PERSUASIVE. Write a paper arguing that the number of international sporting events should be expanded.

ANALYTICAL. Write a paper discussing Chesterton's use of irony.

INVESTIGATIVE. Look at the coverage of an international sporting event in news reports from several different countries. Identify and analyze differences in reporting.

I'd Rather Be Black Than Female

SHIRLEY CHISHOLM

A representative to the US House from 1969–1983, Shirley Chisholm was a dedicated advocate of social justice. She was the first black representative to Congress and she was the first black woman to see the nomination for the presidency. In this essay she makes a case for political activism.

Being the first black woman elected to Congress has made me some kind of phenomenon. There are nine other blacks in Congress; there are ten other women. I was the first to overcome both handicaps at once. Of the two handicaps, being black is much less of a drawback than being female.

If I said that being black is a greater handicap than being a woman, probably no one would question me. Why? Because "we all know" there is prejudice against black people in America. That there is prejudice against women is an idea that still strikes nearly all men—and, I am afraid, most women—as bizarre.

Prejudice against blacks was invisible to most white Americans for many years. When blacks finally started to "mention" it, with sit-ins, boycotts, and freedom rides, Americans were incredulous. "Who, us?" they asked in injured tones. "We're prejudiced?" It was the start of a long, painful reeducation for white America. It will take years for whites—including those who think of themselves as liberals—to discover and eliminate the racist attitudes they all actually have.

How much harder will it be to eliminate the prejudice against women? I am sure it will be a longer struggle. Part of the problem is that women in America are much more brainwashed and content with their roles as second-class citizens than blacks ever were.

Let me explain. I have been active in politics for more than twenty years. For all but the last six, I have done the work—all the tedious details that make the difference between victory and defeat on election day—while men reaped the rewards, which is almost invariably the lot of women in politics.

It is still women—about three million volunteers—who do most of this work in the American political world. The best any of them can hope for is the honor of being district or county vice-chairman, a kind of separate-but-equal position with which a woman is rewarded for years of faithful envelope stuffing and card-party organizing. In such a job, she gets a number of free trips to state and sometimes national meetings and conventions, where her role is supposed to be to vote the way her male chairman votes.

When I tried to break out of that role in 1963 and run for the New York State Assembly seat from Brooklyn's Bedford-Stuyvesant, the resistance was bitter. From the start of that campaign, I faced undisguised hostility because of my sex.

But it was four years later, when I ran for Congress, that the question of my sex became a major issue. Among members of my own party, closed meetings were held to discuss ways of stopping me.

My opponent, the famous civil-rights leader James Farmer, tried to project a black, masculine image; he toured the neighborhood with sound trucks filled with young men wearing Afro haircuts, dashikis, and beards. While the television crews ignored me, they were not aware of a very important statistic, which both I and my campaign manager, Wesley MacD. Holder, knew. In my district there are 2.5 women for every man registered to vote. And those women are organized—in PTAs, church societies, card clubs, and other social and service groups. I went to them and asked their help. Mr. Farmer still doesn't quite know what hit him.

When a bright young woman graduate starts looking for a job, why is the first question always: "Can you type?" A history of prejudice lies behind that question. Why are women thought of as secretaries, not administrators? Librarians and teachers, but not doctors and lawyers? Because they are thought of as different and inferior. The happy homemaker and the contented darky are both stereotypes produced by prejudice.

Women have not even reached the level of tokenism that blacks are reaching. No women sit on the Supreme Court. Only two have held Cabinet rank, and none do at present. Only two women hold ambassadorial rank. But women predominate in the lower-paying, menial, unrewarding, dead-end jobs, and when they do reach better positions, they are invariably paid less than a man gets for the same job.

If that is not prejudice, what would you call it?

A few years ago, I was talking with a political leader about a promising young woman as a candidate. "Why invest time and effort to build the girl up?" he asked me. "You know she'll only drop out of the game to have a couple of kids just about the time we're ready to run her for mayor."

Plenty of people have said similar things about me. Plenty of others have advised me, every time I tried to take another upward step, that I should go back to teaching, a woman's vocation, and leave politics to the men. I love teaching, and I am ready to go back to it as soon as I am convinced that this country no longer needs a woman's contribution.

When there are no children going to bed hungry in this rich nation, I may be ready to go back to teaching. When there is a good school for every child, I may be ready. When we do not spend our wealth on hardware to murder people, when we no longer tolerate prejudice against minorities, and when the laws against unfair housing and unfair employment practices are enforced instead of evaded, then there may be nothing more for me to do in politics.

But until that happens—and we all know it will not be this year or next—what we need is more women in politics, because we have a very special contribution to make. I hope that the example of my success will convince other women to get into politics—and not just to stuff envelopes, but to run for office.

It is women who can bring empathy, tolerance, insight, patience, and persistence to government—the qualities we naturally have or have had to develop because of our suppression by men. The women of a nation mold its morals, its religion, and its politics by the lives they live. At present, our country needs women's idealism and determination, perhaps more in politics than anywhere else.

1970

WRITING ASSIGNMENTS

PERSONAL. Tell a story about a woman you admire.

RESEARCH. Write a research paper explaining the effects of discrimination against women.

PERSUASIVE. Write a paper arguing that women should either become active in one of the political parties or organize themselves outside traditional politics.

ANALYTICAL. Write a paper analyzing Chisholm's use of examples. How do they support her main idea?

INVESTIGATIVE. Identify a female political leader. Devise a survey to determine what people think of her. Report your findings in a paper.

LANGUAGE AND THE ARTS
Style

BEN JONSON

A contemporary of William Shakespeare, Ben Jonson was a highly successful poet and dramatist who influenced many younger poets. These young men were sometimes called "The Tribe of Ben" or "The Sons of Ben." This excerpt comes from a collection of short essays in the collection Timber; or Discoveries Made Upon Men and Matter *(published posthumously in 1640).*

For a man to write well, there are required three necessaries. To read the best authors, observe the best speakers: and much exercise of his own style. In style to consider, what ought to be written; and after what manner. He must first think and excogitate his matter; then choose his words, and examine the weight of either. Then take care in placing, and ranking both matter, and words, that the composition be comely; and to do this with diligence, and often. No matter how slow the style be at first, so it be laboured, and accurate; seek the best, and be not glad of the forward conceits, or first words that offer themselves to us, but judge of what we invent, and order what we approve. Repeat often what we have formerly written; which beside that it helps the consequence, and makes the juncture better, it quickens the heat of imagination, that often cools in the time of setting down, and gives it new strength, as if it grew lustier by the going back. As we see in the contention of leaping, they jump farthest that fetch their race largest: or, as in throwing a dart or javelin, we force back our arms to make our loose the stronger. Yet, if we have a fair gale of wind, I forbid not the steering out of our sail, so the favour of the gale deceive us not. For all that we invent doth please us in the conception or birth; else we would never set it down. But the safest is to return to our judgment, and handle over again those things, the easiness of which might make them justly suspected. So did the best writers in their beginnings; they imposed upon themselves care, and industry. They did nothing rashly. They obtained first to write well, and then custom made it easy and a habit. By little and little, their matter showed itself to them more plentifully; their words answered, their composition followed; and all, as in a well ordered family, presented itself in the place. So that the sum of all is: ready writing makes not good writing; but good writing brings on ready writing. Yet when we think we have got the faculty, it is even then good to resist it; as to give a horse a check sometimes with a bit, which doth not so much stop his course, as stir his mettle. Again, whether a man's genius is best able to reach thither, it should more and more contend, lift and dilate itself, as men of low stature raise themselves on their toes, and so oft times get even, if not eminent. Besides, as it is fit for grown and able writers to stand of themselves, and work with their own strength, to trust and endeavour by their own faculties; so it is fit for the beginner, and learner, to study others, and the best. For the mind and memory are more sharply exercised in comprehending another man's things than our own; and such as accustom themselves, and are familiar with the best authors, shall ever and anon find somewhat of them in themselves, and in the expression of their minds, even when they feel it not, be able to utter something like theirs, which hath an authority above their own. Nay, sometimes it is the reward of a man's study, the praise of quoting another man fitly: and though a man be more prone and able for one kind of writing than another, yet he must exercise all. For as in an instrument, so in style, there must be a harmony and consent of parts.

WRITING ASSIGNMENTS

PERSONAL. Tell about an experience you have had in a writing class.

RESEARCH. Identify several different approaches to teaching writing. Report your findings in a documented paper.

PERSUASIVE. Write a paper advocating that a particular approach to teaching writing should be used.

ANALYTICAL. Analyze the organization of Jonson's essay.

INVESTIGATIVE. Examine several different types of publications (e.g., news papers, magazines, scientific journals, encyclopedias, etc.) and identify the characteristics of the style in each. Report your findings in a paper.

The Heresy of the Didactic

EDGAR ALLAN POE

Most people think of Edgar Allan Poe as a writer of haunting poems like "The Raven" and "Annabel Lee" as well as Gothic short stories like "The Fall of the House of Usher" and "The Cask of Amontillado." He was, however, also an important literary critic and literary theorist. This excerpt comes from "The Philosophy of Composition" first published in Graham's Magazine *in 1846.*

. . . . It has been assumed, tacitly and avowedly, directly and indirectly, that the ultimate object of all Poetry is Truth. Every poem, it is said, should inculcate a moral; and by this moral is the poetical merit of the work to be adjudged. We Americans especially have patronized this happy idea; and we Bostonians, very especially, have developed it in full. We have taken it into our heads that to write a poem simply for the poem's sake, and to acknowledge such to have been our design, would be to confess ourselves radically wanting in the true Poetic dignity and force:—but the simple fact is, that, would we permit ourselves to look into our own souls, we should immediately there discover that under the sun there exists nor *can* exist any work more thoroughly dignified—more supremely noble than this very poem—this poem *per se*—this poem which is a poem and nothing more—this poem written solely for the poem's sake.

With as deep a reverence for the True as ever inspired the bosom of man, I would, nevertheless, limit, in some measure, its modes of inculcation. I would limit to enforce them. I would not enfeeble them by dissipation. The demands of Truth are severe. She has no sympathy with the myrtles. All *that* which is so indispensable in Song, is precisely all *that* with which *she* has nothing whatever to do. It is but making her a flaunting paradox, to wreathe her in gems and flowers. In enforcing a truth, we need severity rather than efflorescence of language. We must be simple, precise, terse. We must be cool, calm, unimpassioned. In a word, we must be in that mood which, as nearly as possible, is the exact converse of the poetical. *He* must be blind indeed who does not perceive the radical and chasmal differences between the truthful and poetical modes of inculcation. He must be theory-mad beyond redemption who, in spite of these differences, shall still persist in attempting to reconcile the obstinate oils and waters of Poetry and Truth.

Dividing the world of the mind into its three most immediately obvious distinctions, we have the Pure Intellect, Taste, and the Moral Sense. I place Taste in the middle, because it is just this position which, in the mind, it occupies. It holds intimate relations with wither extreme; but from the Moral Sense is separated by so faint a difference that Aristotle has not hesitated to place some of its operations among the virtues themselves. Nevertheless, we find the *offices* of the trio marked with a sufficient distinction. Just as the Intellect concerns itself with Truth, so Taste informs us of the Beautiful while the Moral Sense is regardful of Duty. Of this latter, while Conscience teaches the obligation, and Reason the expediency, Taste contents herself with displaying the charms:— waging war upon Vice solely on the ground of her deformity—her disproportion—her animosity to the fitting, to the appropriate, to the harmonious—in a word, to Beauty.

An immortal instinct, deep within the spirit of man, is thus, plainly, a sense of the Beautiful. This is what administers to his delight in the manifold forms, and sounds and odors, and sentiments amid which he exists. And just as the lily is repeated in the lake, or the eyes of Amaryllis in the mirror, so is the mere oral or written repetition of these forms, and sounds, and colors, and odors, and sentiments, a duplicate source of delight. But this mere repetition is not poetry. He who shall simply sing, with however glowing enthusiasm, or with however vivid a truth of description, of the sights, and sounds, and odors, and colors, and sentiments, which greet *him* in common with all mankind—he, I say, has yet failed to prove his divine title. There is still a something in the distance which he has been unable to attain. We have still a thirst unquenchable, to allay which he has not shown us the crystal springs. This thirst belongs to the immortality of Man. It is at once a consequence and an indication of his perennial existence. It is the desire of the moth for the star. It is no mere appreciation of the Beauty before us—but a wild effort to reach the Beauty above. Inspired by an ecstatic presence of the glories beyond the grave, we struggle, by multiform combinations among the things and thoughts of Time, to attain a portion of Loveliness whose very elements, perhaps, appertain to eternity alone. And thus when by Poetry—or when by Music, the most entrancing of the Poetic moods—we find ourselves melted into tears—we weep then . . . through excess of pleasure, but through a certain, petulant, impatient sorrow at our inability to grasp *now*, wholly, here on earth, at once and forever, those divine and rapturous joys, of which *through* the poem, or *through* the music, we attain to but brief and indeterminate glimpses.

The struggle to apprehend the supernal Loveliness—this struggle, on the part of souls fittingly constituted—has given to the world all *that* which it (the world) has ever been enabled at once to understand and to *feel* as poetic.

The Poetic Sentiment, of course, may develop itself in various modes—in painting, in Sculpture, in Architecture, in the Dance—very especially in Music—and very peculiarly, and with a wide field, in the composition of the Landscape Garden. Our present theme, however, has regard only to its manifestations in words. And here let me speak briefly on the topic of rhythm. Contenting myself with the certainty that Music, in its various modes of metre, rhythm, and rhyme, is of so vast a moment in Poetry as never to be wisely rejected—is so vitally important an adjunct, that he is simply silly who declines its assistance, I will not now pause to maintain its absolute essentiality. It is in Music, perhaps, that the soul most nearly attains the great end for which, when inspired by the Poetic Sentiment, it struggles—the creation of supernal Beauty. It *may* be, indeed, that here this sublime end is, now and then, attained *in fact*. We are often made to feel with a shivering delight, that from an earthly harp are stricken notes which *cannot* have been unfamiliar to the angels. And thus there can be little doubt that in the union of Poetry with Music in its popular sense, we shall find the widest field for the Poetic development. The old Bards and Minnesingers had advantages which we do not possess—and Thomas More, singing his own songs, was, in the most legitimate manner, perfecting them as poems.

To recapitulate, then:—I would define, in brief, the Poetry of words as *The Rhythmical Creation of Beauty*. Its sole arbiter is Taste. With the Intellect or with the Conscience, it has only collateral relations. Unless incidentally, it has no concern whatever with Duty or with Truth.

A few words, however, in explanation. *That* pleasure which is at once the most pure, the most elevating, and the most intense, is derived, I maintain, from the contemplation of the Beautiful. In the contemplation of Beauty we alone find it possible to attain that pleasurable elevation, or excitement *of the soul*, which we recognize as the Poetic Sentiment, and which is so easily distinguished from Truth, which is the satisfaction of the Reason, or from passion, which is the excitement of the heart. I make Beauty, therefore—using the word as inclusive of the sublime—I make Beauty the province of the poem, simple because it is an obvious rule of Art that effects should be made to spring as directly as possible from their causes: no one as yet having been weak enough to deny that the peculiar elevation in question is at least *most readily* attainable in the poem. It by no means follows however, that the incitements of Passion, or the precepts of Duty, or even the Lessons of Truth, may not be introduced into a poem, and with advantage; for they may subserve, incidentally, in various ways, the general purposes of the work:—but the true artist will always contrive to tone them down in proper subjection to that *Beauty* which is at atmosphere and the real essence of the poem.

WRITING ASSIGNMENTS

PERSONAL. Write a narrative that tells about a time when you were struck by the beauty of something (a poem, a song, a painting, or a sculpture).

RESEARCH. Identify and discuss different kinds of beauty. Document your sources.

PERSUASIVE. Write a paper arguing that the arts should be encouraged in public schools.

ANALYTICAL. Analyze Poe's use of definition.

INVESTIGATIVE. Go to an art museum and using as many paintings or sculptures as you wish, come up with a definition of beauty.

NATURE AND OTHER HABITATS
Rites of Summer

DONELLA MEADOWS

An important voice in American environmentalism, Donella Meadows was best known for her work on the 1972 book The Limits of Growth. *This essay, written in 1996 reflects her interest in system dynamics as it applies to the natural world.*

The slugs ate the sprouting zinnias right down to the ground.

So we put nine ducklings in the garden to eat the slugs. The ducklings ate the slugs and then they ate the spinach and trampled the peas. So we moved six ducklings down to the pond and left just three to patrol slugs. The raccoon circled the garden fence at night, trying to eat the ducklings. So every sunset we shut the ducklings in a cage to be safe from raccoons, even though slugs come out and eat zinnias mostly at night.

Meanwhile, the fleabeetles ate the sprouting radishes right down to the ground. We replanted the radishes and covered them with a spun-plastic row cover, so the fleabeetles couldn't get at them. That seems to have worked, so far.

We spotted a coyote, hoping to eat lamb, circling the pasture where the sheep are grazing. So we moved the sheep to the orchard near the house. They ate the orchard grass. Then they ate the apple trees. We moved the sheep back to the pasture with an electric fence around them (solar-powered). That has worked, so far.

Meanwhile, the father duck down on the pond keeps attacking the six ducklings. We hatched them out in an incubator, and he doesn't know they're his own children. We throw stones at him to scare him off. It seems to be working, so far.

The witch grass is sending its relentless roots through the bean and sunflower rows. The ground ivy is crowding the lawn grass. The crows are eating the sprouting corn. The old dog is too mellow and arthritic to chase the crows. The fleas are eating the dog. The carpenter ants are eating the house. The mosquitoes and black flies are eating us. The swallows circle overhead, eating the mosquitoes and black flies, but not fast enough.

In the spring and summer on this organic farm where we try to work with the forces of nature, we expend all the energy and cleverness we can summon, trying to keep things from eating things. And nature laughs. We have been farming here for twenty-three years. Nature has worked here for 10,000, since the glacier left, developing a self-balancing system where everything eats everything else, but everything thrives without human help. Nature put white pine and sugar maple here, deer and wolf, beaver, wild grape, wild turkey, salmon, trout, marsh marigold, scarlet tanager, black fly, and smart, lean ducks—not sheep, potatoes, chickens, zinnias, or the stupid, fat, nearly flightless ducks that humans have bred.

Even organic farming distorts nature's system. We push that land to produce the life forms we eat. We don't care about what other creatures eat. If we did, we would, as people did here from the time the glacier melted, catch trout, hunt deer, pick berries, and plant scattered plots of native corn, pumpkins, and beans in a system so stable we could sow in the spring, go wandering all summer, and come back to a successful harvest. There would be many fewer of us, and we would live more simply. But we wouldn't have to twist and prod nature to produce only for us. And we would have enough.

One of nature's laws says that a population growing in numbers or material consumption must be taking sustenance from other populations. The human population is now taking about 40 percent of all that the earth's land produces. We are planning to double our material standard of living sooner than that. We can do so only at the expense of self-balancing natural systems. And we cannot do it for long, because another of nature's laws says that no population can grow in numbers and consumption forever.

Yet another law says that the more we push a natural system our way instead of its way, the more we have to expend muscle energy, fossil fuel energy, and cleverness. As God put it, when he expelled Adam and Eve from hunter-gatherer paradise: "Cursed is the ground for thy sake; in sorrow shalt thou eat of it all the days of thy life; thorns also and thistles shall it bring forth to thee . . . (I)n the sweat of thy face shalt thou eat bread."

This terrific curse does not for a moment dampen our enthusiasm for farming. We like to eat corn, potatoes, and duck; we like to make bouquets of zinnias. In the sweat of our faces, we try to maintain what we call order on twenty acres. We leave fifty acres untouched, so other creatures may have food and so, when we and those who come after us tire, when we run out of fossil fuels, chemicals, and cleverness, nature will still have sugar maples, white pines, beavers, and black flies to work with, to rebuild a system that runs beautifully without any help from us.

1996

WRITING ASSIGNMENTS

PERSONAL. Discuss an experience you have had growing something.

RESEARCH. Write a research paper examining the major causes of environmental destruction.

PERSUASIVE. Write a paper defending the idea that we must conserve our natural resources.

ANALYTICAL. Write an analysis of Meadows' descriptions of the natural world.

INVESTIGATIVE. Observe community gardens, public gardens, or a farmers' market. How do they exemplify the idea of conservation? Report your findings in a paper.

The Woods and the Pacific

ROBERT LOUIS STEVENSON

Robert Louis Stevenson is certainly best known for his novels, especially his two classics Treasure Island *(1883) and* Dr Jekyll and Mr Hyde *(1886). The reading that follows is an excerpt from* Across the Plains, *a travel memoir about a trip across America by train from New York to San Francisco in 1879. It was first published in 1883.*

The Bay of Monterey has been compared by no less a person than General Sherman to a bent fishing-hook; and the comparison, if less important than the march through Georgia, still shows the eye of a soldier for topography. Santa Cruz sits exposed at the shank; the mouth of the Salinas river is at the middle of the bend; and Monterey itself is cozily ensconced beside the barb. Thus the ancient capital of California faces across the bay, while the Pacific Ocean, though hidden by low hills and forest, bombards her left flank and rear with never-dying surf. In front of the town, the long line of sea-beach trends north and northwest, and then westward to enclose the bay. The waves which lap so quietly about the jetties of Monterey grow louder and larger in the distance; you can see breakers leaping high and white by day; at night, the outline of the shore is traced in transparent silver by the moonlight and the flying foam; and from all around, even in quiet weather, the low, distant, thrilling roar of the

Pacific hangs over the coast and the adjacent country like smoke above the battle.

These long beaches are enticing to the idle man. It would be hard to find a walk more solitary and at the same time more exciting to the mind. Crowds of ducks and sea-gulls hover over the sea. Sandpipers trot in and out by troops after the retiring waves, trilling together in a chorus of infinitesimal song. Strange sea-tangles, new to the European eye, the bones of whales, or sometimes a whole whale's carcass, white with carrion-gulls and poisoning the wind, lie scattered here and there along the sands. The waves come in slowly, vast and green, curve their translucent necks, and burst with a surprising uproar, that runs, waxing and waning, up and down the long keyboard of the beach. The foam of these great ruins mounts in an instant to the ridge of the sand glacis, swiftly fleets back again, and is met and buried by the next breaker. The interest is perpetually fresh. On no other coast that I know shall you enjoy, in calm, sunny weather, such a spectacle of Ocean's greatness, such beauty of changing colour, or such degrees of thunder in the sound. The very air is more than usually salt by this Homeric deep.

Inshore, a tract of sand-hills borders on the beach. Here and there a lagoon, more or less brackish, attracts the birds and hunters. A rough, spotty undergrowth partially conceals the sand. The crouching, hardy, live-oaks flourish singly or in thickets—the kind of wood for murderers to crawl among—and here and there the skirt of the forest extends downward from the hills with a floor of turf and long aisles of pine-trees hung with Spaniard's Beard. Through this quaint desert the railway cars drew near to Monterey from the junction at Salinas City—though that and so many other things are now forever altered—and it was from here that you had the first view of the old township lying in the sands, its white windmills bickering in the chill, perpetual wind, and the first fogs of the evening drawing drearily around it from the sea.

The one common note of all this country is the haunting presence of the ocean. A great faint sound of breakers follows you high up into the inland canyons; the roar of water dwells in the clean, empty rooms of Monterey as in a shell upon the chimney; go where you will, you have but to pause and listen to hear the voice of the Pacific. You pass out of the town to the southwest, and mount the hill among pine woods. Glade, thicket, and grove surround you. You follow winding sandy tracks that lead now thither. You see deer; a multitude of quail arises. But the sound of the sea still follows you, as you advance, like that of wind among the trees, only harsher and stranger to the ear; and when at length you gain the summit, out breaks on every hand and with freshened vigor, that same unending, distant, whispering rumble of the ocean; for now you are on the top of Monterey peninsula, and the noise no longer only mounts to you from behind along the beach towards Santa Cruz, but from your right also, round by Chinatown and Pino lighthouse, and from down before you to the mouth of the Carmello River. The whole woodland is begirt with thundering surges. The silence that immediately surrounds you where you stand is not so much broken as it is haunted by this distant, circling rumor. It sets your senses upon edge; you strain your attention; you are clearly and unusually conscious of small sounds near at hand; you walk listening like an Indian hunter; and the voice of the Pacific is a sort of disquieting company to you in your walk.

WRITING ASSIGNMENTS

PERSONAL. Tell about an experience you have had in a scenic place.

RESEARCH. Write a research paper about the most popular kinds of destinations for outdoor vacations.

PERSUASIVE. Write a paper arguing that people should spend time in contact with nature.

ANALYTICAL. Analyze Stevenson's use of descriptive imagery.

INVESTIGATIVE. Go to a scenic place. Identify its unique qualities. Report your findings in a paper.

SCIENCE AND TECHNOLOGY
Sexual Selection

CHARLES DARWIN

Charles Darwin, the British naturalist, is best known for his theory of evolution as explained in his book On the Origin of Species by Means of Natural Selection, *published in 1859. This excerpt is from* The Descent of Man, *published in 1871.*

In the lower divisions of the animal kingdom, Sexual Selection seems to have done nothing: such animals are often affixed for life to the same spot, or have the sexes combined in the same individual, or what is still more important, their perceptive and intellectual faculties are not sufficiently advanced to allow of the feelings of love and jealousy, or of the exertion of choice. When, however, we come to the Arthropoda and Vertebrata, even to the lowest classes in these two great Sub-Kingdoms, Sexual Selection has effected much.

In the several great classes of the animal kingdom—in mammals, birds, reptiles, fishes, insects, and even crustaceans—the differences between the sexes follow nearly the same rules. The males are almost always the wooers; and they alone are armed with special weapons for fighting with their rivals. They are generally stronger and larger than the females, and are endowed with the requisite qualities of courage and pugnacity. They are provided, either exclusively or in a much higher degree than the females, with organs for vocal or instrumental music, and with odoriferous glands. They are ornamented with infinitely diversified appendages, and with the most brilliant or conspicuous colours, often arranged in elegant patterns, whilst the females are unadorned. When the sexes differ in more important matters, it is the male which is provided with special sense-organs for discovering the female, with locomotive organs for reaching her, and often with prehensile organs for holding her. These various structures for charming or securing the female are often developed in the male during only part of the year, namely the breeding-season. They have in many cases been more or less transferred to the females; and in the latter case they often appear in her as mere rudiments. They are lost or never gained by the males after emasculation. Generally they are not developed in the male during early youth, but appear a short time before the age for reproduction. Hence in most cases the young of both sexes resemble each other: and the female somewhat resembles her young offspring throughout life. In almost every great class a few anomalous cases occur, where there has been an almost complete transposition of the characters proper to the two sexes; the females assuming characters which properly belong to the males. This surprising uniformity in the laws regulating the differences between the sexes in so many and such widely separated classes, is intelligible if we admit the action of one common cause, namely Sexual Selection.

Sexual Selection depends on the success of certain individuals over others of the same sex, in relation to the propagation of the species; whilst Natural Selection depends on the success of both sexes, at all ages, in relation to the general conditions of life. The sexual struggle is of two kinds; in the one it is between the individuals of the same sex, generally the males. In order to drive away or kill their rivals, the females remaining passive; whilst in the other, the struggle is likewise between the individuals of the same sex, in order to excite or charm those of the opposite sex, generally the females, which no longer remain passive, but select the more agreeable partners. This latter kind of selection is closely analogous to that which man unintentionally, yet effectually, brings to bear on his domesticated productions, when he preserves during a long period the most pleasing or useful individuals, without any wish to modify the breed.

The laws of inheritance determine whether characters gained through Sexual Selection by either sex shall be transmitted to one and the same sex, or to both; as well as the age at which they shall be developed. It appears that variations arising late in life are commonly transmitted to one and the same sex. Variability is the necessary basis for the action of selection, and is wholly independent of it. It follows from this, that variations of the same general nature have often been taken advantage of and accumulated through Sexual Selection in relation to the propagation of the species, as well as through Natural Selection in relation to the general purposes of life. Hence secondary sexual characters, when equally transmitted to both sexes can be distinguished from ordinary specific characters only by the light of analogy. The modifications acquired through Sexual Selection are often so strongly pronounced that the two sexes have frequently been ranked as distinct species, or even as distinct genera. Such strongly-marked differences must be in some manner highly important; and we know that they have been acquired in some instances at the cost not only of inconvenience, but of exposure to actual danger.

The belief in the power of Sexual Selection rests chiefly on the following considerations. Certain characters are confined to one sex; and this alone renders it probable that in most cases they are connected with the act of reproduction. In innumerable instances these characters are fully developed only at maturity, and often during only a part of the year, which is always the breeding-season. The males (passing over a few exceptional cases) are the more active in courtship; they are the better armed, and are rendered the more attractive in various ways. It is to be especially observed that the males display their attractions with elaborate care in the presence of the females; and that they rarely or never display them excepting during the season of love. It is incredible that all this should be purposeless. Lastly we have distinct evidence with some quadrupeds and birds, that the individuals of one sex are capable of feeling a strong antipathy or preference for certain individuals of the other sex.

Bearing in mind these facts, and the marked results of man's unconscious selection, when applied to domesticated animals and cultivated plants, it seems to me almost certain that if the individuals of one sex were during a long series of generations to prefer pairing with certain individuals of the other sex, characterized in some peculiar manner, the offspring would slowly but surely become modified in this same manner. I have not attempted to conceal that, excepting when the males are more numerous than the females, or when polygamy prevails, it is doubtful how the more attractive males succeed in leaving a larger number of offspring to inherit their superiority in ornaments or other charms than the less attractive males; but I have shown that this would probably follow from the females—especially the more vigorous ones, which would be the first to breed—preferring not only the more attractive but at the same time the more vigorous and victorious males.

Although we have some positive evidence that birds appreciate bright and beautiful objects, as with the bower-birds of Australia, and although they certainly appreciate the power of song, yet I fully admit that it is astonishing that the females of many birds and some mammals should be endowed with sufficient taste to appreciate ornaments, which we have reason to attribute to Sexual Selection; and this is even more astonishing in the case of reptiles, fish, and insects. But we really know little about the minds of the lower animals. It cannot he supposed, for instance, that male birds of paradise or peacocks should take such pains in erecting, spreading, and vibrating their beautiful plumes before the females for no purpose. We should remember that fact given on excellent authority in a former chapter, that several peahens, when debarred from an admired male, remained widows during a whole season rather than pair with another bird.

Nevertheless I know of no fact in natural history more wonderful than that the female Argus pheasant should appreciate the exquisite shading of the ball-and-socket ornaments and the elegant patterns on the wing-feathers of the male. He who thinks that the male was created as he now exists must admit that the great plumes, which prevent the wings from being used for flight, and which are displayed during courtship and at no other time in a manner quite peculiar to this one species, were given to him as an ornament. If so, he must likewise admit that the female was created and endowed with the capacity of appreciating such ornaments. I differ only in the conviction that the male Argus pheasant acquired his beauty gradually, through the preference of the females during many generations for the more highly ornamented males; the aesthetic capacity of the females having been advanced through exercise or habit, just as our own taste is gradually improved. In the male through the fortunate chance of a few feathers being left unchanged, we can distinctly trace how simple spots with a little fulvous shading on one side may have been developed by small steps into the wonderful ball-and-socket ornaments; and it is probable that they were actually thus developed.

Everyone who admits the principle of evolution, and yet feels great difficulty in admitting that female mammals, birds, reptiles, and fish, could have acquired the high taste implied by the beauty of the males, and which generally coincides with our own standard, should reflect that the nerve-cells of the brain in the highest as well as in the lowest members of the Vertebrate series, are derived from those of the common progenitor of this great Kingdom. For we can thus see how it has come to pass that certain mental faculties, in various and widely distinct groups of animals, have been developed in nearly the same manner and to nearly the same degree.

The reader who has taken the trouble to go through the several chapters devoted to Sexual Selection, will be able to judge how far the conclusions at which I have arrived are supported by sufficient evidence. If he accepts these conclusions he may, I think, safely extend them to mankind; but it would be superfluous here to repeat what I have so lately said on the manner in which Sexual Selection apparently has acted on man, both on the male and female side, causing the two sexes to differ in body and mind, and the several races to differ from each other in various characters, as well as from their ancient and lowly-organized progenitors.

He who admits the principle of Sexual Selection will be led to the remarkable conclusion that the nervous system not only regulates most of the existing functions of the body, but has indirectly influenced the progressive development of various bodily structures and of certain mental qualities. Courage, pugnacity, perseverance, strength and size of body, weapons of all kinds, musical organs, both vocal and instrumental, bright colours and ornamental appendages, have all been indirectly gained by the one sex or the other, through the exertion of choice, the influence of love and jealousy, and the appreciation of the beautiful in sound, colour or form; and these powers of the mind manifestly depend on the development of the brain.

Man scans with scrupulous care the character and pedigree of his horses, cattle, and dogs before he matches them; but when he comes to his own marriage he rarely, or never, takes any such care. He is impelled by nearly the same motives as the lower animals, when they are left to their own free choice, though he is in so far superior to them that he highly values mental charms and virtues. On the other hand he is strongly attracted by mere wealth or rank. Yet he might by selection do something not only for the bodily constitution and frame of his offspring, but for their intellectual and moral qualities. Both sexes ought to refrain From marriage if they are in any marked degree inferior in body or mind but such hopes are Utopian and will never be even partially realized until the laws of inheritance are thoroughly known. Everyone does good service, who aids towards this end. When the principles of breeding and inheritance are better understood, we shall not hear ignorant members of our legislature rejecting with scorn a plan for ascertaining whether or not consanguineous marriages are injurious to man.

The advancement of the welfare of mankind is a most intricate problem: all ought to refrain from marriage who cannot avoid abject poverty for their children; For poverty is not only a great evil, but tends to its own increase by leading to recklessness in marriage. On the other hand, as Mr Galton has remarked, if the prudent avoid marriage, whilst the reckless marry, the inferior members tend to supplant the better members of society. Man, like every other animal, has no doubt advanced to his present high condition through a struggle for existence consequent on his rapid multiplication; and if he is to advance still higher, it is to be feared that he must remain subject to a severe struggle. Otherwise he would sink into indolence, and the more gifted men would not be more successful in the battle of life than the less gifted. Hence our natural rate of increase, though leading to many and obvious evils, must not be greatly diminished by any means. There should be open competition for all men; and the most able should not be prevented by laws or customs from succeeding best and rearing largest number of offspring. Important as the struggle for existence has been and even still is, yet as far as the highest part of man's nature is concerned there are other agencies more important. For the moral qualities are advanced, either directly or indirectly, much more through the effects of habit, the reasoning powers, instruction, religion, etc., than through Natural Selection; though to this latter agency may he safely attributed the social instincts, which afforded the basis for the development of the moral sense.

The main conclusion arrived at in this work, namely that man is descended from some lowly organized form, will, I regret to think, be highly distasteful to many. But there can hardly be a doubt that we are descended from barbarians. The astonishment which I felt on first seeing a party of Feugians on a wild and broken shore will never be forgotten by me, for the reflection at once rushed into my mind—such were our ancestors. These men were absolutely naked and bedaubed with paint, their long hair was tangled, their mouths frothed with excitement, and their expression was wild, startled, and distrustful. They possessed hardly any arts, and like wild animals lived on what they could catch; they had no government, and were merciless to every one not of their own small tribe. He who has seen a savage in his native land will not feel much shame, if forced to acknowledge that the blood of some more humble creature flows in his veins. For my own part I would as soon be descended from that heroic little monkey, who braved his dreaded enemy in order to save the life of his keeper, or from that old baboon, who descending from the mountains, carried away in triumph his young comrade from a crowd of astonished dogs—as from a savage who delights to torture his enemies, offers up bloody sacrifices, practises infanticide without remorse, treats his wives like slaves, knows no decency, and is haunted by the grossest superstitions.

Man may he excused for feeling some pride at having risen, though not through his own exertions, to the very summit of the organic scale: and the fact of his having thus risen, instead of having been aboriginally placed there, may give him hope for a still higher destiny in the distant future. But we are not here concerned with hopes or fears, only with the truth as far as our reason permits us to discover it; and I have given the evidence to the best of my ability. We must, however, acknowledge, as it seems to me, that man with all his noble qualities, with sympathy which feels for the most debased, with benevolence which extends not only to other men but to the humblest living creature, with his god-like intellect which has penetrated into the movements and constitution of the solar system—with all these exalted powers—Man still bears in his bodily frame the indelible stamp of his lowly origin.

WRITING ASSIGNMENTS

PERSONAL. Write about a time when you observed a sexual display in an animal (like a peacock displaying its tail).

RESEARCH. Discuss the different kinds of sexual display in a group of animals (birds, for example).

PERSUASIVE. Write a paper advocating that people should rise above barbaric behavior.

ANALYTICAL. Analyze Darwin's use of inductive reasoning.

INVESTIGATIVE. Conduct a survey among classmates and friends to find out the level of tolerance for barbaric behavior among your peers.

What Is a Scientific Paper?

ROBERT A. DAY

Robert Day has written extensively about the IMRAD method of reporting research. The following essay outlines some of the most important features of that approach.

A scientific paper is a paper organized to meet the needs of valid publication. It is, or should be, highly stylized, with distinctive and clearly evident component parts. The most common labeling of the component parts, in the basic sciences, is Introduction, Methods, Results, and Discussion (hence, the acronym IMRAD). Actually, the heading "Materials and Methods" may be more common than the simpler "Methods," but it is the latter form that was fixed in the acronym.

I have taught and recommended the IMRAD approach for many years. Until recently, however, there have been several somewhat different systems of organization that were preferred by some journals and some editors. The tendency toward uniformity has increased since the IMRAD system was prescribed as a standard by the American National Standards Institute, first in 1972 and again in 1979 (American National Standards Institute, 1979). A recent variation in IMRAD has been introduced by *Cell* and several other journals. In this variation, methods appear last rather than second. Perhaps we should call this IRDAM.

The basic IMRAD order is so eminently logical that, increasingly, it is used for many other types of expository writing. Whether one is writing an article about chemistry, archeology, economics, or crime in the streets, the IMRAD format is often the best choice.

This is generally true for papers reporting laboratory studies. There are, of course, exceptions. As examples, reports of field studies in the earth sciences and clinical case reports in the medical sciences do not readily lend themselves to this kind of organization. However, even in these "descriptive" papers, the same logical progression from problem to solution is often appropriate.

Occasionally, the organization of even laboratory papers must be different. If a number of methods were used to achieve directly related results, it might be desirable to combine the Materials and Methods and the Results into an integrated "Experimental" section. Rarely, the results might be so complex or provide such contrasts that immediate discussion seems necessary, and a combined Results and Discussion section might then be desirable. In addition, many primary journals publish "Notes" or "Short Communications," in which the IMRAD organization is abridged.

Various types of organization are used in descriptive areas of science. To determine how to organize such papers, and which general headings to use, you will need to refer to the Instructions to Authors of your target journal. If you are in doubt as to the journal, or if the journal publishes widely different kinds of papers, you can obtain general information from appropriate source books. For example, the several major types of medical papers are described in detail by Huth (1990), and the many types of engineering papers and reports are outlined by Michaelson (1990).

In short, I take the position that the preparation of a scientific paper has less to do with literary skill than with organization. A scientific paper is not literature. The preparer of a scientific paper is not an author in the literary sense.

Some of my old-fashioned colleagues think that scientific papers should be literature, that the style and flair of an author should be clearly evident, and that variations in style encourage the interest of the reader. I disagree. I think scientists should indeed be interested in reading literature, and perhaps even in writing literature, but the communication of research results is a more prosaic procedure. As Booth (1981) put it, "Grandiloquence has no place in scientific writing."

Today, the average scientist, to keep up with a field, must examine the data reported in a very large number of papers. Therefore, scientists (and of course editors) must demand a system of reporting data that is uniform, concise, and readily understandable.

Understanding the Signals

Scientific writing is the transmission of a clear signal to a recipient. The words of the signal should be as clear and simple and well ordered as possible. In scientific writing, there is little need for ornamentation. The flowery literary embellishments—the metaphors, the similes, the idiomatic expressions—are very likely to cause confusion and should seldom be used in writing research papers.

Science is simply too important to be communicated in anything other than words of certain meaning. And that clear, certain meaning should pertain not just to peers of the author, but also to students just embarking on their careers, to scientists reading outside their own narrow discipline, and especially to those readers (the majority of readers today) whose native language is other than English.

Many kinds of writing are designed for entertainment. Scientific writing has a different purpose: to communicate new scientific findings. Scientific writing should be as clear and simple as possible.

Language of a Scientific Paper

In addition to organization, the second principal ingredient of a scientific paper should be appropriate language. In this book, I keep emphasizing proper use of English, because most scientists have trouble in this area. All scientists must learn to use the English language with precision. A book (Day, 1992) wholly concerned with English for scientists is now available.

If scientifically determined knowledge is at least as important as any other knowledge, it must be communicated effectively, clearly, in words of certain meaning. The scientist, to succeed in this endeavor, must therefore be literate. David B. Truman, when he was Dean of Columbia College, said it well: "in the complexities of contemporary existence the specialist who is trained but uneducated, technically skilled but culturally incompetent, is a menace."

Although the ultimate result of scientific research is publication, it has always amazed me that so many scientists neglect the responsibilities involved. A scientist will spend months or years of hard work to secure data, and then unconcernedly let much of their value be lost because of lack of interest in the communication process. The same scientist who will overcome tremendous obstacles to carry out a measurement to the fourth decimal place will be in deep slumber while a secretary is casually changing micrograms per milliliter to milligrams per milliliter and while the compositor slips in an occasional pounds per barrel.

English need not be difficult. In scientific writing, we say: "The best English is that which gives the sense in the fewest short words" (a dictum printed for some years in the Instructions to Authors of the *Journal of Bacteriology*). Literary devices, metaphors and the like, divert attention from the substance to the style. They should be used rarely in scientific writing.

1979

WRITING ASSIGNMENTS

PERSONAL. Recount an experience you have had in a science laboratory.

RESEARCH. Write a research paper about the kinds of evidence that can be used as proof in scientific research.

PERSUASIVE. Write a persuasive paper arguing that students should make sure that their papers on scientific subjects are presented simply and accurately.

ANALYTICAL. Write a paper analyzing Day's method of organization.

INVESTIGATIVE. Find two lab reports. How close are they to Day's formula? Report your findings in a paper.

PHILOSOPHY AND RELIGION
The Allegory of the Cave

PLATO

Plato is perhaps the most famous philosopher in history. Alfred North Whitehead said, "The safest general characterization of the European philosophical tradition is that it consists of a series of footnotes to Plato." This famous passage is from Book VII of Plato's The Republic *written in 360 B.C.E. It is a conversation between Socrates and Glaucon, Plato's older brother.*

And now, I said, let me show in a figure how far our nature is enlightened or unenlightened: —Behold! human beings living in a underground den, which has a mouth open towards the light and reaching all along the den; here they have been from their childhood, and have their legs and necks chained so that they cannot move, and can only see before them, being prevented by the chains from turning round their heads. Above and behind them a fire is blazing at a distance, and between the fire and the prisoners there is a raised way; and you will see, if you look, a low wall built along the way, like the screen which marionette players have in front of them, over which they show the puppets.

I see.

And do you see, I said, men passing along the wall carrying all sorts of vessels, and statues and figures of animals made of wood and stone and various materials, which appear over the wall? Some of them are talking, others silent.

You have shown me a strange image, and they are strange prisoners.

Like ourselves, I replied; and they see only their own shadows, or the shadows of one another, which the fire throws on the opposite wall of the cave?

True, he said; how could they see anything but the shadows if they were never allowed to move their heads?

And of the objects which are being carried in like manner they would only see the shadows?

Yes, he said.

And if they were able to converse with one another, would they not suppose that they were naming what was actually before them?

Very true.

And suppose further that the prison had an echo which came from the other side, would they not be sure to fancy when one of the passers-by spoke that the voice which they heard came from the passing shadow?

No question, he replied.

To them, I said, the truth would be literally nothing but the shadows of the images.

That is certain.

And now look again, and see what will naturally follow if the prisoners are released and disabused of their error. At first, when any of them is liberated and compelled suddenly to stand up and turn his neck round and walk and look towards the light, he will suffer sharp pains; the glare will distress him, and he will be unable to see the realities of which in his former state he had seen the shadows; and then conceive some one saying to him, that what he saw before was an illusion, but that now, when he is approaching nearer to being and his eye is turned towards more real existence, he has a clearer vision,—what will be his reply? And you may further imagine that his instructor is pointing to the objects as they pass and requiring him to name them,—will he not be perplexed? Will he not fancy that the shadows which he formerly saw are truer than the objects which are now shown to him?

Far truer.

And if he is compelled to look straight at the light, will he not have a pain in his eyes which will make him turn away to take and take in the objects of vision which he can see, and which he will conceive to be in reality clearer than the things which are now being shown to him?

True, he said.

And suppose once more, that he is reluctantly dragged up a steep and rugged ascent, and held fast until he's forced into the presence of the sun himself, is he not likely to be pained and irritated? When he approaches the light his eyes will be dazzled, and he will not be able to see anything at all of what are now called realities.

Not all in a moment, he said.

He will require to grow accustomed to the sight of the upper world. And first he will see the shadows best, next the reflections of men and other objects in the water, and then the objects themselves; then he will gaze upon the light of the moon and the stars and the spangled heaven; and he will see the sky and the stars by night better than the sun or the light of the sun by day?

Certainly.

Last of he will be able to see the sun, and not mere reflections of him in the water, but he will see him in his own proper place, and not in another; and he will contemplate him as he is.

Certainly.

He will then proceed to argue that this is he who gives the season and the years, and is the guardian of all that is in the visible world, and in a certain way the cause of all things which he and his fellows have been accustomed to behold?

Clearly, he said, he would first see the sun and then reason about him.

And when he remembered his old habitation, and the wisdom of the den and his fellow-prisoners, do you not suppose that he would felicitate himself on the change, and pity them?

Certainly, he would.

And if they were in the habit of conferring honours among themselves on those who were quickest to observe the passing shadows and to remark which of them went before, and which followed after, and which were together; and who were therefore best able to draw conclusions as to the future, do you think that he would care for such honours and glories, or envy the possessors of them? Would he not say with Homer,

Better to be the poor servant of a poor master, and to endure anything, rather than think as they do and live after their manner?

Yes, he said, I think that he would rather suffer anything than entertain these false notions and live in this miserable manner.

Imagine once more, I said, such an one coming suddenly out of the sun to be replaced in his old situation; would he not be certain to have his eyes full of darkness?

To be sure, he said.

And if there were a contest, and he had to compete in measuring the shadows with the prisoners who had never moved out of the den, while his sight was still weak, and before his eyes had become steady (and the time which would be needed to acquire this new habit of sight might be very considerable) would he not be ridiculous? Men would say of him that up he went and down he came without his eyes; and that it was better not even to think of ascending; and if any one tried to loose another and lead him up to the light, let them only catch the offender, and they would put him to death.

No question, he said.

This entire allegory, I said, you may now append, dear Glaucon, to the previous argument; the prison-house is the world of sight, the light of the fire is the sun, and you will not misapprehend me if you interpret the journey upwards to be the ascent of the soul into the intellectual world according to my poor belief, which, at your desire, I have expressed whether rightly or wrongly God knows. But, whether true or false, my opinion is that in the world of knowledge the idea of good appears last of all, and is seen only with an effort; and, when seen, is also inferred to be the universal author of all things beautiful and right, parent of light and of the lord of light in this visible world, and the immediate source of reason and truth in the intellectual; and that this is the power upon which he who would act rationally, either in public or private life must have his eye fixed.

I agree, he said, as far as I am able to understand you.

Moreover, I said, you must not wonder that those who attain to this beatific vision are unwilling to descend to human affairs; for their souls are ever hastening into the upper world where they desire to dwell; which desire of theirs is very natural, if our allegory may be trusted.

Yes, very natural.

And is there anything surprising in one who passes from divine contemplations to the evil state of man, misbehaving himself in a ridiculous manner; if, while his eyes are blinking and before he has become accustomed to the surrounding darkness, he is compelled to fight in courts of law, or in other places, about the images or the shadows of images of justice, and is endeavouring to meet the conceptions of those who have never yet seen absolute justice?

Anything but surprising, he replied.

Any one who has common sense will remember that the bewilderments of the eyes are of two kinds, and arise from two causes, either from coming out of the light or from going into the light, which is true of the mind's eye, quite as much as of the bodily eye; and he who remembers this when he sees any one whose vision is perplexed and weak, will not be too ready to laugh; he will first ask whether that soul of man has come out of the brighter light, and is unable to see because unaccustomed to the dark, or having turned from darkness to the day is dazzled by excess of light. And he will count the one happy in his condition and state of being, and he will pity the other; or, if he have a mind to laugh at the soul which comes from below into the light, there will be more reason in this than in the laugh which greets him who returns from above out of the light into the den.

That, he said, is a very just distinction.

WRITING ASSIGNMENTS

PERSONAL. Write about a time when you experienced an awakening, when you discovered something significant that you hadn't known before.

RESEARCH. Identify other belief systems that seek to explain a truth beyond reality. Report your findings in a documented paper.

PERSUASIVE. Write a paper arguing that students should search for eternal truths rather than being satisfied with learning facts.

ANALYTICAL. Analyze the structure and effect of the dialogue.

INVESTIGATIVE. Create a survey and use it to discover the core beliefs most students hold. Report your findings in a paper.

Where I Have Lived, and What I Lived For

HENRY DAVID THOREAU, 1854

Walden, an account of Thoreau's two-year stay in the woods near Walden Pond just outside Concord, Massachusetts, is the acknowledged classic of American nature writing. In this selection, the second chapter of the work, we encounter Thoreau's wide-ranging and challenging observations about himself and his culture. Many of his assertions are as surprising to us now as they were to his contemporaries.

At a certain season of our life we are accustomed to consider every spot as the possible site of a house. I have thus surveyed the country on every side within a dozen miles of where I live. In imagination I have bought all the farms in succession, for all were to be bought, and I knew their price. I walked over each farmer's premises, tasted his wild apples, discoursed on husbandry with him, took his farm at his price, at any price, mortgaging it to him in my mind; even put a higher price on it,— every thing but a deed of it,—took his word for his deed, for I dearly love to talk,—cultivated it, and him too to some extent, I trust, and withdrew when I had enjoyed it long enough, leaving him to carry it on. This experience entitled me to be regarded as a sort of real estate broker by my friends. Wherever I sat, there I might live, and the landscape radiated from me accordingly. What is a house but a sedes, a seat?—better if a country seat. I discovered many a site for a house not likely to be *soon* improved, which some might have thought too far from the village, but to my eyes the village was too far from it. Well, there I might live, I said; and there I did live, for an hour, a summer and a winter life; saw how I could let the years run off, buffet the winter through, and see the spring come in. The future inhabitants of this region wherever they may place their houses may be sure that they have been anticipated. An afternoon sufficed to lay out the land into orchard woodlot, and pasture, and to decide what fine oaks or pines should be left to stand before the door, and whence each blasted tree could he seen to the best advantage; and then I let it lie, fallow perchance, for a man is rich in proportion to the number of things which he can afford to let alone.

My imagination carried me so far that I even had the refusal of several farms,—the refusal was all I wanted, I never got my fingers burned by actual possession. The nearest that I came to actual possession was when I bought the Hollowell place, and had begun to sort my seeds, and collected materials with which to make a wheelbarrow to carry it on or off with; but before the owner gave me a deed of it, his wife—every man has such a wife—changed her mind and wished to keep it, and he offered me ten dollars to release him. *Now*, to speak the truth, I had but ten cents in the world, and it surpassed my arithmetic to tell, if I was that man who had ten cents, or who had a farm, or ten dollars, or all together. However, I let him keep the ten dollars and the farm too, for I had carried it far enough; or rather, to be generous, I sold him the farm for just what I gave for it, and, as he was not a rich man, made him a present of ten dollars, and still had my ten cents, and seeds, and materials for a wheelbarrow left. I found thus that I had been a rich man without any damage to my poverty. But I retained the landscape, and I have since annually carried off what it yielded without a wheelbarrow. With respect to landscapes,—

I am monarch of all I *survey*, My right there is none to dispute."

I have frequently seen a poet withdraw, having enjoyed the most valuable part of a farm, while the crusty farmer supposed that he had got a few wild apples only. Why, the owner does not know it for many years when a poet has put his farm in rhyme, the most admirable kind of invisible fence, has fairly impounded it, milked it, skimmed it, and got all the cream, and left the farmer only the skimmed milk.

The real attractions of the Hollowell farm, to me, were; its complete retirement, being about two miles from the village, half a mile from the nearest neighbor, and separated from the highway by a broad field; its bounding on the river, which the owner said protected it by its fogs from frosts in the spring, though that was nothing to me; the gray color and ruinous state of the house and barn, and the dilapidated fences, which put such an interval between me and the last occupant; the hollow and lichen-covered apple trees, gnawed by rabbits, showing what kind of neighbors I should have; but above all, the recollection I had of it from my earliest voyages up the river, when the house was concealed behind a dense grove of red maples, through which I heard the house-dog bark. I was in haste to buy it, before the proprietor finished getting out some rocks, cutting down the hollow apple trees, and grubbing up some young birches which had sprung up in the pasture, or, in short, had made any more of his improvements. To enjoy these advantages I was ready to carry it on; like Atlas, to take the world on my shoulders,—I never heard what compensation he received for that,—and do all those things which had no other motive or excuse but that I might pay for it and be unmolested in my possession of it; for I knew all the while that it would yield the most abundant crop of the kind I wanted if I could only afford to let it alone. But it turned out as I have said.

All that I could say, then, with respect to farming on a large scale, (I have always cultivated a garden,) was, that I had had my seeds ready. Many think that seeds improve with age. I have no doubt that time discriminates between the good and the bad; and when at last I shall plant, I shall be less likely to be disappointed. But I would say to my fellows, once for all, As long as possible live free and uncommitted. It makes but little difference whether you are committed to a farm or the county jail.

Old Cato, whose "De Re Rustica" is my "Cultivator," says, and the only translation I have seen makes sheer nonsense of the passage, "When you think of getting a farm, turn it thus in your mind, not to buy greedily; nor spare your pains to look at it, and do not think it enough to go round it once. The oftener you go there the more it will please you, if it is good." I think I shall not buy greedily, but go round and round it as long as I live, and be buried in it first, that it may please me the more at last.

The present was my next experiment of this kind, which I purpose to describe more at length; for convenience, putting the experience of two years into one. As I have said, I do not propose to write an ode to dejection, but to brag as lustily as chanticleer in the morning, standing on his roost, if only to wake my neighbors.

When first I took up my abode in the woods, that is, began to spend my nights as well as days there, which, by accident, was on Independence day, or the fourth of July, 1845, my house was not finished for winter, but was merely a defence against the rain, without plastering or chimney, the walls being of rough weather-stained boards, with wide chinks, which made it cool at night. The upright white hewn studs and freshly planed door and window casings gave it a clean and airy look, especially in the morning, when its timbers were saturated with dew, so that I fancied that by noon some sweet gum would exude from them. To my imagination it retained throughout the day more or less of this auroral character, reminding me of a certain house on a mountain which I had visited the year before. This was an airy and unplastered cabin, fit to entertain a travelling god, and where a goddess might trail her garments. The winds which passed over my dwelling were such as sweep over the ridges of mountains bearing the broken strains, or celestial parts only, of terrestrial music. The morning wind forever blows the poem of creation is uninterrupted, but few are the ears that hear it Olympus is but the outside of the earth every where.

The only house I had been the owner of before, if I except a boat, was a tent, which I used occasionally when making excursions in the summer, and this is still rolled up in my garret; but the boat, after passing from hand to hand, has gone down the stream of time. With this more substantial shelter about me, I had made some progress toward settling in the world. This frame, so slightly clad, was a sort of crystallization around me, and reacted on the builder. It was suggestive somewhat as a picture in outlines. I did not need to go out doors to take the air, for the atmosphere within had lost none of its freshness. It was not so much within doors as behind a door where I sat, even in the rainiest weather. The Harivansa says, "An abode without birds is like a meat without seasoning." Such was not my abode, for I found myself suddenly neighbor to the birds; not by having imprisoned one, but having caged myself near them. I was not only nearer to some of those which commonly frequent the garden and the orchard, but to those wilder and more thrilling songsters of the forest which never, or rarely, serenade a villager,—the wood-thrush, the veery, the scarlet tanager, the field-sparrow, the whippoorwill, and many others.

I was seated by the shore of a small pond, about a mile and a half south of the village of Concord and somewhat higher than it, in the midst of an extensive wood between that town and Lincoln, and about two miles south of that our only field known to fame, Concord Battle Ground; but I was so low in the woods that the opposite shore, half a mile off, like the rest, covered with wood, was my most distant horizon. For the first week, whenever I looked out on the pond it impressed me like a tarn high up on the side of a mountain, its bottom far above the surface of other lakes, and, as the sun arose, I saw it throwing off its nightly clothing of mist, and here and there, by degrees, its soft ripples or its smooth reflecting surface was revealed, while the mists, like ghosts, were stealthily withdrawing in every direction into the woods, as at the breaking up of some nocturnal conventicle. The very dew seemed to hang upon the trees later into the day than usual, as on the sides of mountains.

This small lake was of most value as a neighbor in the intervals of a gentle rain storm in August, when, both air and water being perfectly still, but the sky overcast, mid-afternoon had all the serenity of evening, and the wood-thrush sang around, and was heard from shore to shore. A lake like this is never smoother than at such a time; and the clear portion of the air above it being shallow and darkened by clouds, the water, full of light and reflections, becomes a lower heaven itself so much the more important. From a hill top near by, where the wood had been recently cut off, there was a pleasing vista southward across the pond, through a wide indentation in the hills which form the shore there, where their opposite sides sloping toward each other suggested a stream flowing out in that direction through a wooded valley, but stream there was none. That way I looked between and over the near green hills to some distant and higher ones in the horizon, tinged with blue. Indeed, by standing on tiptoe I could catch a glimpse of some of the peaks of the still bluer and more distant mountain ranges in the north-west, those true-blue coins from heaven's own mint, and also of some portion of the village. But in other directions, even from this point, I could not see over or beyond the woods which surrounded me. It is well to have some water in your neighborhood to give buoyancy to and float the earth. One value even of the smallest well is, that when you look into it you see that earth is not continent but insular. This is as important as that it keeps butter cool. When I looked across the pond from this peak toward the Sudbury meadows, which in time of flood I distinguished elevated perhaps by a mirage in their seething valley, like a coin in a basin, all the earth beyond the pond appeared like a thin crust insulated and, floated even by this small sheet of intervening water, and I was reminded that this on which I dwelt was but dry land. [. . .]

Every morning was a cheerful invitation to make my life of equal simplicity, and I may say innocence, with Nature herself. I have been as sincere a worshipper of Aurora as the Greeks. I got up early and bathed in the pond; that was a religious exercise, and one of the best things which I did. They say that characters were engraven on the bathing tub of king Tching-thang [Confucius] to this effect: "Renew thyself completely each day; do it again, and again, and forever again." I can understand that Morning brings back, the heroic ages. I was as much affected by the faint hum of a mosquito making its invisible and unimaginable tour through my apartment at earliest dawn, when I was sitting with door and windows open, as I could be by any trumpet that ever sang of fame. It was Homer's requiem; itself an Iliad and Odyssey in the air, singing its own wrath and wanderings. There was something cosmical about it; a standing advertisement, till forbidden, of the everlasting vigor and fertility of the world. The morning, which is the most memorable season of the day, is the awakening hour. Then there is least somnolence in us; and for an hour, at least, some part of us awakes which slumbers all the rest of the day and night. Little is to be expected of that day, if it can be called a day, to which we are not awakened by our Genius, but by the mechanical nudgings of some servitor, are not awakened by our own newly-acquired force and aspirations from within, accompanied by the undulations of celestial music, instead of factory bells, and a fragrance filling the air—to a higher life than we fell asleep from; and thus the darkness bear its fruit, and prove itself to be good, no less than the light. That man who does not believe that each day contains an earlier, more sacred, and auroral hour than he has yet profaned, has despaired of life, and is pursuing a descending and darkening way. After a partial cessation of his sensuous life, the soul of man, or its organs rather, are reinvigorated each day, and his Genius tries again what noble life it can make. All memorable events, I should say, transpire in morning lime and in a morning atmosphere. The Vedas say, "All intelligences awake with the morning." Poetry and art, and the fairest and most memorable of the actions of men, date from such an hour. All poets and heroes, like Memnon, are the children of Aurora, and emit their music at sunrise. To him whose elastic and vigorous thought keeps pace with the sun, the day is a perpetual morning. It matters not what the clocks say or the attitudes and labors of men. Morning is when I am awake and there is a dawn in me. Moral reform is the effort to throw off sleep. Why is it that men give so poor an account of their day if they have not been slumbering? They are not such poor calculators. If they had not been overcome with drowsiness they would have performed something. The millions are awake enough for physical labor; but only one in a million is awake enough for effective intellectual exertion, only one in a hundred millions to a poetic or divine life. To be awake is to be alive. I have never yet met a man who was quite awake. How could I have looked him in the face?

We must learn to reawaken and keep ourselves awake, not by mechanical aids, but by an infinite expectation of the dawn, which does not forsake us in our soundest sleep. I know of no more encouraging fact than the unquestionable ability of man to elevate his life by a conscious endeavor. It is something to be able to paint a particular picture, or to carve a statue, and so to make a few objects beautiful; but it is far more glorious to carve and paint the very atmosphere and medium through which we look, which morally we can do. To affect the quality of the day, that is the highest of arts. Every man is tasked to make his life, even in its details, worthy of the contemplation of his most elevated and critical hour. If we refused, or rather used up, such paltry information as we get, the oracles would distinctly inform us how this might be done.

I went to the woods because I wished to live deliberately, to front only the essential facts of life, and see if I could not learn what it had to teach, and not, when I came to die, discover that I had not lived. I did not wish to live what was not life, living is so dear; nor did I wish to practise resignation, unless it was quite necessary. I wanted to live deep and suck out all the marrow of life, to live so sturdily and Spartan-like as to put to rout all that was not life, to cut a broad swath and shave close, to drive life into a corner, and reduce it to its lowest terms, and, if it proved to be mean, why then to get the whole and genuine meanness of it, and publish its meanness to the world; or if it were sublime, to know it by experience, and be able to give a true account of it in my next excursion. For most men, it appears to me, are in a strange uncertainty about it, whether it is of the devil or of God, and have somewhat hastily concluded that it is the chief end of man here to "glorify God and enjoy him forever."

Still we live meanly, like ants; though the fable tells us that we were long ago changed into men; like pygmies we fight with cranes; it is error upon error, and clout upon clout, and our best virtue has for its occasion a superfluous and evitable wretchedness. Our life is frittered away by detail. An honest man has hardly need to count more than his ten fingers, or in extreme cases he may add his ten toes, and lump the rest. Simplicity, simplicity, simplicity! I say, let your affairs be as two or three, and not a hundred or a thousand; instead of a million count half a dozen, and keep your accounts on your thumb nail. In the midst of this chopping sea of civilized life, such are the clouds and storms and quicksands and thousand-and-one items to be allowed for, that a man has to live, if he would not founder and go to the bottom and not make his port at all, by dead reckoning, and he must be a great calculator indeed who succeeds. Simplify, simplify. Instead of three meals a day, if it be necessary eat but one; instead of a hundred dishes, five; and reduce other things in proportion. Our life is like a German Confederacy, made up of petty states, with its boundary forever fluctuating, so that even a German cannot tell you how it is bounded at any moment. The nation itself, with all its so called internal improvements, which, by the way, are all external and superficial, is just such an unwieldy and overgrown establishment, cluttered with furniture and tripped up by its own traps, ruined by luxury and heedless expense, by want of calculation and a worthy aim, as the million households in the land; and the only cure for it as for them is in a rigid economy, a stern and more than Spartan simplicity of life and elevation of purpose. It lives too fast. Men think that it is essential that the Nation have commerce, and export ice, and talk through a telegraph, and ride thirty miles an hour, without a doubt, whether they do or not; but whether we should live like baboons or like men, is a little uncertain. If we do not get out sleepers, and forge rails, and devote days and nights to the work, but go to tinkering upon our lives to improve them, who will build railroads? And if railroads are not built, how shall we get to heaven in season? But if we stay at home and mind our business, who will want railroads? We do not ride on the railroad; it rides upon us. Did you ever think what those sleepers are that underlie the railroad? Each one is a man, an Irishman, or a Yankee man. The rails are laid on them, and they are covered with sand, and the cars run smoothly over them. They are sound sleepers, I assure you. And every few years a new lot is laid down and run over; so that, if some have the pleasure of riding on a rail, others have the misfortune to be ridden upon. And when they run over a man that is walking in his sleep, a supernumerary sleeper in the wrong position, and wake him up, they suddenly stop the cars, and make a hue and cry about it, as if this were an exception. I am glad to know that it takes a gang of men for every five miles to keep the sleepers down and level In their beds as it is, for this is a sign that they may sometime get up again.

Why should we live with such hurry and waste of life? We are determined to be starved before we are hungry. Men say that a stitch in time saves nine, and so they take a thousand stitches to day to save nine to-morrow. As for work, we haven't any of any consequence. We have the Saint Vitus' dance, and cannot possibly keep our heads still. If I should only give a few pulls at the parish bell-rope, as for a fire, that is, without setting the bell, there is hardly a man on his farm in the outskirts of Concord, notwithstanding that press of engagements which was his excuse so many times this morning, nor a boy, nor a woman, I might almost say, but would forsake all and follow that sound, not mainly to save property from the flames, but, if we will confess the truth, much more to see it burn, since burn it must, and we, be it known, did not set it on fire,—or to see it put out, and have a hand in it, if that is done as handsomely; yes, even if it were the parish church itself. Hardly a man takes a half hour's nap after dinner, but when he wakes he holds up his head and asks, "What's the news?" as if the rest of mankind had stood his sentinels. Some give directions to be waked every half hour, doubtless for no other purpose; and then, to pay for it, they tell what they have dreamed. After a night's sleep the news is as indispensable as the breakfast. "Pray tell me any thing new that has happened to a man any where on this globe,"—and he reads it over his coffee and rolls, that a man has had his eyes gouged out this morning on the Wachito River; never dreaming the while that he lives in the dark unfathomed mammoth cave of this world, and has but the rudiment of an eye himself.

For my part, I could easily do without the post-office. I think that there are very few important communications made through it. To speak critically, I never received more than one or two letters in my life—I wrote this some years ago—that were worth the postage. The penny-post is, commonly, an institution through which you seriously offer a man that penny for his thoughts which is so often safely offered in jest. And I am sure that I never read any memorable news in a newspaper. If we read of one man robbed, or murdered, or killed by accident, or one house burned, or one vessel wrecked, or one steamboat blown up, or one cow run over on the Western Railroad, or one mad dog killed, or one lot of grasshoppers in the winter,—we never need read of another. One is enough. If you are acquainted with the principle, what do you care for a myriad instances and applications? To a philosopher all news, as it is called, is gossip, and they who edit and read it are old women over their tea Yet not a few are greedy after this gossip. There was such a rush, as I hear, the other day at one of the offices to learn the foreign news by the last arrival, that several large squares of plate glass belonging to the establishment were broken by the pressure,—news which I seriously think a ready wit might write a twelve-month or twelve years beforehand with sufficient accuracy. [. . .]

Shams and delusions are esteemed for soundest truths, while reality is fabulous. If men would steadily observe realities only, and not allow themselves to be deluded, life, to compare it with such things as we know, would be like a fairy tale and the Arabian Nights' Entertainments. If we respected only what is inevitable and has a right to be, music and poetry would resound along the streets. When we are unhurried and wise, we perceive that only great and worthy things have any permanent and absolute existence,—that petty fears and petty pleasures are but the shadow of the reality. This is always exhilarating and sublime. By dosing the eyes and slumbering, and consenting to be deceived by shows, men establish and confirm their daily life of routine and habit every where, which still is built on purely illusory foundations. Children, who play life, discern its true law and relations more clearly than men, who fail to live it worthily, but who think that they are wiser by experience, that is, by failure. I have read in a Hindoo book, that "there was a king's son, who, being expelled in infancy from his native city, was brought up by a forester, and, growing up to maturity in that state, imagined himself to belong to the barbarous race with which he lived. One of his father's ministers having discovered him, revealed to him what he was, and the misconception of his character was removed, and he knew himself to be a prince. So soul," continues the Hindoo philosopher, "from the circumstances in which it is placed, mistakes its own character, until the truth is revealed to it by some holy teacher, and then it knows itself to be *Brahme*." I perceive that we inhabitants of New England live this mean life that we do because our vision does not penetrate the surface of things. We think that that *is* which *appears* to be. If a man should walk through this town and see only the reality, where, think you, would the "Mill— dam" go to? If he should give us an account of the realities he beheld there, we should not recognize the place in his description. Look at a meeting-house, or a court-house, or a jail, or a shop, or a dwelling-house, and say what that thing really is before a true gaze, and they would all go to pieces in your account of them. Men esteem truth remote, in the outskirts of the system, behind the farthest star, before Adam and after the last man. In eternity there is indeed something true and sublime. But all these times and places and occasions are now and here. God himself culminates in the present moment, and will never be more divine in the lapse of all the ages. And we are enabled to apprehend at all what is sublime and noble only by the perpetual instilling and drenching of the reality that surrounds us. The universe constantly and obediently answers to our conceptions; whether we travel fast or slow, the track is laid for us. Let us spend our lives in conceiving then. The poet or the artist never yet had so fair and noble a design but some of his posterity at least could accomplish it.

Let us spend one day as deliberately as Nature, and not be thrown off the track by every nutshell and mosquito's wing that falls on the rails. Let us rise early and fast, or break fast, gently and without perturbation; let company come and let company go, let the bells ring and the children cry,—determined to make a day of it. Why should we knock under and go with the stream? Let us not be upset and overwhelmed in that terrible rapid and whirlpool called a dinner, situated in the meridian shallows. Weather this danger and you are safe, for the rest of the way is down hill. With unrelaxed nerves, with morning vigor, sail by it, looking another way, tied to the mast like Ulysses. If the engine whistles, let it whistle till it is hoarse for its pains. If the bell rings, why should we run? We will consider what kind of music they are like. Let us settle ourselves, and work and wedge our feet downward through the mud and slush of opinion, and prejudice, and tradition, and delusion, and appearance, that alluvion which covers the globe, through Paris and London, through New York and Boston and Concord, through church and state, through poetry and philosophy and religion, till we come to a hard bottom and rocks in place, which we can call reality, and say, This is, and no mistake; and then begin, having a point d'appui [base], below freshet and frost and fire, a place where you might found a wall or a state, or set a lamp post safely, or perhaps a gauge, not a Nilometer, but a Realometer, that future ages might know how deep a freshet of shams and appearances had gathered from time to time. If you stand right fronting and face to face to a fact, you will see the sun glimmer on both its surfaces, as if it were a cimeter, and feel its sweet edge dividing you through the heart and marrow, and so you will happily conclude your mortal career. Be it life or death, we crave only reality. If we are really dying, let us hear the rattle in our throats and feel cold in the extremities; if we are alive, let us go about our business.

Time is but the stream I go a-fishing in. I drink at it; but while I drink I see the sandy bottom and detect how shallow it is. Its thin current slides away, but eternity remains. I would drink deeper; fish in the sky, whose bottom is pebbly with stars. I cannot count one. I know not the first letter of the alphabet. I have always been regretting that I was not as wise as the day I was born. The intellect is a cleaver; it discerns and rifts its way into the secret of things. I do not wish to be any more busy with my hands than is necessary. My head is hands and feet. I feel all my best faculties concentrated in it. My instinct tells me that my head is an organ for burrowing, as some creatures use their snout and forepaws, and with it I would mine and burrow my way through these hills. I think that the richest vein is somewhere hereabouts; so by the divining rod and thin rising vapors I judge; and here I will begin to mine.

WRITING ASSIGNMENTS

PERSONAL. Write about an experience you have had when your possessions have proved to be a burden.

RESEARCH. Explain the effects of a technological innovation that has created problems for the modern world. Document your sources.

PERSUASIVE. Defend the claim that people should simplify their lives. Use examples from your own experience and knowledge.

ANALYTICAL. Write a paper explaining how Thoreau reveals the essential details of his value system and his identity through his use of narrative.

INVESTIGATIVE. Examine your life style. Identify those aspects of your life that are unnecessarily complicated. Interpret the meaning of your findings in a paper.

14

Student Writing

An Analysis of "Higher Uneducation"

D. A. Fultz

"Higher Uneducation" by Eldridge Cleaver is a work that gives the reader a rather disturbing insight into the personality and character of its author. The essay is an expressive reaction in which the author makes use of evaluation to condemn the injustices and inequalities he perceives to be present in a racially biased and therefore oppressive American society.

With an expressive purpose, Cleaver exposes his reader to his own attitudes regarding his being a Black, socially militant individual who embraces a value system that rejects the established precepts and goals of modern white, middle-class America. Cleaver defines himself as "a Negro" and "a rapist" who has "a Higher Uneducation." His writing clearly reveals the emotional responses of anger and resentment toward the "fat-assed American geeks," who are in control of the structure which oppresses and judges him. Cleaver writes in his own style of conversational slang when he expresses his desire to get as clean as, "an Esquire square with a Harlem touch," or a "Snicker" in "a pair of bib overalls" and in so doing, he attempts to create a feeling of familiarity and acceptance with his audience. At the end of the excerpt we see Cleaver expressing a personal need to achieve the goal of becoming a new Black leader by gaining his liberation from prison and returning to Berkeley to "frolic in that sty of funky revolution," and "look with roving eyes for a new John Brown, Eugene Debs," and "a blacker-meaner-keener Malcolm X." The excerpt ends with a kind of ritualistic, repetitive chant that engages the emotions of the reader at a different, perhaps more primitive level.

In the very first sentence of the selection, Cleaver challenges the prevailing white value system through his evaluation. He boldly states that he is "a rapist, and that" he has "a Higher Uneducation," but that he has never known "what significance" he is "supposed to attach to these factors." Instead of accepting the established value system prescribed for "'free-normal-educated' people," Cleaver creates his own criteria for social acceptance in a system which would excuse his criminal behavior, or at least find it forgivable, because he is a member of a social structure that accepted, participated in, and promoted the atrocities of the Vietnam war. Cleaver writes that in his judgment, the Vietnamese people "have canceled all" of his "IOUs" to white society "through their sufferings" in a war where we decorated and made military heroes out of those people whose duty it was to "gas" the Vietnamese "burn them up, or blow away their humble pads in a hail of bombs."

This expressive evaluation certainly challenges the reader's own acceptance of and compliance toward our political and social structures. The essay is very effective in creating this challenge even though we may ultimately decide that Cleaver's value system, judgments, and goals for the future are outside the limits of those that we, as a functioning society, are willing to accept.

An Analysis of "Coyote"

FRANK GRAY

In "Coyote," a literary essay, Mark Twain takes every opportunity to delight and entertain his audience by employing his own special talents for looking at ordinary events through the eye of a humorist. By using narration and description, Twain reveals the interactions between a dog and coyote involved in a chase out on the prairie. The interactions suggest the theme that overconfidence can lead to disappointment and embarrassment.

The work's literary purpose is apparent throughout. Twain uses graphic literal images to recreate the tranquil atmosphere of the prairie. He also uses personification to give the animals their human characteristics. Twain writes that the prairie has "fresh breezes" and "vast expanses of level greensward . . . utterly without visible human beings or human habitations." With personification, the author is so successful at giving human characteristics to the animals that at times we almost forget who or what is actually involved in the chase. Twain says, "The coyote will go swinging gently off on that deceitful trot of his, and every little while he will smile a fraudful smile over his shoulder," at the dog. Twain informs us that this behavior fills the dog "full of encouragement and worldly ambition." Once involved in the chase the dog becomes "aggravated" and "madder and madder" when he realizes that the coyote has goaded him into an unfair competition. Twain indulges himself so fully in his use of personification that he actually engages the animals in conversation and dialogue. The coyote "seems to say," to the dog that "'. . . I shall have to tear myself away from you, bub—business is business.'"

Twain creates conflict and tension between the animals when the coyote teases the dog into the chase knowing all along that he is the swifter and more cunning of the two. The dog raises to the challenge because he is self-confident. Twain says the dog has "a good opinion of himself," which is the result of his being "brought up to think he knows something about speed."

Twain uses description and first person narration to tell his story. He makes it fairly clear that he is fictionalizing an actual event he has observed while out on the prairie. He recounts the different stages of the narrative using the first person pronouns of "I" and "we." He begins with the narrator's initial impressions of the day upon waking up in the morning, sighting the coyote "about an hour after breakfast," then describes the chase between the coyote and the dog. He finally resolves the episode by relating that "as much as a year after that" chase whenever the dog hears "a great hue and cry after a coyote," he decides "without emotion," not to get caught up in the game he has lost before.

We see description when Twain recalls the setting and the animals. He tells us that when he looked out over the prairie he could see "prairie-dog villages, the first antelope, and the first wolf," and states that the prairie was "the world-wide carpet about" him. In recreating the coyote for us he describes an animal that is "a long, slim, sick and sorry-looking skeleton," that "blends with the gray of the sage-brush."

It is, then, through literary description and narration that Twain recreates an episode from his own experience to provide his audience with a humorous look at the disappointing consequences of overconfidence. His effective use of personification allows the reader to identify with the animal characters in the narrative.

Amsterdam

JAMES HENDERSON

Amsterdam is a world class city with some truly unique characteristics perhaps found nowhere else in the world. The city is extremely beautiful and historic. Having been built largely in the 1600s, Amsterdam was designed with a system of canals that traverse the city allowing for both commercial transport and leisure travel by boat. Often it has been referred to as the "Venice of the North." Located in the Netherlands, the city of Amsterdam has a government that invests extensively in its people while emphasizing personal freedoms, tolerance, and diversity to a level found nowhere on earth. This noble endeavor is reflected throughout society including its accommodations, entertainment, and especially, its people.

When visiting Amsterdam, a guest in the city has an extraordinary range of choices for accommodation. Like all major metropolitan areas, there are many hotels to choose from, and some of Amsterdam's are among the best I've seen. With European amenities and impeccable service, there is no lack of comfort. Many of these hotels are historic and the Dutch architecture offers an ambiance and atmosphere characteristic of the region.

Many tourists choose to stay in the city's wonderful canal homes. Often run as "bed and breakfasts," many of these houses are older than the hotels and, as a result, offer more insight into traditional Dutch life in Amsterdam.

Generally, they are tall, thin buildings with ornate triangular upper facades. Perhaps the most unusual features of these homes are the staircases. Many of the stairs are so thin and curving that furniture is hoisted up and through the large windows that overlook the trees and canals. Individually, these homes cater to different kinds of tourists. Some have a family clientele, while others cater especially to young party people, business people, the elderly tourist, gay people, or people of various nationalities. The choices are unlimited.

Perhaps the most interesting choice of accommodation is staying on a canal boat. Waking in the morning, opening the cabin porthole and listening to the waves lap against the hull while watching other boats go by is an experience not soon forgotten.

Amsterdam provides an array of entertainment unmatched elsewhere. The city is full of historical sites ranging from the Royal Palace to the city's old churches, including *Oude Kerk* (Old Church), the city's oldest cathedral which was built in the 1300s. Monuments erected over the centuries are found everywhere as are some very ornate medieval clock towers. One of the best ways to take the sights in is to take the canal tour. Day or night, the canal tour offers spectacular sights, during the day, the architectural details and at night, the lighted facades.

For the traveler who wishes to be pampered, the European spas are a must. They offer seemingly every service imaginable to enhance the way people look and feel.

Nightlife in Amsterdam is extremely festive and draws people from around the world. Music and dancing in the clubs goes on until the early hours of the morning and the sense of abandon is possibly the most carefree anywhere. There are many theaters and music venues that attract acting troups and bands from all over Europe and the world.

The city seems to operate on the principle that there's a time and place for everything and that people can do what they want just as long as it doesn't hurt anybody. The red light district (absolutely legal) is a case in point. It even attracts sightseers who have no interest in participating in the activities associated with the area.

Of all of the wonders of Amsterdam, its greatest treasure is its people. Having traveled to a great many places, I've never been more warmly received than in Amsterdam. Perhaps the great diversity of the populous breeds tolerance and acceptance. Perhaps liberal politics that champions freedom breeds cohesion. Whatever the case, the genuine hospitality of the people of Amsterdam puts so many of the world's travel destinations to shame, making Amsterdam one of the world's greatest places to visit.

With so much to offer the tourist—accommodations, entertainment, and hospitality—its no wonder so many people visit Amsterdam each year. Its uniqueness makes it a refreshing stop in anyone's itinerary and one that will be remembered for many years. Amsterdam is certainly one of the best destinations for anyone visiting Europe.

An Analysis of "The Roots of Altruism"

KAY JONES

"The Roots of Altruism" by René Dubos is a referential interpretation of the origins of altruism, a term that means selfless behavior. He says that "altruism has become one of the absolute values by which humanity transcends animality." Further he suggests that the "philosophy of nonviolence," even though we associate it with great religious teachers like Jesus and Buddha, must be much older than that. Dubos contends that altruism was present even before the advent of modern civilization. The essay presents descriptions of the discoveries of prehistoric artifacts that suggest that Neanderthal and other Stone Age people exhibited "charity" and "attitudes of affection."

In this referential essay, Dubos puts forth the thesis that "the social attitudes" denoted by altruism and love existed in prehistoric times. He offers, as evidence of these attitudes, a number of examples of Neanderthalian and Stone Age skeletons found in Europe and in North America which suggest that those societies took special care of the young and the disabled. The thesis is an interpretation of this evidence, an inductive generalization from the evidence offered. The generalizations are consistent with the evidence offered. Since the definition of the term *altruism* is central to his interpretation, he defines it using the synonyms "charity" and "self-sacrifice."

The evidence is presented with both description and narration. The details of the descriptions serve to support the thesis. The condition of the blind Neanderthalian adult male with an amputated arm strongly supports the thesis that the society must have exhibited altruism; otherwise the man would not have survived to the age of 40. The condition of the 50 year-old Neanderthal with arthritis leads to a similar conclusion. The descriptions of the other Stone Age sites in North American add more evidence to support the idea that attitudes toward children reflect feelings of love and affection. The narratives associated with these descriptions are incomplete. They are speculations about the probable circumstances and activities suggested by the artifacts. Dubos speculates that the Neanderthal with arthritis would "have been unable to hunt or to engage in other strenuous activities," and that the blind Neanderthal would "have been incapable of fending for himself. . . ." The entire essay is structured as a historical narrative that traces the existence of altruism from prehistoric to modern times.

Dubos' discussion is a compelling interpretation of the existence of altruism. His presentation of the evidence through description and narration is clear and logically consistent. The inductive generalization he makes based on that evidence is a valid one. The essay is an effective explanation of the origins of a complex social phenomenon.

Beauty Becomes the Beast

SARAH MATTHES

Throughout the generations, women have been regarded as the fairer of the sexes. While many have seen this as a point of pride, it has also created an obligation to maintain this standard of beauty and near perfection. This in and of itself is not such a terrible thing. However, over time it has created impossible standards, unrealistic ideas of beauty, and a sense of dissatisfaction among millions of women. Instead of fixating on flaws, we should redefine our society's idea of beauty and focus more on what we like about ourselves and other women, even daring to go beyond just the physical aspects of beauty. By changing the way we view it, we can turn beauty into something to be found within us, instead of an impossible goal, always just beyond our reach.

In 2009 almost 9.9 million Americans received plastic surgery, and that included roughly 311,000 breast augmentations and 243,000 liposuctions ("2009 Top 5"). In other words, over half a million women have felt so pressured by societal requirements for women to have small waists and large breasts that they were willing to undergo invasive surgery in order to conform to these ideals. Over the years the quest for beauty has made women do ugly things. However, some women have managed to strike the balance, something we all should try to achieve. "Like French women, we, too, need to understand that a healthy approach to beauty is neither pretending it's unnecessary or unimportant nor making it important beyond all else" (Alkon 2).

The question now becomes, how do we break this cycle of vicious self-attack and the insatiable desire to achieve perfection? The answer lies in a shift in thought. Instead of seeing our differences as imperfections, we must learn to see them as aspects of ourselves that make us unique and add diversity to physical appearance. When I was in middle school, people made fun of me because of how skinny I was. I used to eat and eat and eat in hopes of filling out to stop all the teasing. As I grew older though, people treated it differently, some even envied my figure, something I wasn't used to. More importantly though, I learned to accept my own slenderness, even like it, regardless of what I saw in other people. I received the same ridicule and felt the same way about my freckles as well. But as time went by, I saw them less as a telltale sign of a nerd, and more of a sign of distinction, one more thing that made me different from everybody else. If everyone learned to appreciate the little things about themselves instead of covering them up, women in general would be much happier about the way they see themselves.

Along with impossible comparisons come the impossible attempts to change ourselves to meet those standards set for us. This is what drives women to anorexia, bulimia, and extreme exercise. The focus is always on making ourselves look like somebody else, when instead it should be on making you into a better version of yourself. The primary goal should always be on being healthy and fit. If this does not turn you into a size 0 supermodel, *that is okay.*

Perhaps a more extreme shift in thought, women should also learn to see beauty as more than the sum of physical aspects. It is also the spirit of a woman, her kindness, her humor that grants her the title of beautiful. In a study conducted by Dove, researchers found a correlation between a woman's perception of her own beauty and what she considered beautiful. Those who were dissatisfied with their appearance seemed to think that cosmetics and physical perfection make a woman beautiful, while women who found themselves beautiful placed importance on happiness, kindness, confidence, humor, and intelligence (Etcoff and Orbach). These are the legacies that should be passed down from mothers to daughters, and these are the attributes of beauty that will free women from the beauty trap that tells us we must be a slave to our own good looks. In her essay "Beauty," Susan Sontag observes that beauty is "a crude trap" that makes it easy to define "women as caretakers of their surfaces" and then "disparage them (or find them adorable) for being 'superficial'" (134).

Many women feel that being attractive is the only way to appeal to men. While it is true that men are visually wired, they are not completely oblivious to a girl's personality. I do not suggest that women completely ignore their hygiene and overall appearance, but a relationship formed solely on the basis of attraction will have no depth or substance; it would be like buying a house just because you like the color of the paint. Other women feel that there is no beauty trap from which to escape. The system allows women to use their looks as a leverage to get ahead, and this can't be such a bad thing. I cannot argue with any woman who is willing to promote herself through her vanity; that is her own prerogative. I can warn her, however, that her success may not bring her the fulfillment she expects. Success rarely brings happiness unless it is achieved through values that one can be proud of, values that are consequently connected to the true idea of beauty.

With media bombarding our culture with images of anatomically ideal models, women have come to look in the mirror with dread as they prepare to analyze everything that needs to change in order to meet the criteria. Before society becomes a congregation of "beautiful" drones, we must teach ourselves to look in the mirror and see the good-hearted, unique, capable, and funny woman. We must teach the next generation of women to see themselves in this way as well, before the next vicious cycle of self-degradation begins and it is too late.

WORKS CITED

"2009 Top 5 Cosmetic Surgeries." *American Society for Aesthetic Plastic Surgery.* 2009. Graph. Web. 12 March 2011.

Alkon, Amy. "The Truth About Beauty." *Psychology Today.* November 2010.1–2. Web. 3/12/11.

Etcoff, Nancy, and Susie Orbach. "The Real Truth About Beauty: A Global Report." *Dove, a Unilever Beauty Brand.* September 2004. 1–48. Web. 12 March 2011.

Sontag, Susan. "Beauty." *75 Readings: A Freshman Anthology*. Ed. Emily G. Barrose. New York: McGraw-Hill, 1987. 132–34. Rpt. of "Women's Beauty: Put Down or Power Source." 1975. Print.

The House

KIM KRUPP PEPE

The house sits on the highest hill in the county. It's a big old two story structure of no discernable architectural style. It was built in stages over the last few centuries and is a series of styles from different times. The huge trees in the lawn cover the house and grass in dappled shade. The breeze constantly rolls over the emerald farmland and meets on the hilltop to make the sunlight dance and play over everything. It's a very pleasant place. My sisters and brother and I grew up there, and my memories still live here.

As I walk up the driveway, I glance at one of my old climbing trees. When I was little, I'd climb up into the giant maple to read. I'd lay myself on one of the massive branches and live many adventures in my mind. Sometimes I'd climb up the branches as high as I could and jump. The dizzying effect is something I can only compare to being pleasantly drunk, just for an instant. I still climb the tree when I go home to see if it feels the same. Of course it doesn't, and I jump down with a half sad smile on my face when I realize that those feelings and adventures are now just a memory.

As I look around, so many memories flood through my head. There's the big boulder that was unearthed one summer when the new septic system was laid. I used to give speeches standing on the top of this rock. Sometimes I'd be Lincoln at Gettysburg or Martin Luther King with a dream or I'd give a talk of my own contrivance about things that were very profound to my young mind. All the solutions seemed simple from the top of that rock. There's the path into the woods where my sister broke her leg one rainy day. The woods also contain a tree with branches very much like parallel bars. Here I was a world class gymnast on afternoons after school. On the far left side of the lawn is a hedge row broken by a tractor path that leads to the back fields, the old barn, and my childhood Shangri-la. Many mornings I remember running barefoot, always barefoot, breathlessly and ceaselessly through the dewy grass to the fields beyond. The sharpness of the newly cut wheat stalks would sometimes cut my feet, all unheeded. If the grain crops were still high, I could swim through them, holding my breath if I fell, as if I were actually in water.

The porch which surrounds the front of the house was the setting for many lazy summer afternoons—eating peaches and swatting flies—and freezing winter mornings waiting for the school bus to arrive. The porch was where my mother gave food to hoboes and then shooed them along before my father saw them. Under the porch I used to hide and secretly look at the world through the gingerbread trim. No one ever found me there.

All my childhood memories still live in that house and out in the fields and woods. When I visit now, many things are much the same, but nothing is exactly the same or nearly as big as I remember them. Now I'm always kind of torn between being sad because I feel like a child and yet knowing I am not and can never be again. Another part of me feels happy for having a place where all my past is stored and secreted away, always waiting for me to come back and make the little girl dance and laugh and run through the dewy grass.

Crime Scene Investigations and Forensic Analysis

Marcia Salazar

Most people in today's society are familiar with forensic science and how it relates to crime scene investigations. With television shows like CSI, we are able to get a tiny glimpse of what it takes to solve a crime using forensic science. During a crime scene investigation there are several procedures that must be done in order to ensure that the investigation is conducted properly. The scene must be secured and evidence must be collected in order to establish the nature of the crime that has occurred. Crime scenes are a vital piece of evidence in and of themselves. They must be managed in such a way that nothing gets overlooked. Murder investigations, for example, often use the four most important types of forensic analysis: photography, pathology, toxicology, and anthropology.

The most crucial piece of evidence that can be collected from a crime scene is photographic evidence. A forensic photographer will take accurate pictures depicting exactly what has taken place. It is not a simple as clicking a button and taking a picture. There are several steps involved in the process of crime scene photography. Taking photographs of the area surrounding the crime scene is very important, but also paperwork must be in place to assure that the information is documented accurately. A photo identifier will be used to and will include the case number, the date the image was taken, the address/location of where the photographs were taken, the name or badge number of the photographer, and the roll number of the film which is being exposed (Robinson 305). There are also other forms that must be used in order to ensure proper documentation. Robinson states in *Crime Scene Photography*, "Every individual photograph should be logged on a photo memo sheet, which is a form to log all specific data related to the camera, film, and specific variables used to capture each individual photograph" (308). Oftentimes these photos are submitted in court; along with the photographs, a witness must testify that the photographs being submitted are authentic and that they accurately portray the crime scene (Buckland 38). Crime scene photographs are long term evidence, making it even more important that they are documented properly.

Another area of forensic analysis that plays a major part in murder investigations is forensic pathology. Prahlow notes that "Forensic pathology represents a subspecialty area within the larger field of pathology that specifically deals with the investigation of sudden, unexpected and/or violent death" (32). In order to be able to determine a cause of death, the forensic pathologist must examine the body. An autopsy has to be conducted which is made up of an external and internal examination of the entire body, but also includes ancillary procedures that must be done. The external examination is more of a visual exam that documents injuries, postmortem changes, and various physical characteristics of the body. The internal examination is much more complicated and involves surgically opening the body and removing the organs. Once the organs are removed they are dissected in order to determine whether or not disease is present. In the process of the autopsy various ancillary procedures may take place as well. One of the major ancillary aspects is toxicology testing, which evaluates the blood and tissue for toxins (Prahlow 33). Toxicology testing must be conducted by a forensic toxicologist.

A forensic pathologist works hand in hand with a toxicologist. A forensic toxicologist can determine whether a toxic substance is present in a human body and if it may have played a part in the death that has occurred. In the reference work *Forensic Science* we find that "In cases of suspicious deaths, pathologists collect at autopsy the specimens that will be subjected to toxicological analysis. In general, the specimens collected from a body for this purpose include urine, blood, stomach and intestinal contents, bile, bone, fat, tissues of the brain and liver, and one whole kidney" ("Forensic Pathology" 542). Once the specimens are collected, the toxicologist will decide what type of testing is needed and will repeat the procedure several times in order to assure that the results are accurate.

Another specialty of forensic science that is sometimes used in crime investigations is forensic anthropology. In *The Use of Forensic Anthropology*, Robert Pickering explains that a "forensic anthropologist can help recover and analyze human remains, particularly those that are decomposed or skeletonized, in a rapid effective manner" (17). The thorough training that forensic anthropologists receive allows them to be able to assist in the reconstruction of the crime scene. Pickering notes, "At minimum, the forensic anthropologist can determine the major biological characteristics, such as age, sex, stature, and possibly race or ethnicity of skeletonized human remains" (15). Although, forensic anthropologists are normally called in to identify remains, they may also aid the pathologist or toxicologist if needed. Many times a forensic anthropologist helps give the skeletal remains an identity by way of facial reconstruction. All of a sudden the bones come to life and are often able to give some insight to the mystery.

A crime scene can be very complicated and as Pickering observes "A forensic investigation requires a team of specialists from many different scientific fields of study along with legal and law enforcement specialists" (xi). These specialists have to work together in order to be able to solve the crime. Televisions shows like CSI can often distort certain aspects of such investigations making it seem that the completion of an investigation is immediate, when in fact it can be a lengthy process. Many crimes would go unsolved if it were not for the several different methods of forensic analysis. Not all methods may be used at once, but there is a good chance that some form of forensic analysis will be used in a crime scene investigation. Although, there are a number of other fields of forensic science, from psychology to accounting, these four—photography, toxicology, pathology, and anthropology—are among the most essential in solving a crime.

WORKS CITED

Buckland, Gail. *Shots in the Dark*. New York: Bulfinch Press, 2001. Print.

"Forensic Pathology." *Forensic Science*. Ed. Embar-Seddon, Ayn and Allen D. Pass, Vol. 3. Pasadena, CA: Salem Press, 2009. *Gale Virtual Reference Library*. Web. 2 Mar. 2011.

Pickering, Robert B. *The Use of Forensic Anthropology*. Boca Raton: 2nd Ed. CRC Press, 2009. eBook Library. Web. 2 Mar. 2011.

Prahlow, Joseph. *Forensic Pathology for Forensic Scientist, Police, and Death Investigators*. New York: Springer, 2010. eBook Library. Web. 2 Mar. 2011.

Robinson, Edward M. *Crime Scene Photography*. Burlington: 2nd Ed. Academic Press, 2010. eBook Library. Web. 2 Mar. 2011.

The Ford

LAURA SCARBOROUGH

I saw my crazed, absent-minded aunt charging full speed in reverse coming straight towards us. I awaited the impact. . . . When metal hit metal, my mom and I were jerked a bit. Not bad. My aunt's sickly yellow, ugly Continental smashed into the side of our huge pickup truck. My aunt didn't bother to use her rearview mirror. Our truck received a smashed-in driver's side door. We never fixed it—my aunt didn't have insurance, it didn't seem worth the money, and it's not the right thing to sue a relative.

Our family pickup truck is a 1974 Ford. All black, red interior. It has this useless "customized" shelf built above the rearview mirror that matches the red design of the inside. It was bought by my father the same year I was born, 1974. I was about eight years old when I started learning how to drive. I'd sit on my mom's lap and steer the truck down a gravel road while she operated the accelerator and brakes. The truck was basically the "second car." We only used it if the other car was in the shop, or if we needed to haul or move something (like picking up hay for the horse). Therefore, the truck stayed in pretty good condition, collected few miles, and ran well.

As I grew older, my fondness for the truck grew less and less. I was turning into a snot-head teenager with an attitude. To me the truck was too outdated, too big, too long, too noisy, too "redneck" looking. When I was nearing sixteen, I started bugging my parents about getting me a car. "Well," they said, "you can drive the truck." I started fuming and argued, "No way! It's ugly! It's a gas guzzler! It only has an AM radio! It's got a smashed door! I'll look stupid being a girl having to drive that big old monster around!"

So, like many parents, they wanted the nagging to cease and wanted to make their (bratty) daughter happy. They bought me a 1987 Nissan Sentra hatchback in royal blue. It was sporty. It had a sunroof. It was soooooo coooool. I immediately had the windows tinted, put in new speakers and a nice tape deck, and spent all this money getting it fixed up "cool." I didn't spend much time or money for oil changes and putting water in. "Just gotta put gas in it," I thought.

Time went on and my teenage-snot-head self ragged out and abused that wimpy Japanese contraption until it finally overheated so badly (because of the lack of oil) that the engine warped and was destroyed. We spent $1300 to put another engine in it. Within two weeks it overheated, warped, and was destroyed. A couple months later we got the money together to put in engine #3. Eventually, that engine also overheated and warped. Mommy and Daddy finally realized—no more of this. The insurance was taken off, and the dead Nissan still sits under a tree in my parents' yard.

Being without a car for a year and a half taught me that one must respect the transportation they own. I also learned that Nissans are pieces of dookie even despite my bad maintenance. When I moved to South Austin six months ago, I was stuck. I had to persuade my boyfriend to be may chauffeur to and from school, or I had to take two hour bus trips (each way) to get to ACC. I whined and complained to my parents until they gave me the same offer: "You can drive the truck." So I did.

Now, I really appreciate and enjoy driving my baby (as I call it). It still has a smashed-in door and still guzzles gas. In fact, it only gets 8-10 miles per gallon, so I spend a fortune on gasoline. I deserve it, for wasting so much of my parents' money on that worthless Nissan.

I feel a bond with all the other early Ford truck drivers I see. They look at me and I look at them. Occasionally, some wave. It's weird. I get more looks from people at gas stations than I ever did driving a Nissan. People just don't expect a girl in a long flowery skirt and Dock Martins to jump out of a dented up, old Ford truck.

I'm not worried when I drive on the roads. I'm not an obvious cop magnet. I feel safe being surrounded by one ton of American-made steel. Other car owners know they would suffer a lot more than I would if we were to have a collision. So they stay away from me and my smelly pollutant exhaust.

I'm a good driver. Driving such a huge, long massive machine makes you a good driver. It's taught me to judge distances better. If I can parallel park in one try, I know I'm doing something admirable.

I've learned about car maintenance. I know that automobiles need gas, oil, water, brake fluid, etc. (gee, I'm a genius). Since I give the truck a lot of care and love, it has never failed to start since it's been with me in Austin. It's reliable, safe, and very special. I find it ironic that I'm the person it ended up with after all these years—especially since I had the worst attitude towards it in my high school daze. I'll be holding on to my baby for awhile because I'm happy with it and wouldn't really want anything else. So, if you see a girl cruising down Lamar in a big black Ford with a smashed-in driver's door, you know it's me.

An Analysis of "The Rights of Women"

SALLY SMITH

Mary Wollstonecraft's "The Rights of Women," a persuasive evaluation of the role of women in a male-dominated society, makes a strong feminist statement about the destructiveness of conventional gender roles. In an effort to refute common female stereotypes and to make women "more respectable members of society," she uses carefully constructed, strong arguments and vows to "avoid flowery diction." "The Rights of Women" is her impassioned, yet logical defense of the true nature of women which is hidden by false perceptions.

She makes a persuasive claim that women ought "to endeavor to acquire strength. . . ." In trying to persuade both sexes to reject the social and cultural myths that women are inferior to men, she uses both rational and emotional appeals. Part of her support for the claim is the rational appeal created by the assertion that if women do not establish their own identities, then they become "ridiculous and useless when the short-lived bloom of beauty is over. . . ." Wollstonecraft uses emotional appeal when she refers to women's "slavish dependence," to women being "ridiculed and pitied," and to marriage creating the impression that women "are only fit for a seraglio" (a harem). She tries to validate her arguments by the general warrant that all human beings deserve equal treatment. This warrant is suggested by the statement "the first object of . . . ambition is to obtain a character as a human being," and by the reference to the need to "educate a rational and immortal being for a nobler field of action."

The entire work is organized as an evaluation. She evaluates a number of subjects related to women's roles: women themselves, men, and the education of women. Her judgments of women are that they are seen as "weak beings," who are "in a state of perpetual childhood," and as "insignificant objects of desire" who are "mere propagators of fools." She sees men as condescending, and she thinks that women's education does not cultivate "their understandings. . . ." Throughout the work, the subject, women and their roles, is presented by using narration of process. Examples of her use of narration of process are contained in the references to how women spend "the first years of their lives," to marriage as "the only way women can rise in the world," and to "the strength of body and mind" being "sacrificed to libertine notions of beauty. . . ." In this argument evaluation is essential to the success of the persuasion. The argument that women need "to acquire strength" is based on the evaluation of women that reveals how they are weakened and suppressed by traditional roles and by traditional social institutions.

Mary Wollstonecraft's persuasive argument presents a powerful case for a change in the status of women. Her evaluation of the plight of women makes us aware of the repression of women in the eighteenth century and the need for equal rights. Her powerful message is still relevant, even after two centuries.

An Analysis of "On Androgyny"

SARAH TORRES

Virginia Woolf's "On Androgyny" is a referential, although personal, examination and analysis of human mental processes and the role of gender in the human psyche. Woolf relies on her own mental reactions to the scene of a man and woman coming to-gether in a street to demonstrate her viewpoints and explain her conclusions.

Woolf's primary purpose is referential because she purports to reveal certain innate characteristics of the human psyche by using herself as an example. She relates that "the ordinary sight of two people getting into a cab had the power to communicate something of their own seeming satisfaction," and that, "to think . . . of one sex as distinct from the other . . . interferes with the unity of the mind." She conveys detailed information as she deciphers human mental processes, and she reports each step of her mental journey to certain conclusions. Although she often expresses an idea as a personal "feeling," she merely uses this characterization as an initial vehicle for ultimately stating her viewpoints as acceptable and reliable information. For example, Woolf says, "Why do I feel that there are severances and oppositions in the mind, as there are strains from obvious causes on the body?" Although here she expresses this idea as a subjective personal feeling, she proceeds to rely on this idea as established fact in her following statements. On another subject, she explains as a matter of fact that, "the mind has so great a power of concentrating at any point at any moment that it seems to have no single state of being. It can separate itself from the people in the street, for example. . . . Again if one is a woman one is often surprised by a sudden splitting off of consciousness, say in walking down Whitehall, when from being the natural inheritor of that civilisation, she becomes, on the contrary, outside of it, alien and critical." She also informs us, "Clearly the mind is always altering its focus, and bringing the world into different perspectives."

Woolf's secondary purpose is to persuade the reader that her viewpoints and conclusions are reliable and acceptable. First, she uses her personal mental reactions as a sort of primary source example to support the statements she makes about the human mind in general: "When I saw the couple get into the taxi-cab the mind felt as if, after being divided, it had come together again in a natural fusion. The obvious reason would be that it is natural for the sexes to cooperate." Second, she follows a methodical path of purportedly supporting logic. First attaching much significance to the natural mental reaction that occurs when she witnesses the man and woman, she notes, "The sight of two people coming down the street and meeting at the corner seems to ease the mind of some strain . . .," and from there begins to conclude, "Perhaps to think . . . of one sex as distinct from the other is an effort." She says that making this distinction "interferes with the unity of the mind." Woolf then uses the universal sense of "satisfaction" derived from the physical union of a man and woman to support her idea that each individual's satisfaction requires a mental union of the male and female genders: "in each of us two powers preside, one male, one female. . . ."

Woolf uses narration as her primary writing pattern. Beginning by describing the street scene she witnesses from her window, she tells a chronological story of how and when she came to think certain thoughts, have certain impressions, or conclude certain concepts: "The mind is certainly a very mysterious organ, I reflected. . . ." And later: "For certainly when I saw the couple get into the taxi-cab the mind felt as if, after being divided, it had come together again in a natural fusion." In her concluding sentences she says, "And I went on amateurishly to sketch a plan of the soul. . . ."

Within a narrative framework, Woolf organizes her information by classification. In explaining what she means by the "unity of the mind," she uses examples to categorizes the various types of mental states the mind can adopt which change one's perspective of the world: "[The mind] can separate itself from the people on the street . . . and think of itself as apart from them. . . . Or it can think with other people spontaneously, as, for instance, in a crowd waiting to hear some piece of news read out. It can think back through its fathers or through its mothers. . . ." She distinguishes two main types of mental states: "some of these states of mind seem . . . to be less comfortable than others," but "there may be some state of mind in which one could continue without effort . . . And this perhaps . . . is one of them." She also categorizes where male and female powers ought to reside within men as opposed to women: "two powers preside, one male, one female: and in the man's brain, the man predominates over the woman, and in the woman's brain, the woman predominates over the man . . . If one is a man, still the woman part of the brain must have effect; and a woman also must have intercourse with the man in her."

Woolf ultimately concludes that it is with the "fusion" of male and female "powers" within a single individual that the mind is "fully fertilised and uses all its faculties" and that "the normal and comfortable state of being is that when the two [powers] live in harmony together, spiritually cooperating." Using metaphorical symbols of the physical union of a man and a woman, she seems to say that as the unity of a man and woman succeeds, so succeeds the unity of mind in each individual—with the fusion of male and female powers. While the train of thought that leads Woolf to her conclusions is in a sense only as persuasive as the reader can relate to her experiences or accept her logic, and while in most cases Woolf's logical path seems heavily subject to her personal mental experiences and impressions, her intent seems to be merely to use what information is available to her by direct analysis of personal mental experiences to conclude certain truths about human nature. She appears to consider herself a reliable source at least for attempting to glean information about the human mind in general. Woolf's mental journey is intriguing because the reader is given a way to systematically examine ideas regarding male and female powers from a personal perspective and also because the reader is indirectly offered a deep window into the mind and philosophy of Virginia Woolf, however limited the topic, and often subtly given a uniquely sympathetic perspective of how she views herself in the world.

Index